Independent Animation

With the advent of advanced hand-held technology and the widespread nature of the Internet, the world of animated filmmaking is more exciting and accessible than ever. Due to this cultural and technological development, the success of independent animated film makers is on the rise. *Independent Animation: Developing, Producing and Distributing Your Animated Films, Second Edition* showcases some of the greatest, most innovative giants in the field and helps guide readers through the artistic process and production techniques. Story development, casting, color theory, distribution and the intimidating aspects of production are elucidated using various examples of acclaimed, viral and award-winning animated films from all over the world. Readers will also explore the changing nature of audiences, festivals and distributors' relationships with animation and be granted first-hand guidance in navigating the diverse fields of animated film-making.

Key Features:

- Covers the entire process of creating an independent animated film from story development and casting to editing and distribution
- Presents a comprehensive array of classic and contemporary case studies covering all manner of production methods from traditional pipelines to avant-garde, auteur and experimental approaches
- Features input and exclusive insight into the working processes of some of the industry's most noteworthy indie animation talents, including Signe Baumane, Adam Elliot, Don Hertzfeldt, Kirsten Lepore, Robert Morgan, David OReilly, PES, Bill Plympton, Rosto, Chris Shepherd and dozens more

Additional resources and interviews are available through a special section of Skwigly Online Animation Magazine.

Independent Animation
Developing, Producing and Distributing Your Animated Films

Second Edition

Ben Mitchell

CRC Press
Taylor & Francis Group
Boca Raton London New York

CRC Press is an imprint of the
Taylor & Francis Group, an **informa** business

Second edition published 2023
by CRC Press
6000 Broken Sound Parkway NW, Suite 300, Boca Raton, FL 33487-2742

and by CRC Press
4 Park Square, Milton Park, Abingdon, Oxon, OX14 4RN

CRC Press is an imprint of Taylor & Francis Group, LLC

© 2023 Ben Mitchell

First edition published by CRC Press 2016

Reasonable efforts have been made to publish reliable data and information, but the author and publisher cannot assume responsibility for the validity of all materials or the consequences of their use. The authors and publishers have attempted to trace the copyright holders of all material reproduced in this publication and apologize to copyright holders if permission to publish in this form has not been obtained. If any copyright material has not been acknowledged please write and let us know so we may rectify in any future reprint.

Except as permitted under U.S. Copyright Law, no part of this book may be reprinted, reproduced, transmitted, or utilized in any form by any electronic, mechanical, or other means, now known or hereafter invented, including photocopying, microfilming, and recording, or in any information storage or retrieval system, without written permission from the publishers.

For permission to photocopy or use material electronically from this work, access www.copyright.com or contact the Copyright Clearance Center, Inc. (CCC), 222 Rosewood Drive, Danvers, MA 01923, 978-750-8400. For works that are not available on CCC please contact mpkbookspermissions@tandf.co.uk

Trademark notice: Product or corporate names may be trademarks or registered trademarks and are used only for identification and explanation without intent to infringe.

Library of Congress Cataloging-in-Publication Data
Names: Mitchell, Ben, 1983–author.
Title: Independent animation : developing, producing and distributing your animated films / Ben Mitchell.
Description: Second edition. | Boca Raton : CRC Press, [2023] |
Includes bibliographical references and index.
Identifiers: LCCN 2022040984 | ISBN 9781032103105 (paperback) |
ISBN 9781032103112 (hardback) | ISBN 9781003214717 (ebook)
Subjects: LCSH: Animation (Cinematography)
Classification: LCC TR897.5 .M58 2023 | DDC 777/.7–dc23/eng/20221017
LC record available at https://lccn.loc.gov/2022040984

ISBN: 978-1-032-10311-2 (hbk)
ISBN: 978-1-032-10310-5 (pbk)
ISBN: 978-1-003-21471-7 (ebk)

DOI: 10.1201/9781003214717

Typeset in Minion Pro
by codeMantra

Access the Companion Website: https://www.skwigly.co.uk/independent-animation

Contents

Acknowledgments

It goes without saying that this book would not have been possible without the insight of the talented people responsible for its major case studies. My tremendous gratitude to the following for taking the time to be interviewed:

Benjamin Arcand, Kieran Argo, Bjørn-Erik Aschim, Signe Baumane, Pierre Baussaron, Ant Blades, Philip Brookes, Helen Brunsdon, Emma Burch, Seb Burnett, Tom Carrell, Jeff Chiba Stearns, Elliot Cowan, Garrett Davis, Ellys Donovan, Adam Elliot, Michael Frei, Daniel Gray, Daniel Greaves, Robert Grieves, Alex Grigg, Luce Grosjean, Don Hertzfeldt, Melissa Johnson, Tony Johnson, David Kamp, Robert Kondo, Kirsten Lepore, Joost Lieuwma, Ruth Lingford, Peter Lord, Andy Martin, Aidan McAteer, Greg McLeod, Robert Morgan, Sam Morrison, Rob Munday, Vincent Oliver, David OReilly, Lauren Orme, Nick Park, Adam Pesapane, Sarah Phelps, Jonti Picking, Bill Plympton, Emmanuel-Alain Raynal, Chris Robinson, Rosto, Tom Schroeder, Chris Shepherd, Jason Sondhi, Thomas Stellmach, Daniel Šuljić, Sam Taylor, Daisuke Tsutsumi, Marie Valade, Nag Vladermersky, Tünde Vollenbroek, Matthew Walker, Adam Wells, Joe Wood and Robertino Zambrano.

For the love, kindness and support that kept me going throughout this project:

Laura-Beth Cowley, Erica Mitchell, Elspeth Mitchell, Lynn Mitchell, Derek Cherrington, Jane Davies, Joanna Hepworth and Luca Kiss.

Much gratitude also to those whose time and assistance contributed greatly to the overall organization of the book:

Cordell Barker, Marco de Blois, Jessica Casano-Antonellis, Mike Dietz, David Fine, Corrie Francis Parks, Nancy Gerstman, Pauline Ginot, Chris Hinton, Shanta Jethoe, Sophie Klevenow, Sarah Littman, Anna Mantzaris, Mary Murphy, Adam Smith and Alison Snowden.

Special thanks to my Skwigly Online Animation Magazine colleagues, Steve Henderson and Aaron Wood, as well as our fantastic team of enthusiastic contributors and supporters who keep it going.

Extra special thanks to my technical editor, Katie Steed, as well as Lauren Mattos, Haley Swan and Sean Connelly at Taylor & Francis Group.

Author Biography

Ben Mitchell is an animator, motion designer, composer, award-winning independent filmmaker and writer/researcher. As a freelancer he has produced work for WildBrain, CBeebies, Channel 4, Shy Guys, Plymptoons, Animortal, Wonky Films, A Productions, Slurpy Studios, Makematic and Rumpus, to name a few.

As an independent director he has produced six multi-award-winning short animated films that have been showcased at over 200 international film and animation festivals including Clermont-Ferrand, BFI London Film Festival, ITFS Stuttgart, Encounters, London International Animation Festival, Pictoplasma, London Short Film Festival and Anima Mundi. Alongside his work in animation production he is an active writer and researcher on the industry and is Editor-in-Chief of the leading UK animation resource, Skwigly.

As an educator he has lectured and tutored at AUB Bournemouth, University of the West of England, University of Gloucestershire and UAL Central Saint Martins. He has also been actively involved in a variety of capacities spanning curation, programming, awards jurying, hosting and panel moderation for such international events as Animafest Zagreb, ITFS Stuttgart, Encounters Film Festival, the British Animation Awards, Manchester Animation Festival, Cardiff Animation Festival, Fredrikstad Animation Festival, Big Cartoon Festival and Dublin Animation Film Festival.

1

Introduction

Figure 1.1

Wackatdooo (Dir. Benjamin Arcand) ©2014 Benjamin Arcand.

We're living in a particularly exciting time for all forms of independent creativity, perhaps especially animation (Figures 1.1–1.5). Throughout the world, we have seen a rapid acclimation to some very sudden shifts and advances in technology. Entertainment media has evolved to a point where consumers from all walks of life can engage with it in almost any circumstance, thanks largely to the

DOI: 10.1201/9781003214717-1

portability of tablets, smartphones and other such gadgetry. How we experience entertainment has also drastically changed; with content so readily available on-demand, these demands are being raised and, with them, our expectations of quality. Matching this is an increasing prevalence of sophisticated, user-friendly, affordable software alongside a vast ocean of equally affordable, online educational resources to teach auteurs how to use them.

During this same period of recent technological advancement, the changing economy has hugely reconfigured the funding options that were once so key to getting any kind of animated film project off the ground. Depending on where you are in the world, some grants and schemes in support of the arts remain while those not so geographically fortunate have been forced to up their game. This coupling of new circumstances has turned out to be a tremendous positive, with true ingenuity manifesting itself out of the limited resources available to filmmakers.

As such, the cultural significance – and, indeed, effect – of independent animation is thriving, and the future is bright for small studios, collectives and individuals who are able to put strong ideas out in the world in ways they would not have been able to in the not-too-distant past.

My aim with this book, as an animation enthusiast, freelancer and independent director myself, is to lay out some of the essential tenets, philosophies and creative processes behind the independent animation community's most prominent, prolific and respected artists, so that other creatives and artists such as yourself can be motivated to put them into practical effect when it comes to your own projects.

An important thing to clarify is that this is not another book that goes through the fundamentals of animation and storytelling itself, as there are plenty of those out there, a fair few of which will most likely be on your shelves already. This book is for when you have worked through the basics of animation – your bouncing balls, flour sacks, walk cycles, lip sync exercises and layouts – and are asking yourself how precisely you wish to apply this knowledge to a film. This includes

Figure 1.2

The External World (Dir. David OReilly) ©2011 David OReilly.

those of you who have determined that the type of animated film you wish to make will throw these fundamentals out of the window, to develop an entirely personal process from scratch. Here you will read about how popular animated films have come from such unique approaches – whether animated on laptop trackpads, using ink sprayed from syringes or on sticky notes attached to the backs of farmyard animals (seriously).

The most consistent observation I've witnessed at all points of my career as both an animator and animation researcher is that whether you are a student, professional or hobbyist, the call of directing, writing and/or producing one's own projects is often a strong one. Of course, many of those who work in the animation industry are less creatively driven, practically minded individuals with essential talents and specialist skills. Chances are that if you're reading this book you don't consider yourself amongst that group, or perhaps you do but wish to branch out and try your hand at some new territory. Not that there's anything that puts creatives above specialists and other equally hard-workers; specialist skill is invaluable and oftentimes the real key to a project's success, and as such it's worth considering to what degree you wish to "go it alone," so to speak.

To whatever extent this may be, it's a safe assumption that the ultimate goal is the same: To create a standout film that makes your mark on the animation world, one of the few goals aspired to at all stages of one's career. These stages include but are not limited to:

- Animation students who wish to have something to show for their hard work and studies, which will make a name for them and help grab the attention of hiring studios.
- Animation hobbyists looking to channel their interests into something they can make a legitimate career out of.
- Freelancers with work experience and a fundamental knowledge of the industry, eager to create a piece of work with their own stamp and creative identity.
- Studio owners who might benefit tremendously from the visibility and industry credibility a standout film would generate for their business.

Figure 1.3

The Planets (Dir. Andy Martin) ©2014 Andy Martin.

- Industry specialists eager to expand their body of work through collaboration or simply trying something new.
- Even those who have made a film – or several – before, searching for the motivation to create more or possibly pursue an exciting new artistic direction.

Wherever you are in the industry the ultimate goals will most likely be to entertain, be noticed and have your work be seen and appreciated. My personal enthusiasm for the subject comes from having forged an animation career in part from the creation of my own independent film work, alongside my role as Editor in Chief of the UK-based Skwigly Online Animation Magazine. Beginning my involvement with the website as a contributing features writer in 2011, before long I began to truly appreciate just how multi-faceted, entertaining and inspirational animation's independent sector could be. Since then Skwigly has grown to include regular written features, industry exclusives, several long-running podcast series featuring an assortment of guests from all imaginable manner of

Figure 1.4

Phantom Limb (Dir. Alex Grigg) ©2013 Alex Grigg.

Figure 1.5

Splintertime (Dir. Rosto) ©2015 Studio Rosto A.D/Autour de Minuit/S.O.I.L.

animation backgrounds, micro-documentaries, not-so-micro-documentaries, specially curated animation screenings and a great deal more. Through our regular contact with some of the industry's most inspiring figures and the opportunities we have had to spread awareness of rising animation talent, it has become resoundingly clear that independent animation has entered its most innovative era to date.

Throughout this book will be a number of case studies from the world of independent animation. Some are recent, others long-established industry game-changers, but all of which ultimately encapsulate the "spirit" of independent animation. Which begs the rather vital question:

What Exactly *Is* "Independent Animation"?

Our own individual take may be relatively cut and dry, but putting it to the artists themselves paints a wider picture altogether:

Adam Elliot (*Oscar-Winning* Director, *Harvie Krumpet*)

"I never really used the word 'independent' until a few years ago when I thought *I should use it more, because it means many things and it's a good summary of all the things I aspire to do.* I still don't have a business card because I don't know what to put on it. Storyteller, producer, writer, what am I? I do like the word 'auteur' because of the Frenchness and because it suggests that you had a hand in everything, it's a complete artistic expression. It says to not just the audience but to people who want to get involved in your project that 'This is mine, this is an expression of me, I'm in control and I want creative freedom.' So for me independence means many things – it can mean poverty, it can mean creative control, it can mean that you're choosing a path that's probably a bit insane from an audience's perspective but you're being brave, taking a risk and delivering content people may have never seen before and will hopefully get something out of."

Bill Plympton (*Oscar-Nominated* Independent Director)

"It's a very tough question, because technically George Lucas could be considered 'independent' in that he finances his own films and can make whatever he wants, though we don't really think of him as such. To me that's the definition, if the money is your own rather than government money, Hollywood money or from some big producer, because if it's your own money then you can dictate the content. Whoever pays usually has a say in the content, it's very rare that someone will give you money and not care what you do with it. That's just the way it goes. So I believe that if you finance your own film and create it then it's truly independent."

Ruth Lingford (Independent Director and Animation Professor)

"I think it's fantastically important to have animators making work that does not depend on pleasing an awful lot of people. I think we couldn't grow this art form if we were always under the compulsion to make megabucks and to avoid unsettling or upsetting our audiences. There are commercial companies doing really wonderful work and I think in the UK especially there is a wonderful crossover between commercial work and independent animation. Independent animators are, I think, more cognizant of their audience's time, it's a type of filmmaking that has real discipline and muscularity."

Figure 1.6

Rocks in my Pockets (Dir. Signe Baumane) ©2014 Signe Baumane.

Signe Baumane (Independent Director, *Rocks in My Pockets*)

"I pay a lot of attention to how and why films are made. A lot of big studio films are made because somebody wants to make money or somebody *has* to make money. A filmmaker says 'I have an idea' but then needs a producer who won't come on board unless the film will make money. In the credits when you see how many wrote the script you realise these are films made by a committee. They'll strip it of the things that certain groups won't like to make a film that appeals to a very broad audience, not one artist's vision. That is not what interests me and it's not what drives me. I am an individualist, I guess. I want to survive, I want to live, I want to make films that are primarily one person's point of view." (Figure 1.6)

Kieran Argo (Animation Programmer)

"I think it *could* be summarized as filmmaking without the commercial or financial constraints of longer-form work; it's art for art's sake, to use the old cliché. Short form animation is an art form and it should be respected as such, it's not just, as so many people consider it to be, a stepping stone onto bigger and better things, especially not for animation. I think the word that kind of grates on me is 'independent.' Even some of the bigger studios like Aardman still make short films, they still see them just as worthy as any other solo project by an animator in his bedroom. Films are being made for the love of it and I think that's the great thing about short-form work. There's so much dedication and pure love for the art form. So that's what it is for me, it's unconstrained by finance and it's done for the love of it."

Sam Taylor (Independent Director, The Line)

"I feel like the distinction between independent and commercial animation has become more blurred recently. There's so much good commercial work out there that it's less of a dirty word than it used to be. The level, and prevalence of technical skill has definitely increased in line with the explosion of access to content and instructional material online. Its terrifying how good people are at such a young age now. I feel like the main difference is that people are making stuff for more varied audiences. Its not so much about getting into the rarefied world of festivals or awards, and more about producing things that will engage people with similar sensibilities across disciplines."

Tom Schroeder (Independent Director and Documentarian)

"I think that I'm so independent that I'm really an 'amateur' in the strictest sense of the word – making films for the love of making films. My musical metaphor for my students is as follows: if Disney is an orchestra and the Warner Brothers' cartoons of the fifties were made by a jazz ensemble, then independent animators are the folks on a street corner with a guitar and a hat. It implies that you can't achieve the scale or ambition of the grander organizations, but you have complete control over the content and presentation of the work. I'm interested in the expressive relationship between style and content in how an animated film can communicate to an audience simultaneously as a graphic form and as a narrative form, which is one of the most compelling aspects of animation to me. If you're not controlling all aspects of the production, it's more difficult to pursue these goals."

Tünde Vollenbroek (Producer, Studio Pupil)

"One possible meaning of independent animation is when it's simply not commissioned, it came out of the filmmaker's wish. I think about subsidies, where funding comes from, and is a film really still independent if a film gets funding? One core meaning of independence is that you don't do it with any money, you just do it in your free time. In a way, the animated short film is always kind of independent because there's not really an established financial model for it, so at the start there's rarely any other reason to make it other than for yourself."

Robert Morgan (Independent Director)

"It's a feeling of doing it for yourself, not waiting for anybody and being liberated in every way, in terms of production but also in terms of the kinds of stories you want to tell. I think on every level it's about doing it yourself, being yourself and not bending to anyone else's preconceived idea of what you should be doing. To me, that's what it is, it's freedom really." (Figure 1.7)

Figure 1.7

Bobby Yeah (Dir. Robert Morgan) ©2011 Swartz Can Talk/blueLight.

Robertino Zambrano (Creative Director, KAPWA Studioworks)

"I guess it's something that's been started without a financial safety net, so obviously there's grey areas but I would describe it…when someone says 'independent animation' I see a small handful of people or a solo artist getting together off their own back with their own savings and trying to put something together without a large media network behind them. I would say that'd be my attempt at an empirical definition!"

Kirsten Lepore (Independent Director)

"To me, it signifies that I'm largely the one in charge of how the film turns out; that there isn't a client or studio head I'm answering to that has the last word. Because of this, one would generally have more personal responsibility for the film, but I enjoy that responsibility. I don't answer to anyone when I do my personal work. I get to control everything – it's a controlling animator's dream! The downside is that I don't get paid." (Figure 1.8)

Garrett Michael Davis (Animator and Designer)

"It's about having the freedom to make the rules, to be ambiguous. Freedom from 'style,' models, and submitting to other peoples' limitations. There aren't any limitations to animation, but people's minds deceive them into thinking there are. The potential of animation has barely been tapped. In my experience people (in the entertainment industry) tend to see animation as just a less expensive version of live action, like in order for a form to morph and change it has to be written into the script as a drug-trip scene or something. That is absurd – it's making the most basic qualities of animation (change and transformation) require some kind of extraneous explanation in order to be put into practice. Of course the commercial approach is so deeply enmeshed in the baffling complexity of the web of commerce that it doesn't really have a choice, so it's best for artists not to worry about it and use that machine to their advantage if they can, and never lose the true creativity that should only ever be checked by the artist and not by any outside force."

Figure 1.8

Move Mountain (Dir. Kirsten Lepore) ©2013 Kirsten Lepore.

Chris Shepherd (Director)

"I suppose it is animation that's out of the clutches of the big corporations. The thing is, the nature of animation has changed – as time's gone by animation has become very democratised, where now everybody can do it, whereas before it would be a select few who had all the resources and equipment. After 2000 it sort of opened up with Flash and all those other programs. I like that somebody on a council estate in Leeds can make an animation and put it online, and their viewpoint is just as valid as anybody else's. I think that making it more democratic as a medium is a good thing and it can also make it more powerful, it has more strands, it means more to more people."

Robert Grieves (Animation Freelancer and Independent Director)

"It's animation that you don't have to ask anyone's permission to do, you don't need approval, you just crack on. One of the reasons I do it is, having had a perfectly nice career doing attractive enough stuff and making money, with none of my projects could I stand back and say that all of the creative decisions were mine. The ego in me wanted that. Not just from the point of view of taking all the glory, but I was fed up of apologizing. Every project had that moment of 'The client made me do it,' so I wanted something where I could say 'This baby is mine.' At which point it moves into the world of art, it's a self-expression."

It is within the parameters of this reasonably broad series of definitions that the book will operate, and ultimately it's up to you to consider which definition best applies to your processes and how it may very well add to your perspective – or change it altogether. As you read on, you will glean invaluable insight from all of the artists and experts above, plus many more, with practical guidance along the way to help you determine exactly how you can develop, produce and distribute your independent project and have audiences sit up and take notice (Figure 1.9).

Figure 1.9

Risehigh (Dir. Adam Wells) ©2013 Adam Wells.

2

Story Development

To some, story development can be broken down as a methodical process, predicated on heavy research of successful character dynamics, story structure, action beats, etc. In all forms of independent filmmaking, be it animation or otherwise, there generally tend to be more inherent creative freedoms when it comes to how rigidly a story is developed and structured. Outside of the mainstream world of major feature films that are obliged to adhere to a more classical approach, animation has generally managed to sidestep convention.

Immersing yourself in the culture of animated film across the board – from the sunniest, most character-driven box-office smash to the bleakest, most obscure arthouse navel-gazer – is obviously valuable in determining where you lie on the spectrum, and I'm sure many of you reading this will have done as much already. Breaking down the gamut of story into its two most simplified categories, what we end up with are films driven by written scripts and films driven by visual concepts. It follows that if your film has a strong narrative at its core, where the conversational interplay between your characters is the driving force behind their characterization, then written story development is most likely the way to go. By extension, of course, if you're going for physical humor, with less reliance on dialogue, the visual approach will be the best method.

It's not quite so cut and dry, of course. More often than not the process of crafting a story tends to combine both approaches in some measure, depending on artistic background, style, sense of narrative, sense of drama, sense of humor and directorial intent. Sometimes the writing process can even be completely invented by the writer themselves. Filmmaker Adam Wells (whose work we'll

DOI: 10.1201/9781003214717-2

look at in greater detail later in the book) has his own particularly organic way of developing original ideas:

"I listen to a lot of podcast storytelling, sometimes second-guessing how the stories are going to end. When they don't actually end how I imagined I have an original story. It may sound really weird but whenever stuff like that happens I try to write it down."

This method is one I'm sure most of us can appreciate; how often do we wish we could change elements of a story to better suit our tastes? Of course, in Adam's case more is being done than simply tacking on a presumed ending, as one can't effectively plagiarize and claim originality by altering one detail. Working backward to craft a story completely independent of the one that inspired the original, alternate ending results in an end product that is, ipso facto, an original overall idea.

Generally speaking, this isn't an approach that most would adopt, but it warrants mention as an example of just how individual our creative process can be. Circumstances and scenarios that can prompt our own original ideas are multitudinous, so let's take a look at some recent examples of modern animated films taking an atypical approach to story development and examine the main virtues of each to help determine what best suits a project or the artist at the helm of it.

The Character-Driven Approach

As we'll explore in later chapters, the freedoms animation allows can accommodate virtually any approach to story crafting, be they adapted from pre-existing source material, predicated on thumbnail doodles barely legible to anyone other than their artist, or even stream-of-consciousness fantasies animated chronologically. As overused – and, oftentimes, misused – as the saying "the possibilities are endless" can be, on the subject of story generation for an animated project it genuinely applies.

Just because any and every approach *can* be taken, however, doesn't mean it will be the right choice for those who take more solace in a nice, detailed plan of action with an old-fashioned script at its center. Certainly, the independent scene is a playground for the avant-garde and the experimental, yet a more straight-laced method is easily as effective as long as the hook is strong. Oftentimes a short film will be developed with a hope to generate more of the same, either as a pilot for a potential television show or formative outing for a series of shorts that share a central character or premise. The success of Bill Plympton's visually scripted Oscar-nominated *Guard Dog* (2004), for example, inspired the director to return to the character time and again between other projects, for the subsequent shorts *Guide Dog* (2006), *Hot Dog* (2008), *Horn Dog* (2009) and *Cop Dog* (2017). Don Hertzfeldt similarly created a trilogy of shorts in 2006, 2008 and 2011, that all centered around an ailing man named Bill, each film effectively building on what had come before. These three shorts were ultimately edited together to create the acclaimed 2012 feature *It's Such a Beautiful Day*. Since then Hertzfeldt has embarked on another series beginning with 2015s *World of Tomorrow*, again followed by subsequent episodes that build up the same world established in the first (wherein a young girl named Emily is visited by a clone of herself from the future).

In the UK, another independent trilogy of films were produced over a span of six years, beginning with 2007s *Rocket Science* (Figures 2.1–2.3). The film, written by Andrew Endersby and Sam Morrison (also director), was scripted with the full intention of being used as a pilot that might branch off into a series. As is often the case, timing and circumstances – combined with what the TV network perceived as *niche* appeal – ruled out this option, although its functionality as a standalone short made it a successful venture in its own right. In lieu of episodic production, the film eventually spawned two "sequel" shorts – *Grime City P.D.* (Figure 2.4) in 2010 and *The Patsy* (Figure 2.5) in 2013, also directed and co-written by Sam. With a focus on dialogue-driven, movie-trope heavy scripted comedy and effective, minimal visuals, the combined length of the three comes to nearly an hour.

"As we like to think of ourselves as creative people, we thought we should maybe do something creative" Sam says of the project's origins. "It started out as prose actually, writing stories. It's quite possible that we just didn't discuss what it was going to be, but someone wrote a first line and it just went off from there. What we did then was the same thing we do when we write: Get in a room together, take it in turns to write a bit and read it back to one another, and basically just try and make each other laugh."

When working with a co-writer, there are multiple variations on what precisely the working dynamic will be, though it's important you both play to your strengths.

"It's quite a reductionist, sweeping statement but I think I'm probably better at structure and Andrew's definitely better at coming up with funny one-liners and crazy left-turns in the story."

Figure 2.1

Early character sketches/concept for the *Rocket Science* universe ©Sam Morrison. Image courtesy of the artist.-

Figure 2.2

Early *Rocket Science* illustration ©Sam Morrison. Image courtesy of the artist.

Character Development

The *Rocket Science* stories themselves draw upon some of the most familiar conventions of film noir (updated to the crime television genre in later films), as does the leading player of the trilogy, Jack Hersey; a concentrated siphoning of every cop character cliché – such as casual misogyny and arrogance paired with misguided determination. Jack is flanked by two supporting characters with similarly obvious characterization – level-headed Patricia and earnest, unintelligent deputy Billy. It is, in Sam's words "satire with a very small 's,'" though the films stand out as not coasting off personas that could very easily write themselves, a trap that many genre parody films can easily fall into. As far as the writing itself, Sam freely admits that these films are far more script exercises than animation showcases.

"While I'm writing I do occasionally conjure up an idea, I might think *This'll be a different film-noir type shot of looking down through the staircase*, think of the shadows, stuff like that, but most of the time I'm guilty of just thinking up stupid things for Jack to say and not thinking massively visually about it."

The strength of this trio of characters comes from a dynamic that allows them to carry scenes individually, together or in respective pairings. While a story headed up by a single led is reliant on their ability to carry a story on their own, one headed up by a pair is reliant on their chemistry. It follows then that three characters must extend that chemistry, so one person's yin serves as another's yang; Jack Hersey's bullheadedness will be effectively counterbalanced by Patricia, who coddles Billy's naivety and earnestness that in turn will exacerbate Jack while moving the story forward.

"I think that Jack was really well-defined from the outset and has remained pretty much the same. The stories evolved to a point where we were trying to pitch them as a series, they became more focused as a result of that and maybe he became more satirical in his attitudes rather than his actions.

"Billy started out more stupid and I guess evolved to be more of an innocent while still a bit of a doofus; that was played up because it was the nice contrast to Jack. Patricia, being caught between them, I think probably evolved the most, in the sense that at the start everyone in it was just sort of idiotic. With the first draft of *Rocket Science*, she turned up as a scientist, was revolted by Jack but ended up falling in love with him just because that was the way those films were, kind of what you expected. Partly because that made her a less interesting character – and

Figure 2.3

Rocket Science (Dir. Sam Morrison) lobby card design ©2006 Evil Genius Ltd.

partly because we wanted to do more films – we realised that she couldn't fall in love with Jack because that was a resolution, of sorts. Comparatively Jack doesn't evolve, that's his key characteristic."

In substitution of a writer's bible, the universe of the films is largely predicated on amassed pitch materials from when trying to sell the series. Even outside of a formal style or content guide, when dealing with script-based film work that has the potential to expand to a series or, at the very least, further films, having your world mapped out in some form or other will prove beneficial. Breaking down character personalities, motivations and even things the audience won't see such as secret yearnings and past history will give you a sense of acquaintance with your characters and, in turn, give your characters a sense of dimensionality.

At all points of production, feedback is also important. Though the world of Jack Hersey did not find footing as a television series, the pitching process yielded valuable insight into how to improve the next outing. Two prime examples being the automatic limitations of making a film in black and white, as Rocket Science was, and jettisoning their original plan to enforce a timeline by having each outing for the characters be set ten years apart.

"Our original idea for this was so we could visit a whole load of different genres and have Jack in a different decade, being exactly the same. But we realised that wasn't going to work, partly because television commissioners don't like serials,

Figure 2.4

Grime City P.D. (Dir. Sam Morrison) poster artwork ©2010 Evil Genius Ltd.

Figure 2.5

Still from *The Patsy* (Dir. Sam Morrison) ©2013 Evil Genius Ltd.

they like to be able to show programs in any order at all, with no chronology, and partly because Jack would be dead after about four episodes because he'd be too old.

"The main sort of feedback is people who like it, or affect to like it, is saying they think it's funny, because that's all it's trying to be. The main thing that evolved was that *Rocket Science* never made it clear what era it was in, but it was very easy for everyone to assume it's the fifties. In our own heads we were probably thinking that, but commissioners made it clear they weren't interested in stuff set in the past, so we brought Jack and his characters into the present day. That was a really brilliant bit of feedback, actually, because it made it even more satirical, more observed and brought the whole relevance of questioning those old attitudes to the surface."

Telling the Harder Truths

It is a hard truth in itself that animation is often regarded by the masses as little more than frivolous entertainment. We can certainly be amused, moved, even angered by animation; we can be awed by its spectacle and its ability to communicate concepts which live action and other means of storytelling simply cannot. Ultimately though, like any form of artistic expression, it is ephemeral, its appeal bound by shifting cultural attitudes and political climates. As such, there is an inevitably smaller percentage of animators whose work has a lasting value, either through technical advancement or social messages.

Born in Australia and a long-time resident of Melbourne, Adam Elliot is an *important* animator whose work, on an aesthetic level, is purposefully entrenched in a traditional and pleasingly nostalgic era of plasticine animation, while as a storyteller he is able to put across earnest social messages without being either preachy or maudlin. What has so far tied all his work together is an underlying theme of living with affliction. This work began with his Victoria College of the Arts student short *Uncle* in 1996, followed up in quick succession by the government-funded *Cousin* (1998) and *Brother* (1999), rounding out a quasi-autobiographical trilogy of shorts focusing on family members who have led troubled lives (Figure 2.6). Venturing further into outright fiction, Adam's 2003 short film *Harvie Krumpet*, detailing the life of a Polish migrant with Tourette's syndrome, went on to win the 2004 Academy Award for Best Animated Short. The accolade, referred to by Adam as "the golden crowbar," ultimately facilitated the production of his first full-length feature *Mary and Max* in 2009; a critically acclaimed exploration of two pen pals who led tremendously disparate lives yet maintain a bond throughout.

Regarding the latter film, his former producer Melanie Coombs observed "I see the pattern in all of Adam's work is about accepting difference. That we all look for acceptance and love is probably a universal truth; that we are all different, is another."[1]

Adam's films also have a shared sense of national identity, in a manner similar to the distinctly British politeness of *Wallace & Gromit* and the celebration of Americana and family values that was *The Simpsons* in its heyday. It's a quality

Figure 2.6

Character sculpts for Adam Elliot's *Uncle, Cousin* and *Brother* trilogy ©2015 Adam Elliot.

that, alongside the bold choices of topics covered in his work, has made Adam such an important figure in contemporary Australian film and culture. Alongside his affinity for plasticine animation, a constant in Adam's work has been the casual incorporation of subject matter that mainstream television and cinema (even, to a large extent, the world of independent film) feels compelled to handle with kid gloves. Though no doubt well intentioned, this hypersensitivity toward the depiction of important social impairments, physical disabilities and mental illnesses has in many respects only served to fuel the sense of alienation that accompanies them. Adam Elliot's storytelling, by contrast, indulges a far healthier and more socially aware impulse to bring these issues out into the open. Said issues span birth defects, Tourette's syndrome, Asperger's syndrome, cerebral palsy, alcoholism, depression and all manner of limitations of social and cognitive development. The undeniably tragic inherences of these afflictions are married with the far more taboo notion of their comedic mileage. Rather than cheapening or trivializing the plight of each character, this gallows humor instead rounds out and humanizes all of them, making their stories all the more poignant (Figure 2.7).

"I always try to write funny films," Adam maintains. "Unfortunately I can't help myself – they end up being quite tragic! No one has a perfectly happy life or a completely miserable one, I think it's all shades of light and dark. Comedy-tragedies have been around for centuries, and to tell stories which are authentic, empathetic and relatable to an audience. You can't just do gags, you have to dig deeper. I try to create very authentic characters and, while my aim is to make the audience laugh, I *really* feel like I've achieved something if I've caused them to cry. I know that's a strange ambition, to upset your audience, but I don't like them leaving the cinema indifferent or apathetic. I really want them to have experienced *something* – even if they've just laughed, at least I've pushed *some* buttons."

When it comes to the actual process of getting these ideas together, Adam concedes that it can be a struggle. While much energy is expended on draft after draft of each screenplay, more often than not stories only fully come together in the dying hours.

"That's annoying, to just spend so much time trying to construct a scene or a sequence and then you throw it all out at the last minute and go with something intuitive and spontaneous! It's a necessary part of the process, of course, but

Figure 2.7

Adam Elliot with *Ernie Biscuit* character sculpts ©2015 Adam Elliot.

2. Story Development

I feel like a fraud so often when people say that my films have such strong writing! I think all writers try and aim for perfection and we certainly don't feel like we ever really get there."

As frustrating as it may be in the moment, it stands to reason that without the effort spent on story construction that will ultimately be jettisoned, the last-minute change-all might not indeed manifest itself at all. In that respect, the act of writing itself, even if it doesn't contribute directly to the final film, is never a waste of time. It is, truthfully, a far healthier impulse to feel a fraud, rather than feel we are owed. Entitlement and arrogance has rarely led to a creative product that rises above mediocrity, as there is no driving force behind it. As Adam insists, confidence is a curse.

"I think the moment you become confident you tend to rest on your laurels. You don't want your self-esteem to get too low and you don't want to wallow in self-pity, but feeling like you're only at the beginning of your career just forces you to keep writing harder and with more determination. I mean, determination is a silly word, I don't wake up in the morning with this 'determination' to write, I write when I'm angry, I write when I'm tired, I write in all sorts of modes. Feeling inadequate, I think, is an important ingredient, certainly it's a stimulus."

What binds all of Adam's work to date is a staple of an earlier era of film-making: Narration. Going back to his original trilogy of 'clayographies,' the minimally animated visuals and sparse (effectively nil) use of dialogue are undeniably bolstered by the humanity of the narration, performed by Australian actor William McInnes. *Uncle, Cousin* and *Brother* are all recollections of an unnamed, ostensibly fictional protagonist regarding each titular family member. Through both writing and delivery, the films are infused with palpable regret, warmth and humanity. Subsequent films modified the use of this device insofar as the narrator becomes an entirely faceless entity, overseeing the events of the films rather than remembering them. Such is the nature of narration-driven films, Adam is compelled to embrace the English language and, when appropriate, use it as a character almost in itself.

"I can't stop using my thesaurus all the time. I probably overuse it, but I think we're all striving for that perfect sentence, or something that's poetic and original." There are also elements of fastidiousness and caution we should always be aware of regarding the originality of our work. "You go through these periods of self-doubt, thinking *Oh hang on, maybe this has been done before? Have I subconsciously ripped somebody off?* I'll Google sentences I write now just to check that I haven't. For example, in *Ernie Biscuit*, the line 'Somedays you're the windscreen, somedays you're the insect,' I heard it years ago and I still cannot find who came up with that. I certainly didn't write it and I don't claim to have."

The writing process itself is one Adam analogizes with baking a cake ("Which is a cliché in itself") and the selective approach one needs to take with whatever 'ingredients' are appropriate, "An ingredient might be a piece of music, it might be a conversation I heard in an airport lounge, it might be something I found on the ground on one of my walks in the morning. I have notebooks, like a lot of writers do, and they are a mishmash of sights and smells; I try and use all my senses when I'm writing, I try and create imagery that you could almost smell or taste, so when I go to write the scripts I go through my notebooks and I pick out all the ingredients I want. In *Mary and Max* (Figure 2.8), for example, I knew that there had to be a scene in the film where three old men jump off a jetty into freezing cold water and they get erect nipples – I just *had* to have that in the film

Figure 2.8

"Max" character sculpt for Adam Elliot's *Mary and Max* ©2015 Adam Elliot.

somewhere! So I sort of do it the opposite way to how a lot of writers work: I start with the detail and hopefully by the third or fourth draft a plot magically starts to appear, and by the very last draft, a very obvious three-act structure."

One school of thought would insist that structure in filmmaking is a skill that needs to be learned methodically. Having gone the route of reading scriptwriting books himself, Adam maintains that for many it is in fact a natural intuition. What qualifies as three-act structure, an inciting incident and a climax is something we are exposed to our whole lives, virtually anywhere we look, throughout literature, television, cinema, documentaries – even advertising and news reports are tailored to a fundamental narrative, primarily to ensure that audiences don't change the channel.

"I really believe that storytelling is a primeval act, that we're all storytellers and some of us are better storytellers than others. In many ways, a good story, well told, is just like a very good joke, well told – it's all in the timing, and there's a punchline. For me, with all my ingredients, it's always getting a balance between the humor and the pathos, the comedy/tragedy, it's getting a rhythm to the piece, it's a holistic sort of patchwork. I always say 'Without the dark, the light has no meaning.'" Though Adam struggles to work out exactly how his scripts come together, when broken down they often begin with an assortment of small details that are then gradually woven together. Though his later films such as *Harvie Krumpet* and *Ernie Biscuit* are linear and straightforward, Adam does not obsess over plot. The stories are uncomplicated, which allows for their respective twists to stand out all the more and keep the audience engaged.

"It's a cliché to say that I write for myself, but I do, I really make films that I want to laugh and cry at. I think *Mary and Max*, for me, was a great opportunity

2. Story Development

to really have an hour and a half to fully explore two character's lives in extreme detail and have moments of poignancy and comedy. I certainly love making shorts, because for me shorts are about what to leave out, not what to put in. With a feature you can go off on tangents, you can have stuff purely for visual pleasure as long as you come back to a story eventually. The plot is always secondary – as long as the audience are laughing and engaged then that's my golden rule. The other rule I have is that if a joke falls flat that's okay, the audience will forgive you. If the next joke straight after *that* joke falls flat, okay you might be in a little bit of trouble but you could still be forgiven. If the *third* joke after that joke falls flat, then you're in really big trouble!"

As to whether or not he is more at ease with writing comedy or tragedy, Adam identifies there is an element of trial and error. A danger when setting out to move an audience is that our purpose may become too obvious. A "sad" scene, when clearly manufactured to be so, has not nearly as much impact as a poignant moment that doesn't aim to draw attention to itself. Pathos is best delivered in small, understated doses, and as such, it is more likely to have an effect when incorporated organically, without contrivance.

"Luckily with animation we're forgiven so often, whereas a novel is such high art, aspiring for such poignant, palpable scenes, I just do a lot of toilet humour, whack in a bit of poignancy and a few deaths and there you go! Some people would say comedy is harder, but I think with tragedy, getting someone to cry and squeeze tears out of their eye ducts, I mean that's insane! Some films I achieve that, others I don't quite get there, but I know with *Mary and Max* I've had so many people come up and say 'Oh it's the first animated film I've cried at! Apart from *Toy Story 3*.' And they have all said the same thing – that it's not what they expected from a claymation film."

Amidst its overriding humor, the journey of *Mary and Max*'s story is one of extreme, feelgood highs and gut-wrenching lows, a journey that took an emotional toll not just on the audience but Adam himself. Certainly, the labor of a major feature – produced under tremendously limited resources next to virtually any other stop-motion feature of comparable success at that time – was creatively incapacitating, but it was clear to Adam that another film that carried on the traditions of tragedy was not on the cards immediately. The eventual solution came in the form of paring down his next proposed feature *Ernie Biscuit* (Figure 2.9) into a short film of similar length and tone to *Harvie Krumpet*. Completed in 2015 and crafted and produced almost entirely on his own, the film could arguably be considered his first truly independent short.

"For my own sanity, I wanted to make something a little bit more lighthearted, my version of a romantic comedy of sorts. I wrote it as a feature, which I think is a good exercise in making a short is to write it as a feature first and then pare it back significantly, you distil it and you get to its essence.

"I've discovered the difference between *Ernie Biscuit* and my other films is all my other films are tragedies that have comedy in them, whereas *Ernie Biscuit* is a comedy that has a little bit of tragedy in it. My films certainly don't stand out because of their technique – I'm dreadful at walk-cycles, I'm terrible at lip syncing, my characters are pretty grotesque looking. I have very few camera moves, but I think that one of the reasons my films *do* stand out is because they do deal with difficult themes and subject matter that's a bit more challenging.

"Often audiences feel by the end of the film that they've been wrung out, that I've pushed every button on their body and frightened them with scenes

Figure 2.9

Still from *Ernie Biscuit* (Dir. Adam Elliot) ©2015 Adam Elliot.

of suicide and alcoholism. They're quite dense, and in some ways, the audience are exhausted by the end, but they feel somehow satisfied. I get a lot of emails from people who have just discovered *Mary and Max* in particular, and they say that the film has lingered with them. That, for me, is the biggest compliment."

Films that linger with an audience tend to do so because they have had an impact in terms of characters they can empathize with and circumstances they can relate to. These are elements that apply to all areas of storytelling and make a case for looking outside of animation to fully develop your frame of reference as a storyteller.

"*One Flew over the Cuckoo's Nest* works today as beautifully as it did back in the 70s, because it deals with archetypes, characters that are classical in that they will always be ageless and deal with subject matter that is universal and timeless. That's also why I read a lot of classic literature, for selfish reasons! I read classic literature because I want to find out *How did this become a classic, what is the definition of a classic novel?* It is a never-ending pursuit of trying to work out what is a story I want to tell, what is a story I want to hear and see. Ultimately you get to the point where you think *Alright, well I just want to be moved, I want to have a laugh, I want to smile, I want to understand most of the plot, but ultimately I want to leave that cinema feeling something has* happened *to me.* Whether it lingers or not, I want to feel that I haven't wasted that person's time. The audience are giving up twenty minutes of their busy lives!"

Often when we see perceivably taboo subject matter used for humorous purposes it is for shock value, contrived to provoke. Certainly, there are filmmakers, comedians and television show creators who have capitalized off this device, as that which will offend some will also have an in-built audience of those who enjoy seeing offense being taken. Adam Elliot's films don't take this approach, as easy (perhaps lazy) as it would be to take any of their more sensitive topics and rattle of a series of caustic one-liners, the effect of this would quickly diminish. Instead his writing is more effective for being respectful and honest, incorporating small details that stand out in their truthfulness – recalling, for example, the cerebral palsy afflicted cousin of *Cousin*'s ever-present smell of licorice, the color and size of his pills and the (inexplicable, yet perfectly sensible to a child) envy of his being allowed to pee sitting down.

"I *was* jealous of my cousin, as a child. He got special treatment, he got to do everything first, I remembered going through this weird period where I wished I had no legs, because I'd get all this attention! It was ridiculous now in hindsight."

Although ridiculous in hindsight, there is an authenticity to it that gives the writing far more weight than if the story were laced with condescension and positive affirmation; these are not always films about people who triumphed in the face of adversity. Animation functions superbly as a form of escapism, but it is equally capable of facing real-life issues – be they sociological, political, religious and so forth – head on. To confront, rather than escape, can be equally nourishing to an audience.

"I remember going to Annecy back in 1996 with *Uncle* and realising that my film was very different to everyone else's. Back then I had never been to a film festival and wasn't really an animation buff or fanatic – I didn't know who Jan Švankmajer was! But I quickly realised that I was a point of difference and that, if I was going to have any longevity as a filmmaker then I should just continue making more of the same. Luckily, I had plenty of friends, relatives and people I knew who I perceived as interesting and a point of difference themselves. Then as the years went on, I kept thinking *Why aren't more people making films like mine? I want to see animated films about autism and Tourette's syndrome*. It wasn't so much that I wanted to see films about disability but I wanted to see films about *real* people, which is why I prefer documentaries over animation."

Having always gravitated toward anything biographical or autobiographical, the ripple effect of Adam's success has led to an increase of short, animated films that strive to deal with more challenging subject matter. That there is new work being created that is proving more challenging, if not abstract, to the audience is something to be encouraged by.

Though technically operating outside of the more commonly agreed-upon definitions of independent animation, UK-based animator Matthew Walker has directed several films whose funding circumstances have infused in them a degree of independent spirit. Following his 2005 University of Wales Newport student short *Astronauts* (a major success on the festival circuit depicting two hapless spacemen growing increasingly aggravated by their confined proximity aboard their ship), Matthew joined the Bristol-based studio ArthurCox as an in-house director for commercial work (some of which was produced in association with local powerhouse Aardman Animations, the studio that would eventually produce his children's series *Lloyd of the Flies*) as well as short films when circumstances allowed. The first and most prominent of these has been *John and Karen* (2007), which shared the director's identifiable pacing and unostentatious wit seen in *Astronauts*, applied instead to a lighter, more domestic scenario in which a polar bear awkwardly attempts to repair his relationship with a penguin, a prior *faux pas* having driven a wedge between them.

As with Adam Elliot's work, one notable area where Matt's films succeed is making effective use of minimal resources. With student films often bogged down by the need to showcase the spectacle of CG software in lieu of an engaging story, I have often cited *Astronauts* as a masterclass in what corners to cut to both alleviate the demands of production and benefit the story. As written, the animation requirements are minimal, which allows what little there is to have more time spent on it, resulting in subtle yet highly considered character animation. Labor-intensive sequences that would otherwise require lip-sync and facial animation are alleviated by having the astronauts wearing blacked-out helmets, a device that, rather than limit their range of expression, adds a charming impassivity to their performance when paired with the often-deadpan dialogue. Ultimately all of Matt's animated films tend to share this trait of humor through minutiae, which requires an interplay between dialogue and visuals that warrant a good deal of consideration at the writing stage.

"I feel like I'm always struggling with it, because I kind of work both ways. I usually start with a script and then further develop it in the animatic stage, or storyboarding, but sometimes I'll start with a visual idea, it depends on the film. *Operator* (Figure 2.10) never really had a script, because it was just a very simple idea that I had sketched in a notebook. It was just a few lines of dialogue I wrote on a plane coming back from a festival, and then I just turned that into a little comic, and then that was it. I never sat down and wrote it as a script really, it was just a kind of little series of thumbnails. So then I think when I recorded it I added a few lines or tweaked some of the dialogue. Whereas all my other films have started with a script, but then a lot more has been added as I've gone through the animatic stage. I think the animatic stage is where I do most of the creative stuff. So the script is just a starting point, and then I'll refine it in an animatic."

Operator is perhaps the most minimal of Matthew's work in terms of story, being essentially a one-sided phone conversation between a man and God. The film, made while an Artist in Residence at Newport International Film School Wales, benefits from an assortment of visual embellishments in a manner similar to *John and Karen* (Figures 2.11 and 2.12), in particular the use of cutaways to paint an incomplete yet intriguing portrait of a man compelled to call upon a deity to enquire as to why humans cannot lick their own elbow. In the single room that the film takes place, we glimpse an assortment of sticky-notes with illegible enquiries, possibly of a similar nature, an empty watering can, a sleeping cat and a book on dishwasher safety among other seemingly disconnected bric-a-brac. Small details also serve to flesh out the realism of these endearingly simple premises, such as being halfway through a bite of toffee apple when God picks up on the other end, or a brief moment of struggle in *John and Karen* when the titular polar bear realizes he has overdunked his biscuit to the point of flaccid saturation. For Matt, the point at which these elements are incorporated into the story tends to vary.

"Sometimes when I write a scene in the script I'll have a very clear idea of what's going on in the scene, or the reaction of another character, or anything that's happening in the background, and I might write that in the script. But sometimes stuff like that just comes from doing the animatic, working out the layout of the scene and then thinking of another joke that can be added, or

Figure 2.10

Mockup and final layout for the sparsely detailed *Operator* (Dir. Matthew Walker)
©2007 Matthew Walker.

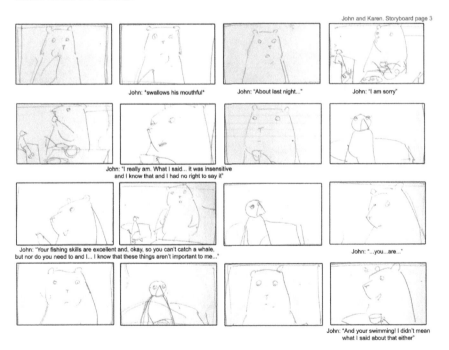

John and Karen. Storyboard page 3

John: *swallows his mouthful*   John: "About last night..."   John: "I am sorry"

John: "I really am. What I said... it was insensitive
and I know that and I had no right to say it"

John: "Your fishing skills are excellent and, okay, so you can't catch a whale,
but nor do you need to and I... I know that these things aren't important to me..."   John: "...you...are..."

John: "And your swimming! I didn't mean
what I said about that either"

Figure 2.11

John and Karen (Dir. Matthew Walker) thumbnail board excerpts. Images courtesy
of Matthew Walker.

another layer of interaction with the characters. There's no rule with it, it just happens as it happens."

Matt Walker's films also represent how some stories are best delivered with restraint and understated humor. Although the characters may have an identifiable arc, or the story a satisfying resolution, the films maintain a consistent low-key tone throughout. This accentuates how a grand denouement that resorts to visual gimmickry can be unnecessary and arbitrary, as seen so prominently in mainstream films or effects-driven, design-oriented studio projects. Similarly, the pacing of the films benefits from being allowed to breathe, not succumbing to the impulse to pepper quiet moments with sight gags or constant activity. While

Figure 2.12

John and Karen (Dir. Matthew Walker) early concept art, storyboard excerpt and final still demonstrating the film's visual development. Images courtesy of Matthew Walker. Still ©2007 ArthurCox Ltd.

2. Story Development

"plussing" (a term coined at Pixar to describe how critiques of in-progress work are used to constructively embellish and enhance their films) is a vital process for some films, in others a more moderate approach that allows the story to speak for itself is far more appropriate.

Taking the above case studies into consideration should help paint a clear enough picture of how a script-based approach to a short film will determine its outcome. Indeed, the hope with all of the examples shown in the book is for you the reader and prospective (if not already active) animation filmmaker to pick up each artist's variety of perspectives and approaches and determine whose you have the strongest creative kinship with. This will be the key to developing your own personal production pipeline, one that may not necessarily be consistent with major studios and mainstream projects but will guarantee your own follow-through on whatever animated undertaking you set for yourself.

If scriptwriting is not your forte, however, then don't be dissuaded. There are many other approaches to story from which a strong animated film can emerge; we've only just begun to scratch the surface.

Note

1 Source: *Mary and Max* EPK.

3

The Visual Storyteller

Figure 3.1

Still from *The Dam Keeper* (Dir. Robert Kondo/Dice Tsutsumi) ©2014 Tonko House LLC.

Having established in the preceding chapter that the line between strictly written and strictly visual storytelling can be a blurry one at best, one key factor that remains is that animation is, first and foremost, a visual medium. So while a scripted approach is often integral to the successful animated short, by animation's very definition it is never quite as essential as the visual component. More to the point, writing a script, like every other type of creative process, is not necessarily easy for everyone. Beyond having the solid germ of an idea, the actual act of describing environments or writing dialogue can be something that is more

DOI: 10.1201/9781003214717-3

organically achieved through a visual process. Fortunately, independent animation is an accommodating medium for those whose films need not be dependent on conversational interactions between characters (or the presence of "characters" in a literal sense at all) and conventional approaches to film structure. In this chapter, we will look at several instances where the "script" of a film is a far more visually driven affair.

Branching Out

Our first major case study for this chapter may not at first seem especially relatable, being in many respects the product of a creative union forged at Pixar Animation Studios; a powerhouse of big-budget, mainstream animation production and, as such, one of the least "indie" operations out there. Following a stint as Visual Developer at Blue Sky Studios, Dice Tsutsumi's talent eventually brought him to Pixar where he worked as an Art Director on such films as *Toy Story 3* (2010). Over the course of seven years, Dice worked closely with Robert Kondo, himself an Art Director on *Ratatouille* (2007), the two of them contributing significantly to *Monsters University* (2013). Having neighboring offices, the two would oftentimes find themselves looking over one another's shoulders and finding excuses to collaborate, Dice in particular harboring a desire to work on his own independent project one day.

"When I met Dice," Robert recalls, "He always made a really clear distinction that I had never really heard anybody else put the same way. He would say 'I'm an artist who works for a studio, not a studio artist.' I think that spirit was really kind of the impetus, very much making the clear distinction that these feature films are a collaboration between artists and a studio rather than a studio having artists that are 'theirs,' it's really more of a collaboration. That also means that it's really important to have your own ideas, to have your own identity as an artist."

This sense of artistic identity was nurtured over time with extracurricular projects such as a promotional film for *Sketchtravel*, a collaborative charity project in which a sketchbook traveled across twelve countries picking up artistic contributions along the way. The animated promo made use of a very striking visual concept, in which the elaborate, painterly aesthetic of an animation film's production art is applied to a series of quickly intercut images that tell a story.

"*Sketchtravel* wasn't really made as a short film," affirms Dice, "Any film artist, when creating concept artwork for films, thinks about story, about how our paintings will turn into actual, moving images. Of course, we don't have the skillset to make it into an actual animation but we do think about it. So when I made Sketchtravel as a kind of PR film, it was as an animatic, albeit totally painted."

Surprised by how effectively this approach could convey a story despite not being fully animated with smooth motion or in-betweening, Dice equated the end result with a moving picture book. Applying a similar approach to a short film, one that maintained the same artistic depth while incorporating a somewhat heightened aspect of the character animation, seemed very achievable.

"I told Robert 'Why don't we make it together? Since I made a seven-minute PR short by myself at two frames per second, if there's *two* of us that means we'll have *four* frames per second.' It came with the naïve idea that we could maybe smooth out the animation if there were two of us. We always dreamed of having a painting animated, but when we decided to do *The Dam Keeper* (Figures 3.1–3.5), we realized there is so much more to animation. It's not just about a series of paintings,

Figure 3.2

Pig from *The Dam Keeper* – early development drawing by Dice Tsutsumi ©2014 Tonko House LLC.

you have to know how to animate, which we didn't." Embracing their own limitations as well as the opportunity for collaboration, Dice and Robert approached a studio friend Erick Oh to become their Animation Supervisor, heading up a crew of contributing animators.

A complicating factor, though one that in many senses reduced the risk element had it been an entirely new venture, was that Dice had initially approached Robert about the prospect of their own film deep in production of *Monsters University*. Getting it off the ground with such a demanding day job was not the only hurdle and, as we'll explore further in Chapter 9, funding was an important reality to face. Rather than go down the now well-trodden route of crowdfunding, realizing the extra demands that campaign management would have on time, energy and resources better spent making the film itself inspired the duo to self-fund as a more viable alternative. *The Dam Keeper* ultimately took the form of many truly independent works, as a passion project and group effort.

"In the beginning," Dice recalls, "We had some savings and talked about paying everybody but there are certain kinds of restrictions that didn't allow us to do that, so everybody on the project was a volunteer. So, by default we saved a lot of money there." In lieu of crowdfunding, a more traditional fundraising approach was used, accruing enough of a budget to get started from selling original artwork they had created for the pre-production of the film through avenues such as eBay. In spite of this, what the film's production hinged on more than anything

Figure 3.3

The Dam Keeper early development by Robert Kondo ©2014 Tonko House LLC.

was dedicated time, effort and commitment, with a total production period of nine months (three of which full-time and the other six alongside their day-job on *Monsters University*).

When it came to story itself, the two certainly benefited from being in a nurturing creative environment, as Robert remembers.

"Being inside Pixar was great for seeing all the parts that it takes to make these multi-million dollar feature films, but at the core of it was this idea of storytelling. I wouldn't even say that we were good at that, we just had a real intérest in it and didn't expect a studio on the scale of Pixar to just hand us the opportunity to play in that world, because we really hadn't done anything within the walls of the studio to warrant that."

The film's visually rich look is bolstered by the story, one that uses simplicity as a strength and acts as an effective platform for the duo to flex their artistic muscles. At its heart, it subscribes to convention of an underdog lead in the form of a porcine narrator recalling his youth as a village dam keeper, ostracized by his schoolmates. Effective visual scenarios are driven by the story elements: The operation of the dam's windmill that keeps a perpetually threatening dust storm at bay, the idyllic visualization of the village itself and the dark turn of the film when the dam keeper, despondent, forgoes his duty and allows the storm to take over. Robert attributes the visual success of the piece to the same reason that the two gravitated toward one another in the first place.

"The absolute, most important thing was us working together, so the visual style really came from the fact that we both paint very similarly and so it felt like the easiest solution for us. It made the most sense, given that we knew story was going to be the most challenging thing for us. We didn't want to create a really challenging visual style that would push us in a different direction where there was potentially another area to have disagreements about. As for the story itself, I think a lot of creative relationships come out of somebody having an idea first and really wanting to make it – we did not have that at all. We really wanted to work with each other, to see what we were capable of."

Figure 3.4

Still from *The Dam Keeper* (Dir. Robert Kondo/Dice Tsutsumi) ©2014 Tonko House LLC.

Figure 3.5

Still from *The Dam Keeper* (Dir. Robert Kondo/Dice Tsutsumi) ©2014 Tonko House LLC.

Embarking on a film with a vague story idea is an uphill journey at the best of times, so embarking on one with no story at all, without a traditional storytelling background or experience would make the prospect especially daunting. It speaks volumes for the duo's certainty that something good would come of the endeavor that they would do just that, though ultimately going into the project completely green when it came to a rather vital area turned out to be to its benefit. "We went through almost five or six versions, completely different stories, before we got to this final story. So I'd say the core of everything was the relationship, wanting to work together. Then after that the look kind of fell into place and the story itself was something we struggled with, knowing that it was going to be our first film, we told ourselves that, while we weren't going to just rush this thing out, let's just make sure we finished. It's our first story, we can't be precious with it, if it's not perfect we'll do another film that's better! So that was our plan."

Nightmare Worlds

Let's take a cross-country trip to the complete opposite and far less sunny end of the independent animation spectrum. While matching *The Dam Keeper*'s ambition in terms of length and impulse to eschew a formal studio hierarchy, in most other respects you could not envisage a more different film than British nightmare-weaver Robert Morgan's BAFTA-nominated *Bobby Yeah* (Figures 3.6–3.10).

Robert's name was established in the late nineties with his stop-motion student short *The Man in the Lower Left-Hand Corner of the Photograph* in which a lonely, corpse-like man who spends his days spying on his suicidal neighbor keeps a photo of himself amongst his minimal possessions. Despite – or, arguably, because of – the relatively meager resources available for the film's production, it perfectly captures the same uneasy, claustrophobic tone conveyed in such nightmare-visions as David Lynch's *Eraserhead* (1977) or Roman Polanski's *Repulsion* (1965).

With a clear precedent set, Robert moved on to professional film production shortly thereafter, with 2001s equally horrific (albeit faster-paced) *The Cat With Hands*, in which a terrifying apocryphal story of a supernatural cat who absorbs the body parts of its victims is told through a mix of live action and irreal stop-motion. The film, partly inspired by a recurring nightmare of Morgan's sister's, began life as an Animator In Residence scheme once run by UK television network Channel 4. The successful end result led to a bigger budget for his

Figure 3.6

Bobby Yeah (Dir. Robert Morgan) poster ©2011 Swartz Can Talk/blueLight.

3. The Visual Storyteller

harrowing, slickly produced third animated short *The Separation* (2003), a horrifyingly violent and tragic tale of twin co-dependence.

In another era and under other circumstances, the idea of returning to independent film would most likely not have been the most logical next step. In truth, Morgan was motivated by the realization that, in a country whose arts funding had been decimated, going solo was the only way forward.

"I remember literally lying on the bed awake at night wondering what was next, because it felt like there were no more opportunities to make stuff, especially as animation is so time-consuming and you need the right gear to make it work. Around the same time it became much more possible to do that stuff; the dropping out of the funding coincided with the arrival of things like Final Cut, DragonFrame and iStop Motion, which I was using for *Bobby Yeah*. So with the arrival of home stop-motion software and kits that could capture HD with a stills camera, I realized I could actually do something. The original idea was just to make a little placeholder, a two-minute short just to remind people I was still here while I worked out how to get funding." Once the film was in motion, however, Robert quickly developed a renewed enthusiasm for the process, mainly for the freedoms that automatically come with being independent. It soon became clear that, liberated by not requiring permission from funders or clients to make a film, something far more substantial than a two-minute placeholder was on the cards. "The biggest, most exciting thing was to not have to 'okay' everything with a higher authority, which is what you normally have to do when you're making a

Figure 3.7

Bobby Yeah (Dir. Robert Morgan) character sketch and film still ©2011 Swartz Can Talk/blueLight.

film. That's why I think the film is so unhinged because there was no-one telling me 'You can't do that!'" Three years later, I was still making it."

"Unhinged" is certainly apropos. While Robert's prior work never shied away from troubling premises and visuals, *Bobby Yeah* is a masterpiece of unrelenting, hallucinogenic excess, one that earned him a BAFTA nomination in 2011.

"This film was a stream of consciousness. Previously I have written scripts when I have a story to tell, and the visuals come second to the story, but this time around there was no story. I just started filming and the first shot of the film is the first shot I filmed, the last shot is the last, and everything in between was chronological. All I had at the start was just a visual sense, I just had a puppet and a set and just started animating that, had this character run into the room, watched it back, thought *Okay, now what can happen?* and went from there. So it was only visual to begin with, and then you start noticing you're subconsciously telling a story."

To fully appreciate just how unconventional said story is, here is a beat-by-beat breakdown of the first five minutes of the film:

- We open on a sparse, minimally furnished room bathed in blue light, into which scurries Bobby Yeah, a creature of indeterminate species (though resembling a squat man with rabbitlike ears and a mammalian tail).
- Seemingly anxious, Bobby retreats from the room and, shortly afterward, re-enters carrying another inexplicable creature in his arms. It resembles an earthworm with a cluster of fingernail-clippings for a head, out of which a pair of squinting eyes peer. Both Bobby and the creature's body language suggest it has been either stolen or rescued.
- Placing his find on a bed, one of the room's few furnishings, Bobby examines it as it writhes around the mattress.
- Bobby gently strokes the creature's wormlike torso, calming its frantic movements, then spies a stark red, metallic button protruding from it.
- Clearly tempted by what may occur if he presses it, Bobby visibly attempts to resist doing so until the suspense is too much to take.
- Once the button is pressed, we briefly cut to a shot of a dramatic sunrise, then return to the room where the creature and Bobby find themselves joined by two new monstrous entities. One is faceless save for a toothy mouth, the other all tongue and beady eyes, both fleshy, amorphous and protruding from tanklike machines.
- Bobby approaches as the two creatures gyrate disconcertingly, acknowledging the anticipatory twitching of one creature's tank barrel.
- The barrel eventually secretes two tasseled globules. The two creatures briefly pause, inspect what they've produced, then resume their gyrations with fervor.
- As more and more globules pile in front of him, Bobby takes action and muzzles the barrel with his fingerless hand.
- Pressure builds until the mechanism clogs and breaks, the backed-up secretia instead coming out of the creatures' faces.
- Pressure continues to build until the tank explodes, sending Bobby hurtling across the room followed by a rapidfire succession of globules from the splayed barrel.
- Globules continue to fly, ricocheting off of every surface and item in the room.

- Bobby races over to the creature whose tank is (one assumes) malfunctioning and, in desperation, punches it, which has little effect.
- Bobby's Plan B is to grab the creature's protuberant tongue and pull with all his might, eventually removing it along with what looks like a spinal column, attached.
- The creature is seemingly felled, one final globule leaking out of its destroyed mechanism. The second malformed creature remains alive.
- Bobby surveys the bizarre detritus around him, his attention soon taken by the cry of his wormlike, fingernail-headed kidnappee.
- The wormlike creature's shimmering tail opens and expands like a trunk, growing and spilling onto the floor where it proceeds to vacuum up (or consume) the spilled globules.
- Once all the globules have been absorbed, the wormlike creature lays a blood-smeared egg on the floor and returns to its original shape.

At this point, we're less than a quarter of the way through the film, with nearly twenty minutes to go. Though obviously Morgan's machinations are not for the weak of stomach, this is excellent news to an audience who delights in the animation's weirdest, darkest and most surreal potential – an audience I'm staunchly amongst. As Robert freely admits, a pitch meeting or funding application for *Bobby Yeah* could only boil down to "A list of disgusting events that wouldn't work as a document" – so what *does* make it work? In the midst of the hypnagogic nightmare-fare, the success of the film ultimately comes down to an unexpectedly traditional trope: The sympathetic lead.

"What links it all is the character of Bobby," Robert offers, "I think he's a very relatable character in that he becomes the audience's eyes. In a slightly perverse way he wants to see it all but at the same time he's squeamish about it. Once the game is revealed, that every time he presses these buttons that appear something really weird happens, the audience becomes him: They want to see what happens, yet at the same time they're afraid. So there is that push and pull of being

Figure 3.8

Bobby Yeah concept sketch. Image courtesy of Robert Morgan.

Figure 3.9

Still from *Bobby Yeah* (Dir. Robert Morgan) ©2011 Swartz Can Talk/blueLight.

tempted that I think satisfies a certain perverse feeling within the audience. I never expected anyone would like this film, but the fact that so many people did, I think that's why, because they relate to the character, he becomes the thread through which the audience can relate to events."

The events themselves continue in a vein similar to the opening as outlined above, and accompanying the thread of Bobby himself a story slowly starts to emerge; Bounding from scenario to scenario at the push of a succession of mysterious, enticing, red buttons, we come to learn that Bobby is indeed a thief, and it soon transpires that those he has stolen from are not to be trifled with. When called to be accountable for his behavior, the turns the action takes are wholly unpredictable, utterly surreal and yet very easy to make sense of. As with the practice of free-association writing, a method of idea generation in which a writer will put pen to paper without thinking of what they will write until the moment it's being written, oftentimes with surprisingly creative results, the improvisational approach to *Bobby Yeah*'s story does build up a comprehensible narrative around itself.

"It was completely ad-libbed. I would shoot in chunks until I would get to a point where I felt like I'd boxed myself into a corner because I didn't know what he was going to do next, then I had the idea of the red button that kind of got me out of it; If this button appears and he presses it, then literally anything can happen. So my process was animating a little bit, watching it and then fantasizing about what could happen next. I set myself a little rule that, whatever occurred to me, I wouldn't analyze its meaning; If I liked it, it would go in. If I *had* analyzed anything it would've killed it, so I forced myself not to."

This process extended to the creation of the ensemble cast, a silicone mishmash of intricately detailed, hyperreal features set against a mess of detritus and viscera, evocative of Francis Bacon's furies, Clive Barker's cenobites and the mixed-media sculptures of David Lynch. When it came to the point in which Robert felt a new character should be introduced, the animation itself would be halted so that a new puppet could be built from scratch. One example of character development in particular perfectly exemplifies just how circumstantial the progress of the story could be:

"I had gotten to the point where this bird-headed creature and Bobby are fighting. Bobby kicks him and his head goes into the wall. When I reached that bit,

3. The Visual Storyteller

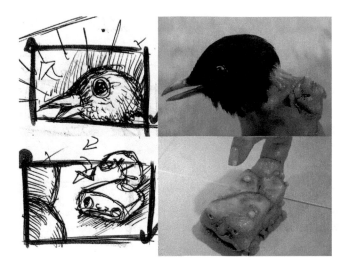

Figure 3.10

Bobby Yeah (Dir. Robert Morgan) storyboarded characters to final film comparison ©2011 Swartz Can Talk/blueLight.

I stopped for Christmas for a two-week break. I'd left the set as it was, with this bird-headed man's head in the wall and I was going to continue after, he was going to pull his head out and the two would continue fighting. Then for Christmas a friend, for some bizarre reason, bought me this weird little ragdoll keyring. As soon as I opened that present the image popped in my head that when the bird-headed man pulls his head from the wall and turned around he'd now have this ragdoll's head. It made me laugh because it was so, so weird, I just thought *That's going in the film, no analyzing, that happens now!* I went back and then that's how I carried on, the creature pulls his head and he's got this new head. That type of opening yourself up to anything that occurs to you is what really frees you up to do some really surprising things on this journey that you go on.

Idea Generation

While Robert's spontaneous method of idea generation is incredibly freeing, it carries with it a high risk factor if applied to most other types of film than the surreal or horrific. Even the ever-present humor of *Bobby Yeah* owes its success to the director's intuitive sense of comedic timing, something that is especially tricky to pull off when dealing with such unconventional characters and events. As seen in the accompanying illustrations, some of the most outlandish visuals of the film are rooted in sketched-out character concepts and basic thumbnail boards, which can be a huge contributor to a film's cohesion in the absence of a script.

Returning to a comparatively lighter side of stop-motion production, acclaimed LA-based animator Kirsten Lepore, perhaps best known for such auteur short films as the multi-award-winning *Bottle* (2010), *Move Mountain* (2013, Figure 3.11) and *Hi Stranger* (2016), has her own personal process that assists with idea generation.

"I have no way of just coming up with ideas out of the blue, however there are certain things I can do to help get inspired. I keep a sketchbook/notebook of ideas I get and always write them down, so I can go back and reference those once

Figure 3.11

Still from *Move Mountain* (Dir. Kirsten Lepore) ©2013 Kirsten Lepore.

I need to generate ideas for a project. I also get inspired by browsing the aisles of craft stores, driving and being out in nature.

"I've never written a script, as my ideas are almost always visually driven. My sketchbooks, however, mostly contain writing (such as a quick note I will have jotted down) and the occasional thumbnail to help jog my memory further once I revisit it. When I first have an initial seed or spark of an idea that feels right, it usually includes a technique, color palette or sense of movement that excites me. From that starting point, I branch outwards until I can narratively justify that element."

Striking visual concepts are a mainstay of Kirsten's work, going back to her first stop-motion project *Sweet Dreams*, an undergraduate thesis film produced in 2008 at the Maryland Institute College of Art (MICA). From a production values standpoint, there are certain tells that the film is a formative outing, especially in contrast to her later work, but the marriage of an inventive visual approach (the film is made almost entirely out of food, presenting a world where sugary snacks build structures out of sugar cubes) and a well-thought-out story (a bored cupcake sets sail to start a new life and finds itself stranded on an island occupied by healthier food, quickly adapting to their simpler yet more fulfilling – and ultimately pragmatic, as it learns on its return – way of life) would prove to be one of Kirsten's major strengths.

This quality is further refined in *Bottle*, a stop-motion/pixilation film that sees two lone figures on opposite sides of the ocean – one made of sand, the other of snow – communicate with one another via a bottle sent back and forth between their respective shores. Using actual sand, snow, foliage and miscellaneous detritus, a sense of growing friendship is conveyed to the audience to the extent that, when the film concludes, they are emotionally invested in the connection between these two and the poignancy of their geographical separation.

While *Bottle* would ultimately prove the more acclaimed and visually sophisticated project, both films are grand in scope when considering the circumstances of their production. Yet both also began life as relatively simple ideas.

"Both *Bottle* and *Sweet Dreams* were created as university projects – it's doubtful that they would exist had I not had an assignment to fulfill. The idea for *Sweet*

3. The Visual Storyteller

Dreams was sparked because I thought the idea of using kale and leafy greens as foliage in a film would be interesting. I built out that world and story from there. For *Bottle*, I had the initial spark for that idea while I was watching a snowfall at my parents' house in New Jersey a year prior. I had the realization that packable snow behaved much like clay and was curious about animating with it."

That such engaging work can be built upon these types of idle musings goes to show that even a passing thought might be worth expanding on. A great film has to begin somewhere, after all.

Returning to the Scene

The approaches explored above both go to show the potential independent animation can have to still succeed even when throwing the rulebook out of the window (or in the case of *Bobby Yeah*, setting it aflame and stomping it into oblivion). Sometimes, this does not prove to be the case, and entering into a film's production blindly may very well be reflected in the final result. To elaborate on this, we will take a look at *Sausage* (Figures 3.12–3.17), a playful, high-energy short by Robert Grieves about "two artisan stallholders whose idyllic world is invaded by a devious fast-food vendor."[1] The film would be considered successful in terms of both its execution and reception. This, as it happens, was very nearly not the case, as the largely unseen first attempt at the film demonstrates.

One of the major considerations when it comes to personal work is knowing precisely when to draw a line under a project. Without deadlines or a client, it can be very hard to tell impartially when a film is truly finished and deliverable. When it comes to student films, however, the lines can tend to be a little blurrier. Technically speaking, a student short *will* have a deadline in terms of its assessment, but in a great deal of instances the door is open to return to it and tighten things up before sending it out in the world. Allowing yourself a week or so to take a second swipe at the edit of your film might increase its festival performance immeasurably (I speak from firsthand experience here). As the months go by, the urge to open up the project files and tinker around more and more eventually fade to be replaced, hopefully, with the urge to create something new.

In the case of *Sausage*, however, Robert rightly identified the unrealized potential for a film that could make his name, but would have no chance of doing so as made. Several months after completing it for his Master's degree, he realized

Figure 3.12

Sausage (Dir. Robert Grieves) lobby card art ©2013 Robert Grieves.

that despite the high marks it had earned, it simply wasn't a professional enough piece of work to appropriately convey his true vision of its story.

"After a couple of weeks of just being a bit depressed about it, I got that wave of *No, these things aren't* meant *to be easy.*" Robert recalls, "So I ended up fixing it, which ended up being a process of complete deconstruction. I suppose it was mainly the story, but to be honest every discipline needed rethinking – the editing, the storyboarding, the animation, the music, everything had to be reworked, because this style of narrative animation was very new to me.

"To me just designing interesting characters doesn't work, I have to build the world first, the reason for it all to exist. I want to see the narrative take shape and I want to see where it's going to end up. You hear novelists talk about how they developed some characters, set them on a journey and they don't know how it's going to end. While I respect that, it's *nothing* like how I write. I tend to build it up in that layered way, I want to know that everything works and is in place and then I'll start going into details."

This approach being contrary to that taken by those who would start with details and then develop outwards does not make either right or wrong. You will know as a creative that is right for you based on the obvious – which approach yields more by way of actual results? For Robert, the emotional place he wishes to take his audience to is the most important catalyst for character development.

"It's just not the kind of person I am, so I can't worry about it too much, but one of the issues I have about my work in general is that I wish I was more of a doodler. I never doodle. Everything I do is for a purpose, it's all functional, to go towards whatever it is that I am making. I think doodlers are similar to the novelists who start with a character and 'take the lion for a walk.' I definitely start with the bigger picture and then narrow down, I did that on *Sausage* and I would say I continue to do that."

Having made a fair amount of short form animation, both narrative and experimental, the duration of *Sausage* had presented Robert with challenges that had been entirely unfamiliar at the time. One particular area of weakness boiled down to not appreciating how best to approach the character animation itself which, given how character and performance-oriented the film's premise was, proved a major pitfall. Conceding that the fundamental issues with the film were, in fact, issues with the fundamentals of animation production itself, Robert realized he needed outside assistance.

"My use of character animation didn't really give much emotional depth. Fortunately, I had worked with someone on some random little commercial job in Sydney, this English guy Simon Williams who was storyboarding on the job, but his previous life had been in London where he was an animation director on various animated series. I went to him and said 'I've got this film I really need to work out' which led to the classic moment of 'What do you want to hear? Do you want me to just tell you enough to get it finished and out there, or do you *really* want to know the deal?' 'Yeah, c'mon, hit me with it!' So he basically started that deconstruction process."

During their evenings after work, Robert and Simon tried for several months to work out fixes for the film as made. Eventually both admitted defeat, that time was only being wasted and that the only realistic option was to put the existing animation to one side and return to the storyboard stage where the story issues could be resolved before embarking on new animation. Although such an undertaking is far from appealing, Robert acknowledged it as an exercise in correcting

Figure 3.13

Sausage original storyboard excerpts Images courtesy of Robert Grieves.

the missteps of his first attempt; by redoing the film in this way, it would become far easier to appreciate how best to create a dynamic flow and marry shots properly for better cohesion. In a direct sense, it was a matter of learning from one's own mistakes.

"It wasn't hitting the audience at the right time, all those things that you don't have to deal with in two minutes. Two minutes is jazz-hands, it's eye-candy, it's punchlines, whereas anything over five minutes – and this was eight minutes – you will need to have an arc and things have to deliver, you have to let the audience know where you are in any given moment. All those things that keep the audience engaged. Although he was outraged at my lack of knowledge and my audacity to make a film, he was wonderful, and with his help we built it and got it to a point where I could not only watch it again without retching, but I was actually really excited! And now I watch it and I am entertained by it, it carries an audience and it carries me."

One way to rationalize the failings of a short would be that there was not enough time, and that with more hours and more commitment might come the fixes necessary. The truth of the matter is that, no matter how much time is available, knowledge of the craft itself is what is required more than anything, and there is no shame in reaching out to others with a more expansive skillset than us for help; in fact, what better way is there to learn?

"One of the big things that I have learned to appreciate is how sophisticated the audience is. It isn't as though we're in the twenties inventing cinema and people are going to be impressed by anything, our audiences have grown up on what is not just random kids' television; some of the *best* animators and filmmakers out there make kids' television and then go on to make adult television. You could choose to ignore the three-act game, but you have to know what that game is because the audience certainly knows it. They might not know enough to teach a course on it but they instinctively feel when things are working or not. So you have to respect the audience by understanding what it is they already come to any screening with. The reason we make these films is to get better, it's an opportunity to get stuck in."

Despite the massive reworking of the short, efforts were made to preserve some of the original character animation that had actually proved successful the first time around. As a result, the overall style of the film – modern digital animation processes applied to a retro approach to 2D character construction – needed to remain the same, as did the general arc of the story.

"There were things that got dumped, like a minute at the beginning with a whole backstory of the two main characters as children – talk about killing your

Figure 3.14

Sausage early sketches ©Robert Grieves.

3. The Visual Storyteller

babies; it was a baby slaughter! But that's all part of the process, and sometimes you need someone to come along to make you realize which babies need to die."

The major limitation regarding the character work for the original film was an absence of emotional range that could translate to visual performance. Without dialogue or a narration, their acting would be needed to carry the entire film, so that an emotional journey could be communicated. Though a largely whimsical story, every major character conveys a vital emotion at some point throughout – the hero and heroine running the gamut of contentment, elation, fear, horror, sadness, anger, confusion, joy and despair, the villain smugness, malice, revulsion and fury. While the final film boasts all of these with no ambiguities, the performances of the original pass at the film were far more stilted.

"My characters weren't good enough actors, it was like putting someone with a stroke on screen and expecting them to be Marlon Brando. So I was in that situation where stylistically I had gone through that limited animation look, but I was telling a story that was more sophisticated and had more requirements. This is all stuff that you learn, isn't it? If your story asks for this degree of emotional range, either you need a voiceover that tells you 'This character's sad,' or you need a character that can really *be* the particular type of sad that the script calls for. So I did keep the stylistic thing, but there was a big discussion about whether that should change."

Most of us will have past projects that, were we to dust them off and take a second run at, would doubtless be improved by the newly accrued and more finely honed skills we've developed in the interim. When, then, is doing so an advisable, practical idea?

"You've got the two levels, one is where I'm at personally, having done the film, that definitely it was worth it because I'm now a confident filmmaker – I wasn't before. It also gave me a product – which these things are – that was able to go

Figure 3.15

Sausage revised storyboard excerpt. Image courtesy of Robert Grieves.

Figure 3.16

Sausage character design sheets demonstrating poses and actions ©2013 Robert Grieves.

3. The Visual Storyteller

Figure 3.17

Still from *Sausage* (Dir. Robert Grieves) ©2013 Robert Grieves.

out and have life. I'm now getting the kind of jobs I *wanted* to do, that I wouldn't have been able to without the film, and I'm able to *do* them having done the film. So it's a double bonus!

"If I ever spoke to a bank manager he'd think I was an idiot! The amount of time I was working and spending on my own, I would have been better off doing something more simple. Watching the younger graduates who are doing sensational stuff at the moment and really using the internet as a way of connecting with the world, I don't know if it's instinctively or not but people just seem to be doing these much shorter, sweeter things, and it makes a lot of sense, doesn't it? You get it out there, throw something at the world, if it sticks, great, if it doesn't then move on to the next thing. The other approach, of putting all your effort and spending years working on one thing that's seven minutes long, it takes forever to do. So of course you learn from doing it but you might have learned just as much from doing some shorter, quicker things in a short amount of time."

Pleasing Abstractions

One of *Sausage*'s other appealing attributes is how the liveliness of the visuals is bolstered by composer Dan Radclyffe's playful musical score. Indeed, the interplay between music and visuals is obviously a huge consideration when it comes to animation. We'll look at this further when considering animated music videos in Chapter 5 and score composition in Chapter 19. Music also has a part to play in the conceptual and visual development of a film, and it's worth taking a look at work whose "stories" are far more open to interpretation, if not outright abstract. Canadian experimental film artist Steven Woloshen (Figure 3.18) began making films at around seventeen years old in the 1970s, making use of the Super 8 cameras and projectors his parents had lying around their house in Laval. Beginning as a means to pass the time in lieu of much by way of quality TV entertainment, Steven joined forces with his friends, an assortment of artists, designers and musicians, to dip his toes in the waters of experimental filmmaking.

These freeform efforts, primarily involving the destruction of Super 8 film cartridges and scratching over the negatives, paired with unplanned musical

Figure 3.18

Steven Woloshen scratching on film. Image courtesy of the artist.

improvisations, would prove to be the first step of a long career. Indeed, Steven's formative years of playful experimentation would heavily foreshadow his eventual – and quite extensive – filmography. The first major turning point came during his studies at Vanier College in Montreal.

"My professors were experimental film teachers who were really interested in Stan Brackhage, Len Lye and all these formalist experimental filmmakers. They kept on talking to me about the surface of the film, the surface of the screen, the materiality of the film. I told them I had been bashing up film cases and having a really good time, so they said 'That's perfect, bring it in!'"

Spurred on, Steven began making films with hole punchers and pins, beginning with an experimental use of the projector as a filmmaking tool in itself. The positive response and high marks this early student effort garnered cemented his affection toward this particular area of filmmaking, not looking back since. During his studies, he was educated on the works of Len Lye, such as *Free Radicals*, a four-minute short incrementally created over a twenty-one year period (from 1958 to 1979) by scratching 16 mm black film leader with needles. The stark simplicity of this process appealed to Steven, and no further encouragement was needed to actively fill the remaining gaps in his knowledge about the culture, the process and its terminologies.

"I didn't know until later on that it had all these designations, terms like 'Absolute film' and *Cinéma Pur*, but all I did was what I wanted to do in my parent's basement, like letra-film on top of film, ink, paint, dipping it, rolling it over with bicycles, setting it on fire. I didn't know what I was supposed to do or what I wasn't supposed to do, I just did it anyway and it was a lot of fun.

"I used those films to get into university, but there I made documentaries. The documentaries were not going my way because they were 16 mm Bolex. I would waste a lot of film forgetting to take off the lens cap, so instead of throwing the film away, I would paint and scratch on it a little bit more. So how it started was basically the result of bad documentary filmmaking!

Figure 3.19

Still from *When the Sun Turns into Juice* (Dir. Steven Woloshen) ©2014 Steven Woloshen.

"I've always considered the films that I make to be a kind of document of the way I'm feeling about something, or the way my hand moves, the way my eye moves, the light that's in a room, the tools that I have on hand, if I find a marker or a bottle of ink that I really like – it's always just a reflection of what's around me. If I can get the material to make the film, if I hear music I really like, it's a reflection of that too. So it's not really about a story *per se* except the story of me, as a document of what I'm going through at the time. This isn't really a linear document, like a narrative, but it's still what I perceive as being really important in my life. A lot of times that's music, colour, movement, light – in the early 1980s, for example, I started getting into calligraphy. I wanted to exercise my skills, so instead of making letters on paper I made them on very small squares of film. So it's just a reflection of the things I thought were important."

The projects that followed share certain fundamentals approaches throughout; manipulation of existing film is a dominant theme, as is the role of carefully selected musical accompaniments and a tactile physicality to the variety of textures and images, however briefly glimpsed. To give some small sense of Steven's variety of approaches, these films include *Bru Ha Ha!* (2002), a film timed to a found brass musical piece that had been previously transferred to 35 mm magnetic film, on which Letraset symbols are strategically placed; *When the Sun Turns Into Juice* (2011, Figure 3.19), making use of both sides of film leader using both ink and paint and lighting the results from both sides during the optical printing stage; and *Crossing Victoria* (2013), combining hand-painted rotoscoping with the projection of imagery onto raw stock using a self-constructed variation on an optical printer.

Noteworthy amongst this body of work is *1000 Plateaus (2004–2014)* (Figures 3.20–3.22), so subtitled because of its decade-long production history.

"It started when I was a driver on film sets in Montreal. I drove actors, directors, technicians, directors of photography – and as a driver you usually want to make your passengers comfortable. What I did was I tried to get their mind off my bad driving skills and just let them talk about something (of course you're not allowed to be the one who talks first). So I placed a roll of film on a little wooden box with a glass surface and a flashlight in it between the passenger's seat and the driver's seat. What I wanted to do was just scratch on film while I was waiting for the actors to come out of their hotels, just so I could work on the film a little bit, here and there. They would ask 'What is that thing?', 'I'm glad you asked, I'm

Figure 3.20

Still from *1000 Plateaus (2004–2014)* (Dir. Steven Woloshen) ©2014 Steven Woloshen.

making an animated film in the car!', and they'd respond 'Are you sure you're allowed to do that?' We started a process where I could tell them a little bit about what animation was, and slowly they encouraged me. So over time whenever I was free I'd do a foot here, a foot there, and by the end of it I'd done about 300 feet."

Even when it comes to experimental film, discipline and forethought are important – one might argue, in fact, that experimental film by its very nature demands even further consideration in these areas. When dealing with a film that has no characters or linear narrative, it is more of an uphill battle to wind up with an end result audiences will consider watchable. As loose and freeform a visual medium as scratch-on-film is, the visuals have to make some kind of sense. An abstract film can, in the right hands, prove curiously entertaining; an assortment of arbitrary and thoughtless visual noise, however, cannot carry itself. When it comes to Steven's work, great pains are made to ensure his end result falls into the former category. In lieu of a script, his films are often structurally dependent on their soundtracks.

"What I had to do was chart out what piece of music I was going to use, how long it would last, where the changes would happen and stick to that 'script' from the beginning of the film to the end of the film. So it all landed in sync, I would have to count perforations just like an animator would do with a dope sheet, counting where events would occur. So there was no digital technology for me to use, it was just the box. It started in 2004 on a magnetic strip, an audiomagnetic tape with perforations, and that's where it continued!"

Ten years later, the finished *1000 Plateaus* (*2004–2014*) was released to much festival success, picking up major awards at festivals such as the Melbourne International Film Festival. Steven has accompanied the film as it has traveled, bringing workshops to various international festivals and events to showcase the tactile joy this branch of experimental filmmaking can evoke.

"I really find that I've made it my goal to make an imaginary toolbox of all the things I can do with film, either by stapling it, burning it, glueing it, peeling stuff off from it or combining it all together. I just want to make a very big compendium of what animated films could be. I do a lot of workshops and everybody always moves towards scratching on it or painting on film, so I suggest 'Well, why don't we try doing both?' or 'Why don't we try bleaching it, or putting paint underneath, or scratches underneath? Why don't we try combining what we already know with something that we don't know? To me that has always

3. The Visual Storyteller

Figure 3.21

Still from *1000 Plateaus (2004–2014)* (Dir. Steven Woloshen) ©2014 Steven Woloshen.

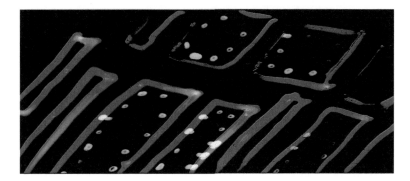

Figure 3.22

Still from *1000 Plateaus (2004–2014)* (Dir. Steven Woloshen) ©2014 Steven Woloshen.

been the most important thing, just to move forward with something that's been around since the 1930s."

Later in the book, we will look at other projects whose creative approaches have been similarly informed by music and experimentation, such as Thomas Stellmach and Maja Oschmann's *Virtuos Virtuell* (2013) and Benjamin Arcand's *Wackatdooo*. If you've skimmed or skipped ahead in the book, you will have gleaned that in many instances the films and artists we have discussed serve as prime case studies for a number of areas, and not just within production. Now that we have canvassed a range of script-based and visual-based storytellers, for the next few chapters we will expand on other types of approaches and genres that can kick a film idea into gear.

Note

1 Vimeo synopsis, *Sausage* (Dir. Robert Grieves).

4

Consider the Source

There's no shame or failure in conceding that we are not all of us storytellers. In truth, it's something of a rarity for directors, animators and/or producers to be responsible for the story on top of everything else they have to deal with. So where to turn for a great film idea? In the upcoming chapters, we will hear from animators whose work spans musical interpretation, non-fiction, meta-fiction, skit-based vignettes and interaction-driven, multimedia projects, amongst others, to assuage any potential concerns that there are limits to what form your independent project will eventually take. For this section, we will be presenting a cross-section of animated projects that used pre-existing source material as their jumping-off point.

It is worth establishing the fundamental difference between a respectful adaptation of another artist's work and just outright stealing their ideas. It's sad to say, but on occasion it's not been unheard of for some people, in lieu of their own original concepts, to go the lazy route of either stylistic or narrative plagiarism, sometimes even justifying the practice as simply taking inspiration. Have you ever seen a bold, ingenious approach to an independent film online or at a festival, then seen more or less the same idea replicated with a higher budget in a television commercial a few months later? In some instances, the original creative will have been hired to direct a variation of their idea or brought on as a creative consultant, but it isn't unheard of that some poor, meek, non-litigious soul has just been ripped off.

In terms of being taken more seriously as a creative and artist, this is obviously not a route you want to take. It can be a thorny business, and one that further hammers home the need for audience feedback not just after but during

DOI: 10.1201/9781003214717-4

production. So if, as it turns out, the process of idea generation does indeed turn out to be a constant battle wherein every idea or concept is second-guessed or falls flat – or, frankly, if you simply want to direct or animate a film but have no impulse to write it – then it's advisable to look elsewhere for your story.

One of the most rewarding creative partnerships can thus be predicated on a pairing of a writer and director, mutually beneficial especially if both are at a similar stage of their career. It may even be the case that the story you want to tell has already been written.

Adaptation is far from a filmmaking cheat or hack – it can be a tricky process and effectively translating one storytelling medium to another is a skill in itself. The process of finding a story that proves a fit as far as your artistic sensibilities are concerned may eliminate the initial ideas phase of the process, but rarely will a story as written translate immediately to film. Some concepts may need to be

Figure 4.1

Love in the Time of March Madness (Dir. Melissa Johnson/Robertino Zambrano) poster ©2014 High Hip Productions/KAPWA Studioworks.

embellished, others significantly edited down, focus may shift and, structurally, the narrative may require much by way of tweaking. To stay true and respectful to your source material while creating a film that stands up on its own is a gentle art that warrants a great deal of communication.

Depending on the circumstances of your initial arrangement, it may very well be that the story's original author is perfectly content for you to adapt it in whatever way you please in which case it makes sense to proceed as you would under any other circumstances. However, keeping lines of communication open with a story's originator gives you a direct line to the humanity of its characters, the intended narrative arcs and help guide you toward defining a response you want from your audience.

Standing Tall

Love in the Time of March Madness (2014, Figures 4.1–4.4) is an animated memoir written by filmmaker and writer Melissa Johnson. With a background predominantly focused on live-action documentary films, her work has leaned toward rites of passage stories focusing on women athletes, such as *No Look Pass* (2011), a feature documentary project for Showtime, as well as *Brittney Griner: Lifesize* (2014) and *Queen Vee* (2015) for ESPN. Alongside her documentary work, she is also an acclaimed humorist, co-creating the Comedy Central web series *The Worst Speeches of All Time* along with a number of first-person essays published in the New York Times, Boston Herald, GOOD Magazine and Salon.com. Posted on the latter in March 2011, Melissa's essay *The tallest woman in the room tells all* proved a huge hit for the website.

"I received a lot of positive feedback about the essay, which was hugely encouraging. It was based off a series of anecdotes drawn from a twenty-year span of my life. The film is a pared down version of the Salon piece."

The essay, an endearingly candid series of her own recollections and personal conflicts as a 6'4" basketball player often prone to romantic misadventure, seemed to Melissa to be best suited to an animated film adaptation over any other approach. Not having had any direct experience in this arena, a mutual contact introduced her to Robertino Zambrano, then working at a New York ad agency having hailed from Sydney.

With some early dabblings in animation and CG during high school, Robertino's enthusiasm for motion graphics kicked into gear when he embarked on a Visual Communications degree at University of Technology Sydney. With a knowledge of design, illustration and animation, he would eventually branch out into other areas such as advertising, though the call of more creative projects remained strong.

"The piece immediately resonated with Robertino and it felt like creative kismet." Melissa recalls of their initial meetings, "I mean, he's not a 6'4" white American woman, but that didn't matter a bit. Robertino just *got it*. We started going back and forth, refining the script and creating the storyboard. I don't think I've ever had such an experience of total alignment in a creative collaboration from the very start."

For Robertino collaborating on *Love in the Time of March Madness* with Melissa was an ideal incentive to make the shift back into the creative side of animation and motion graphics. "I think starting on that project was one of the big factors in what propelled me to leave my job there in New York. I moved back

Figure 4.2

Love in the Time of March Madness concept sketch by Robertino Zambrano. Image courtesy of KAPWA Studioworks.

home to try and start up my own practice where I'd just try and focus solely on animation and motion and film."

Similarly, Melissa was feeling the call to step out from under her agency life and establish herself in the world as an independent artist. With Robertino having moved back to Australia, setting up shop as KAPWA Studioworks, and Melissa leaving New York for Los Angeles, the two began the transcontinental process of adapting her resonant essay to an animated short, sharing the directorial reins.

"It then took about three years to complete because of the complexity of the animation," explains Melissa. "We wanted an *Alice In Wonderland* meets Alexander McQueen aesthetic – dark, ornate, irreverent – with exaggerated plays on perspective and a dry sensibility to the humour. I don't normally talk deadpan like I do in the narration, but I wanted it to have this insider, intimate feeling which I think animation complements so well. I want you to feel like I'm speaking only to you. Maybe we're driving in my car and I'm telling you this story, or it's just the two of us over candlelight and I'm sharing something that I don't share often. But of course, in reality, I'm sharing it with everyone."

The pair began working with a first draft of the script in early 2011. With Robertino producing the film as a side-project to his commercial projects, they were able to indulge a year or so of visual development, experimenting with a variety of different styles to determine what would be the best fit for the script.

With the project initially quite ambitious in scope, it was then essential to edit down the script to make its completion more feasible. Ultimately tightening up the film at this stage proved to be beneficial, especially as Robertino's initial hope was to produce it using traditional, frame-by-frame animation.

"By then we had a fifteen minute script that we hacked down." Robertino recalls, "I tried to get it to seven but I think we settled on around nine. That was when I thought *I don't think I'm gonna do this in 2D, let's start doing some 3D and cheat our way through compositing to get it looking nice!*"

The most important factor was creating a piece of art that would reflect the tone of its source material, especially when considering the personal nature of the original essay. In this respect, *Love in the Time of March Madness* also serves as an additional case study alongside other works of animated non-fiction we will look at in Chapter 7. It is clear when comparing the two that the film is a faithful adaptation of the essay, albeit streamlined to create a flow more suited to a short film narrative. Condensing the film in this way chiefly fell on Melissa's shoulders.

"As a writer I had to cut a lot of words and trust the visuals to do the work. For example in the essay I say: 'I was a walking Rorschach, mirroring their self-image'; I cut the line in the film because Robertino took it on and was able to visually communicate it. So I think for me I had to really go in with a red pen and strip away a lot of language, and then explore the complexity of his animation and think about what to simply."

"At the start I was very informal about storyboarding and doing all the layouts," says Robertino of the earlier stages of production. "It was only as we started getting deeper into making the film when I really realized that I should have been as disciplined with this as with commercial work!"

A major motivator for laying out a solid production plan came with bringing on other animators and delegating tasks. With a crew to be accountable for, production on the film began proper, using a combination of approaches to the animation itself.

"We built most of the raw elements, such as the characters and most of the main props, in Maya. There are a couple of shots in the film that are actually just frame-by-frame 2D, done in Flash, but the majority of it is generated through CG. We brought all the footage into After Effects and did all our compositing in there, adding any treatments and other little elements, backgrounds, layouts et cetera."

The result is a truly unique and seamless blend of digital animation processes. Rendered in start black and white, Melissa's animated counterpart occupies an ethereal world of visual metaphors, inventive transitions and wry onscreen gags that perfectly complement the humor of her original essay. An extra detail that gives the production an instant identifiability is the line work, which runs together to create a painterly effect, something Robertino had previously experimented with for a commercial project *TED Ed: The Science of Stage Fright*.

"Photoshop has this oil-paint filter which looks really hokey if you just apply it, straight-up, to any image, but the thing I saw that it did – which most effects didn't do – was it actually picked up a lot of the contours in the image, so you could extract some really cool painterly effects." With this in mind, the Maya render settings were adjusted so that each shot would contain enough visual information to be picked up on in this way. To reduce the artificiality of the effect, the footage was combined with an assortment of hand-generated digital textures during the compositing phase in After Effects.

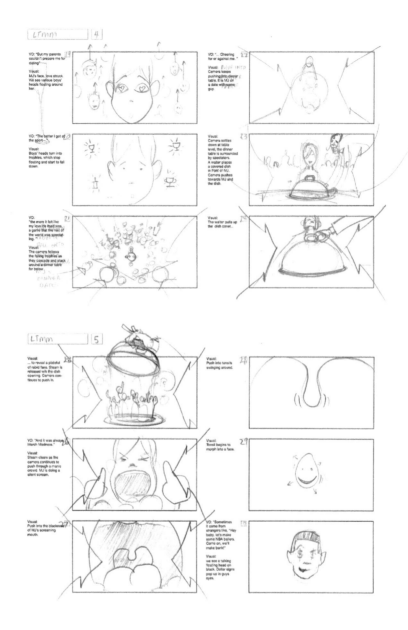

Figure 4.3

Love in the Time of March Madness storyboard excerpts. Image courtesy of KAPWA Studioworks.

"It really helped, especially when we had some of the more frame-by-frame Flash generated stuff, where I was wondering how we were going to marry these two animation styles together. A lot of the scenes at the start, where they're all coming out of Maya, were looking very 3D, so it was trying to break up the perspective so it didn't look so 'nice.' When you get to that point where someone who's watching it wonders *How Did They Make That?* then you've done something right!"

Figure 4.4

Stills comparison demonstrating the textural effect applied to the animation of *Love in the Time of March Madness* ©2014 High Hip Productions/KAPWA Studioworks.

Like Mindedness

Were it not for the synchronicity and mutual understanding of Melissa and Robertino's creative partnership, both artistically and circumstantially, it's hard to say whether or not *Love in the Time of March Madness* would have come together in as successful a way, if at all. Though from notably disparate backgrounds, it is encouraging to see that the pair's instances of common ground revolved around an art form they both clearly care about. This is important to remember when contemplating any type of collaboration; pairing up with somebody with whom you share little by way of empathy or interests will probably not result in a successful film. Certainly, you can have differences, or even wildly dissimilar personality types, but it's crucial to know for sure that, on some level, there is an understanding and focused idea of what you both want out of the project.

Amongst the variety of genres and filmmaking methods covered in the extensive filmography of director Chris Shepherd is one particular adaptation that came about from an artistic rapport with Cheshire-born humorist and Turner Prize-nominated artist David Shrigley. The eventual collaboration began during Chris's stint on the BBC sketch show *Big Train*, for which he animated a series of vignettes – *The World Stare-out Championship Finals* – whose minimalist absurdity would foreshadow the short to come. Discovering David Shrigley's work through a collection of his drawings titled *Why We Got the Sack from the Museum*, Chris was immediately enamored.

"I looked at it and thought it was really great, because when I was a kid I always used to draw crazy pictures and, in a sense, his book reminded me of that. It reminded me of the drawings that I'd do that would in fact be very dysfunctional. I always think it's like graffiti – in London you can get graffiti that is super-ornate and beautiful, but when you go up North it's just your straight, four-letter expletives on a wall with no frills. This book was like that, these moments that are really raw, they just go BANG and there it is. That really appealed to me."

With David's star having not yet risen within the art world, the possibility of collaboration appealed to a mutual fondness for animation, but a suitable

Figure 4.5

Still from Who *I Am and What I Want* (Dir. Chris Shepherd/David Shrigley) ©2005 Chris Shepherd/David Shrigley.

concept couldn't be decided on. In 2003, the binding premise of a new David Shrigley collection titled *Who I Am and What I Want* (Figures 4.5–4.8) served to finally get the ball rolling. The following year, with the assistance of Arts Council England's animate! Projects and Channel 4, the pair embarked on an animated adaptation of the book.

"What was great about that book for adapting was that it was all stories of one person. Most of his other books are like snapshots of time, vignettes; they're all different moments so they don't have that narrative. I remember the first thing I did was scan all the pages in the book and put them in a timeline. What I ended up with came to something mad like forty minutes, with no shape to it."

The absence of a narrative in any strict, traditional sense was remedied by the addition of a framing device in a manner bearing some similarity to that of Magic Light's *Grufallo* adaptations, though wildly different in terms of tone and audience. With the addition of scenes set in a forest in which the protagonist (voiced by natural born oddball Kevin Eldon) is established as a societal outsider and woodland-dwelling hermit. In this context, the disconnected musings as presented in the original book are presented as remembrances of a life he has left behind. Despite maintaining the nonsensical nature of the narration's array of non-sequiturs, the film effectively builds a structure for itself.

"It starts off in the woods and ends in the woods, to give the illusion that it has a story. Then when we did the animation, I drew the animatic all in Flash, the animatic, really roughly and just in my own style. Then I'd ask Dave, who was getting really mega-famous then, and sort of super-busy, to give me some

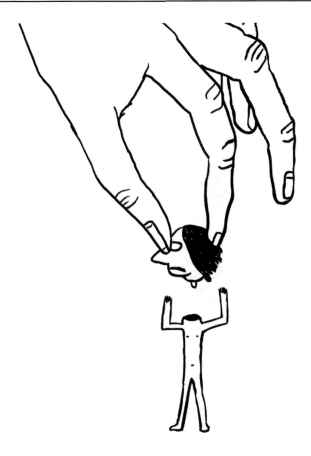

Figure 4.6

Still from *Who I Am and What I Want* (Dir. Chris Shepherd/David Shrigley) ©2005 Chris Shepherd/David Shrigley.

drawings of buildings or some trees, different things, street furniture. He'd give me pages of those and then I just assembled it, a bit like Letraset, in the computer. That way of doing it worked really well because it meant he didn't have to draw the whole world."

With Chris taking the lead on the animation itself, David maintained an active involvement in the co-direction of the film and the adaptation of the script.

"When we did the script we did it together, I'd write and bounce it back to him, he'd come along to come up with ideas, do voices. We changed some things and created some great inversions on the film. There's a line where he says 'I want to be in a cage with the lions and dress like a clown,' but I think it was different in the book, I think it was 'I want to be in a cage with clowns and dressed like a lion.' At the last minute he said 'I know, why don't we just swap it?' and it was much more surreal. It was a good collaboration because nobody was precious about it, we just got on with it."

The final film, an appealingly bizarre affair all at once filthy, violent and curiously thoughtful, proved a major hit on the festival circuit, winning thirteen major awards in its first year of release alone. In 2014, nine years after its production, it also won the Filmmaker Grand Prix at Japan's esteemed Sapporo Film Festival, a further testament to its relevance and longevity.

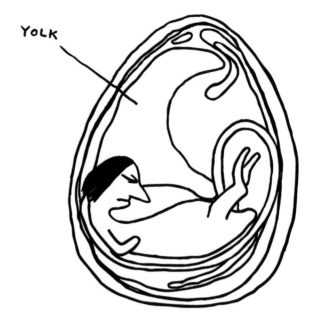

Figure 4.7

Still from *Who I Am and What I Want* (Dir. Chris Shepherd/David Shrigley) ©2005 Chris Shepherd/David Shrigley.

Figure 4.8

Still from *Who I Am and What I Want* (Dir. Chris Shepherd/David Shrigley) ©2005 Chris Shepherd/David Shrigley.

Traveling in creative circles will generally lead to opportunities for collaboration, but a more pro-active approach may be handy too. If the concept of applying your knowledge, skill and passion for animation to an adaptation of a pre-existing work is something that appeals, then it may be worth stepping outside of your comfort zone and reaching out to writers directly. Montreal-based animator Claire Blanchet's understated and haunting National Film Board of Canada short *The End of Pinky*, for example, began life as a film noir short story by Heather O'Neill that appeared in a magazine the director happened upon fortuitously one day. Instantly enamored of the writer's style of humor and feeling a connection to its evocative tone and use of familiar Montreal locations, Blanchet made contact with O'Neill. The eventual film was able to both showcase the director's own sense of mood while complementing the original text, even featuring O'Neill as the film's narrator.

Writers' groups, literature festivals, meet-ups and of course the internet are all good facilitators for potential collaboration. At the risk of sounding drippy, it may very well be that making the effort and reaching out will become the catalyst for something special.

5

The Beat of a Different Drum

Figure 5.1

Still from *Dub of a Preacherman* ©2011 Rumpus Animation.

The composition, production and performance of music are creative exercises not without their animation parallels. It's no surprise then, that music and animation have so often made fine bedfellows. From the very dawn of animation throughout its golden age, music was often the thrust behind the early shorts and feature films of every major studio. From Norman McLaren's work for the GPO and NFB to the musical sequences of The Beatles' *Yellow Submarine*, music has been an established linchpin of the animation world since long before the

DOI: 10.1201/9781003214717-5

dawn of MTV. Once the concept of music videos became mainstream, animation was quickly integrated and, on occasion, propelled forward as a medium. While showing their age nowadays, early videos showcased exemplary animation techniques, such as rotoscoping for A-ha's *Take On Me* (Dir. Steve Barron, 1984), early CG in Dire Straits' *Money For Nothing* (Barron again, the following year), stop-motion in Michael Jackson's *Speed Demon* (Dir. Will Vinton, 1989) and the mixed-media masterwork of Peter Gabriel's *Sledgehammer* (Dir. Stephen R. Johnson, 1986) which depicted the singer alternately through live-action, plasticine animation and pixilation against a predominantly stop-motion backdrop, serving as a formative outing for the talents of Aardman and the Brothers Quay.

As time has gone by, the role of the music video as a promotional tool has hugely diminished in importance. With the nature of music sales a completely different beast than it was in the eighties and nineties, along with the oversaturation of music-based channels (their originator MTV having long succumbed to the lure of cheap 'n' cheerful "reality" shows making up the bulk of its schedules), music videos are no longer considered an indispensable branch of an artist, band or album's advertising. They do, however, remain quite vital in the cultivation and preservation of a band's image, and the viral potential today's online outlets allow for is mutually beneficial to both musicians and filmmakers. Mainstream examples of modern animated music videos remain plentiful; outfits as diverse as Queens of the Stone Age, Radiohead, R.E.M., Daft Punk, U.N.C.L.E. and The White Stripes making up a mere fraction of those who've had their work represented through animation in some form or other, not to mention the entire branding of Damon Albarn's Gorillaz.

Alas, this isn't a history book you're holding (which is a bit of a shame for me as I'd rather love to bang on about this subject at tiresome length), though hopefully the above helps to legitimize a music-oriented project as a tenable prospect for short-form animation.

Bristol-based studio Rumpus Animation began life as far back as 2007 in the way many studios do, as an assortment of hypothetical film ideas and character concepts discussed between animator Joe Wood and designer Seb Burnett. The two would officially begin the company proper in 2010 and work together for the next decade, with Joe remaining solely at the helm from 2020 onward. Though now a firmly established operation, in the early days of the studio the pair would see a long road ahead as far as forging their brand and reputation, as is often the case.

One formative project that served as a valuable exercise in establishing Rumpus's identity was *Dub of a Preacherman* (Figures 5.1–5.4), a collaboration with DJ Count Skylarkin, a mutually beneficial exercise that also served to develop his own visual branding. The music video embraces some of Rumpus Animation's major strengths, a wide variety of quirky character designs coupled with short, endearing, loopable animations (a perfect fit for the up-tempo music), composited together to create a showy animated bar-room scenario.

An issue to consider is that "independent," be it animation, music or otherwise, tends to go hand-in-hand with nil budget. As Seb reasons, "Most record labels or indie bands who might want you to produce work for them as an indie studio, are going to be broke as well. So unless you're working with big bands through an agency it tends to have to be more of a labour of love."

"But it's the only one where they probably *can* pay you in exposure," adds Joe, in reference to the dubious lure most emerging creatives find themselves faced with when embarking on the first stage of their career. "It actually works some-times, as opposed to lots of project that offer to 'pay' you in the exposure. At least with music videos, sometimes you can get quite a free reign to do what you want."

As a means of getting the ball rolling for the studio itself, the advantages are fairly obvious. There may very well be a plethora of half-formed film ideas, char-acter concepts and vanity projects that come with establishing a studio's identity, though without a focus for these creative energies it's likely that they won't take flight. "Apart from having the musician chasing us all the time to make sure we've actually done it, all you need is the music and the animation and it's done. Our job is to make some cool stuff to go over this music, so it's quite a nice thing to do. Although it took us a while to get it done, we were chased up quite a lot, which made us do it."

"Because it was our first project, instead of doing something quite simple, we put as much as we could into it," explains Seb. "The idea was to keep everything really simple, reuse, loops – that's the thing with music videos, they're sort of made for re-using visuals. We started enjoying the fact we could put any character we wanted in there, it sort of mushroomed a bit." The assortment of characters, a tradition that Joe and Seb enthuse is paramount to the Rumpus MO, regard-less of medium, was amassed from sketchbooks, stalled projects and pitches. The premise of the video itself uses simplicity to its advantage, with bar patrons and soul singers animated in a variety of dance loops. To Joe, this simple setup made the overall process "Quite fun, because you can pretty much use anyone you like the look of and they won't be out of place in the film."

"In fact, it was a chance to just do the funniest stuff we'd normally not make for a commercial film," adds Seb. "We had a bit more free-range. I think origi-nally it was set in the woods – I just like setting everything in the woods – it would be the same except at the start you would go down into an old tree trunk. For whatever reason we decided to change it to a city, that way it's sort of based on an area in Oxford he does a lot of DJing in. We're mostly interested in funny characters or funny stories. Whether that's for a game or an animation or comics doesn't matter, as long as we're enjoying making something funny happen that

Figure 5.2

Dub of a Preacherman character designs ©2011 Rumpus Animation.

hopefully people will enjoy – light relief, daft little characters falling over or pulling things out of their pockets in a funny way. It's always the story and characters that are the most interesting."

Producing work for friends carries with it a diminished risk factor when compared to producing work for major clients who are less accommodating about missed deadlines. Though it took longer than expected, it served as a ropes course in the realities of production that, as well as making their mark on the animation community, cemented their more disciplined approach when the commissions began.

The film and song both performed well, with the music video making the Annecy International Animation Festival official selection and the song receiving extended airplay from prominent UK DJ Craig Charles, leading to a significant boost in YouTube hits. Since then Rumpus has dipped their toes in the waters of music video production with a follow-up Count Skylarkin video *Dubplate Iko* in collaboration with live-action director Miho Lomon in 2014, preceded by 2011s *Dresinen* for the Norwegian band Casiokids. Though the opportunity didn't offer up a huge budgetary advantage, weighing up their own fondness for the song itself as well as the opportunity to appeal to an entirely new, international audience again proved vital to the company's visibility. Seb, who took the lead on the project creatively, looked at it as "A chance to experiment for the first time by combining stop-motion and Flash. So it's all cut-out characters arranged in Flash, then animated as if it were stop-motion, with real fingers. I'm still quite proud of that one because it looks quite different, it's still got identifiably Rumpus characters but it looks quite different as a technique to what we've normally done, so that made it worth it."

The chance to develop a technique the studio most likely would not have happened on otherwise proved another advantage, with Seb drawing upon influences such as the 1977 Polish adaptation of Tove Jansson's *Moomins* series. "I had been playing around with ideas of how we could make it, and the song was a really good opportunity because they're Scandinavian and the sound of the music fits rather well with the imagery. That was probably one of our more successful projects because it was for a more established band." The opportunity originally arose through the brother of a studio friend owning the independent record label the band were signed to, which makes a case for exploring all avenues of networking when they present themselves.

As with *Dub of a Preacherman*, Rumpus was afforded creative reign in lieu of a hefty budget which, hand in hand with the exposure, made for a successful end result. This too makes its own case, that the circumstances under which monetary compensation need be strictly proportionate to the labor involved are not necessarily that cut and dry. Whether a studio or individual, we are all of us aware at some level of our own worth and the value that being associated with a certain project can bring. If a high enjoyment factor, genuine visibility that will lead to more regular work and an excuse to try new approaches all align, then accepting the odd honorarium or stipend now and again will not grind our careers to a standstill, so long as they can be time-managed effectively.

"Definitely the indie stuff we've done, like the music videos, have led to getting some work in." Seb reflects, "Then when you're pitching work as well you can show stuff you've made to prospective clients. It just shows that you're making work as well. We try and keep Rumpus so that funny animation comes first. Occasionally we do quite a lot of work where there's no humour involved

Figure 5.3

Artwork demonstrating the visual development of a sequence in *Dub of a Preacherman* ©2011 Rumpus Animation.

Figure 5.4

Still from *Dub of a Preacherman* ©2011 Rumpus Animation.

whatsoever, but they've seen some of our work and realised technically we can animate, but the project will be in a completely different style than what we usually do. We work with different illustrators as well, I've got constant freelancers coming in, it's quite a flexible way of working but the basis of it all is the humour, basically.

"We've tried to keep a balance doing our own little experiments, and as visual language changes and different things become fashionable, new techniques emerge. You need to keep trying to experiment with different approaches to different films, so you're not just 'that' studio with 'that' style."

Going Solo

The ways in which music and animation can complement each other need not even be dependent on collaboration, as plenty of animators with a musical bent have demonstrated.

There is clearly a place for music and its potential to take hold of an audience in the world of web-based animation (an area we shall explore in more depth in the following chapter). The viral success of self-propelling online personalities such as Jonti Picking, a prolific producer of online content under the moniker Weebl, is often peppered with animated musical numbers.

The roots of Jonti's enthusiasm for bringing music and visuals together began before his first major strides in the world of design and animation, taking a Music Tech course which introduced him to Macromedia Director (an early incarnation of Adobe Director) which ran alongside Flash in the development of interactive CD-Roms which, at the time, were quite prevalent.

"Music was hugely important to me," Jonti recalls, "Until I became sort of disenfranchised by the whole music scene. Eventually, I decided to write tunes to amuse myself and try to annoy other people, which made it all fun again. Songs like *Badgers* and *Scampi* use the most obnoxious melodies and sounds possible, so that they are really hammered into the brain."

Said clips, as well as a smorgasbord of others including *Narwhals* (Figure 5.5), *Magical Trevor* and *Kenya*, serve less as music videos than hook-centric microshorts

Figure 5.5

Narwhals – a viral phenomenon ©2009 Weebl's Stuff.

which take advantage of their Flash SWF file format to play on a perpetual loop. As with many of Weebl's viral companions from the earlier days of webtoons, they use simple visual concepts, oftentimes random and surreal, combined with musical earworms that linger with their audiences for days. While these have frequently proved extremely popular, racking up millions of views, Jonti has been keen to evolve and embrace the broader role music can play in his work. More recent song-oriented projects include Savlonic (Figure 5.6), a series of animated music videos for a faux-electro band that has quickly developed a considerable fanbase in its own right, with a successful crowdfunding campaign ensuring the professional production of its first studio album. "As I've gone along, the technology and equipment I've been able to buy has improved, so it's been nice to dabble with slightly more sensible stuff. Hence Savlonic, which will possibly become a proper, full-on electro band. It was meant to parody electro bands but their lyrics became as daft as ours. There's not much point in parodying something that's become a parody of itself anyway, so we may as well write proper music.

"People attach themselves to tunes, they're easy to share and understand, straight away, music videos are engrained on our psyche. You can come back to them as well; with a comedy script obviously with each viewing the comedy will be less and less, generally, whereas with music you can get the comedy element and then go back and watch it for the tune because that's stuck in your head. I think that's why music is so successful with animation. It's rewatchable."

Even when dealing with the super-short, absurdist subsection of music-driven animation, there are certain disciplines that differ from standard webtoon production. "You don't generally have a script to begin with, so the tune very much drives what's going to happen. With a script you'll write it, then you'll do the audio, then you'll animate everything to the script and add background music

Figure 5.6

Still from Savlonic music video *The Driver* ©2012 Weebl's Stuff.

last, so for music videos it's sort of the reverse of that. It means you can do things quite quickly as well which, when dealing with online content, is a bonus."

From Scratch

Another virtue of collaboration, in a manner not dissimilar from that explored in Chapter 4, would be one in which a piece of music is not only the basis of an animated short but created specifically for it. A project preceding her success with *Bottle* and later films saw Kirsten Lepore joining forces with fellow undergrad, animator and songwriter Garrett Michael Davis.

The two met during their time at MICA (Maryland Institute College of Art), when Kirsten was working in the Experimental Animation department and Garrett in Interdisciplinary Sculpture. Over time they would begin a series of creative collaborations, Kirsten providing ideas and concepts to prompt improvisational monologues and character performances from Garrett. In their senior year, finding themselves both studying animation, they decided to work together on their final project, having composed a piece of music originally titled *The Spider Song*, in which a frightened boy entreats his father to dispatch of a spider and is instead met with a series of increasingly surreal and existential hypotheticals (Figure 5.7).

"The spider song was written well before we had the film in mind," confirms Garrett, "I wrote it while spending a summer in Colorado, working in the gift shop of a whitewater rafting company and trying to write songs. Lacking ideas, I asked my girlfriend at the time what I should write a song about and she suggested a girl asking her Dad to kill a spider in her room. Obviously it became about a little boy, but the seed of the idea came from her, hence she's thanked in the credits.

Deciding to animate a video for it, the two collaborated on the retitled *Story from North America* (Figures 5.8–5.10), originally intending to professionally re-record the song but ultimately preferring the raw, hastily recorded demo version.

"It was the natural preference. I recorded it on my Nikon Coolpix digital camera that had an audio recording function. I recorded it very soon after writing the song, and since at that point I had not yet memorized the lyrics, the page turn

5. The Beat of a Different Drum

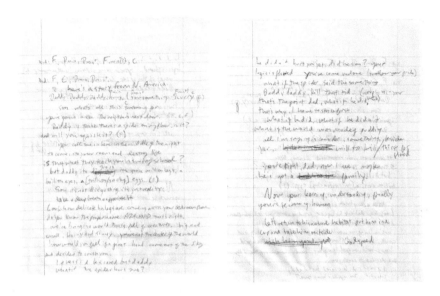

Figure 5.7

Original lyrics for *The Spider Song* by Garrett Michael Davis. Image courtesy of Garrett Michael Davis.

that got animated as the narrator turning the page in a barren field was me turning the page of my notebook as I read the lyrics. Aesthetically though, recording in such a low-fi way was just how I liked to do things then, and still do now, though that process has evolved quite a bit.

"I'm not impressed by the technical slickness which is so idolized at the moment (and was back in 2007 as well). We re-recorded the song with an extra guitar in a sound booth and it was just so obvious that the original version was better. On this point I also must mention that having a finished audio track like this to work with is a dream come true. There is no need to think about sound effects if you don't want to, as the skeleton of the timing is already present. Working with music has such a rich history in animation and having a set audio track to animate to, whichever way it has been generated, simplifies things a lot. It gives you set limits within which to explore, makes a lot of decisions for you at the outset so you have more time and energy to go wild generating ideas of how to fill it."

Though Kirsten contributed, mainly in so far as the animation of the spider itself and the ever-beseeching child tormented by it, obligations toward her own production and thesis meant that Garrett ultimately took the lead on the visuals, though the idea generation behind them harkened back to their earlier, improvisational collaborations.

"I animated all of the Dad's parts, and things like the narrator, the devil in the cloud of smoke in the kid's room, the spider family blessing their feast, the scene where the kid has a glass of blood on his nightstand, the spider at the end. Our working dynamic was very natural and effortless. For any given line of the song we'd just say, 'What should this be?' We would think of ideas, decide on one, and go do it. We both understood each other's sense of humor intuitively, so it just flowed."

"Garrett did most of the animation and made most of the design decisions on the film." Kirsten assures, "We definitely approached the visualization in a very

Figure 5.8

Still from *Story from North America* (Dir. Garrett Michael Davis/Kirsten Lepore) ©2007 Garrett Davis/Kirsten Lepore.

unique way where we wouldn't plan too far ahead, but instead meet, assign each other a verse, loosely figure out what we think we'd animate for our respective verses, and then go off and animate separately. We never boarded anything; the animation itself was relatively stream of consciousness. When we'd meet back up, it was always exciting to show the other person what we had animated. Since we had not pencil-tested, it felt like Christmas every time we shot a scene because we were seeing our finished animation for the first time."

This sustained commitment and fondness for the process is what Garrett credits the success of what, on its surface, might not be the most accessible of films. Through the scratchy designs and fuzzy audio, a film with no small amount of appeal shines through, something that never would have happened without their combined forces.

"It was also just the friendship and camaraderie of it," says Garrett. "Staying up all night in Kirsten's apartment drawing and then her cooking up some ingenious meal out of the scraps she had in her kitchen. Making the rounds of the computer labs taking paper out of the school printers to draw it on, and bringing giant stacks to this one particular security desk that had a three-hole punch that would punch about a hundred sheets at a time."

Alongside these rituals was an overall rejection of how "best" to approach the production pipeline, instead opting to wing it without tests or storyboards. Working to a primitive dope sheet in Flash for timing reference, the pair wound up working straight-ahead for the most part.

"Our classmates were completely shocked that we didn't storyboard it. We didn't care about the accepted way of doing things. We found those methods stiff and boring, an unnecessary layer of tedium heaped onto the already nearly unbearable tediousness of the animation process itself. While everyone was busy imitating those who had influenced them by drawing off-brand anime, we were doing our own thing.

"I think the spider with the knife up to the kid's throat is one of my favorite of Kirsten's contributions. It's hard to say, people always ask who did this, who

Figure 5.9

Still from *Story from North America* (Dir. Garrett Michael Davis/Kirsten Lepore) ©2007 Garrett Davis/Kirsten Lepore.

did that, but really it all blends together when the collaboration is successful, and it doesn't matter who did what. I guess it matters to other people 'cause they are curious and they always ask, but I don't really care as long as the final product is good. And honestly with animation, when it's done, you're just glad that it's over!"

Certainly amongst Kirsten Lepore's work, oftentimes focused on tactile stop-motion projects and digital 2D, *Story of North America* stands out as unique, again attributed to Garrett's taking the lead on the look of the film. "Although this was probably because I was trying more to match Garrett's style of drawing. I really had only done 2D/drawn animation up until that point. *Sweet Dreams* was pretty much my first stop-motion film. We also decided from the beginning that we wanted *Story from North America* to remain a fun, super loose project where we resolved never to pencil test anything, but instead to embrace all the weirdness and shiftiness that came naturally. It was such a wonderful, liberating way to work."

Completed in 2007 during their senior year, the film's ensuing viral success validates the time spent on it as a university side project. Despite it being mostly Garrett's vision, the most-viewed versions of the film have been uploaded to Kirsten's YouTube and Vimeo channels, a decision made for pragmatic reasons, chiefly that Garrett had neither of his own at the time.

"I was living in a converted air-stream trailer inside a warehouse in Philadelphia for $140 a month, working as a furniture mover and a slough of other weird jobs. Kirsten was building her freelance career and 'had her stuff together' way more so than I did." Though this has generated a modicum of confusion amongst audiences, as stated earlier by Garrett, the film stands up either way. "The overall audience response has been overwhelmingly positive. I've received loads of nice messages from people who've enjoyed the film, and it's been a point of connection with so many people I've met in the animation world in Los Angeles." The visibility of the film would also help Garrett secure freelance commissions and festival exposure the world over.

Figure 5.10

Still from *Story from North America* (Dir. Garrett Michael Davis/Kirsten Lepore)
©2007 Garrett Davis/Kirsten Lepore.

"It usually gets interpreted as a political statement, though it was not consciously intended to be one. Overall I think what people respond to is its 'rock and roll' spirit." The film would also eventually be followed up by *Story from South America*, though the alternate funding circumstances (it being commissioned for Fox's Animation Domination HD late-night programming block) and absence of Kirsten's input would make both production of the film and the end result quite a different beast, as we'll learn in Chapter 9.

Playing with the Majors

When it comes to independent animation figurehead Bill Plympton, music videos make up a percentage of his output and help him fund his more independent work. Though these are more often than not commissioned and not entirely "independent" by some classifications of the term (see Chapter 1), the independent *spirit* of his style and creative approach has become, over the years, a valued commodity to a diverse array of mainstream artists, from Kanye West to "Weird Al" Yankovic. As such his approach remains applicable to those approaching their own indie music video.

"I think that the union of music and animation is one of the great duets of culture, putting the two together is always beautiful. I mean, look at some of the old Fleischer Brothers films with Cab Calloway. *Fantasia* of course is another great example of the union of music and animation. It's just a fun art form for me. There's a lot more freedom and a lot more chance for experimentation. There's not necessarily a story you'll have to deal with and it's a lot of fun creating images that are really fascinating, interesting and, hopefully, compelling. Sometimes the money's great, sometimes the money's not so good, but more than anything you've got to love music."

From the earliest days of Bill's work, this passion has been evident, most notable in *Your Face*. The film, made in 1987 to an original song by Maureen McElheron, introduced the world to his capacity for hypnagogic insanity, as a well-dressed man simplistically lip-syncs the song's eerily slowed-down lyrics while his face melts, contorts and metamorphoses throughout. The wide-reaching effect of Bill's striking imagery extended to Kanye West who, in late 2005, eschewed the live-action video Michel Gondry had directed for the song *Heard 'Em Say* in favor of an animated interpretation from Bill. Shortly afterward, Bill was recruited as one of several prominent animators to direct a video for "Weird Al" Yankovic's twelfth studio album *Straight Outta Lynwood*, animating the album's closing track *Don't Download This Song*.

"Kanye West was very hands-on, in fact he came to my studio for two days and actually looked over my shoulder while I was drawing. He definitely has certain ideas, and they're great ideas. He's a very smart, talented guy and he's very visual, whereas other people like 'Weird Al' Yankovic are much more easygoing to work with. Al doesn't need to see the storyboards, he just wants to see it when it's finished." Bill was brought on board again with Al's 2011 follow-up *Alpocalypse*, to direct and animate the video for *TMZ* (a parody of Taylor Swift's *You Belong with Me*, the new lyrics and video depicting the hounding of an unsuspecting celebrity desperately trying to avoid the titular website's notorious paparazzi). "I also did one for Joe Cartoon, the guy who does *Frog in a Blender*. He has a wonderful album out and asked me to do a music video for one of his songs, which was a lot of freedom, it was really fun.

"There was another one I did called *Mexican Stand-Off* by Parsons Brown from the Netherlands, a cowboy-themed one. I really had fun doing the cowboys because I'd loved to draw them since I was a kid, so I sort of developed a whole new side with that."

Bill's experience on this particular video proved to be an informative new creative direction. Approaching the animation entirely using ballpoint pen, something he had never tried with animation before, the process and overall look of the end result inspired him to apply a similar approach to a subsequent independent short. 2013s *Drunker Than A Skunk* is an animated poem created during the last year of production of his feature film *Cheatin'* (see Chapter 8), mainly with the (successful) aim of inclusion at that year's Annecy festival. The film is visually reminiscent of *Mexican Stand-Off*, also adopting the ballpoint pen look. Previously, Bill had used the opportunity of creating *Heard 'Em Say* to take his style in a more extreme direction that he had previously, using highly caricatured proportions and ambitious approaches to layout. This was an approach which ultimately determined the overall aesthetic of *Cheatin'*, a film which might have had an entirely different tone and comedic sensibility otherwise. These further serve as a testament to the value of taking on different creative projects for the sake of one's own artistic direction, and music videos have a demonstrable ability to give artists an outlet for experimentation they may not find elsewhere.

Here we have looked at how songs themselves, from chart hits to hastily recorded indie offerings, can serve as a basis for an animated music video. This is, of course, quite a different practice than an animated short that uses a musical score as its thrust, something we will explore more in Chapter 19. Before then, however, let's venture into one of independent animation's more anarchic arenas, the internet, and consider how viable an option it remains so many years since the birth of the online webisode.

6

Going Webisodic

Figure 6.1

Still from *Carpark* (Dir. Ant Blades) ©2013 Ant Blades/Birdbox Studio.

It is a sobering thought to look back and see how swiftly web culture of all varieties has blown up over the past couple of decades. Humankind can barely get anything done for the glut of vlogs, cute animal clips, video game playthroughs and Autonomous Sensory Meridian Response (whispering, basically) videos out there. It may seem a distant memory now, but the sheer quantity of today's procrastination bait was not always within such easy reach, calling to us like a siren song from our smartphones and minimized browser windows. As most of you

DOI: 10.1201/9781003214717-6

reading this are probably aware, it is animation in its most independent form that started that particular ball rolling.

In many respects, we live in a very different world to that of the dawn of animation on the web. Video content and the internet were rarely a comfortable pairing, short MOV clips taking up *entire megabytes* of hard disk space, provided one's household dial-up connection had the fortitude to survive the hourslong download process. The concept of streaming HD content was so far out of the general public's grasp that the very phrase "streaming HD content" most likely wouldn't even have made sense to anyone who heard it. By the late 1990s, however, several enterprising creatives began taking advantage of a fortunate loophole facilitated by both the possibilities of creating animation, however rudimentary, in a program called Macromedia Flash. Said loophole was the software's ability to export its projects with small enough file sizes to be watched online with relative ease. The mechanics of the hows and whys are surely well known to anyone who knows their vectors from their bitmaps (which I'm cautiously optimistic includes anyone who is reading this). An entire subculture was born, in a semi-lawless online world where broadcast regulations had no authority and content could be as provocative, daring and gratuitous as their creators desired. Though originally leaning toward juvenilia, some of the Internet's most significant webtoon pioneers got their start through a mix of Flash-animated animal misfortune and vaguely risqué celebrity impersonations. In the decades since, online animation has spanned a larger range of genres, though its independent roots have remained (Figure 6.1). While there are certainly major corporations that have capitalized on the revenue-generating potential of streaming animation, with the advent of social media and influx of platforms through which to showcase original, self-made content, the monetary potential for an independent artist is still strong. To get a clear sense of how this corner of the independent animation world has developed, it is worth looking at webtoon creators who have consistently produced original content to this day, forging entire careers out of it.

A Life in Webtoons

Having begun his career as an Interactive Developer at AMX London, Jonti Picking (Figure 6.2) mainly worked on Flash development for blue-collar clients until the dot-com bubble burst at the start of the millennium. In the ensuing lull, Jonti took to using Flash for his own purposes, animating cartoons for the web, initially through the website B3TA. At this point, the phenomenon was slowly building serious momentum.

"There was Joe Cartoon's *Frog in a Blender,* you had Joel Veitch of Rather Good doing his dancing kittens and *Homestar Runner* who were fantastic and still are. There were loads of Newgrounds people obviously, using their horrible speech synthesis to do stuff. Newgrounds was big noise back then. It was definitely a more creative environment."

Starting with small, quirky GIFs, Jonti soon graduated to using Flash for web shorts that would accommodate the limitations of most household internet capabilities. With most of the public connecting to the web with 56k or 28k modems, even the small file sizes of Flash cartoons could prove taxing to people's connections. In creating his own animated characters, Jonti opted to bypass this concern as much as he could through sheer minimalism, creating the duo *Weebl and Bob* (Figure 6.3) as a consequence.

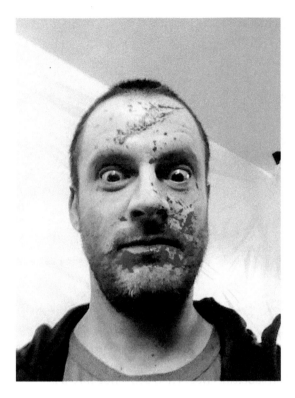

Figure 6.2

Jonti Picking, AKA Weebl. Image courtesy of the artist.

"Obviously the simpler the shape the smaller the file size. The sound was designed around short little music loops and snippets of speech to try and keep everything as tiny as possible, which just about worked."

Whether or not the asset-light approach made the cartoon easier to stream, its immense audience reaction when it debuted in June of 2002 was a clear indication of the mileage in the characters. Cemented by a two-month stint producing *Weebl and Bob* shorts for MTV, Jonti quit his day job and used the funds to host his work on his own site Weebl's Stuff. Since then his output has extended to multiple series, with a variety of writers and animators to add in extra dynamic visual range. As for what grabbed the attention of the public initially:

"It's really hard to say. I think it's that there is a lot of catchphrase-oriented material, easily quotable lines and such. The fact it had quirky music choices I guess helped it along, that it was very simple and iconographic, so that you knew instantly what it was. Ambient comedy was quite big at that point as well and looking back on the early *Weebl and Bob* shorts there were massive pauses between each line. It had this weird flow to it that wasn't really seen, which I think helped."

Having taken on corporate work alongside his web-based output, Jonti has a firm concept of how web-based production differs from the more business-driven animation industries.

"It's very improvisational, though if it's scripted then obviously that will give some direction. We tend not to bother with animatics because if you're making Flash video correctly it should be done in a way where you can make changes

Figure 6.3

Online animation superstars Weebl and Bob ©Weebl's Stuff.

fairly quickly. I like the improvisational approach because people often bring their own approach, their own style or timing, which is why I like to pick certain animators over others.

"Generally I'll do a callout for animators via social media. People will send their stuff, link me up to a few of their videos and if I like the style then we'll chat more on email. I generally give them one short test animation, a tune or a short script, to see what they would do with it. This gives a better idea of what their sensibilities are, because I like to bring people on for their methods as well. I don't force them down a specific route unless it has to look or be a certain way, generally I think it's nice to mix it up. I like the sense of community, I can link to their other work, it's important to me that people get to appreciate them for who they are rather than what I've made them do.

"A lot of the mistakes that people working in Flash will make is to put everything on one layer or timeline. It makes things a lot easier to break everything down into layers so you can change anything within the project really quickly. I'll spend the extra time setting things up, building the asset library and then I can change assets on the fly as and when I need to. I think that's the best way of doing it, especially if you're doing advertising work where the client will often do rewrites. You don't want to lose months of work when you can get it right in two hours. So I'm very much about that, just build your assets, then animate, then change as need be."

Different Worlds

As hugely popular as the phenomenon of independent webtoons has grown to be, it remains curiously separate from the comparatively insular world of broadcast

Figure 6.4

Assassin Babies – skit from the webseries *Wobble Box* ©2013 Jelly Penguin.

animation production. In many respects, the initial sense of individuality and informality that allowed for such creative freedom has been retained, with prominent practitioners achieving online celebrity rather than industry notoriety. In this universe, the type of viral success a major studio would dream of achieving is noticeably less earned by the ingenuity of a piece of work than the established fan base of the online personalities who have produced it. I myself had never truly appreciated this disparity until my first rolling contract producing animation for web content developers Channel Flip in 2012–2013. While it served as an especially gratifying gig with many creative freedoms, I was aware throughout that I was disconnected somewhat from the other artists, many of whom had their own YouTube channels and established following. My comparative anonymity gave me some free reign to take risks that might have had greater ramifications working on a broadcast series at an animation studio. For others, however, the work produced was a very visible extension of their online persona and there were significant audience expectations to meet. At the reins of Channel Flip's specially developed online channel was Jonti Picking, contracted to produce consistent, rapidfire animation content over the course of that year. With this certain mainstays of the Weebl universe were brought over, notably *Weebl and Bob* themselves.

"We've got a *Weebl and Bob*-only channel, so every single episode is now uploaded in HD with better sound. I decided not to put them on the main channel because of the way YouTube works – if you put something up that people aren't expecting, don't necessarily like or aren't aware of its context, then it's going to affect everything else."

The demand for regular original material with new characters in this environment was high, with numerous interwoven series' boasting their own independent, ensemble casts. Amongst these was *Wobble Box* (Figure 6.4), an animated skit show where each episode required an assortment of one-time characters, premises and styles created from scratch.

"We generally have a writer's meeting round our house, with everyone at the table bouncing ideas around. If we think there's something to an idea we'll do maybe a rough block of what would happen in the sketch and then assign writers.

If I need to fill time then I will simply draw the first things that come to mind and ask myself what would happen."

From these intense sessions are occasional instances of ideas and characters with enough of a hook to recur in multiple episodes. The potential appeal of a concept beyond its first outing is a major consideration for all of Jonti's work. Sometimes ideas intended as one-offs or throwaway gags organically evolve into the basis for an entire series in its own right. The opposite, inevitably, has also been known to happen:

"There's stuff we've written as a series from the off which has just not picked up. We did a short called *Zombie Street* that we thought would be popular; it wasn't until it was finally animated that we realised it probably wasn't going to work. Then there are one-off ideas like *Rescue Whale* and *Bad Advice* where the audience response was 'This'd be a great series!' The ideal thing about YouTube is that you receive brilliant feedback straight away, we learn what people like so we can do things without giving up the ideals we have. Instant feedback has always been there on the internet, when you can read comments straightaway you just go with it – if people are liking it then do more, if they don't then don't be afraid to just dump it and move onto the next thing."

So of this feedback, what are the main recurring wants and needs of an online audience that have been picked up on? After so many years of evaluation Jonti has some idea.

"The songs are generally popular. A few people have a bit of a bee in their bonnet about the more puerile jokes but they've always been there and always will. They actually seem to be more popular, they get shared a lot more because people

Figure 6.5

Cat Face (Dir. Sarah Darling) ©2007 Weebl's Stuff.

want the world to think they're above something, while secretly they're chuckling away. These days people have quite a short attention span when it comes to online videos. You shouldn't spend too long developing a character, you have to hit it straight away and start moving the plot along quite rapidly. If you're doing something that is slow, then *maybe* you can get away with it if it's beautiful, but that's a big risk, I would say. It's nice to do something along those lines occasionally, but mainly it's all rapidfire.

"The internet's always been quite segmented in a way, so specific websites that you deal with will have their own preferences. The original ethos was 'Bad equals Good,' which kind of worked back then; it was punk, it didn't matter what it looked like as long as you had the core idea. I think this was carried across on Newgrounds to a certain extent, but their idea was to push yourself and become better, which is why you have people like Harry Partridge[1] and Egoraptor[2] who really started pushing what Flash could do, more in the direction of traditional animation in many ways.

"Then there's YouTube, who like catchphrases and memes. There's still an appreciative audience there but the main audience who are the driving force tend to just like the things they already know reinforced. There's a 'tipping point,' as Malcolm Gladwell put it. In television, there are rewrites, they like to hone ideas and there's time to do it, for the most part. Their budgets have dropped quite extensively but they still have a mind for production values. With online content there's an attitude of wanting the same values, except the money's terrible and you have to upload something new three times a week!"

Amongst the core team who makes up Weebl's Stuff is Jonti's spouse Sarah Darling, who became heavily involved in producing content during a commission for the iconic children's series *Sesame Street*. Sarah's natural inclination toward writing for younger audiences led to her commandeering some of the website's more innocuous fare such as *Cat Face* (Figure 6.5), a series whose titular protagonist floats through the air due to his inflated head. Though tinged with occasional innuendo, this series is largely stripped of content that would limit its audience. Directing these energies into an outlet more focused on child-friendly content, the pair developed the online channel JellyBug in 2014. The channel, for which Sarah is head writer, serves to accommodate the increasing demand for quality children's entertainment through such staples as catchy music, repetition and bright, simplistic visuals, occasionally remaking existing family-friendly Weebl's Stuff videos such as *Badgers* with a more distinctly children's aesthetic (Figure 6.6).

"We've got two young kids now, and when we sit them with a tablet and YouTube, they just swipe away. It's good that they're using computers and there is a lot of stuff on YouTube that's well made but mostly stuff that isn't. If you're out with your family and your kids start screaming while you're trying to have a nice chat, now we can show them something safe on their tablets and have a little break. But we were sick of them watching really shoddily animated stuff, some with millions hits that were really poorly sung, looked atrocious and were of zero educational value. So we thought we'd make something better, some great kids' stuff in our own little style. Around that time YouTube really started pushing that side of things as well, there are some interesting things happening on that front. It's something we're really passionate about, I really want good kids' animation to be out there for people to watch."

Figure 6.6

Badger Badger Badger – original and redesigned (for online preschool channel Jellybug) versions ©2003 Weebl's Stuff/©2014 JellyBug.

The Virility of Virality

The career potential of a viral short, one that transcends ephemera and the fickle attention spans of online audiences, has been proven elsewhere. Matt Stone and Trey Parker's satirical animated sitcom *South Park*, a show presently in its third decade, would never have existed without their first, ostensibly halfhearted stabs at animation going viral before the term even existed in such a context. The duo's seasonally themed short *Spirit of Christmas* (a loose remake of their 1992 University of Colorado student film of the same name, commissioned by Fox for a video Christmas card) was a word of mouth sensation following its initial distribution in December 1995, ultimately serving as a style guide and precursor to the show's eventual pilot which aired in 1997.

More recent examples of virality translating into mainstream success largely take advantage of the new relationship that has developed between creators and audiences. When an established fanbase reached the millions, it is more than just opportunities for merchandising which become valid; a supportive viewership can nowadays further the animation itself. Web series such as Simon Tofield's *Simon's Cat* and Natasha Allegri's *Bee and Puppycat* have been able to successfully crowdfund (a phenomenon we shall explore more in Chapter 9) proposed projects more ambitious than their standard output, audience enthusiasm for both exceeding their proposed goals by hundreds of thousands of dollars. Other artists, such as Cas van den Pol[3] whose series of "recap" cartoons brilliantly condense standout animated feature films into 2D animated parodies less than five minutes long, or Vivienne Medrano (AKA Vivziepop)[4] whose sensationally popular animations would lead to the series *Hazbin Hotel* and *Helluva Boss*, have made use of platforms such as Patreon that allow their established fanbases to subsidize their art through monthly tiered payments in exchange for exclusive content and access to their process.

Nowadays, the influx of original, auteur web series and one-offs is so voluminous that to stand out and achieve a significant viewership is especially challenging. As always, there are key components that will serve as a leg-up, such as quotability, anarchic/surreal humor and effective use of music, but it's all too easy to miss the mark; for every hit like Jason Steele's *Charlie The Unicorn*, there will be hundreds, if not thousands, of forgettable imitators who do little more than replicate these traits on an entirely superficial level.

Breaking this mold somewhat is British animator and cartoonist Ant Blades,[5] whose work has proved that today's broader web audience can be as impressed and bowled over by technical skill as by comedic hooks. Having worked as an animation freelancer at Tandem and Prism Entertainment, Ant eventually found himself disheartened with working on other people's animations, gravitating more toward the world of online design. Working for Google as part of YouTube's creative team, Ant found his enthusiasm for animation began to rekindle over the years.

"It was fairly limited in terms of what I could do creatively, so there was an itch to do stuff on the side. Being very aware of YouTube, I knew of the stuff that was out there and thought it would be quite nice to have some really short but nicely animated stuff, to put it out there. After I had put about four of those out then people started getting in contact and saying they wanted me to do some work for them. That was always the plan, though I never quite thought it would come off. Then work started coming in, so that was the point to jump and then go for it. It's weird though, as soon as what you enjoy becomes your job, suddenly it's not quite the same anymore. Now it suddenly seems like work, but it's work I want to be doing."

An early motivator for Ant's work was via a local comedy festival that would showcase short films and up-and-coming comedians. Setting himself a monthly deadline tied in with each festival event spurred him on to create new, short-form work that was not unreasonably labor intensive or demanding on his time.

"I'd be amazed that students would be making a film for a year or two that was a five-or-ten-minute masterpiece. It just seemed such a commitment. So I quite liked that I was only trying to get these quick-as-possible ideas and, because that was successful I've tried to keep them going, keep them short and very funny and try to remember what got them started in the first place.

Birdbox has since served as an avenue for Ant's personal creative work, creating a series of unfailingly viral sensations that go against the grain of established webtoon culture, instead indulging the public's appetite for more sophisticated humor rich in physical comedy and slapstick. Rarely longer than a minute and a half, every second is meticulously thought through, a process which required some adaptation after his prior career as a newspaper cartoonist.

Working on his weekly strip *Bewley* would, from time to time, present an opportunity to execute a sight gag without the aid of dialog balloons. Although this proved a rare instance in the strip itself, taking that approach with the Birdbox shorts of physical comedy-based payoff humor was essential. One of the major concerns about appealing to a broader audience are the automatic

Figure 6.7

Still from *Chop Chop* (Dir. Ant Blades) ©2012 Ant Blades/Birdbox Studio.

limitations the inclusion of dialog can incur; a particular regional accent, in spite of whatever the creator's intentions may be, can appeal to one audience while simultaneously alienating another. A particular intonation, characterization or turn of phrase can similarly cordon off a presumed target age rage. Consider shows such as *South Park* or *Beavis and Butt-Head*, made for adults but ultimately finding maximum viewership amongst the demographic they were in fact skewering, due undoubtedly to the well-observed and effective use of relatable vernacular. Naturally, if a filmmaker wants to target a specific niche audience, then dialog can be used advantageously, but in the world of viral appeal, the more universal the better.

"If I can avoid words then I will. If, in a script, it looks like someone can say something, I will do my best to think how can we avoid them saying it, or have it be a mumble. Or how can we avoid there being writing anywhere in the background, things that will keep it as open as possible. That probably leads to more slapstick than anything else.

"To be honest I've actually got out of the habit since the cartoon ended some years ago. It was a weekly strip, so I was definitely used to having to sit down, trying to churn out ideas, having to throw away the bad ones that weren't working and then having that deadline, so even if something wasn't working, to have to push through the barrier of thinking what I had was awful until *something* eventually emerged. Translating that to shorts worked quite well. Going off and spending an hour or so without getting any good ideas didn't dishearten me because I knew that was part of the process, that if I just kept pushing eventually something would turn up that would be worth doing. I used to put aside a morning just to sit down and even at the end of the morning not have anything at the end of it, but it definitely helped with the process of hammering out bad ideas."

The earlier shorts made their way online via the BBC, who at the time were after original comedic content for their website. Accompanying similarly short and punchy commissioned vignettes created to raise awareness for World Mental Health Day in 2010, the first handful of Ant's shorts premiered on the network's official channel exclusively, an arrangement that worked well in terms of initial visibility. From 2012 onward, new content was put out independently through

Figure 6.8

Chop Chop character animation in Flash ©2012 Ant Blades/Birdbox Studio.

Figure 6.9

Chop Chop background colors in Photoshop ©2012 Ant Blades/Birdbox Studio.

Birdbox's own channel to better serve the studio's interests. "For what I was getting back I thought I'd rather have this bank of my own shorts on my own channel rather than selling them off. Even though you only get pennies back from YouTube, it made more sense as a brand to have them all together."

Relying less on repetition, music or asset-based design, Ant's shorts have more of an archetypal focus on silent comedy, with an assortment of visual gags leading up to a main payoff. The only concession made to the first handful of shorts is retaining a rough, digital line-test style, presenting the films without cleaned-up line work and sometimes without color. Rather than devalue the work, this "sketchy" quality of *Guard*, *Duel*, *Blues* and *Ice Creams* (the most popular of the four, in which a hapless father is left disastrously in charge of his children for mere seconds) the presentation allows the fluidity of movement, timing and

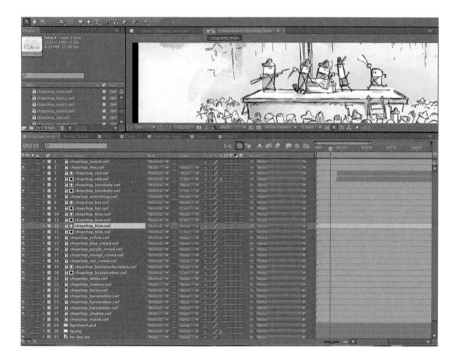

Figure 6.10

Chop Chop compositing in After Effects ©2012 Ant Blades/Birdbox Studio.

sound design to speak for itself. These sensibilities would reoccur in subsequent projects such as *Chop Chop* (Figures 6.7–6.10) in 2012. As each of the films play out in one continuous shot against a single background, special attention is paid to the character animation itself (which by and large makes use of the entire lay-out of the shot) so that the viewer is visually engaged throughout. This approach rules out the idea of mass-produced, weekly content, though producing several films over the course of the year provides the dual benefits of a maintained view-ership and higher quality ideas. As a result, the films play as standalone works of art whose presentation happens to be well-served online.

"I tend to have around ten personal works on the side at any point. I'll have an idea and quickly sketch it out in Flash, which is a very easy way to sketch out an animatic of the idea. I normally have other work on, so I will spend the first morning working on it, show it to other people and leave it for a month. I always know that if people are after something I will have a few things to one side that can be used." Although over time this style has veered in numerous directions, from Ant's perspective this hasn't had any aversive effect on the audience. With public feedback on most of the work largely visible, it's clear that the substance of the content itself is what has kept his viewers on board. "I think *Wildebeest* (Figure 6.11) could have worked in a different style. As you're coming up with an idea, you sense certain styles will lend themselves to it better. With *Wildebeest*, it definitely helped to have that look where it felt like a wildlife documentary, some-thing a bit more realistic. It also helped because there was minimal movement in it anyway, so it was quite nice to make something that looked a bit more plush, a bit more colorful. It might have been a bit boring if it had just been a line-drawing because so little is going on."

Figure 6.11

Stages of production for *Wildebeest* (Dir. Ant Blades) ©2012 Ant Blades/Birdbox Studio.

Regardless of these shifts in visual style (it is worth noting, despite all of the above, that the most successful of Ant's work in terms of viewers alone is the more traditionally webtoon-designed, asset dependent *Wildebeest*), each short carries with it equivalent economic concessions that accentuate the artistry of the animation; more often than not, Ant's shorts have been approached with speed in mind and, as such the production carries with it an acute awareness of its circumstances.

Dinner, for example, uses simple digital painting in lieu of sketched line work. Carrying on the tradition of the original *Sketchy* quartet is 2012's *Chop Chop*, where a gallant knight crashes an execution too late to rescue an already beheaded maiden. Of all Ant's work it is this film in particular which required the most fine-tuning.

"Certain films were labor intensive just because I was messing around with them for so long. *Chop Chop* could have been done months before, but I was just fiddling around with it for ages, with no real point at all. The original idea I came up with four years before finally finishing it, and looking back at it the first pass almost worked as well or better than the others. Having no deadline just makes it so much worse, you just keep messing around with stuff forever. I'm sure as I try and make them a bit more polished, they're gonna stretch out a bit more, and more time will go into them."

Setting Ant's work further apart from standard online fare is his altogether more traditional approach to the production itself, which is a major contributor to timing and choreography. "As the animatic is kicked off, I definitely am aware of the kind of rhythm that the films will need to be, so you can see as it's starting *Okay, this is kind of building up to something, so we need to pick up the pace.* Then you can start to feel that there's some kind of rhythm to it. You'll get that in most of them or you play with the rhythm and as you feel it's going somewhere then you just cut it short and end it. When it comes to *Chop Chop*, that's playing in a slightly different way in that you know it's going somewhere and then just kind of tails off. That's part of the humor, I suppose, that it's not really ramping up in any way, it's just tailing off to nothing, to failure. "The timing is definitely in the back of my head as I'm planning it out, that I know there will be a certain rhythm to getting there, getting the best comedy from it. When you look at a film like *Car Park*, with the dog in the car, you know that you'll need a slow build up because he's got the shopping and you need to wonder what's happening, there's a tease and then the jump. Mostly, the ending has to be fairly snappy – bam bam bam, then there has to be a finish."

Work produced since (Figures 6.12 and 6.13) has continued to range in quality and ambition, animations such as 2011s *Singing Christmas Hedgehogs* making use of YouTube's in-video hyperlinks to present the viewer with an interactive, "choose your own adventure"-style film. Perhaps the most visually "slick" of Ant's films is 2013's *Carpark*, which retains all of the hallmark strengths of his earlier work with additional cleanup and a well-rendered, textural quality. One of the reasons behind the alternate approach was the short's origin.

"*Carpark* was a personal idea I wanted to get out there. This was actually a rejected idea from the *Life is full of Ups and Downs* BBC Headspace campaign from a couple of years ago. It was put to one side as it was too long and not quite the right message, but it made me laugh so thought it was worth tidying up. The approach is pretty similar. The difference between commissioned and personal work is mainly how time is spent on them. Commissioned work forces ideas through to completion a bit quicker which can be helpful. It feels more productive. Personal work can drag out longer than it needs."

As time has worn on and commissioned work has increased in direct correlation with Birdbox's visibility, the speed at which new original work makes its way online has inevitably slowed down. Given the ruthless nature of YouTube's tendency to favor consistent output in its rotation, the quality versus quantity argument bears some evaluation.

Figure 6.12

Stages of production for *Carpark* (Dir. Ant Blades) ©2013 Ant Blades/Birdbox Studio.

6. Going Webisodic

"I suppose a bit more time's gone into them, because they do have to stand out from the rest of the content people are quickly churning out. A lot of that stuff is really funny, such as the *Cyanide and Happiness* shorts."

It stands to reason that if you produce a lot of videos on your channel, there's a far greater chance of building and maintaining a strong following. In terms of sheer volume, however, each new film will be far less likely to strike an audience – or traffic-generating outlets such as comedy blogs – as especially

Figure 6.13

Ant Blades in studio. Photo courtesy of the artist.

ingenious. The vitality of a filmmaker such as Ant Blades, however, hinges on the notion that each film is served by its own uniqueness.

"If you wait a bit longer to do something new, then it does have to be something a bit standout that makes people think *This is funny in a slightly different way and I'm gonna share it with my mates.* It does pile on a lot of pressure, because the longer I wait until the next one comes out, the more it feels like it has to do well. Obviously, it is better if you want to build an audience to do one or two or month – even one every couple of months is enough to keep an audience aware of what you're producing, and make sure they keep coming back. It can be a bit more forgiving, because it doesn't matter if you haven't produced anything particularly great as long as you have another one coming along. So if you haven't made something new in over a year, your next film really needs to have something especially funny or quirky about it that's going to make people want to send it round."

Although Ant himself confesses a tendency to hammer out ideas for years without ever seeing them cross the finish line, the number of his successfully completed undertakings affords him some perspective on when and, more crucially, when not to persevere.

"If I was talking to myself I'd say not to get hung up on one idea too much and, if it's not working quite as you want, move on to the next one. I think it is quite easy to think you've come up with some genius idea and then get stuck on it for so long because you can't quite get it to work, when you might find that three ideas down the line is one that works a lot better – if only you could actually get there!

"Also if you are kind of trying to come up with ideas, do a vague sketch of what you think will happen. It doesn't need to be sketched, but as soon as you're doing the animatic, just try and get as much of it done in the first pass. It's quite easy to do half an idea and think *This Could Be Good* and think you'll come back to it, but then by the time you do you've lost your energy for it. If you've got that first spark you have to make use of it while you're interested and excited about it – try and get it finished as soon as possible, in terms of an idea."

Instant Gratification

As part of the Utrecht-based animation studio Frame Order, Dutch animation filmmaker Joost Lieuwma has directed his own short films alongside his freelance animation career since 2011s energetic crowdpleaser *Things You'd Better Not Mix Up* (Figure 6.14), an ostensibly simple premise around the consequences of confusing one item for another that escalates with increasing intensity, surrealism and perfectly timed sight gags. Joost would start as he intended to go on, with subsequent short film projects seeing him go from strength to strength, harnessing an ability to interweave an accessible, friendly animation style with truly bizarre scenarios, such as 2012s *How Dave and Emma Got Pregnant* (that sees as a couple raise a mound of liposuctioned fat as their child in the aftermath of a phantom pregnancy), 2013s *Leaving Home* (in which a young man finds himself inexplicably tethered to his childhood home whenever he attempts to move on) and 2015s frenetic *Panic!* (a story of a woman driven to distraction by increasingly horrific fantasies about what could go wrong at her house when she's not there), co-written and directed with Daan Velsink.

In 2016, Joost began focusing his energies on the series *Cartoon Box* (Figures 6.15–6.19), a project that siphons his gift for gag-driven visual ideas into a collection of standalone micro-shorts. Beginning with its inaugural episode *Crying*

Figure 6.14

Still from *Things You'd Better Not Mix Up* (Dir. Joost Lieuwma) ©2010 Joost Lieuwma.

Child posted in September of that year, the series instantly established a sense of identity for itself as setup/punchline vignettes that manage to (for the most part) evade predictability by subverting whatever expectations you may have for the outcome in the last moment. Characters often meet gruesome fates yet, in the grand tradition of animated comedy going back to its inception, are back again the next episode for more punishment.

It was punishment of a different sort, the self-inflicted kind we animation filmmakers are often drawn to, that put *Cartoon Box*'s wheels in motion.

"Often after making a short film, I experience some form of creative crisis. Sometimes I have worked for years on a film and invested so much time that, when it's finished, the result hardly lives up to the expectations I had at the start of the project. So several times after finishing a short, I would start making fast, gag animations in a couple of days, just to experience the difference compared to having spent years on a project."

These cathartic mini-film exercises wouldn't see the light of day until Joost's Frame Order colleague Lukas Krepel suggested that a series made in the "typical Joost style" might have potential on YouTube. Following the launch of *Cartoon Box* as a series, Joost made a personal commitment to himself to produce a short each week (allowing for the occasional seasonal break) for at least a year. Several years, hundreds of shorts and hundreds of millions of views later, *Cartoon Box* has become a worldwide phenomenon unto itself. Despite its indie roots, the series has required a certain degree of discipline from a production standpoint to stay on track and avoid descending into incomprehensible chaos:

"On making *Cartoon Box* I've set some technical and story rules for myself. It has to challenge me, but at the same time it has to be realizable within three days as well. So some rules make it easy for me and others are more challenging:

1. First of all, I have to find the joke funny myself.
2. Once I have completed the storyboard, I often show this to my co-workers. If none of them thinks it works, I won't make it or I'll keep working on the story until it does.

Figure 6.15

Cartoon Box ©Joost Lieuwma.

3. The animation really has to be 'animated,' I won't let myself get away with things too easily.
4. I put everything online as fast as I can, without being too critical of the work. It's okay when it's still a bit crude.
5. It can't be *too* ugly and it has to fit the style.

"It almost never happens that I can't get an episode finished. There isn't really a pipeline, it just helps that I always create a pretty elaborate animatic, so I know exactly what I have to do when I start animating. I know my own drawing style very well, and also its limits; I will never try to create complicated camera movements, for example."

As the rise of content apps primarily focused on short form content has demonstrated, audiences have an appetite for micro-shorts more than ever before. The speedy turnaround and constant workflow required to maintain audience engagement would be an overwhelming prospect to some. For Joost, it has turned out to be exactly the creative outlet he has always craved.

Figure 6.16

Storyboard image from *Cartoon Box #1: Crying Child* ©Joost Lieuwma.

"Working on a longer short film can take up so much of your time, time in which you're *not* actually creating. In these micro-shorts I *am* working on the actual creation for the greatest part. The challenge is big enough and there is a regular deadline every single week. I would say that the biggest advantage is that you get to spend more time on the actual creation instead of sitting around thinking about what you want to make.

"Starting something on YouTube always takes a lot of time and patience. So I think you should accept that you will have to spend a lot of time making it work. But on the other side you should let go of some things. You can't do everything and there is always more to do."

Joost would go into the world of YouTube relatively blind, save for some fundamental advice other content creator friends of his were able to impart. While there is a lot of uncertainty as regards what will and won't resonate with audiences, not to mention the mechanics of YouTube's algorithm or that of other streaming platforms one might be inclined to cross-post to, the director feels that the platform has grown to be more "creator-friendly" in the years since he began.

"It's hard to see how big the following exactly is, because some new episodes on YouTube get over a million views and others 'just' get about 300k–400k views. I think an important thing to keep in mind as a creator is that sometimes you can't do anything about it when a video doesn't get the views you hoped for. There are always a lot of influences that make a video 'fly' or not, and sometimes it can be a pitfall as a creator to think you can make it work better by spending more and more time interacting with everybody in the hope the new video will do better."

One inconvenience of the algorithm when it comes to creating micro-shorts is the general understanding that users are far more likely to be directed toward longer videos. With Joost's *Cartoon Box* formula and three-day turnaround rarely resulting in episodes longer than a single minute, a key strategy for traffic generation would be to start packaging up longer "compilation" videos, usually exceeding eight minutes, once enough episodes had piled up. With the episode count eventually numbering in the hundreds, each new release would take this compilation approach, leading with the newest entry followed by an assortment of previous episodes. Another way Joost has kept on top of the system is through

Figure 6.17

Making *Cartoon Box* ©Joost Lieuwma.

paying attention to his metrics over time and identifying content consumption patterns when they present themselves.

"A big part of my audience is located in Asia. I always post at the end of the morning European time, because the most traffic is generated between 4–6pm. So the video will have some time to get momentum."

In spite of the success of the series, which often leads to the expansion of a creative team, for the most part *Cartoon Box* and its signature style remains largely a solo affair for Joost: "Most of the stories I write myself but sometimes an intern will pitch a story to me and a couple of times the people from our animation studio Frame Order helped me out with a story idea.

"There is no formula. I just sit on the couch with my *Cartoon Box* sketchbook and a pencil, and stare at the white empty piece of paper hoping that an idea will pop up. Every week again I think that I can't do it anymore. And then all of a sudden, I come up with something – most of the time. It helps that I write everything down, also the bad ideas. Bad ideas can turn into better ones when you read them again later."

One certainty when looking back through the series is that virtually nothing is off the table as far subject matter is concerned. Through the inherent cartooniness of Joost's style and the universe of the show, Joost is able to plumb the depths of gross-out, frequently scatological humor and intensely violent scenarios, but in an appealingly cheeky way that doesn't ruffle many feathers. Given the degree to which the shorts involve bodily fluids, mutilation and death, to say they're suitable for all audiences would be a pretty big reach, although any elements of threat or danger are offset by the playfulness of their presentation to be legitimately disturbing.

"In the beginning it was pretty hard to find this balance. I think Youtube also didn't know where to draw the line, but now most of the time my videos always get a 'green' icon (to allow monetization) by manual review. As long as you avoid sex topics and make the bloody parts cartooney, you will be safe."

Figure 6.18

Storyboard image from *Cartoon Box #2: The Traffic Light* ©Joost Lieuwma.

Figure 6.19

Still from *Cartoon Box #21: Chocolate Ice-Cream* (Dir. Joost Lieuwma) ©2017 Joost Lieuwma.

With the series firmly established and a heaving back catalog of episodes already in the rear-view mirror, *Cartoon Box* would ultimately become Joost's primary career focus. While a perfect fit for his comedic sensibilities and talent for turning economic animation around while keeping it appealing, Joost still treats it as a job that he has managed to effectively incorporate into his lifestyle.

"I learned to manage my time very well. I can easily make one episode a week and repeat this week after week. It still takes a lot of effort but at this moment I don't experience any stress. I work about 35–40 hours a week and the most difficult part is the pressure I'm sometimes under to always come up with new ideas. That is something that doesn't compare with other freelance work I did before."

Something we learn from Ant and Joost's successes is that internet audiences are a very different beast than they were at the dawn of the online animation revolution. As with every major cultural shift, it usually takes one practitioner to make the first move so that others may follow. From Ant's perspective in his preceding years working with Google and YouTube, there is one pioneer in particular he cites as being especially influential.

Simon Tofield, whose formative animation influences were such Saturday morning fare as *Transformers* coupled with the more artistically valuable (one might argue) work of Bill Watterson and Gary Larson, set himself the personal task of getting to grips with Flash by creating a short animated skit inspired by the behaviors of his cat Hugh. Fast-forward to 2012, four years after the short was originally uploaded to YouTube, and Tofield is regarded as the creator of one of the most recognizable characters of modern animation, producing new work through Disney with an audience in the tens of millions. Since then, his popularity has stayed consistent, but how did one short have such a monumental cultural effect to begin with?

There are many qualities of *Simon's Cat*, now a long-running series, that are worth dissecting in determining its public response. Luck and circumstance will always be a factor in anything that goes viral, certainly, but in this instance the sheer volume of enthusiasm and fundamental staying power of the premise stands out as exceptional. This is owed in no small part to its sense of visual comedy and the fact that audiences from all walks of life – even those who don't own cats – can engage with. Certain varieties of humor will always be universal, and as with much of Ant Blades' work, the absence of dialog is another major win as far as international appeal is concerned.

Subscribing more to the storytelling approach outlined in Chapter 3, Simon's process generally begins with writing a "visual script"[6] in the form of a rudimentary storyboard. With the animation itself being especially sophisticated, the economics at play are largely regarding post-production. This is best exemplified by the disparity between most standard episodes of *Simon's Cat* and the crowdfunded,

Figure 6.20

Simon's Cat: Off to the Vet crowdfunding campaign image ©2014 Simon's Cat Ltd.

6. Going Webisodic

full-color and significantly longer outing *Off to the Vet* (Figure 6.20) - again, to be explored further in Chapter 9.

To wrap up on this subject, the somewhat manic glut of arbitrarily rewarded web animation has definitely subsided two decades on, or at the very least, the arbitrary rewards are being designated elsewhere, to online "personalities" and the worlds of commentary, gaming and other such easy-to- produce ephemera. The advantage of this is that animation is no longer a novelty on the internet, but as respected a medium as any other form of filmmaking. So is the era of the animated webseries behind us? As we once knew it, very possibly, but in its place more doors are open for creatives to use the web for collaboration and to keep one another inspired.

Notes

1 http://happyharry.newgrounds.com/.
2 http://egoraptor.newgrounds.com/.
3 https://www.youtube.com/user/CAS.
4 https://www.youtube.com/user/SpindleHorse.
5 https://www.youtube.com/user/Birdboxstudio.
6 http://www.skwigly.co.uk/simon-tofield/.

7

The Animated Documentarian

Figure 7.1

Making animation with *Yellow Sticky Notes* (Dir. Jeff Chiba Stearns). Image courtesy of Jeff Chiba Stearns.

Just as with live-action, some animation filmmakers can find themselves more at ease with the world of non-fiction (Figure 7.1). Of course, dealing with real-life as the subject of a film isn't some hidden cheat to sidestep the labor of coming up with an original work of fiction; it carries with it its own set of disciplines, some even trickier to master. Crafting a structure that an audience acclimated to the pacing of television and cinema can appreciate – be it drama, comedy or

DOI: 10.1201/9781003214717-7

everything in between – requires a great deal of forethought and attention to detail at all stages of production. The story a documentary filmmaker might hope to tell at the outset can turn out to be wildly disparate from the final product. Henry Joost and Ariel Schulman's *Catfish*, for example, begins as a fairly unremarkable study of a child prodigy, one which only becomes compelling when it takes a bizarre turn and winds up an alarming portrait of psychological delusion and deception over social media. Seth Gordon's *The King of Kong: A Fistful of Quarters* starts off as a fluffy look back at retro video gaming, escalating into a surprisingly emotional underdog story. Joe Berlinger and Bruce Sinofsky's famous *Paradise Lost* trilogy is a series of films spanning fifteen years, beginning with a chilling case of a group of allegedly homicidal teenagers which unravels as a jaw-dropping dissection of how manipulatable and presumptuous society (including, by the third film, us as the audience itself) can be, with little provocation.

While all of the above are examples of live-action documentaries, the veracity of all questionable in varying measure (there is, naturally, some artistic license taken in the construct of a non-fiction "story"), the same major principles should apply to any filmmaker who appreciates the potential a documentary film can hold, regardless of the medium they choose to make it in.

So, given that it can hardly be considered a labor-saving device, what *are* the main advantages of choosing animation over live-action? Largely it depends on the subject matter, tone and artistic direction best suited to the director. Animation, whether used exclusively or in conjunction with live-action, can be an ideal way in which a director might experiment with visual concepts in a freer, less-linear fashion.

A film dependent on talking heads can be made visually rich or even have its meaning subverted, as with *Wallace & Gromit* creator Nick Park's groundbreaking and often-imitated 1989 Aardman film *Creature Comforts*, in which the accounts of British citizens alongside recent immigrants acclimating to life in the UK are ingeniously recontextualized as those of animals evaluating their quality of life in a zoo. *Creature Comforts* carried on the tradition of Aardman's prior short films that were largely based on recordings of the general public set to animation. While earlier shorts such as *Down and Out* (1977), *Confessions of a Foyer Girl* (1978) and *Late Edition* (1983) relied on eavesdropping, feasibility issues forced Nick to deviate from his original plan of doing likewise.

"I went around Bristol zoo with a hidden microphone," Nick describes, speaking to Skwigly in 2014, "the idea being to try and record what people said about the animals but reverse it, so in the animation the animals were saying these things about people – 'Look at that strange looking thing, what's he doing?' But the recording situation was never that good or easy and the zoo didn't really want me to record there either! Afterwards I thought *Why not just go up to people?* We had done some vox pops as a test – approaching people outside the zoo and asking for their thoughts about zoos and animals in cages. It was good but people all said the same thing, that it was nice to see the animals, but a pity they were locked up.

"So myself and an interviewer went to people in their houses, small flats, old people's homes and foreign students to get a view on what it's like living in the UK, things that had parallels to animals being dissatisfied with their environment. And I happened to find this student from Brazil, who just loved ranting about how he hated living in Britain compared to the hot, Brazilian weather. He stole the show.

"What I had liked about what Aardman had done before was that it was different to how you thought about animation. It wasn't whiz-bang, exciting, fast-quipping, big cartooney jokes but it was like minimal and realistic."

The Brazilian student's vocal contribution to the film was, as an example of the film's contextual subversion, animated to a mountain lion, who in the film comes across as yearning for the plains of his home country. Granted, this type of subversion takes the film a step away from straight-ahead documentary but it serves as a prime indicator of how banality can be repurposed to become engaging and visually rich. The film was produced as one of five films for Aardman's *Lip Synch* series commissioned in 1989, two others being Aardman co-founder Peter Lord's *Going Equipped* and *War Story*. While the former is rich in atmosphere, the focus of the animation is largely a straightforward interpretation of the interviewee, detailing the lamentations of a former convict through the minutiae of plasticine character animation. *War Story*, by contrast, incorporates vibrant, witty and occasionally slapstick interpretations of the stories told, more fully making use of the freedoms of animation without changing its overall context.

While animation and non-fiction had undoubtedly crossed paths before, the cultural impact of this early, comparatively independent work (from a studio who has since grown to become an industry powerhouse) is undeniable, as Peter Lord himself is aware. "I couldn't take credit, but I do feel a certain satisfaction that we kind of started a genre. Nowadays if you go and see any student degree show there will be three or four films based on these self-revealing soundtracks. It's quite a big deal now, when no-one had thought of it before."[1]

To get a greater sense of how non-fiction can serve as a legitimate basis for powerful, witty and emotionally engaging animated films, let's take a look at a sampling of some recent exceptional filmmakers who have taken it on.

Anecdotal Value

A traditional hand-drawn animator based in Minnesota, Tom Schroeder's various films have been screened at major festivals including Sundance, Annecy, Edinburgh and Ottawa. Having been active since 1990, it was the 2000 documentary tale *Bike Ride*, his fourth self-directed film, which served as his first significant step into the waters of animated non-fiction. The film is a seven-minute tragicomic recollection of James, a man who travels fifty miles by bike to see his girlfriend, only to have to return home after getting dumped immediately, with an improvised drum track from musician Dave King (of The Bad Plus and Happy Apple) "reacting" to the events of the narration. It was from this soundtrack that Tom took an adventurous, creative cue in his approach to the animation.

"When you're animating off of an audio track, the first step is to chart out the sound frame by frame on an exposure sheet. When I'm drawing I'll have the structure of both the story and the drum performance to use as a guide. My original idea with *Bike Ride* was to have Dave King record his drums to the story, to animate to both tracks and then pull out the voice in the final audio mix, so that you just had the visuals and the drums with the story hopefully implied. When I tried that it was clear the film didn't work as well. The quality of (narrator) James Peterson's personality and the conversational tone of the film were lost.

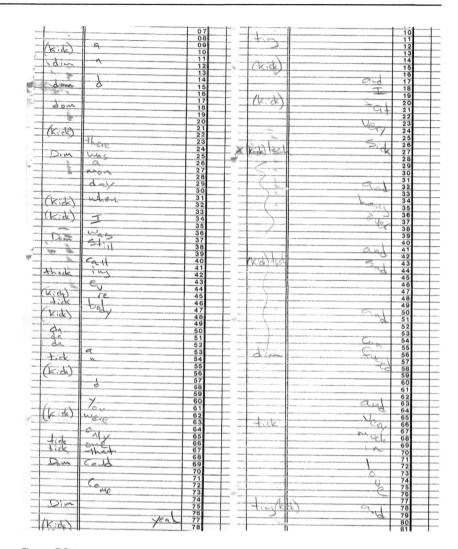

Figure 7.2

Bike Race dope sheet. Image courtesy of Tom Schroeder.

I think a lot of the appeal of the film is that people can identify with the situation very readily and find something appealing in James' self-deprecation.

"In general, I'm following the vocal tracks first as a guide for the content and the acting of the characters and then I'm following the drums for accents and beats in the rhythm of the movement. Having both of these structures as a kind of architecture that exists before the animation gives me the freedom to improvise and work loosely without much of a plan.

"In the improvisational spirit of the audio track I draw straight-ahead without a storyboard or plan. I don't think I revised anything that I drew, the simple graphic white on black ink drawing style helped with that." The first of Tom's film to prove a hit on the festival circuit, *Bike Ride*'s success led to a series of commercials with Klasky Csupo's commercial division Ka-Chew, making use of the film's unique style. In 2010, Tom produced *Bike Race* (Figures 7.2 and 7.3), not a follow-up film so much as a companion piece, dealing with a completely different

7. The Animated Documentarian

story albeit retaining some of the crucial themes of love, relationships and misunderstanding. Though many of the qualities of *Bike Ride*'s aesthetic remain, there is a discernible style shift partly brought about through bringing on board additional techniques from his commissioned work.

"When I was working on the commercials in the *Bike Ride* style I was compositing photographic color cereal boxes into the line animation and I liked the way that it looked against the black field. So when I made *Bike Race*, I hired a former student of mine from the Minneapolis College of Art and Design, Lindsay Testolin, to do the inventive photo collage sections that you see in the film. I always liked the style that Lindsay developed in After Effects and gave her a lot of freedom as regards her contributions to the film. She provided another layer of improvisation in the conversation, so to speak.

"When I started designing the characters for *Bike Race*, I intended to use the same thick ink line style as I used in *Bike Ride*. But I found that the complexity of the story and the subtlety of the acting demanded from the characters required more detail than the thick lines would allow. So I used a thinner pencil line; the film really is an inverted, cleaned-up pencil test in the traditional sense of how character animation is created. I liked the feeling when I inverted it that it looked perhaps drawn on a blackboard with chalk. Both *Bike* films were drawn and rendered on paper, scanned into the computer and composited in After Effects. I like to think of the films as representing the manner in which thought flows, because a long period of my thinking gets compressed into a short duration in the finished film. I would aspire to make a film that is 'thought' rather than 'told.'

"There was no initial plan to make *Bike Race*. But people really responded to the combination of elements in *Bike Ride*; the sound, the picture and the story worked very well in support of a single idea. So I decided that perhaps there should be a trilogy of films exploring this approach and thematic content, one every 10 years, thus *Bike Race* in 2010. I have just recorded the vocal tracks for *Bike Trip*, which I plan to finish around 2020; it's in a queue of other films that I have planned. When the third film is finished I imagine them playing together as one half hour program."

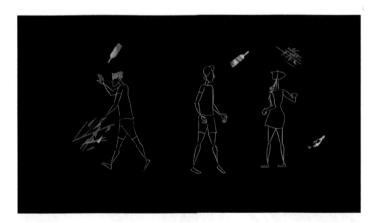

Figure 7.3

Still from *Bike Race* (Dir. Tom Schroeder) ©2010 Tom Schroeder.

Since *Bike Race* Tom has gone on to produce another, entirely separate documentary with 2012s *Marcel: King of Tervuren* (Figures 7.4 and 7.5), another festival hit and crowdpleaser. This film serves as a prime example of how animation can infuse anecdotal storytelling with wit, passion and visual gravitas, chronicling the dramatic life of a Belgian rooster belonging to Ann Berckmoes, a friend of his wife and the film's narrator.

"Each time we visited Ann in Tervuren on the outskirts of Brussels, we would drink Belgian beer and she would give the latest update on Marcel her rooster, while chain smoking, drinking and punctuating each section of the story with a throaty 'cuculurucoo' – Ann is the archetypal *bon vivant* and reminds me of Jeanne Moreau in the 1960s. During May of 2011 Ann visited my wife and I in St. Paul, Minnesota and I took the opportunity to record her telling Marcel's story. She recorded the story in English, Dutch and French. I speak Dutch and my wife Hilde helped with the French, so between us we edited three versions of the story in the different languages."

The film, described by Tom as "Greek tragedy enacted by Belgian roosters" also deals with a love triangle, this time of the bestial, *crime passionel* variety. The story tells of Marcel who, having lived through a rooster cull during a bird flu pandemic, finds himself ostracized from the farm where he lives after being half-blinded and cuckolded, essentially, by his own offspring. The bloody battle that ensues when Marcel seeks to reassert himself as the "King" of Tervuren is evocative of numerous Grecian myths, carrying with it a curious sense of humanity.

"I remembered a specific line from Albert Camus's essay on Sisyphus: *There is no fate that cannot be surmounted by scorn.* I saw in Marcel an attractive, wilful defiance, but also the comic possibilities of contrasting the grandiosity of 'King of Tervurven' with the ordinariness of the backyard setting."

Tom's approach with the film made use of developing technology in a manner which worked to its aesthetic advantage, drawing the animation directly on computer using a Cintiq.

"Somewhat ironically, the loose, painterly style of the film developed from working digitally rather than drawing on paper. The animation was about half rotoscoping from live action footage I shot and half traditional character

Figure 7.4

Still from *Marcel, King of Tervuren* (Dir. Tom Schroeder) ©2012 Tom Schroeder.

7. The Animated Documentarian

Figure 7.5

Still from *Marcel, King of Tervuren* (Dir. Tom Schroeder) ©2012 Tom Schroeder.

animation. I gravitated to the rotoscoping initially because I was still a little uncomfortable drawing with the tablet.

"As for the abstract transitional sections, these came about as a formal expression of the main theme of the film. As Marcel fights to stay alive, his representation in the film struggles to fight against the forms breaking into an abstraction of line and color. Form and abstraction, life and death, matter and energy. I've always felt that the most successful animated films demonstrate an awareness of the relationship between the technical aspects of the production and the narrative content. My sense of this really comes from modernist literature rather than graphic design, from having read James Joyce at a formative age.

"Between *Bike Ride* and *Bike Race* I was gaining experience with the software as a creative tool in making the films and in the storytelling. When you arrive at *Bike Race* and *Marcel*, I'm thinking less in terms of traditional film language and more in terms of continuous flow and transition. The technology has obviously evolved very quickly and you can see it in the period between *Bide Ride* and *Marcel*. In *Bike Ride* I'm still drawing on paper, but it's the first film I made that I didn't shoot with a film camera. By *Marcel* the last vestige of a physical process has disappeared – no graphite, no paper. It's a bit of a challenge to continually make these transitions demanded by the technology, but the new tools always present opportunities in reinventing how you tell a story. From *Marcel* onward I've drawn directly in Photoshop with a Cintiq. At first I found the feeling of working this way alienating, but now I like it a lot. I can still get the illusion of naturalistic media but with the advantages, versatility and speed of working digitally."

Introspection

Of Tom's work it's *Marcel, King of Tervuren* that most represents a perfect marriage of animation and storytelling, though the strengths of all his work are in the audience's relatability to the stories being told themselves. Themes of love, loss, victory, humiliation, redemption and revenge are all staples of highly effective narratives, whether fictional or otherwise. How effective, then, can venturing into comparatively unknown territories be?

Harvard Animation Professor Ruth Lingford's path into animation is a particularly atypical one, stepping away from a career as an occupational therapist to pursue the arts, eventually studying at the Royal College of Art. Having gone on to work with the NFTS, Animate! Projects and Shynola among others, her Harvard role as Professor of the Practice of Animation came about following a stint as visiting instructor in 2005. Her filmography frequently explores strong, pervasive and sometimes sexual themes, notably the shorts *What She Wants* (1994), *Death and The Mother* (1997) and *Pleasures of War* (1998), and upon receipt of a Harvard Film Study Center Fellowship, she set about applying these to an independent documentary project.

"It's important to me that when I tell people the germ of the idea, they react to it as something they would like to see. Provoking curiosity in an audience is something I really do value, so giving them something that they would be interested in is important."

The result was 2011s *Little Deaths* (Figure 7.6), which proved a strong talking point of the major festivals it screened at. As with many affecting documentaries, the film tackles a subject rarely discussed in casual conversation, in this case the nature of orgasm as articulated by an expansive cross-section of the public.

"I'd been working for some time on a documentary called *Secrecy*, directed by two of my colleagues at Harvard, which was a film about government secrecy. The animation's role was to kind of be the unconscious of the film and to try and look at what secrecy means to humans. A lot of that was images of Adam and Eve, the tree of knowledge and sex. I ended up doing a lot of animation that wasn't used in the end, some of which I liked. I was a bit embarrassed having been at Harvard a few years and not having made a film of my own, so I was thinking of ways to use this leftover footage to make a quick, two-minute film. I hit on the idea of taping interviews of people and asking them to describe orgasm, thinking *obviously you can't describe orgasm, so people will run out of words.*"[2]

When dealing with a documentary that depends on a handful of outside contributors, there are certain questions of handling and etiquette. One might assume that anything pertaining to human sexuality might be automatically

Figure 7.6

Still from Little Deaths (Dir. Ruth Lingford) ©2010 Ruth Lingford.

7. The Animated Documentarian

taboo and off-limits; in the case of *Little Deaths*, however, this turned out to not be the case:

"My plan was to edit together the moments where people ran out of words accompanied by vague sexual images, and that would be the film – but when I started doing the interviews, I found that nobody ran out of words at all. I live in Cambridge, Massachusetts, which is the home of Harvard, MIT and a lot of very clever and articulate people, so that may be why – but I found people were really wanting to talk about it. People would say 'I've never put this into words before,' then make a big attempt to do so, getting really interested in what their own experience was, and of course I got quite interested in the differences and the similarities between people. So then it became a quite different project and the animation had to start from scratch."

This serves as an important reminder to documentarians that you should not be dissuaded before you have even tried. Our internal self-doubts – or perhaps even the voiced doubts of our peers and immediate social circle – may not necessarily line up with the realities of the matter. Indeed, in this case the documentary highlights how society's mores quell discussion of a subject about which many people have a lot to say.

Self Reflection

While other people's stories may be compelling and offer you as a filmmaker a variety of new perspectives to work with, this should not rule out the option of turning to one's own firsthand experiences for inspiration. As we saw in an earlier chapter, Melissa Johnson's Salon.com memoir *The tallest woman in the room tells all* proved tremendously engaging and popular when adapted to the animated film *Love in the Time of March Madness* (Figure 7.7). Though the visual execution predominantly fell to co-director Robertino Zambrano, which of course allowed for a fresh twist on the film's aesthetic, Melissa's own involvement with the film version of her story was also integral to its success. Though not previously versed

Figure 7.7

Still from *Love in the Time of March Madness* (Dir. Melissa Johnson/Robertino Zambrano) ©2014 High Hip Productions/KAPWA Studioworks.

in animation production, her established talent as a live-action documentary filmmaker had a considerable part to play when turning the focus on herself.

"I think when you've made films about other people, when you tell a story about yourself, you must operate on two levels. One: go deep into yourself and your experience. Two: You have to take a step back and say objectively as a storyteller, *If I was making this about someone else, what does the story need? Let me get some distance here and figure out from a story arc and character development from the perspective of someone who does not know me at all* (i.e. the majority of people seeing this) – *does this make sense? Is it compelling? What else does the subject – in other words*, me – *need to reveal here?* So, absolutely, my background in documentary storytelling was a huge asset. It's just helpful at times to forget that the story is about me, so as to make it a better film."

As *Love in the Time of March Madness* proves, putting forward our own non-fictional stories and observations as fodder for animation can yield tremendously appealing results, especially when combined with visual invention and self-effacement. Another such example is Latvian animator Signe Baumane's *Teat Beat of Sex* (Figures 7.8 and 7.9), a series of semi-fictionalized personal recollections that stem from the artist's firsthand experience and array of viewpoints on the subject. As with Ruth Lingford's *Little Deaths* (to which Signe also contributed as an interview subject), the films are uncompromising yet refreshingly candid, oftentimes dealing with somewhat taboo areas that can serve as discussion points.

The series has perhaps the broadest appeal amongst Signe's other short film work, though they very easily could not have come to be at all, as the director recalls:

Figure 7.8

Teat Beat of Sex poster ©2009 Signe Baumane/Pierre Poire.

7. The Animated Documentarian

"*Teat Beat of Sex* came to life by accident. A few years ago there were these websites that were looking for content, and one of the sites contacted me and said 'We really love your work, would you come over and pitch us your ideas?'

"So I gathered all my ideas that I had and brought everything to the meeting. There was this big table in the middle of the room, with three men in suits and jackets sitting around it. I wanted to make small talk, but when I'm nervous I always have to talk about sex, for some reason."

With a gift for ribald anecdotal storytelling, Signe's small talk ultimately became the pitch itself – a series of films in which she would present her personal perspectives on sex through a series of recorded monologs set to animation.

"I was so excited, because this project was a combination of three of my favourite things – animation, ranting and sex. So when I started to work on the film, I was so excited until I thought *Wait, it's a really original story, with original character designs, I wonder how much they're gonna pay me?* So I called them up and asked how much. They were offering $1000 for each episode along with all the rights."

Her enthusiasm soured by that caveat, she proceeded with *Teat Beat of Sex* on her own should a better offer come along. During the production of the second of these micro-shorts she was approached by Pierre Poire Productions, an Italian production team looking for a new project dealing with love, sex and bridging misunderstandings between genders. Fitting in perfectly with the spirit of *Teat Beat of Sex*, the partnership would eventually yield a full series of fifteen uncompromising and "explicitly educational" shorts. Each film of the series makes consistent use of bold jump-cuts stringing together minimally animated visuals, some of which so steeped in visual metaphor that they require repeat viewings to be fully appreciated.

At face value, these films come across initially as more shallow than in fact they are. To a casual viewer, or one perhaps not interested in the complexity of Signe's explorations of psychosexuality, the films may appear to be little more than a succession of dirty jokes and visual innuendos. Once acclimated to the strange appeal of her truly unique style and energy, however, the series proves to be something deeper altogether.

The narration is provided by Signe herself (as is also the case with her feature film *Rocks in My Pockets*, explored in Chapter 8). At times, these monologs are scripted, quasi-autobiographical anecdotes that tie several films together consecutively, though more often than not each episode is a standalone recollection, musing or venting session. The candor of each film's monolog enables a tremendous range of visual expression when translated to animation, and few efforts are made to temper Signe's enthusiasm, passion, anger or, at times, unabashed naivety. Though all of these make for compelling visuals, it is perhaps the latter that leads to the most effective, with glimpses of endearingly literal visual analogies peppering the narrative as a consequence. The subject matter veers from the amusingly frivolous (*Hair, Juice*) to the poignant and introspective (*Envy, Respect*), with Signe's onscreen counterpart renamed Cynthia in acknowledgment of the blurred lines between fiction and non-fiction.

"It is a composite of both, because if I really launched into the 'true' story then that story would be an hour long, so since the premise of each final episode is one minute, you can imagine how many layers are stripped off. But mainly I chose to call the main character Cynthia because the depiction of the mother is not really accurate. In *Teat Beat of Sex* she comes off as very odd, dressed in strange garbs

Figure 7.9

Still from *Teat Beat of Sex – "Juice"* (Dir. Signe Baumane) ©2009 Signe Baumane/
Pierre Poire.

and so on. But for me the mother in the films represents the conservative voice, the voice of society that you sometimes hear in your head, of what you 'shouldn't be doing' because of what society might think. So the mother is really not my real mother, it's that conservative part of society that tries to get you to fit to its standards. And so that's why I choose to be in character as 'Cynthia.'"

Sticking Points

Independent Canadian animator and documentarian Jeff Chiba Stearns trained in animation at the Emily Carr University of Art and Design in Vancouver, graduating in 2001 and immediately embarking on a career in animation filmmaking and teaching. Governed by a fastidious need to plan and make lists, he found himself at the mercy of a barrage of yellow sticky notes covering every available surface of his office by the mid-2000s (Figure 7.10).

"I need my life organized but I still live in a sense of chaos, so my life is organized by sticky notes and to-do lists that are scattered haphazardly around my office. I think I was going through a bit of a crisis because I had just finished a film and was broke. I needed to find work, there wasn't a lot of animation work out there so I became a teacher. All of this was being written down on sticky notes, to the point where I was feeling really overwhelmed with the fact that these to-do lists were running my life, and as fast as I was writing stuff down I couldn't accomplish all the stuff on these lists in time.

"I realized that when I self-reflected on the last nine years of my life to the point where I decided I wanted to pursue animation, some major world events had an impact on those decisions. I had just graduated and was looking for work when 9/11 happened. That's when the entire animation industry in Vancouver kind of crumbled again – Disney left town, a lot of the studios were closing, senior animators couldn't find work – and so for a recent graduate it was the worst time to be in the job market. So I started to look back on that, starting to sense this connection and I figured I'd take revenge on these sticky notes, make a film on self-reflection based on these to-do lists."

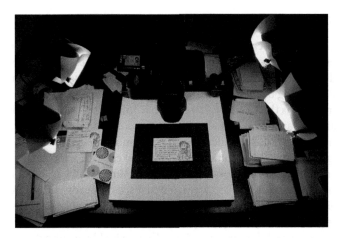

Figure 7.10

Behind the scenes of *Canadian Anijam*, Jeff Chiba Stearns' follow-up (see Chapter 14) to *Yellow Sticky Notes*. Image courtesy of Jeff Chiba Stearns.

Without a deadline, funding or a budget of any description, Jeff embraced the organic nature of the process. The film, titled *Yellow Sticky Notes*, was progressed in fits and starts, the sporadic nature of his process entirely down to whether or not he felt the impulse to do so on any given day. Coining the term "animation meditation," the making of the film became a therapeutic, self-reflective exercise where ideas could flow freely from his subconscious. This was largely enabled by his production approach, which called for little more than the sticky notes themselves.

"It was all straight-ahead animation, without even a backlight. I don't in-between, in fact I don't know if I have the patience for it. I like the idea that I can draw from one drawing to the next, and the next, and the next; I think if you can do that right you can capture some really nice animated motion. I was teaching animation at the same time so it was a good way for me to get back into just drawing, pen-on-paper, and with sticky notes themselves being very portable, I could take them wherever I needed to, including hotel rooms and aeroplanes.

"It took me about nine months to do all the drawing. When I finished the film all I had were these sticky notes stacked about the place, I just arranged them from the earliest date to the latest date, put them in little sections, spread them across the room and said 'I guess I'm done!' Then I just sat myself in a dark room with a camera stand and shot it all. The editing took a few days because it was already kind of in the right sequence, I just pulled drawings out here and there to make it succinct."

After testing a rough cut of the film to an audience of students at a Taiwanese animation festival, the positive reception inspired Jeff to move past his doubts about the film and package it properly for festivals.

"I kept saying it was either going to be the greatest thing I ever made or the worst, there was no middle ground, it would either tank or take-off. It ended up winning for Best Animation at an Asian festival in Toronto, and the guy who ran What Media saw it and called me personally to say it was brilliant! That's when I started to catch on, then when it hit Tribeca it just took off, YouTube saw it and from there it screened everywhere, won People's Choice at Clermont-Ferrand, racked up all these awards, so luckily it became that film that resonated with people."

The Animation Advantage

Certainly, non-fiction can be a rich and invaluable resource for exciting short-film content. Another crucial factor to address is the necessity of animation as a medium. In the preceding case studies, all of the films discussed were subjectively improved by having been animated as opposed to taking a live-action approach, but why precisely is this? What is the edge that animation itself has in this realm?

Jeff Chiba Stearns makes a strong case for animation's practical ability to, more than anything, make a documentary film more entertaining. "In the world of creating a documentary, sometimes if it's spoken with a lot of talking heads, where it's not so much *cinéma-vérité* but more a survey film, animation makes a kind of sense because it gets us away from just seeing heads talking. Animation has the ability to bring those stories to life in a way that's appealing for the audience, an appeal that helps keep people's attention spans, helps keep them within the film, helps expand their imaginations. That's why I love animation and documentary, because it goes hand in hand. Sometimes you can't always find the right b-roll, you can't find something that's going to bring those stories to life, you can't recreate. I'm not a big fan of documentaries that do re-enactments and I think the great thing about animation is that we can be a little bit more descriptive of these stories, but in a way that's more imaginative rather than specific interpretation."

Ruth Lingford's attitude is similar, while also acknowledging the significantly increased range of expression animated imagery can bring to the mix, particularly its ability to visualize the internal: "The thing about animation and documentary is that animation can document the subjective, or can try to. When I was making *Little Deaths*, people would say *Oh, that's been done before*. There have been projects where people's faces are filmed as they have orgasms, which are kind of interesting but don't really tell you too much about what's going on inside. In the way that people were grasping for ways of expressing their feelings in words, I was grasping for images. There are moments where the film gets close but it's always a foreign land, a struggle to communicate this essence of your experience. It seemed to me that animation could get nearer than live-action, just because in this circumstance the superficial isn't very interesting to me. Also there is something to be said for the poetic mutability of animation, a poetic metamorphosis of sorts that seemed to me to get close to one's experience of one's own body during sex; that that is so subjective and so mutable, it seemed to me that animation was the right means to try and approach expressing that feeling.

"It's a side to animation that encapsulates that struggle as well, because people know when they watch animation that the images are hard-won. There's often a poignancy to animation when you feel the animator's time and struggle in their film."

Bearing these qualities in mind, animation can also have a role within live-action documentary, especially if dealing with a longer-form project. While feature-length animation in and of itself will be explored further in Chapter 8, the use of animation as an embellishment of an otherwise live-action film is exemplified in another of Jeff's works, the multi-award winning 2010 documentary feature *One Big Hapa Family* (Figures 7.11 and 7.12).

"I never looked at *Yellow Sticky Notes* or my previous film *What Are You Anyways?* (an autobiographical look at Stearns's mixed-raced heritage, produced in 2005) as though they could be considered documentaries, but when I was at Tribeca and they actually put *Yellow Sticky Notes* in the Documentary category,

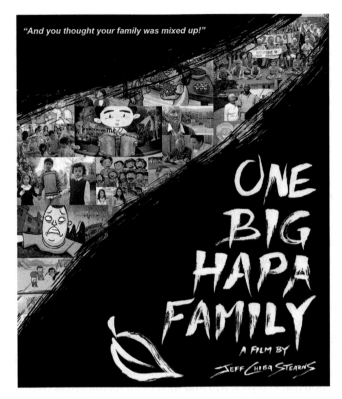

"And you thought your family was mixed up!"

ONE BIG HAPA FAMILY

A FILM BY JEFF CHIBA STEARNS

Figure 7.11

One Big Hapa Family (Dir. Jeff Chiba Stearns) poster ©2010 Jeff Chiba Stearns.

that's when it made sense. When I started thinking of it as a documentation process through animation, it seemed logical to make a documentary of greater length. Even though the majority of the film is live-action, there's a lot of animated components to the film. That's when I started looking at the collaborative animation process, because as I was the one editing the film it meant that I didn't have a ton of time to be animating on it myself."

Having been on the festival circuit since 2000, many years of networking with likeminded independents served to provide Jeff with a pool of talent to reach out to for assistance. Bringing on board six established animators – Jonathan Ng, Louise Johnson, Todd Ramsay, Ben Meinhardt Kunal Sen and Sean Sherwin – who were willing to give their time to the project, Jeff assigned each a segment of the film to animate based on his familiarity with their respective bodies of work.

"As a lot of the interviews are historical or are telling a certain story, I had an animator at the back of my head for each; for example Louise Johnson is really good at doing paint on glass, so for a historical story of Japanese internment one fellow was talking about, I could see it coming alive with that technique. I let everybody animate in their own style, which I think allowed me a chance to work in my own style too, so I could work with chalkboards and different hand-drawn or stop-motion elements. It became what I call a 'candy shop of animation,' very eclectic in its animation approach.

"I didn't give storyboards to the animators, I basically just gave them the chunk of the dialogue and asked them to animate it, so for them they were able to do all the preproduction, design, animate in their own style, do all the drawing themselves and do the post; essentially, they were in charge because I trusted them in their style and ability. Some animators would keep in touch with roughs, they'd send storyboards and we'd go back and forth but for the most part I could trust that they would do what they do best. The long and short of it is that animation both complements and enhances the appeal we need to help the audience get into the mindset of the interviewees. The interviewees are going back into their brain and pulling these stories out and essentially we're bringing these stories to life.

"The other thing that's great is all the animators can work together at the same time, independently of each other, which is a good way to get a lot of animation done quick as opposed to having one animator who's working on twenty minutes of animation that would take them probably six months, if not a year or longer, whereas we can get twenty minutes of animation done in two or three months by having different animators working on it, understanding and being content with the fact that the animation's going to look different. In a film like *One Big Hapa Family*, without the animation it could be a boring film because it's just a bunch of talking heads – at least bringing a visual sense to the film by giving it that kick of animation worked out really nice. If someone's going to sit through an hour and a half of this documentary we better make sure they're entertained as well as being educated, inspired and taken into the film."

Audience consideration is a major factor when it comes to any type of film production, be it animation, documentary or otherwise. Pure self-indulgence, or the assumption that everyone will find what interests you just as riveting, is never an advisable approach. The artistry of non-fiction comes from how it is structured, packaged and presented to the audience, and the success of *One Big Hapa Family* undoubtedly benefited from the addition of these visual representations in a way that an audience sees beyond what is simply being said, to the spirit and relevance of it. While you don't want an audience to feel condescended to, there's something to be said for holding their hand through more challenging territory.

Figure 7.12

Still from *One Big Hapa Family* (Dir. Jeff Chiba Stearns) ©2010 Jeff Chiba Stearns.

7. The Animated Documentarian

As Tom Schroeder sees it, audiences are generally not accustomed to the notion that animation and documentary can co-exist until they see it in front of them:

"Some people are excited by this apparently contradictory idea of a 'poetical truth,' as opposed to the 'truth of accountants,' as Werner Herzog likes to characterize it. Others seem to like the fact that something as simple and immediately accessible as a rooster in the backyard can be material for larger allegorical themes; that the viewer can then project their own content into the situation. With *Marcel* people tend to find appeal in the lived-in rough quality of Ann's voice, as well, her mingled amusement and affection."

While the endearing quality of the narration serves as a firm audience foothold in Tom's case, with Jeff's *Yellow Sticky Notes* it came more in the form of audience-artist solidarity: "I started to realize, when it hit online and I was reading through all the comments, that it was starting to inspire people in really cool ways. I'd get comments from old ladies who hadn't picked up a paintbrush in thirty years who were inspired to paint again after watching the film! I guess the biggest compliment I ever got was that there's an honesty to the film – that we're all busy people and when people see other people's lives as being busy as well they automatically relate to it. It's very voyeuristic too; I think people enjoy, especially in this day and age, glimpsing someone's life and getting to read their to-do lists, you're seeing how they visually reflected on that day through the animation process. Which is sort of what the 9/11 or Tsunami or Columbine sequences were about: Taking in the world around us. I think that's why people gravitated toward the film as much as they did."

Notes

1 Remembering "Lip Synch" with Aardman's Nick Park & Peter Lord http://www.skwigly.co.uk/nick-park-peter-lord/.
2 Skwigly – The Films of Ruth Lingford: http://www.skwigly.co.uk/ruth-lingford/.

8

Going Long

Figure 8.1

Still from *Cheatin'* (Dir. Bill Plympton) ©2014 Plymptoons.

For anyone who has already dabbled in the often laborious, anxiety-inducing process of creating their own independent short, the concept of tackling a feature-length project in the same way probably seems like madness. Surely it's too impossible to even contemplate? If it takes you years to make something that lasts five minutes, anything above forty (this being the official point, categorically, where a short film becomes a feature) will leave you forever friendless and riddled with every kind of thrombosis your veins can throw at you[1]?

DOI: 10.1201/9781003214717-8

Well, in some respects, sure. It's farcical to entertain the idea that going about creating an independent feature won't carry with it some significant sacrifices to time, social life and (worst case scenario) emotional and physical health. I hope I'm not overselling the prospect, here.

All that being said, while it is certainly a taxing and full-on commitment, today's resources have made it considerably more feasible and less intimidating than one might initially think. But first of all, there are some realities worth chewing on.

The cold, hard and most obvious consideration to take on board would be that your indie feature will never look like a major studio production (though it has the advantage of being more likely to retain the signature style of the artist, see Figure 8.1). It should go without saying that the high-performing merchandise machines put out there by the likes of Disney, Pixar and Dreamworks are not going to remotely resemble what you come up with on your lonesome. That needn't be a bad thing, as fortunately we've learned from several major films that, when it comes to features, strength of story and idea can conquer all. Adam Elliot's *Mary & Max*, true to the established style of his earlier independent work, is stop-motion of the purposefully non-slick variety, yet I defy anyone to claim it is neither moving nor hilarious. Ari Folman's *Waltz with Bashir*, rendered in a distinctly non-mainstream animation style by Yoni Goodman, is an undeniably

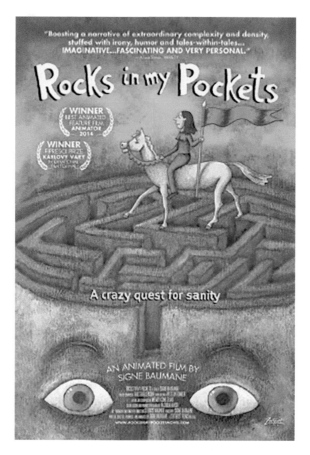

Figure 8.2

Rocks in My Pockets poster Courtesy of Signe Baumane/Zeitgeist Films.

gripping and haunting account of the Lebanon War that bowled over critics and audiences alike.

The same applies to those operating outside of a studio system altogether, where keystone crews and even solitary individuals have proved the seemingly impossible can be achieved with enough passion, dedication and clear thinking. One such filmmaker is Signe Baumane who, after a respectable career as a director of shorts, made the transition to an indie feature. Over the course of four years, she successfully wrote, directed and animated her first full-length film *Rocks in My Pockets* (Figure 8.2), largely from her chilly Manhattan loft.

Following on from the success of her *Teat Beat of Sex* series brought up in the previous chapter, for her first feature Signe instead turned her attention toward an altogether more heavy-going subject: Hereditary mental illness including, but not limited to, observations of her own bloodline's propensity toward depression, anxiety and, on occasion, suicide. Created ultimately as an exercise in learning to better understand and live with her own suicidal thoughts, through her wit and intuition for visual interpretation, the end result is funny, thoughtful and has been met with critical acclaim.

A main motivating factor for Signe to take on such a large-scale endeavor can be attributed to many years spent as a protégé of Bill Plympton once she moved from Latvia to New York. Bill's much-documented history as an artist and filmmaker stands out as being one of the most prolific, with over forty short films and eight features produced independently over the course of his thirty-odd year career. Once his work as a newspaper cartoonist and illustrator evolved into a fondness for short-form animation, the rate of his initial output was the first sign that his own independent feature was not out of the realm of possibility.

"I started making animated short films in 1985. I did a film called *Boom Town*, then I did a film called *Your Face* (1987) which was a huge hit, it got an Oscar nomination and made a lot of money, so I gave up illustration and started to make animated shorts. I did a whole bunch of them: *How to Kiss* (1989), *One of Those Days* (1988), *25 Ways to Quit Smoking* (1989) and *Plymptoons* (1990). I put them all together on a videocassette – they didn't have DVDs back then – with some of my earlier shorts that I did in college and I realized that I had an hour's worth of animation!

"It occurred to me that I'd almost made a feature film in the last three or four years without even trying. Of course, it had always been my dream to work at Disney on some big feature film, but then the thought occurred to me – *I can make my* own *film, who needs Disney?* The films were making money, plus I was doing a few commercials, so I had the finances to spend on a feature film. I did a storyboard with a friend of mine, Maureen McElheron, we did the script together, she did the music and I just started drawing. It took about a year and a half to make the film."

This hard work resulted in *The Tune*, a musical comedy released in 1992. Steeped in hallucinatory visual motifs and incorporating elements from short films produced concurrently, it served as a crucial first long-form outing, one that wears its *naïveté* on its sleeve.

"I was really sort of ignorant about the history of independent filmmaking. I had of course heard of Lotte Reiniger's *The Adventures of Prince Achmed* (a German masterwork released in 1926, animated in silhouette with many qualifiers to be considered the first known independent animated feature) but I didn't know that it was such a breakthrough; that it was so unique for one person to animate an entire feature film. I just thought it'd be kind of fun to do, an adventure and a challenge to see if I could. Then when I finished we entered the film into Sundance and it was a big hit there. We got huge audiences and lots of applause – and the film got distribution. It was just such high, such a *thrill* to actually make a feature film that I decided to do it again!

"So since then I've made seven more animated feature films. What's really interesting now is that anybody can make an animated feature film, it's not nearly so farfetched as when I did it. Back then it was kind of stupid, it was absurd; now it's as though *all* my friends are making animated feature films. I applaud that! I think it's great. Plus it's so democratic now, you don't have to go to Hollywood and get a fifty million dollar budget to make your film, you can do it at home on your computer. I think that's really exciting.

"A lot of people look to me and the film *The Tune* as a sort of breakthrough, something that shows it is possible for one person to make an animated feature film and anybody can do it. I'm proud of that fact and I'm happy to have started this whole revolution."

The original feature-length films produced alongside Bill's subsequent shorts and commissions display an increasing level of comfort and ambition, all embracing the freedoms of content such independence allows. His self-penned features to date (2015s *Revengeance* being a collaboration with writer Jim Lujan) are *I Married a Strange Person!* (1997), *Mutant Aliens* (2001), *Hair High* (2004), *Idiots and Angels* (2008) and *Cheatin'* (2014). It is 2014s *Cheatin'* (Figure 8.3) which presents the most harmonious mix of what are considered to be staples of his work; ribald adult themes, perfectly timed slapstick, cartoon hyper-violence, deftly interwoven musical numbers and impeccable draftsmanship. The film also benefits from elements of emotional pathos introduced in its predecessor *Idiots and Angels* which see themselves further developed in this instance, chiefly the absence of dialogue which allows for greater appreciation of the characters' animation and subtleties of performance.

"An interesting thing about *Cheatin'* is it features better storytelling, I believe, than my other films. It's not so much just a lot of gags, sex and violence; it has a little more emotional impact, especially for women; a lot of the women really love it, they love the story, they love the characters, they love Ella, the lead character.

Figure 8.3

Still from *Cheatin'* (Dir. Bill Plympton) ©2014 Plymptoons.

This is rare for me, that a lot of women really would be moved by my storytelling and characters."

The films mentioned above are all examples of how perseverance and commitment can achieve the seemingly impossible. Realistically, of course, this only scratches the surface as far as the practicalities go. It is important for us to further explore some of the critical areas that led to the success of each of these films.

The Commitment Factor

Realizing one's own limitations is vitally important during such a huge undertaking as an animated feature. In the case of *Rocks in My Pockets*, the success of

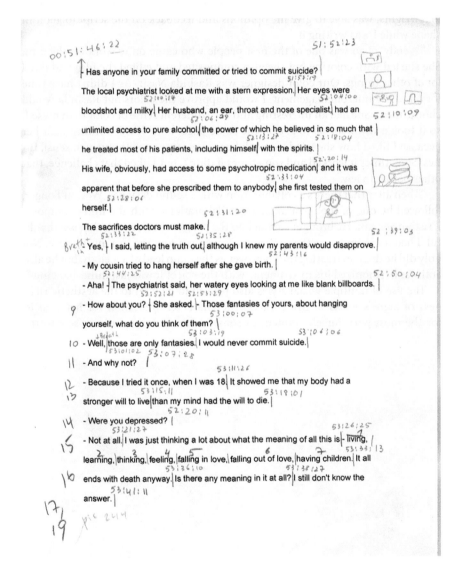

Figure 8.4

Rocks in My Pockets script excerpt with notes on timing. Image courtesy of Signe Baumane.

the film depended in many respects on the skills of others. For Signe Baumane, film has always been a collaborative enterprise:

"For a long time people were asking me 'You make your own short films, why do you need a sound designer when you can do sound yourself?' or 'You work digitally, why do you need a cameraman?' The reason is because I like collaboration, I like when I get given a hard time."

Collaboration provides new perspectives, ways of working and practical solutions that would otherwise never be brought to the table. The *Rocks in My Pockets* (Figures 8.4–8.7) crew consisted of Signe's friends, colleagues and enthusiastic interns whose specialist expertise proved crucial to the final film's overall watchability.

"We had the voiceover director, my boyfriend Sturgis Warner, who directed the film's narration. He is also a theatre director and, because he works with new playwrights, was able to give me opinions and feedback on the script to get it in shape while I was writing it.

"Wendy Zhao was one of the first people who came on to work on the film. She started with coloring but she also composited and edited the film and did a lot of other things. Our color designer was Rashida Nasir. As I didn't have time for all of the micromanagement, I would approve the colors but Rashida would choose them. She had an interesting and very different sense of color than myself, so it took a while for us to get on the same page, but I liked working with her because I liked how she tried to sneak her color sense in with my own sensibilities. Sometimes it worked and sometimes it didn't, but I liked that challenge, that other point of view.

"Then after that there's a collaboration with a sound designer, Weston Fonger, followed by one of the most amazing collaborations, with the film's composer Kristian Sensini. He brought so much to the project that I, to this day, am thankful. I had told him to use the spoken voiceover as a soprano in a music piece. Not only did he do that, treating the voiceover as the main lead of a melody, but he also at times harmonized his instruments with the voice! It was just mind-blowing."

The use of multiple visual styles also proved to be vital to the aesthetic richness of Signe's *Rocks in My Pockets*. The character animation for her film is, for the most part, hugely limited, in some instances taking a back seat to the

Figure 8.5

Signe photographs background elements for *Rocks in My Pockets*. Image courtesy of Signe Baumane.

8. Going Long

narration and story. While this is mainly to serve the long running time and ensure the completion of the project itself, the film remains charming and watch-able throughout for several reasons. Consistent with Signe's approach to prior short films, the action is a mix of literal interpretation of the stories being told intercut with abstract, metaphorical concepts to help elucidate each character's state of mind. Adding real depth to the action is the atypical approach to layout, for which the 2D character animation is composited onto photographed (and occasionally animated, using stop-motion) physical sets sculpted out of paper mache. While this approach blesses the film with a unique visual personality all its own, it represented one of the more intimidating aspects of production.

"The areas that I had no expertise in whatsoever, where I didn't even know where to start, were the most nerve-wracking. The first was the lighting of the sets – I can create paper mache sets and I can draw, but the skill of lighting or the talent and knack to understand it I don't have at all. As a camerawoman I knew what

Figure 8.6

Photographed *Rocks in My Pockets* backgrounds for character animation refer-ence. Image courtesy of Signe Baumane.

looked good and I could make pretty decent pictures, but I couldn't even begin to set up the lights. So Sturgis, because he had a better sense of lighting, was able to help me to light the set. Otherwise, I don't know how that would have happened.

"The other part was creating the voiceover, which was very intimidating. I did *Teat Beat of Sex* with my voice so you would think *Oh, just go ahead and read it*, right? But *Rocks In My Pockets* is a ninety-minute narrative, it has to have an arc and consistency and drive because people have to stay with you for that length of time. So again I asked Sturgis to direct the voice. We worked on it for seven weeks, five hours a day and then we read it in front of a small audience of thirty people. It was really nerve-wracking. I never ordinarily have stage fright but I had stage fright for a week before the presentation, which lasted until it was over. I was so nervous, almost to a point where I felt that I would faint, because I am not an actress. After all, you can't cram in seven weeks and think you'll be as good as Meryl Streep, that's ridiculous."

Aside from working through hurdles of production that seem daunting, the realistic completion of a long-form independent feature hinges on a particular level of dedication one may not be prepared for. As someone who has worked on features since before the digital revolution, Bill Plympton's perspective on just how much more achievable such projects are today holds particular weight (Figures 8.8 and 8.9).

"I think the big help is the digital technology. The cost of making a film has come way down; when I shot my first film I had to use a big rostrum camera, 35 mm film and paint-on-cels. The editing was done on a Steenbeck flatbed and the sound mix was really expensive, you had to do it in a big lab and pay between fifty to a hundred dollars an hour. The technology was so old-fashioned that it was very expensive, whereas you can now make a feature film on your home computer and it will probably be better than the one I made. I think that's the real key, even more so than funding, it's all down to new technology – and new distribution, now you can distribute it online without worrying about getting someone to distribute the film."

Figure 8.7

Still from *Rocks in My Pockets* (Dir. Signe Baumane) demonstrating 2D character animation against constructed backgrounds ©2014 Signe Baumane.

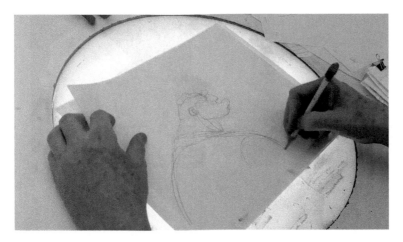

Figure 8.8

Bill Plympton animates 'Thug' from *Cheatin'* ©2013 Plymptoons.

Even bearing such technological progression in mind, the fundamental sacrifices of time and resources remain just as taxing and need to be considered when planning such a large-scale project around other work and life commitments.

"Generally speaking, I do a feature film about every two to two-and-a-half years and I'll do maybe two or three shorts a year. In between I might do a couple of commercial jobs, an ad or part of a documentary or compilation film, that's the kind of work pattern I like. The storyboard and writing process will ordinarily take about a year – though not full-time, it's sort of part-time in between other projects. Then I will do animation for roughly a year (*Cheatin'* took a little bit longer, it took a year-and-a- half because it was a lot more drawings) and then post production takes about six months, so it's about two-and-a-half years to make the film. While I'm doing the storyboards and the writing my studio will be working on the post-production and editing for the previous film, so it kind of balances out, there's always a different part of the production going on all the time."

Story Development's Greatest Ally: Feedback

With such an extensive filmography under his belt, Bill Plympton's sense of his audience's wants and needs is doubtless more attuned than most, although this doesn't get in the way of what, to him, is prerequisite to the development of his story ideas.

"One of the important things that I do – and I think other filmmakers should do – is test it at almost every stage of the production. I do this for my shorts, too. I'll show the storyboards to really close friends in animation, because most animators understand storyboards better than the man on the street. Then I'll do a rough cut of the film, maybe even a pencil test with sound, and I'll show that to a test audience of mostly strangers, not necessarily friends, so I get a hopefully unbiased opinion. Then when the film is close to being done, when it's all colored with rough sound and rough music, I'll show it again to get some feedback as this is my final chance to perfect the film.

Figure 8.9

Compositing pencil art and digital color layers for *Cheatin'* in After Effects ©2013 Plymptoons.

"A lot of people think that since I produce, finance and draw the films myself that there's no censorship. There is, I really censor myself a lot because I want the film to be popular, so if there's a scene in there that I don't think works very well or will be offensive or turn people off, I will cut that scene because I really want this film to be a success. Now I *will* try to put in ideas that I think are kind of crazy and wacky and bizarre, that aren't necessarily 'normal' ideas, and I will fight to keep those in, but if the test audience doesn't like them I will cut them out and put them on the shelf.

"I think an important quality to have is considering the audience as the master I'm working for. I'm not working for myself, I'm not working for good reviews or winning lots of prizes, I'm working for the audience and that's the way it should be."

Signe Baumane similarly doesn't make films for herself (Figures 8.10–8.12): "It's not like I'm going to make the film and lock myself in a room with it and watch it for a year. You make a film to communicate ideas, and before you release the film into the world you want to know if you have somehow succeeded. At the very least I want my points to come across, I want the story to be clear, but there

Figure 8.10

Rocks in my Pockets thumbnail boards to final stills comparison ©2014 Signe Baumane.

is a line of how much you give in to the audience or to the demands of people who are not used to seeing something so utterly different. Very early on, when I presented the first five minutes in screenings and online, the feedback was very strong and very consistent that the voiceover was horrible and that I would have to hire some decent actress or get rid of the voiceover altogether. So for me, early on I had to consider, do I do that?

"The way I conceived the film was like an acorn that I'd planted in the ground, and I had to wait and work on it. The people were saying to me that they wanted to have wheat or barley, or a rose, but the seed that I had put into the ground was for an oak tree, so what can I do? Dig it out and find a seed of a rose, or wait and see how my oak tree grows, how this will turn out and what my options are? So it was very hard for me with this early negative feedback to stay loyal to the acorn that I had put in the ground. I was full of doubt and insecurity but I decided that even if I failed, even if this oak tree came out crippled, I wanted to see it. So I stayed loyal to that idea.

"I didn't just re-record my voiceover, we had a test reading where I read the script in front of a small audience of thirty people who gave feedback. They said which parts were interesting, which parts they liked and where they felt it dragged. So we cut out some stuff, I stayed loyal to my acorn and I worked and worked. Then towards the end, in December 2012 when we had most of the film animated but only half-colored, I had two test screenings. One was at Bill Plympton's studio where we had about ten people crammed around a TV set who we took feedback from afterward. Another took place a week later at a small arthouse café in Sunset Park in Brooklyn. That had roughly seventy people and we had a very intense feedback session. Out of seventy people who saw the film in these two feedback sessions, fifty said they loved the voiceover, seven said they absolutely hated it and then the rest of them said they could go either way. For me that was interesting, that people still hated the voiceover, but only ten percent of them. So if you were to bring it to ten thousand people, then a thousand people would hate it but the bigger percentage loves it. This was at a time when the film didn't have music and was barely colored, when the voiceover was really right in your face. In that instance because way more people loved it than hated it I decided to keep the voiceover.

"Then there's a certain type of feedback where people say 'Oh I think that you shouldn't do this' or 'If I were you I would do that,' where it's them trying to make my film. That feedback is hard to take, because it's not really helping the film."

This degree of awareness to pick and choose which feedback is applicable speaks for one's self-assuredness as a filmmaker, though as Signe herself concedes, the more consistent feedback is usually consistent for a reason: "People were confused in the beginning as to who was the main character, because she doesn't kick in until around fourteen minutes into the film. That was important feedback that I was scratching my head about for a good six months, until in June 2013 I was ready to do something about it. It took me six months to understand what had to be done, which was to create an opening sequence that wasn't there before, of the small woman pushing a big rock up the mountain so that you knew she is the main character; when she reappears in the film, you know that it's her story.

"I cut out the first five minutes of the film, which was very hard because they were fully colored and they were kind of funny but they had to go because they were prolonging the time where you didn't know what was happening, or why.

Figure 8.11

Still from *Rocks in My Pockets* (Dir. Signe Baumane) ©2014 Signe Baumane.

Then we cut out some parts that we felt could be tightened up, parts I was really attached to but ultimately felt were unnecessary. Then we had the final test screening in Fall 2013, after which I did small adjustments for moments where people were confused about how the characters related to each other. Then of course we added the music and sound design, and that was it. So overall there were four testing events."

Staying Visible, Keeping Afloat

Both *Cheatin'* and *Rocks In My Pockets* benefited from coming together at a time when social media and blog culture had firmly taken hold. Signe Baumane's production blog,[2] which began with a cryptic first post in September 2010, would venture into all sorts of territory beyond being a strict breakdown of the making of film. As in the movie itself, her gift for anecdotal storytelling is frequently on display, the site serving a repository for childhood recollections, memoirs of early adulthood and accounts of shambolic relationships that serve as well articulated companion reading to the eventual movie. Though plenty of the posts do explore her process and detail the successes, pitfalls and challenges faced during and after production, it is Signe's unabashedly idiosyncratic personality and the heart of who she is as a filmmaker that shines through and grants the film's potential audience an avenue to communicate with her. "I had no idea what I was doing with social media when I was making the film, but it was very important to me to connect with people. One interesting thing that happened was, after one screening of the film at DOK Leipzig in Germany, a man came up to me and said that he'd followed my blog and the Facebook page for the four years I had worked on the film. He had stumbled across my blog by accident, without any interest in animation at all, but every update that I posted helped him to understand and connect with the project better, and at the end he was a complete fan of the project. When it came for him to be able to see the film in Leipzig at a screening he was just beside himself, he was so thrilled. That was something interesting that I'd never considered, and probably if I had known about it earlier, I would have done a better job maybe, or consciously written things about connecting people to the project. I was just writing random stuff, I'm not really a very well organized

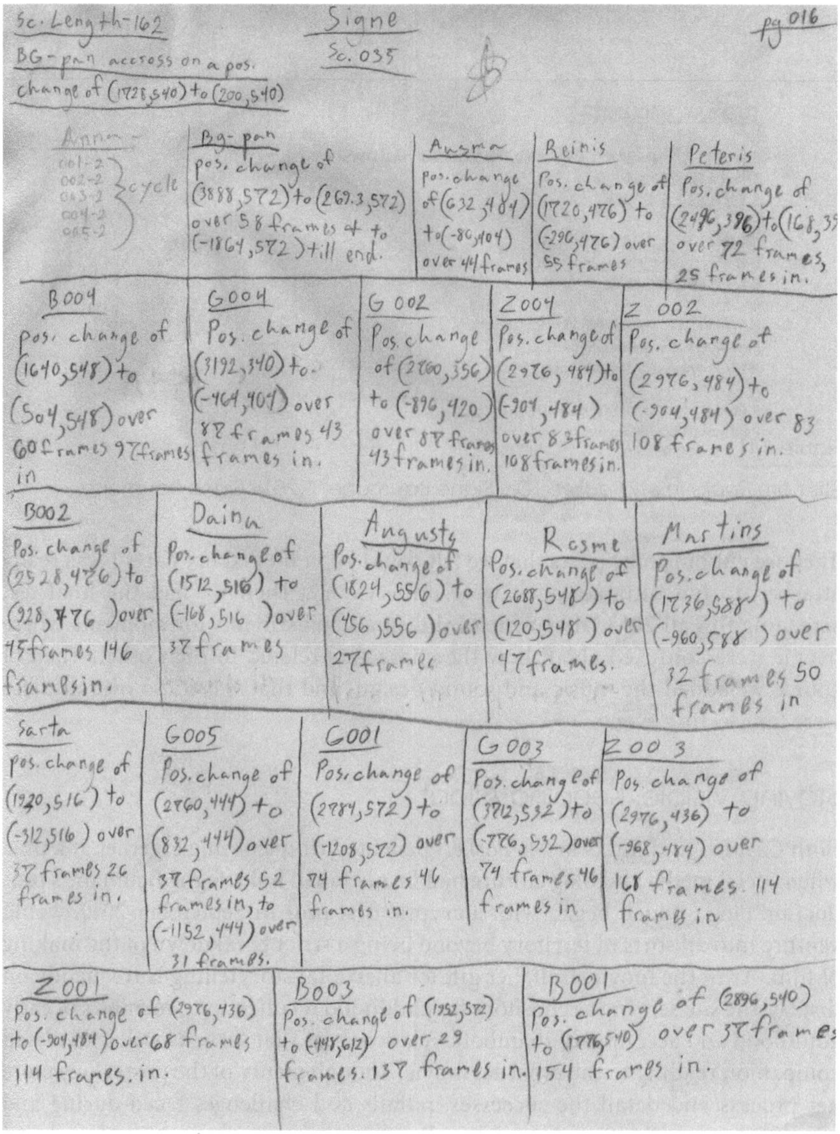

Sc. Length-162 Signe pg 016
BG-pan across on a pos. Sc. 035
change of (1928,540) to (200,540)

Annu~	Bg-pan	Ausra~	Reinis	Peteris
001-2 } cycle 002-2 003-2 004-2 005-2	pos. change of (3888,572) to (269.3,572) over 58 frames + to (-1864,572) till end.	pos. change of (632,484) to(-86,404) over 44 frames	Pos. change of (1720,476) to (-296,476) over 55 frames	Pos. change of (2496,396) to (168,39 over 72 frames, 25 frames in.
B 004	G 004	G 002	Z 004	Z 002
pos. change of (1640,548) to (504,548) over 60 frames 97 frames in	Pos. change of (3192,340) to (-464,404) over 88 frames 43 frames in.	Pos. change of (2800,356) to (-896,420) over 88 frames 43 frames in.	Pos. change of (2976,484) to (-304,484) over 83 frames 108 frames in.	Pos. change of (2976,484) to (-304,484) over 83 108 frames in.
B002	Daina	Augusta	Rosme	Martins
Pos. change of (2528,476) to (928,476) over 45 frames 146 frames in.	Pos. change of (1512,516) to (-168,516) over 37 frames	Pos. change of (1824,556) to (456,556) over 27 frames	Pos. change of (2688,548) to (120,548) over 47 frames.	Pos. change of (1236,588) to (-960,588) over 32 frames 50 frames in
Sarta	G005	G001	G 003	Z 003
pos. change of (1920,516) to (-312,516) over 37 frames 26 frames in.	Pos. change of (2860,444) to (832,444) over 37 frames 52 frames in, to (-1152,444) over 31 frames.	Pos. change of (2884,572) to (-1208,572) over 74 frames 46 frames in.	Pos. change of (3912,532) to (-776,532) over 74 frames 46 frames in	Pos change of (2976,436) to (-968,484) over 168 frames. 114 frames in
Z 001		B003		B001
Pos. change of (2976,436) to (-304,484) over 68 frames 114 frames in.		Pos. change of (1752,572) to (-448,612) over 29 frames. 137 frames in.		Pos. change of (2896,540) to (996,540) over 37 frames 154 frames in.

Figure 8.12

Rocks in My Pockets exposure sheet. Image courtesy of Signe Baumane.

person so I'd just do random posts, there's no real strategy for me, but I guess my personality comes through. Who I am, my passion, the simple pleasures I underwent to make this project happen and my sense of humor also comes through. The tagline 'A funny film about depression' could be many things but if you followed my blog and Facebook page for four years you would know exactly what to expect – or you would hope that it would be what you think it is going to be."

Supplementing her blog is a short series of video entries, a means of documenting the process further also embraced by Bill Plympton throughout *Cheatin'*. The extensive production blog[3] put together by Bill and his Plymptoons studio crew painstakingly covers the key processes and technicalities, offering fans and enthusiasts a look at his unique approach and the ways it differentiates from a traditional feature pipeline. While very different films, these windows into the more or less simultaneous production of *Rocks In My Pockets* and *Cheatin'* (Figures 8.13 and 8.14) - coupled with Signe and Bill's prior working relationship - offer their fanbase an insight into their solidarity as independent creatives and mutual encouragement.

Such support is integral to staying motivated while in the thick of production, especially at points where the light at the end of the tunnel is so hard to see. For Signe, the sacrifices that might otherwise have stood in the way of perseverance were tempered with some good fortune in the sense that collaboration maintained an important personal relationship.

"One thing that, in my case, was extremely lucky was that my boyfriend Sturgis realized early on that I was embarking on a project he could not stop me from, so he integrated himself into it as the voiceover director and the lighting designer. In Q&As when we are together, sometimes people ask the question, 'So why did a theatre director decide to be part of this animated feature project?' And he says 'I had to do it if I wanted to see my girlfriend!' In the last year he became co-producer and we raised money together for the last batch of distribution and marketing, we formed our own LLC did research and prepared marketing materials together. We work quite a lot and we communicate all the time about business. If I was communicating so intensely with somebody else, I wouldn't have *time* for a boyfriend!

"As for the personal sacrifices, they are obvious: I lived very frugally, I lived on the edge of being insanely poor and all the money I had went towards the project. I barely had time for friends – I believe I *had* friends, but I hardly saw them. There are people in our lives who come in and expect a certain level of friendship, a certain level of communication that I couldn't give them and they would get very upset and walk away mad at me. So I can only be friends with people who understand what I do, and why, people who would not try to barge in and take big chunk of my time, that have respect for this thing that I try to do. "Be prepared to work long hours and be prepared to become a family with your team. The other thing I would say is that one has to foster good relationships with people who are wealthy! When people put down wealthy people I don't agree, I think that they're fun, and when you need to raise money for your film a person who believes in you as an artist, who believes in your project and who is able to support you with a little more contribution that just ten dollars, that is also very handy."

Bill Plympton's own resolve is predicated more on having found a working rhythm that feeds his personal contentment. "Well, first of all, just to let you know, I get up every morning around 5 am and go to my drawing board and start drawing – and sometimes I'll draw until 9 pm or 10 pm at night, so it's a long day! Certainly during the day I have to do phone calls or business or write cheques or have meetings, but it is a long day of animation and, I'll be honest with you, it's really fun. If you're doing it right, if you really have an interesting story with interesting characters then it's a really exciting process, it's a joy and a pleasure. That, I think, is the number one reason why I do it, but also at the back of my mind I have this fantasy – and sometimes it's a reality – of *Oh, this one will win the Oscar, this'll win the Nobel Peace Prize, this will get a standing ovation, this will get lines around the block waiting to see the film...*

"And you have to believe that, you have to believe that this is the best film ever made, better than *Snow White and the Seven Dwarves* and *Citizen Kane*, because if you don't then you'll lose your passion, you'll lose your excitement for

Figure 8.13

Cheatin' (Dir. Bill Plympton) drawn animation to final film comparison ©2014 Plymptoons.

the project and it will turn out pretty bad. So I always have a very optimistic attitude about my films, I always fantasize about winning all these prizes and going to all these wonderful festivals. That's the other part, getting a huge response and nice ovation from the audience, that's really what drives me. For some of the films I've gotten that and I must say it's very gratifying after all the work to know that the audience likes what I have produced."

To filmmakers who would follow in the footsteps of those who've run the animated feature production gauntlet, Signe Baumane recommends a soupçon of denial. "When I started *Rocks in My Pockets* I thought it could be done for $100,000. Well, it was not, in the end when we had finished everything including marketing and distribution it was three times that. That number is huge, I will never hold that much money in my hands, so I think that I protected myself from knowing exactly what was going to happen, if I had known how much the film would have cost from the start I might have never begun. So you have to be delusional to start any project and you have to say it's going to be easy, which is how I started. The hardest thing for me was that, once I had been animating for half a year with an assistant who was coloring for four months as fast as she could as I had these drawings piling up, in four months we had only colored around three minutes! That feeling of despair, that I had a ninety minute project to accomplish and in four months two of us had accomplished so little, that feeling of that long

Figure 8.14

Still from *Cheatin'* (Dir. Bill Plympton) ©2014 Plymptoons.

tunnel ahead, I felt like I have to walk across the Earth! But then everybody got faster, it was the beginning, the early stages. We got more help and so things moved along and it went ahead."

Notes

1 This happens, people. I once heard tell of an animator who nearly did himself in when he developed auxiliary vein thrombosis in his shoulder after cramming in too much track-reading in one go. So, if you're planning on an all-nighter or several, treat it like a long-haul flight and try to throw in the odd break.

2 http://rocksinmypocketsthemovie.wordpress.com/.

3 https://vimeo.com/plymptoons.

9
Funding

Figure 9.1

Still from *Virtuos Virtuell* (Dir. Thomas Stellmach/Maja Oschmann) ©2013 Thomas Stellmach.

The international landscape of animation funding is, unfortunately, not evergreen, and even if it were, then the differences between how each nation (or even region) supports the arts are an overwhelming maze of inconsistencies and contradictions. As such, it would be nigh on impossible to sincerely lay out the realities of what funding opportunities might be available to you, the reader and

DOI: 10.1201/9781003214717-9

budding filmmaker, so I won't even attempt it. There are, however, some crucial insights to be gleaned from those who have set out on the journey of securing funds and, for the very reason of said landscape being in a state of constant flux, have been prompted to adapt their strategies on the fly.

Going into one's own pockets may be a grim inevitability, but depending on the perceivable value of your film – whether it has an educational purpose, for example, or examines a major social issue – can help bring in supplemental funds. When seeking support for *Virtuos Virtuell* (Figure 9.1), directors Thomas Stellmach and Maja Oschmann were well aware that the high quality standard they hoped for the film would be far easier to achieve without self-funding alone.

"I had to produce a film which could go to festivals, that was why it was necessary to get this high quality." Thomas assures, "The film had to go to cinemas, that was the only way I could get funding. On the other side, we had some patrons from the city, because the idea was to also produce this film for the exhibition of Kassel's Louis Spohr Museum. At the end of the day, we managed to get roughly half of the production budget, from companies, banks and the mayor, for example."

Funds were gathered from a variety of sources, patrons including The Federal Government Commissioner for Culture and Media, the Hessian Film Fund, companies, banks, stores, individuals, not to mention the Louis Spohr Museum itself. Thomas and Maja's own financial contributions came not through dipping into existing funds as much as countless unpaid hours working to finish it. This was made possible by limiting the film's crew to just themselves. While it might seem that bringing on board a larger crew would have reduced the overall production time down from three-plus years, it's worth remembering that the entire aesthetic and emotion of the film hinged on a very personal system of communication and idea generation – an artistic *folie à deux*, almost – that, if extended to salaried outsiders, may have both cost money and protracted the length of production.

The Snowball Effect

In the case of prolific, Amsterdam-based artist Rosto (who, tragically, is no longer with us, having passed away in March 2019), geographical circumstances also proved fortuitous when it came to securing funds for new projects, even if he had to look further afield than his home country of the Netherlands: "We are very lucky that we are European, and although things can go rapidly in the wrong direction – it's always easy to break stuff down that took a long time to build up – we still have good government funding systems. In my case I often collaborate with other European countries, especially France who have been very good to me – they are a cinephile country and there are a lot of people there sitting on money, so to speak, who really appreciate what I do. So a film like *Lonely Bones* (2013) for example, was only financed by French money; I didn't get any financing from my own country but France was there. But for a film like *Splintertime* (Figure 9.2) (2015), there were three countries involved – Belgium, France and Holland, and some television money. That's basically how we'd gather all the little bits and pieces of funding together."

The additional streams of funding are again owed to the snowball effect of each Rosto project being more visible and aesthetically polished than the last, owed in no small part to his professional association with the production company

Figure 9.2

Still from *Splintertime* (Dir. Rosto) ©2015 Studio Rosto A.D./Autour de Minuit/S.O.I.L.

Autour de Minuit. It is something of a rare case, however, for outside funding to not contribute significantly to the creative side of the process. In the world of mainstream cinema – or any form of marketable art, for that matter – there is an inevitable correlation between the level of outside financial assistance and the amount of creative control a filmmaker has to relinquish. Sometimes this is a good thing (think of all the "director's cuts" of films you might have seen that only serve to belabor or convolute the story, paling in comparison to its tighter theatrical release), though the idea of having your vision as a filmmaker curbed is, in principle, an idea that most people will not be especially fond of. This is especially true in the case of independent film, where the potential to profit from and market your finished film is significantly less.

An example of how the presence of corporate funding can affect the independent spirit of a project refers back to an earlier case study in the book. The viral visibility of *Story from North America* (Figure 9.3), the auteur song-based project by Garrett Michael Davis in collaboration with Kirsten Lepore, ultimately led to a sequel film *Story from South America*, commissioned by the FOX Network's Animation Domination High-Def. Though Kirsten was not involved, Garrett once again took up the roles of writer, composer, performer, designer and animator with the hope of ensuring a film that, although a more "produced" affair with higher production values, would maintain the *outré* spirit of the original. Ultimately, Garrett would wind up approaching the process of this follow-up in an entirely different way.

"I made a full-on animatic for it, in contrast to *Story from North America*, and then the whole thing was animated in two weeks, compared to the six or so months we spent on the original. It was also animated in Flash as opposed to on paper, but (collaborator) Ben Jones had the idea to do all the backgrounds on paper. They were then painted in Photoshop and the result was amazing. Mostly I learned what I already knew, that you don't need a studio to make something good. And it's probably easier to make something good without a studio, if you have vision."

In the absence of former collaborator Kirsten Lepore, *Story from South America* features a larger team of animators and designers: "Working with any

Figure 9.3

The raw edge of 2007s *Story from North America* (Dir. Garrett Michael Davis/Kirsten Lepore) did not prove to be as present in its 2013 successor ©2007 Garrett Davis/ Kirsten Lepore.

kind of crew was totally new for me. It was fun, and I really enjoyed what the background designers did especially. They were all really young kids who just got out of CalArts and everyone was scared of being fired."

Though it proved somewhat difficult to maintain the tone of the piece ("I didn't even really know what the tone *was*"), the final result was not entirely satisfactory to Garrett, but with a fairly tight production window available compromises had to be made.

"I allowed individual people to contribute their own ideas and I didn't shoot anything down. Ultimately I just wanted everyone to have fun working on it. There is always a degree of letting go that has to happen on any collaborative project, but I much prefer working alone or with one other person. The more people, the more diluted the vision gets, unless you are a tyrannical director – which I may become someday, but I wasn't at that point."

Despite the lo-fi approach to its predecessor, the time restraints on the development and production of *Story from South America* ultimately outweigh the benefits of the additional funding and manpower available for it. Embarking on a piece of music that was more of a "skeleton of a song," one not "totally resolved, lyrically or musically," as opposed to the sturdier "Spider Song" on which the first film was built around was another major drawback. The newer song also suffered due to unforeseen scheduling issues conflicting with Garrett's personal process when it came to performing the piece.

"I had been growing the fingernails on my right hand out pretty long because the song used this specific finger style that I came up with. The producer kept telling me 'tomorrow we're going to record, be ready.' So I kept my fingernails. It kept not happening, so after a couple of months of that I figured it was never going to happen so I cut my nails, because they were annoying me. The *next* day we were recording, and we were rushed because we only had twenty minutes in the booth. I got gigantic blisters on my fingertips because I had no nails and couldn't even play the song properly."

In Garrett's mind, it remains clear which of the two works best as a film: "*Story from North America* is far better in every way. The sequel for me is more about an experience of becoming a part of the larger animation world. Through ADHD it's been aired on American television; my friend told me once that it came on the TV while he was eating in an Ethiopian restaurant. That gave me a really nice feeling."

Selling Yourself

While perhaps primarily known for her work as an animation producer/exec producer, UK-based animation stalwart Helen Brunsdon wears several hats within the animation industry including programming, advisory roles, development, events organization, education and, since 2019, heading up the nation's most significant bi-annual industry event as Director of the British Animation Awards. Through her work with and alongside organizations such as the British Film Institute, Animation UK (of which she is also Director) and Creative Skillset, among others, Helen has actively played a role in increasing animation funding within the UK and has been in the unique position of seeing both sides of the looking glass when it comes to how funds for new animated productions are both sought out and allocated.

"Lots of people apply for funding but the chances are that you might not get all that you ask for or you might be rejected from some funding rounds. We've all been there, you've just got to keep going. Sometimes the timing isn't right, but you will learn so much by applying for funding, and how those application forms work. You've got to read the guidelines and ask questions, you've got to see if you're eligible, be sure that it takes on animation. You've got to be really proactive and start to build a relationship with stakeholders and funders in order to understand the mechanisms of how the funding structure works, and you've got to do your own research. Research is so key and it's never all contained in one space. There's lots of different websites to go to seek more information for funding."

The first recommended ports of call are animation industry blogs, newsletters and social media groups, some of which can be particularly focused on niche areas that may line up with your own specific creative aspirations, geographical circumstances or personal background. Although based in the UK, being aware of an international readership, we at Skwigly also work hard to get the word out whenever there are new opportunities available for pitches, training, career furtherance and calls for entries across the globe. Helen also recommends investigating trade organizations within your country that embrace the animation industry – in the UK, these include PACT, Animation UK, UK Animation Alliance and Edge of Frame.

"There's only a certain amount of funds that get awarded but don't be put off by that, keep applying to lots of funding. You've got to be really resilient and a bit hard-nosed about one day getting this funder to support your work.

"I always go wider than animation and I do suggest that people look into the arts spectrum as a whole; you might have elements of an idea that ties into live action or music. There's different funding pots out there that might take on an animation proposal, so you've got to consider how much of it is animated and which pot can you steer your idea towards."

Targeting opportunities that are more realistically lined up with the project you have in mind is an obvious but often overlooked timesaver when it comes to submitting pitches and applications. Make the effort to really consider your film's prospective appeal and who its audience might be. If possible, bounce your idea off of people you can trust to give honest feedback and get their impressions; this is another reason to proactively network at industry events and get some face time with people who can steer you in the best direction.

"Even if you don't have an idea, reach out and meet funders for coffee, get out to festivals or networking events, pitching opportunities, you've got to gain experience from doing that. You need to know what's happening on your doorstep. You need to collaborate, you need to find other people who might be in different countries or regions who can come together to make a film. You might be a director, a writer, an animator, you might need a producer or you might need a director to attach your project. So you've got to build up a who's-who, and keep looking at festival winners, who's directed what."

Oftentimes when a funding opportunity presents itself, there will usually be specific materials that are requested with each submission. When an idea is in a more embryonic state, it can be tricky to fit it into that mold, but doing so is a valuable way of motivating yourself to develop the idea further. If a one-line summary is being solicited and you've only previously conveyed your idea in sprawling paragraphs of brilliance, take it as an opportunity to really hone in on the quality of it that makes it stand out. If visuals are requested (such as concept art, character designs or layouts) and you haven't begun that part of the process yet, then look to the application as your opportunity to do so. There's usually some scope to be inventive and creative as well, although it will probably benefit you to stay within any parameters (per-section word counts, for instance) that have been clearly outlined.

"You've got to get across who's going to work on it," adds Helen, "what some of the key roles are from a creative point of view, the look of the film, the technique – duration is a really key one to put in. Certainly for sound or music, you've got to get across in your application that you have a complete picture in mind of what the soundscape is going to sound like, or what some themes are, or what direction you're imagining it will go. Enthusiasm can assure people that you know what you're doing and it's likely to attract other talent in. Definitely have ideas, not just about story and script, but also about character designs, about what we're gonna hear, what we're going to see when it's finished. What do you want the audience to take away? What do you want the audience to see?

"For those details, or information that you think will enhance your application but they haven't asked for, there might be an opportunity for you to attach some separate documentation to your application. They won't have hours and hours to look through your work, because they might be inundated with applications, so you've got to make an impression."

Standing out in this way isn't just advantageous, it's essential when considering that other artists applying for the same funds may have been at it much longer, with an already established track record. If you're relatively new to the game, Helen recommends drawing on other strengths that will enhance your value as a sure thing in funders' eyes.

"Creatively, be prolific – when I was at university, the people around me who are still in the industry today were always going above and beyond what we were asked to do. So that starts to build up a body of work. Beyond university, the creative progression might be that you try different genres, different durations, you might try to do something in 30 seconds and you build up to something a bit longer. It's always better to cut your teeth on something that's a minute long versus ten minutes. It shows aptitude, of being able to edit yourself down and be able to tell a story. Maybe you've done something for a 24 hour anijam, or took part in a competition by yourself or used it as an opportunity to progress and work with somebody else or even a team. You might get yourself into a style that you really want to explore across a series of films, and it just gets better and better. So a body of work to justify where you are currently at does, absolutely, get taken into account."

A subject not brought up especially often is one of personal comportment. Whether it be a funding application, a job application, a film festival submission (more on this later in the book), a studio pitch or really anything that demands we run the risk of rejection, how we handle ourselves in the aftermath can have lasting effects. Across programming, curation, teaching, industry coverage and jury duty (of the film festival variety), I've seen my fair share of ungraciousness when someone hasn't gotten the results they wanted – and I'm sure in my (hopefully much) younger years a fair few people saw it from me. When you keep at it enough, you do develop a callous for bad news, mainly because you come to realize it isn't going to be the only opportunity that comes your way.

"Remember there's always another funding pot to go after, so keep trying," assures Helen. "When it comes to not being successful in securing money, the last thing you want to do is go rant about it on social media, because you don't know the circumstances, you don't know who *was* successful. Instead, sit back and ask for more detailed feedback. Calm down a bit, don't send an angry email or people will start to associate you with that kind of attitude. There's an etiquette of making yourself shine out for the right reasons and writing polite, well-researched emails is part of that. Nobody teaches you how to network, nor how to spot an opportunity, but if you do find yourselves in front of an industry person, always take advantage of that and ask them questions – but don't ask them to do your homework for you.

"Just be respectful. For me, it's about having a professional face and a personal face, and I think that's really key, to not mix up the two. Even down to having a serious email address, a fun one might be comical to you but in a professional context it's off putting. That can be your personal email but your professional email should be exactly that; there's no better ambassador for yourself than yourself."

The other thing to bear in mind is that the project you have in mind may require more than one funding stream to secure a decent enough budget. If you're going the auteur, homegrown route of being the primary member of a keystone crew, or even doing the whole thing yourself, then it's fair to say you won't need much more funding than what will sustain you for the production period. For loftier concepts that will benefit from a dedicated crew who you can pay decently, one application likely won't be enough. Many animated features and television series come together through what Helen dubs "a jigsaw puzzle of finance" and this is increasingly the case with short film productions as well.

"If you have worked out a £100,000 budget for a short film but you can only raise £50,000 of that from the UK, you've got to either rethink your idea to make it for half, or you've got to find the other £50,000 pounds. There could be another pot of funding in a different country that is worth £30,000 that, if you receive it, will require you to conduct that amount/value of work in that country, so the work and the money doesn't actually come back to the UK. Then you've still got a remaining deficit of £20,000 to find, so you might find that you could do an artist in residency in another country to make up some money, but that would require you going to a different country to do that work. Depending on your individual citizenship, this might be a contributing factor in approaching and securing different finances. So it starts to become a little bit complicated, which is where producers come in – they have to evaluate the conditions attached to those different pots of funding and help exploit."

To expand on this, we'll look at a case study of a director/team who managed to do precisely that. Prolific UK-based animation and puppetry director Joseph Wallace's work has been internationally acclaimed, screened at prestigious festivals and seen him rubbing shoulders (creatively speaking) with musicians including Parker Bossley, James and Sparks as a music video director as well as creating animated documentary segments for Edgar Wright's 2021 documentary feature on the latter, *The Sparks Brothers*. Between commissions, Joseph has built up an impressive filmography of mixed-media short films such as the BAFTA Cyrmu-nominated Newport Film School graduation film *The Man Who Was Afraid of Falling* (2011), the analog paper-cutout "domestic tragedy" *Natural Disaster* (2014) and the live-action puppetry micro-short *La Forêt Sauvage* (2014).

It would be his passion project *Salvation Has No Name* (Figures 9.4–9.9), however, that would prove the longest to gestate, being richer in ambition and scope than his previous work. A fifteen-minute, cinematic folktale exploring the prevalent themes of xenophobia and faith, securing a significant budget beyond his usual method of subsidizing personal projects from his paid work (one that only realistically allowed the films to be five minutes or less in length) would be crucial.

"I felt like I'd hit a limit of duration, but also ambition, in terms of storytelling and scale. From the outset, the scale and ambition of *Salvation Has No Name* was a lot bigger and I knew I couldn't do a film like that on no money."

Initially developing the film on his own, Joseph would eventually partner up with Loran Dunn of Manchester-based Delaval Film. Having known one another through doing theater together at a young age, the pair had kept in touch over the years and saw potential in the new film as a viable project to pitch for funding.

Figure 9.4

Still from *Salvation Has No Name* ©Delaval Film, image courtesy of Joseph Wallace.

"I think we were both quite naive about support for animation at the start. When I started *Salvation Has No Name* around 2014, I really quickly discovered there was no money for independent animation in the UK at all. We were in this hiatus after a kind of 'Golden Age' in the late eighties/early nineties where the BFI, Channel 4, BBC and S4C had been funding things."

It would be several years of hunting and championing the value of animation as an art form (Joseph would eventually join the Animation Alliance UK's advisory board to lobby for new animation funds within the UK) before the first streams of financing would come in, and the road to success was a bumpy one as most of the film funding schemes open for applications weren't set up to accommodate the demands of animation.

"One thing about going through this process is it really steels you to the sight of the rejection letter, because we really were rejected by more places than ever chose to support the film in the end. Due to the fact that there was no one place to go for animation funding, the approach became, 'let's try and apply for all these little grants and see if we can get a bit here, a bit there, etc.' And at a similar time, we decided to look into residencies and development opportunities. I wanted to do design work and write the script and there wasn't any money to do that, so I applied for a development residency at the Open Workshop in Denmark. I'd done the Animation Sans Frontières production course years before, which was part-taught at The Animation Workshop and they have the Open Workshop for residencies; you can go there to make your film or write it, or create concept art etc. So I went out there and did a residency for just over a month writing the script for *Salvation*. They provided me with accommodation, a studio space and some

Figure 9.5

Storyboarding *Salvation Has No Name*. Photo: Nom Tarassenko, image courtesy of Joseph Wallace.

feedback from industry mentors but probably the most useful thing was meeting all the other filmmakers out there and getting feedback from peers."

During his time in residency, Joseph was steered toward the Visegrad Animation Forum (now CEE Forum), which resulted in him being among thirteen participating teams of animation professionals pitching their projects to an international jury in Třeboň. This served as a crucial opportunity to hone his pitch and develop the film further.

"Probably one of my biggest bits of advice in terms of funding and getting interest is to carefully consider how you present your project. The idea might be so clear for you, in your head, but you then have to translate that into something that you can put in front of an audience and get other people to imagine and get excited about and want to support it, whether it's crew, or financers or co-production partners."

This is an area that Helen Brunsdon agrees should be a primary focus: "What you've always got to remember is that you are selling your idea, your team and yourself. When you are putting together a pitch, you've got to think of what people are going to read off the paper. There might be an opportunity to do a piece to camera as part of a funding application, in which case I would definitely encourage you to write a script, practice it and do your piece to camera; don't waffle. Then a funding panel can see the energy and enthusiasm for the project coming off the screen.

"You need to think about what the film is trying to say and then also what it would look like, so you might have to do some key designs. If it's stop-motion, we all get that it's harder to recreate, but that doesn't mean you can't do drawings or a mood board for what the style could be, and start to build it up that way."

In Joseph's case, generating these types of visuals during his residency was especially important in conveying the atmosphere, theatrical tone and overall approach to the cinematography for *Salvation Has No Name* when it came to pitching.

"I had a desk where I was working with these pinboards behind and I used their photocopier and printed off all sorts of reference images from Goya and religious iconography to circus and clown imagery. I also made a prototype puppet of the Priest character and photographed that to use as a lead image for the project."

Although the initial puppet design would change significantly by the time production rolled around, this proved an important stepping stone in the visual development stage of the project. "That process of making a promotional image, concept artwork, choosing a font, thinking how you encapsulate the themes of the piece, is so important. A big realisation for me, which seems obvious, was the importance of the vocabulary you use to talk about the film, the words you choose say so much about the project and your intentions. All of that was really rigorously drilled through pitching and eventually I knew how to tell the whole story concisely in one minute and I knew what terms to use to describe the project and guide people through that narrative.

"The other thing I'd really recommend doing, if you can manage it, is to make a teaser trailer or sizzle reel. These can be quite simple but having something moving that you can show makes such a big difference. Before we pitched at the Visegrad Forum I had a week with my friend Péter Vácz, the Hungarian animation director, I flew him over to Bristol and we made this 2 minute teaser in seven days. That was seven days to make two puppets, props and sets and to animate

Figure 9.6

Salvation Has No Name teaser trailer still ©Delaval Film, image courtesy of Joseph Wallace.

the whole thing! We were lucky to be able to shoot it in a corner at Aardman's Gas Ferry Road site. None of that teaser trailer ended up in the final film, it's all rough and sketchy but it gave an *impression* of the film and captured the story-telling language. I edited the teaser to feel quite dramatic, because the film is a stop motion drama and I wanted it to convey the Shakespearean influences and grab people's attention!"

Joseph's pitch at VAF was successful, winning the project €2000 that, though relatively modest, got the ball rolling in a very real way. In spite of it being the first win for the film in a sea of rejections, the team's proactivity in searching out available opportunities had been extremely beneficial to rounding out the film both visually and conceptually.

"By that point we had a full script, a teaser trailer, a one-pager (which is another useful piece of the puzzle) for people to look at. There was a fair amount of press from winning the pitching prize and it made people aware of the project. I went to Prague afterwards and had a meeting with Animation People, who are a Czech company, and they were interested in doing a co-production but at that point, we didn't have any money from the UK side of things, and for us to main-tain the rights and make it through Delaval Film, you have to be the majority producer. Fortuitously at that time we found a private investor in the UK who came on board, which meant that we could then enter into negotiations with Animation People."

Additional funds would trickle in from various sources – *Natural Disaster*, one of Joseph's earlier films, would be awarded funds from the BFI that could go toward future work; the France-based production and distribution company Autour de Minuit would come on board during production as well as RAPT in the UK. Remaining funds would come from a combination of crowdfunding (a Kickstarter campaign generating a respectable £19,643 to go toward upping the overall production values, post-production and generally bringing it back on track due to complications – such as having to up sticks and shift the entire production from Bristol to Manchester – caused by the pandemic in 2020), pri-vate investors and through taking advantage of the UK tax credit available to

Figure 9.7

Priest on set of *Salvation Has No Name*. Photo: Joseph Wallace.

film-specific projects. While crowdfunding will be discussed further in the next section, these other two methods are perhaps less-known and trickier to come by, though also worth addressing.

"I have to say, the tax credits are fairly complicated. If you are a filmmaker who's self-producing, I don't know if I would recommend doing it because unless you're very good with your spreadsheets and auditing, it's quite a lot of work! But it's also a great benefit to making work in the UK. I think it's a little bit complicated when you're doing European co-productions, because obviously the UK tax credits can only be spent in the UK, but it is a really good system where you can get back something like 19% of your UK spend at the end of the production. So that definitely helped strengthen the budget."

Securing private investment from individuals is no sure thing and certainly shouldn't be an expectation going in, though if a project comes together and clearly shows potential then there may be people who are enthusiastic to get involved and help it across the finish line. In some respects, the process of selling the value of a project to an individual is not so different from pitching to an organization.

Figure 9.8

Painting on set of *Salvation Has No Name*. Photo: Jonathan Garvey, image courtesy of Joseph Wallace.

"One of the investors was somebody who I knew already, I was talking to them, in passing, about the financing of the film. At that point we were in some kind of Catch 22 situation where the Czech company wanted to invest and do this co-production, but we didn't have any finance from the UK side to actually be able to do that. Then the person I was talking with expressed an interest in getting involved as an investor so I later very informally pitched them the story and showed the teaser trailer and they came on board and essentially kick-started the production. They're the reason the film was ever able to happen in the first place because everything else began to fall into place once the first investment was on the table, so I'm incredibly grateful for that. With the second two private investors, it was much more of a kind of business thing where it's an investment and they receive a return if the film makes a profit.

"What's been really humbling is that I think a lot of people have wanted to get involved in *Salvation Has No Name* because it's really trying to *do* something as a film. It's exploring a theme and telling a topical story. Somehow dealing with those kinds of themes has meant people have responded to the intention of the piece and what the film is trying to do from an emotional point of view.

"In an interesting way, the project has grown over the years it's been in development and production in terms of its scale and ambition. People have gotten involved at different stages, more support has come in. I'm certain I will never make any money out of the film, even if it did somehow turn a profit, but we just got to a point where we wanted to do anything we could to get it made. The two most important things for me through this whole process of finding partners have been that the film is the best it can possibly be from a quality and execution point of view and that secondly, as many people as possible can see the film when it's finished. So I suppose the more partners are involved, the more impetus and support there is to get it to festivals, get it on TV and get it out in the world."

Though a long journey occasionally tinged with stress and complications (what animated film isn't?), *Salvation Has No Name* would eventually reach its finish line. Reflecting on the overall experience, Joseph's zen attitude is to focus on the positives – the acts of goodwill and instances of affirmation and validation that nudged the film along throughout, on top of the groundswell of support from followers of the project over social media. Joseph also acknowledges the vital importance of his pairing up with Delaval Films and the working dynamic between himself and producer Loran Dunn.

"Loran is probably my most important collaborator on Salvation. I've worked with producers on commercial stuff before, but I'd always self-produced all my shorts and even some of the commercial stuff. Because I'd studied on Animation Sans Frontières, a lot of which was about budgeting, scheduling, managing teams and developing ideas etc, I'd learned to produce myself over the years just by doing it but it's not something I set out to do necessarily. I have an Associate Producer credit on *Salvation Has No Name*, mainly because I had that animation experience whereas Salvation is Delaval's first animated film. Now Loran's doing two more animations off the back of this! There were a lot of complementary skills in terms of our collaboration, Loran's experience producing shorts, features, specials etc and her connections in the live action scene with the BFI, my experience of budgeting and scheduling animation. So we really worked together on a lot of the production side of things.

"I definitely recommend that filmmakers seek out a producer. Maybe it's reaching out to production companies or maybe it's somebody who you studied with who has a knack for networking and spreadsheets and finding cash down the back of the sofa! Find someone who's work and ambitions and ethics you align with, get a relationship going. It's so useful having somebody else who's invested in the work, somebody who's there figuring things out with you and wanting to get the film made and up on the big screen."

As someone with no small degree of production history herself, to Helen Brunsdon a director/producer relationship, one that can legitimize a project and

Figure 9.9

Salvation Has No Name – Ringmaster on stage ©Delaval Film, image courtesy of Joseph Wallace.

make it more of a serious consideration in the eyes of potential investors, should indeed be actively encouraged.

"Some directors are also used to self-producing. I get that, but I think a producer is important because before a production there's a lot to do, and after a film is finished, there's a lot to do in terms of distributing it. You may not have one dedicated producer (for an independent short), but you should consult a producer and consider how much of this journey you would like them to go on with you. I feel that the brilliant vision of a director can be really enhanced and brought to life further with a really good producer. A producer can come in with solutions, because there are always problems; no matter how big or small a production is, there's always going to be some hurdles to get over."

Digging Deep

When it came to diving in to his fifth short *Ernie Biscuit* (Figures 9.10 and 9.11), Melbourne-based director Adam Elliot eventually had to concede that the funding options that had been in place to enable the completion of such films as his Oscar-winning 2003 short *Harvie Krumpet* and 2009 feature film *Mary and Max* simply did not exist anymore. With the Australian film industry having taken a knock, there were significant compromises to be made should his new short ever be realized. One telling consideration is that *Ernie Biscuit* had not originally been intended as a short film at all, but a second feature.

Self-funding the film was certainly not the plan from the start, especially with the script in its longer-form state. Working alongside executive producer Brian

Figure 9.10

Adam Elliot with *Ernie Biscuit* puppet ©2015 Adam Elliot.

Rosen, whose prior credits included Henry Selick's stop-motion adaptation of *James and the Giant Peach* (1996), the journey to get *Ernie Biscuit* off the ground began shortly after the release of *Mary and Max*. Despite Brian's former position as chief executive of the Australian Film Finance Corporation, this journey proved to be an uphill one.

"I was very lucky to have him on board." Adam recalls with admiration, "He's very proactive, energetic and enthusiastic. He never throws in the towel, he never gives up a battle and he was determined that *Ernie Biscuit* as a feature would one day get fully financed."

Conviction and perseverance are both vital in getting a passion project off the ground but it's important to have enough of a grounded sense of what is and isn't attainable. While it's never the desired outcome to settle for an alternative, knowing when to compromise can save a lot of unnecessary hassle and heartbreak.

"I've always been aware of filmmakers who've been 'developed to death' and I didn't want to be one of those. So I think after about the third year, when we had started to raise some of the money, we had sales agents and distributors all interested and enjoying the script but they all said it wasn't family-friendly enough. We were very lucky to make *Mary and Max*, if we tried to make that film today in Australia there would be no way we'd even get half of the budget, because the average Australian budget has now gone from eight million to one and a half million, and that's just tragic."

As Adam and Brian persevered with the pursuit of feature film funding, the writing incrementally etched itself onto the wall as the proposed budget would continually diminish. Having started at forty million Australian dollars, considered a modest sum to strive for in the world of features, the hypothetical funds eventually dropped to a tenth of that amount. With no viable way to create a film that would remotely resemble Adam's vision as scripted (the final act as written hinged on a dynamic and elaborately animated chase scene) for four million dollars, a rethink was in order. So as not to severely compromise the aesthetic and tone of the film, *Ernie Biscuit* was reinvented as a companion film to *Harvie Krumpet*.

"I said to my executive producer that I was throwing in the towel, that I was going to reinvent the script. I was determined it would get made but I thought it would probably work as a short if I could get the script to under half an hour."

Observing the changing tide of independent film, it occurred to Adam that other filmmakers were beginning to take matters into their own hands in a way they hadn't before. Proactivity and entrepreneurial ingenuity served as an inspiration to Adam, especially when coupled with the realization that concessions need not be a negative thing. In truth the absence of funds and resources and, by association, being beholden to the demands of those who provide either, can be a major positive.

"I thought *It's about time I should stop being one of those filmmakers who just expect government grants. I should start to be a little bit more entrepreneurial and clever, work out other ways of getting a film made.* So *Ernie Biscuit* was an experiment not just in technique but also in financing as well. All my films up until then had been government grants. I don't own *Harvie Krumpet*, I don't own *Mary and Max*, all the royalties from those films go to the government. I only just got the right to *Uncle, Cousin* and *Brother* a few years ago, I thought it would be great if I owned one of my own films so if I sell it to a broadcaster or an airline I get 100% of the royalties. So that's what's happened. I own *Ernie Biscuit* 100% and it's great,

Figure 9.11

Still from *Ernie Biscuit* (Dir. Adam Elliot) ©2015 Adam Elliot.

I don't have to answer to anyone, there's very little paperwork and it's nice to own something that I made!"

A Collective Effort

Depending on the circumstances, crowdfunding can be something of a dirty word. To many, it can be an empowering process to seek out something that excites us and be able to seize the opportunity to play a part in getting it made. It provides a platform to communicate directly with artists on a personal level and it humanizes the production process. With public and general film funds so dishearteningly depleted, it has frequently been a boon to not just independent animation but the animation industry as a whole. So why is there a stigma attached to it nowadays?

As with anything that has been around for more than a handful of years, crowdfunding is just as susceptible to mishandling and misinterpretation as any other form of online transaction. It really should not be underestimated just how much of an undertaking a crowdfunding campaign really is. Even animation studios have been known to struggle with the influx of customer relations if they aren't appropriately prepared.

For this section, I want to take a look at four successfully crowdfunded projects showcasing a range of funding goals. These are:

> Project: Simon's Cat in 'Off to the Vet'
> Creator: Simon's Cat
> Goal amount: £275,850
> Amount raised: £310,734
> Year: 2014
> Platform: IndieGogo
>
> Project: Mister Plastimime
> Creator: Tandem Films
> Goal amount: £33,450
> Amount raised: £34,500
> Year: 2013
> Platform: Kickstarter

Project: Submarine Sandwich
Creator: PES
Goal amount: $30,000
Amount raised: $48,922
Year: 2014
Platform: Kickstarter

Project: The Patsy
Creator: Sam Morrison
Goal amount: £1,500
Amount raised: £2,340
Year: 2012
Platform: Kickstarter

One of the primary benefits of crowdfunding is the ability it affords the creatives at the helm of a project to retain complete creative control. When external funding or investors are brought in, inevitably there will be a proportionate obligation to allow their input on the project itself. Certainly, this can be advantageous if these contributions come from a place of experience or, at the very least, a set of fresh eyes, but that is never a guarantee. On the flip-side, it can be a process that

Figure 9.12

Mr. Plastimime crowdfunding backer poster ©2014 Daniel Greaves.

carries with it the risk of tarnishing an original vision, if not destroying it completely. The desire to eschew this reliance is, as touched upon previously, one of the main lures of independent animation in and of itself.

Simon's Cat, as explored earlier in the book, is something of an animation phenomenon, whose independent roots have led to unforeseeable mass adoration.

Following her association with Tandem Films, producer Emma Burch subsequently went on to work on *Simon's Cat* for the production and campaign management of their crowdfunded short *Off to the Vet*. Her first experience of crowdfunding took place during her tenure at Tandem, overseeing the fundraising of *Mister Plastimime* (Figure 9.12), a mixed-media animated short from Oscar-winning director Daniel Greaves.

"Dan had gotten so far down the line with the film, but had run out of funds. It was frustrating, as we were looking at various public completion or funding schemes, but there were very little in the UK. I had had my eye on crowdfunding for ages, as when Kickstarter was launched in the United States I was researching it for my own film *Being Bradford Dillman*, but they had not launched in the UK at that point. So I suggested Kickstarter to Dan, who was a little reluctant as he didn't want to be asking people for money. After talking about it further, we felt that there was more to lose by *Mr. Plastimime* being shelved half-finished than if we took the plunge and tried crowdfunding. Going with Kickstarter's 'all or nothing' model also meant that if we didn't raise the funds, we didn't owe anything to anyone."

Although *Simon's Cat* found success on IndieGogo, a crowdfunding alternative to Kickstarter, from Emma's perspective their more flexible model – in which all money raised goes to the creator regardless of whether a goal is met,

Figure 9.13

Simon's Cat plush reward for *Off to the Vet* backers ©2014 Simon's Cat Ltd.

and therefore, all obligations to the funders should also be fulfilled – can be more useful for campaigns offering presales of new products (Figures 9.13–9.15).

"If you're trying to make a film and you need a certain amount of money, you might only get £500 out of £25000. You have to plan how you will honour your promises to the people who did support your campaign, by fulfilling the perks or rewards offered, despite not having the funds to complete the project you set out to do. I don't feel that it's worth the risk or the potential stress and work involved."

The risk element was present in both campaigns, even when considering how much more visible and topical *Simon's Cat* is as a franchise. As the audience for Daniel Greaves' *Mr. Plastimime* was less defined, there was more allowance within the campaign itself to be tongue-in-cheek and appeal to a broad range of potential backers. Courting an existing and comparatively voluminous fanbase with the *Simon's Cat* campaign called for a more specific approach.

"*Simon's Cat* was a lot easier because I was better prepared after the *Mr. Plastimime* campaign. We also have a highly engaged audience and a large social reach with 1.5 million likes on Facebook, etc., so in that respect it was a lot easier to put our focus on existing fans. When it came to *Mr. Plastimime*, Dan didn't have an online following when we launched the campaign, so I had to leave no stone unturned to reach people. I was even contacting people I went to school with to help spread the word!

"There were often ten, eleven hour days of constant emailing and trying to think on your feet as to how to reach new people. Then we were really lucky that Kickstarter got behind it and featured it in their newsletter and as one of their Projects of the Day. You cannot guarantee that happening, obviously, and without it I do wonder whether or not we would have made our goal. There was quite a learning curve in terms of what goes into the planning and fulfilling rewards, because you end up setting yourself up as a shop where you manage orders and handle customers. The work that goes into the rewards really shouldn't be underestimated."

Even when factoring in a subscriber base of more than three million, reaching their target proved trickier than anticipated.

"We were expecting far higher numbers of individuals contributing smaller amounts, whereas in fact we had these real diehard fans that just kept putting their hands in their pockets, so in the end our average pledge was higher than Indiegogo's overall average."

Although the final amount raised exceeded the goal amount by over £30,000, the fact that the full tally of contributors came to 10,155 from just 7,500 individuals, roughly 0.3% of their prospective audience of three million should prove sobering.

"Obviously once the campaign's over there's still a lot of administration to be done; the larger the campaign, obviously the more funders you have to keep happy. Coordinating the many combinations of perks has been a bit of a logistical nightmare. Luckily our partners Portico Designs have a warehouse and a production team, so at least they're taking care of all of that, but we're the first point of contact for the funders themselves. So it's a matter of making sure that communication is very clear between *Simon's Cat* and the funders as well as between *Simon's Cat* and Portico."

Customer Etiquette

One of the hardest things to get a handle on for most new to crowdfunding is precisely how you go about directly soliciting funds. For Emma, the answer is the most obvious, yet also most laborious and time-consuming approach:

"Social media is a fantastic tool but direct email communication gets a far higher response. Be personal and make your emails individual and specific to each person, so it takes ages. You *can* send out automated emails but I do think that when you're asking for money, especially if it is people that you have never contacted before or you only know to a certain extent, you need to be personal about it; it's just that it takes so long. Even if you have a template email you still have to personalize each one, even if it's simply adding their first name at the beginning, so just be mindful that there's no mass-mailing everyone. You should think about who you're talking to and how to speak to them. That's why you can't always necessarily have blanket communication across all your target audience, you should tailor it to the different types of people you're trying to reach, categorizing groups if you can. It's about putting in the preparation and planning before you launch which takes time, but improves results."

The human race, delightfully idiosyncratic though we are, are not always the most understanding bunch. Higher profile campaigns always run the risk of

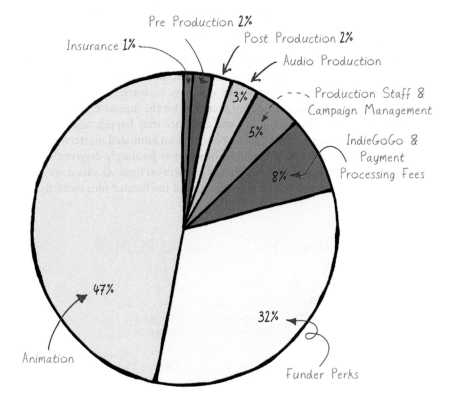

Figure 9.14

Pie-chart from the *Off to the Vet* campaign to clearly communicate to backers how funds would be distributed ©2014 Simon's Cat Ltd.

facing criticism, constructive or otherwise, especially if an audience has their own preconceived notions. The visibility of *Simon's Cat* inevitably carries with it an assumption that it has access to funds that would render crowdfunding redundant.

"There was definitely a backlash to the campaign's target amount. First of all, there's a complete misunderstanding of how much work goes into *Simon's Cat* because it looks so simple. People don't realize that it is traditionally hand-drawn animation, from roughs to clean-up, so there wasn't much of a public understanding of how much production costs. We don't believe in paying people a pittance just because they should feel like they're getting something out of working on a project that's popular; we think people should be paid a fair wage to reflect their skills, so that obviously bumped up our budget. We also believe in delivering quality perks, so a great deal of the money we were trying to raise went to the items that people were then going to receive, including UK postage costs – it's amazing how quickly some things can actually add up."

These cost accumulations boil down to the fact that *Simon's Cat* operates on a business model that puts the public first, in so much as it produces new content on a semi-regular basis to an exceptional standard of animation rarely seen on broadcast television and puts it out into the world for free. Granted, advertising revenue does exist, but not to the extent that would facilitate any project more ambitious than the company's standard fare. A YouTube film produced for somewhere between £10,000 and 20,000 carries with it its own cashflow risks and takes considerable time to break even on.

Another significant oversight often made by those whose crowdfunding campaigns failed is that the obligations to the public don't end when a campaign draws to a close. Some backers may very well have no interest in the film being funded and simply gave their money in exchange for the incentive, as they would any online store. So, while some of your audience may happily accommodate delays in the knowledge that it's for the benefit of an animated masterwork they want to see turn out as good as possible, others may be simply disgruntled that the perk they paid for is not wending its way to them on time. As this stage of the process goes hand in hand with the production of the funded film itself, having

Figure 9.15

Simon's Cat decals perks for *Off to the Vet* backers ©2014 Simon's Cat Ltd.

a campaign manager in place to help deal with such warring stresses is hugely important.

"We always try and respond to emails as quickly as possible, treating it as typical customer service. At peak times, we have been sent three-hundred emails or more in one week, that all need to be replied to. You can't take people's money and ignore them. The main frustration for me at the time was when we had criticism from fellow animators, very talented animators who were saying that they could do it far, far cheaper. These individuals I feel are undermining themselves, their own talent and also the animation industry as a whole by saying how little they are prepared to work for and pay others to collaborate.

"It's really important not to launch until you really feel that you are ready and your diary is clear for the campaign duration. You end up living and breathing crowdfunding when the campaign is live – it probably sounds a bit dramatic, but it took me about two months to recover from the *Simon's Cat* campaign because there was so much riding on it. So much work goes into it that it becomes immensely stressful and immensely personal as well because you feel like you're exposing yourself. It's been extremely important to me that the fans that chose to support us have a positive experience from it, which I hope people have done from both of the campaigns I've managed."

Combined Resources

PES, an animator whose creative process will be scrutinized in Chapter 13, also used crowdfunding to successfully guarantee the completion of his 2014 film *Submarine Sandwich* (Figures 9.16–9.19). The film, in which athletic equipment substitutes deli meat in the construction of the titular sub, is the third of what has been dubbed his "Food Trilogy," following *Western Spaghetti* (2008) and *Fresh Guacamole* (2012). The film drew funding from several sources, firstly his own in the gathering of props and set pieces that were essential to the aesthetic he hoped to achieve.

"The big purchase I had made up to that point was the deli case, I had bought that because I had been watching the eBay space for over a year. I thought it was

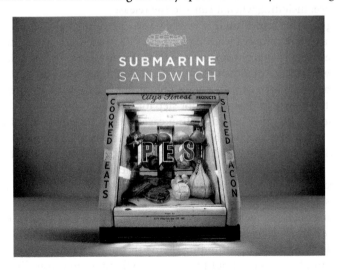

Figure 9.16

Submarine Sandwich crowdfunding promo image ©2014 PES.

gonna be easy to find an old piece of deli equipment that had a bit of personality, that matched my notion of what this cool deli could look like. I always loved the old scales, all that white porcelain and enamel equipment, that real old-school, New York deli feel, and I thought I could go to a junkyard of delis and have my pick of the litter."

It transpired that the deli junkyard of his dreams proved somewhat elusive, and procuring the exact type of deli case required for the film eventually came down to over a year spent scouring eBay listings. When one that conformed precisely to his style demands finally appeared, he bought it instantly, the expense and space it took up in his living room more or less committing him to following through on the film itself.

"I was starting to collect the boxing gloves and the athletic equipment that would go in the case but that process is also one that extended over months. It's not like you can go to one shop and say 'I'd like thirty old boxing bags, all off-white,' I had to shop for those one-by-one and find specific vendors. So that sort of hand-picking was going on, which made me confident to approach Nikon for support."

With a strong track-record of high-quality viral hits under his belt, the camera company became a film sponsor which offset the budgetary concerns associated with purchasing new technical equipment. By timing the proposed launch of the film with a new product release, the final film acts not as product placement but a rather effective demonstration of the technical specs.

"It was fun, like a kid in a candy shop I had all these lenses that I was now able to experiment with."

Although a boon in terms of hardware costs, ultimately Nikon's involvement didn't finance the labor and onscreen materials of the film itself. At this stage, with a great deal in readiness, crowdfunding held the most appeal as a viable option.

"Crowdfunding was something that we had been tossing around for a long time," explains Sarah Phelps, PES's wife and manager. "There was more money available elsewhere, but all that money usually comes with strings. We had both gotten to the point where we were tired of that and PES wanted zero creative compromise, including when it came to the release."

"We agreed that crowdfunding would be an interesting publicity opportunity as well as a different way of working for me." PES says, "In the past, I would just take money from clients or whoever was financing my films, and I would just sort of work away at it for months until one day I would post the film online. So the whole idea of having to explain my vision upfront to people, to get them excited and raise the money for it was a major step for me."

Consistent with other crowdfunding case studies, preparing to solicit funds from fans required a considerable amount of research and forethought. As Sarah recalls, "Going into it we had done a lot of research and knew a lot of the challenges we were going to face. Some of the challenges we ended up facing were unanticipated, so on top of what we knew about was a whole new basket of challenges.

"Figuring out how much to ask for was also a really big deal. Right off the bat, I felt like the biggest decision I made was that we couldn't ask for what we actually *needed*. I feel like with crowdfunding there's this understanding that people are willing to fund your project but they are not willing to fund your life, and that what you get in return is your art project, but you have to figure out how to support yourself. So I decided right there off the bat that we were going to do that.

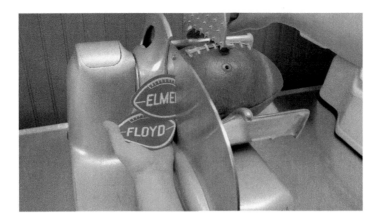

Figure 9.17

Still from *Submarine Sandwich* (Dir. PES) ©2014 PES.

"The second decision I made was we can't ask for how much this film actually *costs* because, while people who understand stop motion and production know how much these things cost and how long they take, when it came to anyone else there was a line I didn't want to cross. Beyond that line people would have thought *There's kids starving out there and you need* how much *money to make a one-and-a-half minute film?* So it was just trying to balance that."

Another issue in PES's mind was the idea that the film's premise and twist would have to be revealed months before anyone might see the final film, which ran the risk of diminishing its impact. "In the past I think I would normally say 'Well, it won't be a surprise anymore! Why would I want to tell anyone about it?' I'm also very suspicious about creating expectations, and with crowdfunding, once you start telling people your idea, you open yourself up to people's expectations."

What makes PES's take on crowdfunding notable is that his experience of it is one of a number of completely separate funding scenarios that have brought his "Food trilogy" into being. The first entry, 2008s *Western Spaghetti* received financial aid from Mike Judge, known to many as the creator of MTV's Beavis and Butt-Head, in exchange for an exclusive launch as part of The Animation Show, a touring program he curated with fellow independent animator Don Hertzfeldt. In 2012, the second film, *Fresh Guacamole*, was commissioned by the cable network Showtime as part of their Short Stories series, a scheme that also commissioned original work from animation directors Bill Plympton and Cyriak.

"All three of these situations have allowed me to make films without making any creative compromises, so there's no real difference in that respect. Crowdfunding was a headscratcher because it was a really positive experience and it is wonderful to be a little bit more connected to the fans but it's so much more work than just making a film! You really have to take into consideration that it exponentially creates work. I try really hard to focus on the quality of the film but it really is like running a pop-up business for six months."

Another perceivable advantage of the crowdfunding process is the ways in which incentivizing can be another creative outlet, rather than a chore. When it came to the rewards for the Submarine Sandwich campaign, PES used it as an opportunity to indulge a desire to experiment with building a merchandise element around the project.

Figure 9.18

Submarine Sandwich model – one of the available backer rewards ©2014 PES.

"It doesn't really just come from the idea of wanting to make money, it's more that I studied printmaking for four years, I love making prints and shirts, so crowdfunding was an outlet for some of my other creative interests."

What makes *Submarine Sandwich* especially noteworthy as a crowdfunding case study is its near-immediate success, reaching its target well within the first week of the campaign. While this would seem on the surface to be a dream come true, pragmatism on Sarah's part was necessary to keep their obligations from spiraling out of control.

"It just burst out of the gate, got picked up by a lot of blogs, was a Kickstarter project of the day, then after we hit our goal it just ticked up slowly for the last three weeks of the campaign. I very quickly saw certain reward categories were more lucrative than others, percentage-wise. Plus you have to subtract the cost of taxes and shipping rewards. The most popular were the t-shirts and screen-prints, which were the most expensive for us, so if we'd have gotten another $10,000–30,000 in backing, we'd have almost directly relative costs yet it would look like we had more money. So after we reached our goal, one of the decisions that I made was to back off."

This means of accompanying the release of his film with an array of products that, to those who missed out during the campaign itself, would still be purchasable online, was a bonus unique to the crowdfunding process, as merchandising options are rarely if ever available to creators if corporate funding has much of a role to play. Indeed, when the same idea was floated to the network during the production of *Fresh Guacamole*, it didn't bear much fruit. Logically, it stands to reason that if a channel has paid for content, they will rather audiences click through to other such content rather than to an independent merchandiser. Beyond the excuse to flex his product-making bent, the positives of his relatively low-key campaign has opened PES to more direct interaction with his fanbase.

"Obviously having people talk about your film for four-to-six months before it comes out is really cool and, frankly, something I didn't do too well in the past. When I got the money for my films I'd work in the dark and put them online, there wasn't much of being in touch with the people who really care about the work and getting to know them a little, so that was a nice addition of that relationship. So all three situations worked out, they seemed to be a bit of the evolution of how things are moving."

Figure 9.19

Still from *Submarine Sandwich* (Dir. PES) ©2014 PES.

Chances are that your means and resources are not equatable with those of the *Simon's Cat* empire, nor as long-established in the indie world as PES. So what makes crowdfunding a reasonable option to the less visible, or those just starting out?

Ultimately, it comes down to perspective and a healthy, realistic sense of self.

What do you think your film and, by extension, your talent is worth?

Be honest. Take the time to systematically break down what your production costs will be, subtract that amount from what you first came up with and evaluate again based on what's left. Now think hard about what you've read so far in this section and ask yourself if it's really within your capabilities. If you have a crewed studio, or a devoted fanbase, or a team of hard-working friends who think the world of you, then certainly your options are going to be more open. But if you're going solo, which is far from uncommon in the independent animation world, it may be practical to bring your level of ambition a little closer to the ground.

Sam Morrison, whose approach to story we looked at earlier in the book, managed to round out his *Rocket Science* trilogy through crowdfunding. Above all, the Jack Hersey films are personal, auteur film projects whose primary function (alongside being entertaining) has been to further establish Sam as a writer and director. While his short film work has been successful, they do not share the same in-built audience factor as PES or *Simon's Cat*, nor are they made more visible by an Oscar-win association, as with Daniel Greaves. The crowdfunding option was therefore approached from a place of relative anonymity.

"We've used crowdfunding a couple of times and found it helpful, but set our sights reasonably low without doing any big promotional stuff." Naturally, as Sam reasons, a lower goal amount necessitates lower demands and far less pressure that would needlessly distract from the end goal of getting the film itself made. "We just sent out little reminders through social media to people for the duration of the Kickstarter campaign, sending out little reminders on Facebook and Twitter and that sort of thing, and just managed to get a couple thousand together for *The Patsy*." (Figure 9.20)

Even considering this low-key approach, your accountability to your audience isn't ruled out entirely.

Figure 9.20

Stills from *The Patsy* (Dir. Sam Morrison) – one available incentive to backers was the option of having their names incorporated into the film ©2013 Evil Genius Ltd.

"We realized that it's quite a lot of work when you've finished your film and sent your pledges. There is a whole new wave of stuff, which you should have anticipated really because you wrote them yourself, but it costs money and takes a lot of time. We did them all, even though I think we've been late some of the time, but we do get them done, and because of the people we've got money off tend to be friends, family or friends of friends, then nobody thankfully has been too angry about us being a little bit late.

"I knew it would be a sort of realistic way to raise a couple of grand, and because we were putting in some of our own money, basically funding the film, crowdfunding sort of topped it up and made it viable for Ian and myself to work on it for a long time. We would have been below the minimum wage or something ridiculous, so crowdfunding just bumped the overall budget to the point where it became more workable for us, just because we couldn't work that long for that amount of money and survive."

To wrap up, here are some important campaign page essentials as outlined by Emma Burch:

- "Images always go a long way. I do actually feel that we didn't have enough development material on the site. When it comes to film or anything creative, people want to see the product that they're actually backing."

- "Certainly showing where the money's going to be spent in a pie chart is quite sobering for the fans."
- "You have to be short, sharp but informative – make sure that you don't repeat yourself by going over the same facts."
- "In terms of the tone of the writing, it can be very tricky to get right. Sometimes you need to step back from it and return to it later, re-read and see how you would feel if you were reading it for the first time."

10

Keeping It Real

Getting a project off the ground is a wonderful feeling. With a script or concept in place, officially being able to categorize a project as "in production" is the first step of a complex, rewarding, exciting – and long – journey. A very long journey, in fact. Long, long road ahead. Good grief it's long. Why did nobody say how *long* it would be?

This is the point where any lingering romantic notions you may have about an animated production just being able to come together are cruelly extinguished. When you're in it, you're in deep – and possibly with funders and a crew to answer to. In this chapter and the next, we'll look at how some of independent animation's best and brightest have soldiered through, whether going it alone, dealing with creative concessions, managing teams or being literally separated from their co-director by the ocean. Yes, depending on the type of project you have set yourself, it can be a long road ahead, but everyone has to go down it.

Having had to strip down the ambition of his feature-cum-short film *Ernie Biscuit* (Figures 10.1 and 10.2), Adam Elliot was insistent on being directly involved in virtually all areas of production, going back not just to the auteur roots of his original trilogy *Uncle*, *Cousin* and *Brother* but delving into entirely unexplored independent territory. This approach to the film was a stark contrast to his previous project, the 2009 feature film *Mary and Max*, going from overseeing a large crew to essentially a one-man operation.

"I wanted to do everything, not because I am a megalomaniac but because I felt that there were certain parts of the process with my previous films I didn't have a full understanding of. I wanted to learn more about producing a digital film and strengthen the areas of the filmmaking process I'd always felt were weak

DOI: 10.1201/9781003214717-10

Figure 10.1

Adam Elliot on the set for *Ernie Biscuit* ©2015 Adam Elliot.

points for me – editing and sound were areas where I felt very inadequate – so by the end of the film, I'd have a better understanding. Now I certainly know a lot more about editing, things like 5.1 digital surround sound, DCPs, digital cameras, megapixels."

Though the familiar funding avenues that had allowed his five films prior to be made had dried up, corporate sponsorship did assist the production in some measure. Making a deal with Apple to produce the film entirely using their products – Final Cut Pro, Aperture and Motion primarily – covered the hardware and software costs.

"I animated blind in many ways, I just had a Leica camera, one lens, three lights, some plasticine, wire and paint. I had no fully articulated armatures, I didn't have any mouldmaking, there's no airbrushing, just three paintbrushes, three jars of paint and that was it! I had a very limited palette if you want to call it that, which was great, it was very liberating having less choices, just having the basics. It forced me to focus more on what was important."

Toward the end of the production, unforeseen personal issues reared their head and demanded Adam's attention. As a consequence, the planned completion date was not met on time, and while certain festivals were understanding enough – and appreciative of his sterling track record – to extend their deadlines, the post-production was not afforded the time and care Adam wished it could have been.

"The biggest regret I have is that the post-production was severely compromised and rushed and that hasn't sat well with me. But that's life, a lot of post-production is rushed and you make mistakes. I would definitely get a sound designer in earlier and allocate more money towards the sound mix – I also would like to have spent more time with my actor, I just would've loved another couple of months of shooting time. I lost my focus and I had to make very quick decisions, such as having to finish off the editing of the film in only two weeks instead of having a month. Some of these things were out of my control but some of them were in my control, so you learn a lot of lessons. Having said that, in all of my films there have been areas where we've had to compromise. With every film I've made I've had to think laterally and be a bit of a renegade in terms of

10. Keeping It Real

Figure 10.2

Still from *Ernie Biscuit* (Dir. Adam Elliot) ©2015 Adam Elliot.

how to get the film completed. With every film I've learned lessons and learned from my mistakes."

Moving forward while having the wisdom of hindsight (more on this later) is doubtless the best option for filmmakers eager to continue to produce new work. Sometimes, a project executed badly is worth revisiting (as with Robert Grieves's *Sausage* discussed in Chapter 3), but when it comes to a largely successful project with mere kinks, most of which only visible to the directors themselves, the best way to apply these lessons learned is toward future works.

Manual Labor

Stop-motion itself is arguably the most difficult animation medium with which to achieve independent success. Not to denigrate 2D, CG or any other approach that requires similarly vast reserves of skill, patience and effort, but the fact remains that digital software has advanced so tremendously that the outright physical labor of animation, not to mention material costs, has rapidly diminished. That being said, stop-motion is certainly benefiting from recent technological advancements that make it increasingly viable with each passing year. On top of this, its relevance as a storytelling medium has barely diminished, flying in the face of prediction. During the making of his student short *Uncle* in 1996, Adam was assured that by producing his film using plasticine, he was "pursuing a dying art form." With the advent of Pixar features and the rise of CG processes ousting stop-motion, animatronics and similarly practical processes from the world of visual effects around that time, it most likely seemed a reasonable theory that within five years the medium would have died off altogether. Cut to twenty years later and, factoring in the peaks and valleys any filmmaking medium will experience, stop-motion remains ever-present in the industry. Mainstream television shows and features are still proving lucrative and critically successful, competing for Academy Awards alongside their digitally animated brethren.

"I think stop motion is alive and well," insists Adam. "Digital cameras and digital technology have liberated stop motion animators, we can now see what we're doing and we can predict what we are doing a lot better. There's software out there that are wonderful tools for stop motion animators, who can go into their studios now with a little bit more confidence. They know that they can make a stop-motion film for a third of what it used to cost.[1] That's mainly because of the 'death' of celluloid and that processing costs have just vanished. So we can edit ourselves, not that that's necessarily a good thing – I still believe you need a good editor – but it's far more egalitarian now to make a film."

For many younger animators presently working in the industry, an era in which digital processes take care of the areas of production that would have proved physically or financially challenging is all they have ever known. There's something to be said for investigating the production processes and materials of old that these digital shortcuts derived from, especially as regards stop-motion. For filmmakers such as Adam Elliot, whose body of work spanned the transitional period in which analog switched over to digital, the benefits of having had feet in both camps are clear.

"The technology has absolutely been a wonderful, timely event, and I wonder whether if I was graduating today, having not ever experienced an analogue world or a celluloid world, I would have had the same career path. I think I'm lucky in many ways that I was on that crossover period of analogue to digital, I got to edit my first two films with a Steinbeck, I spliced the film, I sticky-taped it together, I got to mix my sound on magnetic tape, so I learned the traditional techniques and also watched these new techniques come into the workflows and the pipelines, and then watch stop-motion become popular. I mean, when I started animating, I was considered an odd person and nerdish, geekish, whatever you want to call it, but now stop-motion is quite popular. It's almost fashionable!"

One artist whose attitude toward stop-motion lines up with this observation is Kirsten Lepore, director of *Bottle, Move Mountain* (Figures 10.3–10.5)

Figure 10.3

Kirsten Lepore working on the set of *Move Mountain* ©2013 Kirsten Lepore. Image courtesy of the artist.

10. Keeping It Real

and *Hi Stranger*. Having produced an impressive array of her own films using the medium, she's especially grounded regarding the production realities stop-motion animators must face: "You have to be willing to work your butt off. Stop-motion takes tremendous patience, dedication and time, and if you're one of the rare few that can take on a whole production alone or with a small team, you need to be the type of person that can meet a deadline, be reliable, and have a clear vision."

In Kirsten's view, the trickiest requirements when it comes to stop-motion production (especially if one person is at the helm) are extensive knowledge of cameras, lighting, rigging, fabricating, animating, clean-up post and a locked-down, highly controlled space in which to shoot. "I've worked most of my life on learning as much as I can in all these areas and more. There have been many times someone has told me not to bother learning some very technical thing – instead just to pay a professional to do it down the line – but that attitude just made me want to learn it more. Almost all of those things I'd been discouraged from learning have popped up in random jobs and saved me tons of money since I already knew how to do them myself."

For the most part, Kirsten handles every area of her production process herself. Though this ultimately saves time in having to communicate her ideas to other people, she acknowledges that the limitations of her own skillset can be a significant downside.

Figure 10.4

Armature building for *Move Mountain* (Dir. Kirsten Lepore) ©2013 Kirsten Lepore. Image courtesy of the artist.

"It can be both exhausting and rewarding. Lately I have been much more interested in collaborating and having a studio, since you are able to accomplish much more in a shorter time span, as well as achieving a product of much higher production value." Her current setup is a far preferable arrangement to the circumstances of her student short *Bottle*. Though massively acclaimed, the shoot was far from smooth sailing and plagued by "major issues" throughout. "There were unforeseen obstacles at every step of the way: The snow wasn't packable, the sand would crumble past a half meter, my camera remote broke, seagulls constantly stole my props, I was covered in shortening and lard (part of puppet construction), my car smelled like dead crab, I couldn't take a pee break for the full 8 hrs of shooting, et al. To say making the film was challenging would be a gross understatement, but somehow it still got made."

By contrast, *Move Mountain*, made in the far more reliable indoor environment of her studio, allowed for more by way of experimentation with new materials and an easier production timeframe that afforded her six months in which to educate herself on the mold-making and casting processes for silicones and urethanes. "Constructing and rigging the flexible trees and the clear flexible waterfall pieces were the biggest challenge. I have an entire binder where I would document my process and record data about which castings worked and failed, slowly improving with each prototype.

"I mostly experiment as I go (sometimes to the detriment of the project), because I'm usually too eager to jump into building and shooting to spend the amount of time I should be doing R&D beforehand. *Move Mountain* did require a fair amount of testing in the pre-production phase to figure out how I would even construct certain things – but regardless of how much you plan, there are always problems you will have to solve in the middle of production."

Though Kirsten Lepore's star was already well on the rise, the call of Late Night Work Club[2] (an international collective of indie animators, the origins of which we will expand on in a later chapter) – indeed, the overall spirit of the project – was something she felt drawn to; the feeling was mutual.

"For the first edition of Late Night Work Club, they had actually asked me if I wanted to be involved initially, but at that time I was still in school and in the middle of a million projects, so it wasn't going to work out, timewise. I didn't even know what it was going to be at that point. Then when *Ghost Stories* came out, I saw it and I was kicking myself for not making time for it, because it was just so amazing. The films are so incredible and made such a splash that when they hit me up for the second edition, I was over the moon that they'd asked me again."

Landing an episode of the enormously popular Cartoon Network series *Adventure Time*, in which Kirsten reimagined the world of the show in stop-motion for the season seven episode *Bad Jubies* (which she also co-wrote and co-directed), ultimately proved to be a significant demand on her available time. When Late Night Work Club fans were treated to an early teaser trailer roughly a year before the finished version of *Strangers* came out, there would be some disparities when compared to the final product, including a glimpse of what would be Kirsten's contribution. Although the film we see in *Strangers* is a different piece entirely, her own work and life circumstances ultimately determined that her entry would have to be rethought from scratch, despite production having already begun on the initial idea.

"I hadn't completely kiboshed it to the point of getting rid of the sets I built, because the sad thing is I spent months working on that first film. I had the

Figure 10.5

Casting and molding characters for *Move Mountain* (Dir. Kirsten Lepore) ©2013 Kirsten Lepore. Image courtesy of the artist.

whole thing totally storyboarded, ready to go, I fabricated all the puppets, I built I think two different full sets and I shot two scenes. Then when I came back after *Adventure Time*, I sort of lost my initial motivation for making that first film, because it was really motivated by what I was going through at that very moment. I felt like all of those emotions and feelings had passed, so it didn't really feel totally relevant to me anymore."

There is something to be said for striking while the proverbial iron is hot, and most prolific creatives will be able to recall a fair few projects that have petered out after that initial burst of enthusiasm or motivation passes them by. This, of course, is compounded by the least appealing quality of animation production – that it takes so damn long to do. For Kirsten, the closing of one door ultimately led to the opening of another, one that would unexpectedly take the indie animation world by storm.

"I'm definitely not the type of person that likes to give up on things halfway, especially if you've made all the assets and you've done most of the work. But I couldn't bring myself to do it in the timeframe I had allotted, so I went totally in another direction with something that felt much more on the tip of my brain at that moment. I had just finished going to therapy for a year and I was all about mindfulness. I was doing some meditation and I was thinking about all these things, but I was also just exhausted at the prospect of making another film."

Out of this cornucopia of feelings came *Hi Stranger*, the closing film of the anthology that presents a simple yet immediately engaging concept: a serene, nude, pale, man-like creature (voiced by Kirsten's *Story from North America*

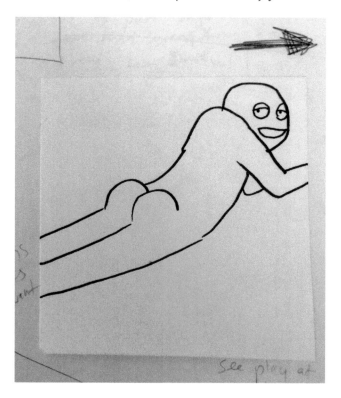

Figure 10.6

Original character doodle by Kent Osborne. Image courtesy of Kirsten Lepore.

10. Keeping It Real

collaborator Garrett Davis) offers platitudes and reassurances to the viewer. The origins of *Hi Stranger*'s concept came from Kirstin's stint on *Adventure Time*.

"I was trying to come up with a new idea, because that old, longer idea just wasn't going to happen. I was going through old sketchbooks to see if I had jotted anything down when I found this sticky note that Kent Osborne – who's the head of story on *Adventure Time* – had had on his desk during our one and only writers' meeting." (Figure 10.6)

Aware of her interest in his doodle (of a similarly strange, naked man lying down and looking over his shoulder coquettishly at the viewer), Kent offered it as a gift to Kirsten, who would keep it in a sketchbook where it would stay, forgotten, until she eventually unearthed it during her hunt for new ideas.

"I asked Kent if I could adapt this character, and he was totally cool with it, which was awesome. So I changed the design a little bit and sort of created a personality for this simple doodle. That's where the design came from, basically." (Figure 10.7)

Originally, Kirsten had hoped to create a fully articulated silicone puppet for the repurposed main character of *Hi Stranger*, although time and budget determined that economic approaches were required wherever possible. Instead, Kirsten used polymer clay over a wire armature, a material chosen for a distinctly translucent shininess that distinguishes it from plasticine. For an elaborate vista cutaway shot, Kirsten went with a similarly lo-fi route using paper cups, crumpled up paper and fluorescent paint with a black light to rather striking overall effect. To an even greater degree than its predecessor *Move Mountain*, the film proves on the whole just how important strength of idea can be in the face of a low budget, something that many of the best independent animators out there are able to embrace. Indeed, in Kirsten's opinion, independent filmmaking and personal projects are vital to artists.

"I think it's probably the most important thing for most animation artists to keep that flame alive, basically making your own work in some way or another. Sometimes it won't happen for years, sometimes it's really difficult to get something out. But I think it's what keeps you sharp as an artist and what keeps you

Figure 10.7

Kirsten Lepore's revised design for *Hi Stranger*'s protagonist. Image courtesy of Kirsten Lepore.

Figure 10.8

Still from *Hi Stranger* (Dir. Kirsten Lepore) ©2016 Kirsten Lepore.

experimenting. You feel like you always have to express yourself in some way. So doing those things, I think, is really important. I think it's what defines someone as an artist."

Following the release of *Strangers* in November 2016, Kirsten would go on to release *Hi Stranger* online as a standalone short in March 2017 (Figure 10.8); it immediately went viral in a massive way, amassing millions of views across Vimeo, YouTube, and inevitably, the assortment of Facebook pages that would appropriate its bizarre appeal for themselves. Further cementing its viral status was a parody segment on *The Late Show with Stephen Colbert* in the US less than a month after its release, substituting the film's main character with a 2D animated caricature of then-President Donald Trump. Certainly, beyond the predictable layer of befuddled viewers, it's clear that the film has a resonance to it that has spoken to audiences, going to show that the films can have just as much of a life of their own outside of the anthology as within it. Similar degrees of individual success can be seen in the standalone postings and international festival success of other Late Night Work Club films including Alex Grigg's *Phantom Limb*, Sean Buckelew's *Lovestreams*, Nicolas Ménard's *Wednesday with Goddard* and Charles Huettner's *The Jump* to name just a few. Despite not being a full realization of her initial concept, *Hi Stranger* clearly proved to be a worthwhile endeavor, one which further established the director's already-glowing reputation. In part, it was the informal pressure of remaining involved with the *Strangers* anthology that bolstered Kirsten to follow through.

"I definitely function well when I have deadlines. That's why I was always making films in school. I do really well when someone above me is telling me 'do this by a certain time,' because I'm that kind of person where, if you give me a deadline, I've gotta hit it. But if I'm left to my own devices, I'll probably be lazy and float away and go watch movies and things."

"It was definitely a struggle to get a film out on time, even though we had probably two and a half years, but work happens; *Adventure Time* happened in the middle of that and it just becomes difficult to get personal work done. But I still wanted to make this happen somehow, on the one hand because I really wanted to make a new film but also because I didn't want to disappoint these cool people that are part of this club. So I'm glad I finally got to. It feels good to be in an anthology and in the company of such talented indie animators."

Kirsten's occasional collaborator Garrett Michael Davis has his own perspectives on how his methods of producing his auteur work differ from more traditional production pipelines.

- "The real advantage of a studio pipeline is that it includes a step that deposits funds into your bank account. And also it allows you to focus on one aspect of the process rather than having to wear all the hats yourself. It's nice to only have to think about storyboards, or only animation, or only design. Thinking about all of those things is very challenging, but people everywhere are doing it all the time."
- "The present ease and accessibility of technology makes it very simple if you use your ingenuity. You don't need a studio. You really just need access to a computer. You don't need a fancy camera if you have a phone. You don't have to storyboard. Werner Herzog has some devastating things to say about storyboards, and with a much more expanded view on filmmaking in general. If you watch his films, you know he is involved in something that goes way beyond filmmaking."
- "That said, working in a studio pipeline is just like being in school, or boot camp. You learn a lot and you sharpen your skills to a very high degree. I'm an example of the kind of artist I would never think could work happily at a studio, yet I have and I do. But to me, it's more about taking everything you learn there and then applying it in way more interesting ways in your own projects."
- "I throw off the illusory shackle that is 'being on model.' If you are doing frame by frame animation, that means every frame is a different drawing, and a character is going to morph and change and grow just like a living thing. I do try to place limitations on that to some degree, but in my opinion the only reason to 'stay on model' is if someone is paying you to do so. Even then I find it excruciatingly painful and my whole being rebels against it."
- "Animation is tedious enough as it is. Japanese artists are masters of fearlessly representing characters in wildly different ways even within the same scene, but nobody says 'wait, for a second there I didn't recognize that character, I'm lost: shut it off!' when that happens. This art is supreme illusion, illusion of movement, illusion of change. People care so much about consistency, about reality, but personally I can always tell when I'm watching an animation. I don't confuse it with real life, no matter how high-res the CG is."
- "I'm interested in bringing in a much wider range of things to animation, to the point where it becomes a kind of life philosophy. I get ideas from dreams. I use collage in many different ways, a method which has been around since at least Picasso but still seems untouchable to some people."
- "I don't feel guilty about rotoscoping something if I want to. I pack too much stuff into a scene to even see, I include things that are 'distracting,' I don't want people to 'get it' on the first watch. I want them to watch it a million times and see something new every time."

Outside Assistance

While Sam Morrison's *Rocket Science* trilogy of films conformed to convention as far as his and co-writer Andrew Endersby's approach to scriptwriting, the animation process itself proved to be an altogether different affair, relying on a small crew with the bulk of the animation taken on by Ian Hickman and Sam himself.

"Obviously the actors contributed a good deal as well, but there certainly wasn't a big production team that moved into place. Basically I was Producer, Editor, Director and Animator but I don't think I credited myself as I don't like those films where you see the same name, over and over. I'm not *averse* to seeing my name, it's good, but it felt like a two-man band once we got past the voice record – essentially it's just myself and Ian from then on, with Andrew periodically looking in to see how things are progressing."

Other assistance did come in the form of students in search of work experience, thanks largely to ties with local universities, though some made the approach of their own volition.

"I generally get people contacting me every year from the Bristol School of Animation at the University of the West of England. I usually say 'Yes', as long as there's something for them to do. I don't like people just to come in if there's nothing happening in the studio, because then it's really boring for them and I feel really self-conscious about it as well. So if there's a project they can work on, such as a commercial then they can get involved, and I can pay them as well. If it's a short film then there probably won't be money in it, so they have to decide if it's good for work experience. I sort of like to feel like I'm helping people out and not exploiting them; if there's money in the production they work on, they'll get some of it, and if there isn't they'll get some experience."

Kirsten Lepore's *Move Mountain* benefited greatly from artistic collaboration for one of the film's most elaborate and appealing sequences, in which the wounded protagonist hallucinates a mountainside dance party (Figure 10.9). The assortment of characters who appear in this sequence was designed by fellow animators including Garrett Davis, David OReilly, Mikey Please and Julia Pott.

Figure 10.9

Still from *Move Mountain* (Dir. Kirsten Lepore) ©2013 Kirsten Lepore.

"Using friends' characters for the dance scene in *Move Mountain* was part of the concept from the conception of the idea and also one of the things I was most excited about executing. All of the contributors are close friends who work in animation – many of whom were attending CalArts alongside me. For those people who lived nearby, I threw a puppet making party where we all sat around, drank, and designed and built armatures for our puppets. I finished the puppets from that point on, using their initial sketch as reference. For the few people who were overseas, I either created the puppet for them or borrowed their existing puppet. It was a fun challenge, but it also served a larger purpose in the conceptual scheme of the film."

The idea of international collaboration need not just be limited to the occasional contribution to a film, especially in an era where networked production pipelines are common and online transfers of entire project files or fully rendered footage files are the work of minutes. Even a film whose entire visual production is based across the world from one of its directors can be achieved, as was the case when it came to the majority of the production of Melissa Johnson and Robertino Zambrano's *Love in the Time of March Madness*. Taking place with the two directors living on opposite sides of the Pacific Ocean, the animation itself was made entirely by the in-house team at Robertino's KAPWA Studioworks in Sydney, while Melissa contributed to its direction from Los Angeles.

"I feel like Skype almost deserves a credit in the film, in terms of how we actually used it for communication – and as a digital media management tool – when you don't actually have the luxury of being in the same room with the other person for almost the entire time," says Melissa of the team's unconventional setup. "I've been conditioned as an athlete to be on teams my entire life and a lot of the fun of that is getting to banter with people, and go back and forth in real-time, in person. So it was a challenge. We definitely surmounted it but it was hard dealing at a greater distance, when you have to do a lot more coordination.

"You have to figure out the time zones and when you can talk, so I think that the only way to get a project like this done, with the kinds of challenges we have

Figure 10.10

Character designs for *Phantom Limb* ©2013 Alex Grigg.

in terms of distance and no budget, was to be obsessed with doing it and getting it done, there's just no-one behind you cracking a whip; you *are* your own whip! You have to just continue it and finish it to that high degree, or the sacrifices you've made so far are for naught."

While working on his segment for the first Late Night Work Club anthology *Ghost Stories*, director Alex Grigg was motivated to bring on other talents for certain areas of the film that he felt were not his strengths, as well as a crew of animation generalists who would be able to expedite the overall turnaround time of the film by taking on shots simultaneously. Despite the fact that *Phantom Limb* (Figures 10.10–10.13) was essentially an unfunded personal project, the strength of its premise and that of the overall anthology proved to be an appealing enough incentive for people to volunteer their time and skills.

"I think everyone had their own individual reasons for being excited about it. If I wanted to work with someone I'd just email a friend and say 'Hey I've got this film project, would you be interested in doing a couple of shots?' While just really defining the scope of their involvement and trying to make sure they have enough ownership that it can be fun and they can really flex their muscles on the shot."

Being candidly upfront and respecting the time people are giving to your project are both vital. Even though it is potentially an opportunity for people to refine certain skillsets, try something new, embellish their showreel and potentially get exposure, they are still giving time and expending effort for your benefit in a way that, in any other circumstances, would have a monetary value. As such, it's important that everybody who gets involved with the project is on the same page and has a clear idea of exactly what they might get out of it as well as what the plan of action is for the film once completed. As with any creative collaborative effort, it is also important to have a clear idea of what precisely the project will

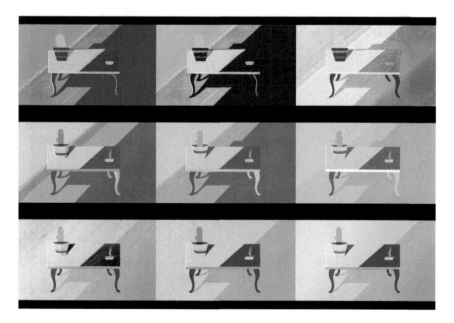

Figure 10.11

Phantom Limb color boards by Colin Bigelow. Image courtesy of Alex Grigg.

10. Keeping It Real

be and how it will come together. For Alex, *Phantom Limb* proved a far better attempt than any that had come before due to its forethought and focus.

"I think when I first started trying to collaborate with people ages ago, we'd come into it all as equals and we'd say 'Hey let's make something together!' And we'd sort of 'um' and 'ah' while being really polite to each other and no one would actually make anything. So I found that in this situation, giving a really clearly defined role and giving it a defined timeline saw me more committed to the project. I knew that I didn't want to waste that time, so there was no chance that I could *not* finish the film, because other people had put their time into it for free and that would do them a disservice."

The end result was undoubtedly successful, and bringing on additional talent to help realize the film was beneficial in many respects, but along the way the value of just how much contributors were actually helping the production along came into question. Although it could not have been predicted, during the latter stages having a crew in place would actually add unnecessary complications and slow things down.

"Eventually I would be at a point where I could just largely do it myself, so in the end there were parts where it probably was more work to get someone else to do a couple of shots than it would have been for me to just do it, just because I needed everything to be on style."

In spite of this, the primary benefit – and the one that makes the entire endeavor worth the effort – is the opportunity that collaboration creates to observe the working processes of others whose skillsets lie in different production areas than our own and learn from them.

"There was a bunch of stuff, like sound and backgrounds, that I really needed people on and I will continue to use people for that stuff. I worked with Colin Bigelow, who is a phenomenal designer and helped with the backgrounds in the early stages. It's hard to learn from someone that good, you sit in awe of them. It did mean that future projects were really easy to work together on as well, I just

Figure 10.12

Phantom Limb production spreadsheet. Image courtesy of Alex Grigg.

knew how to work with him. The process that he uses, this iteration process I have sort of transferred onto other designers that I've worked with, as it's a great way to work and it's how I now prefer to work. So I did learn a lot from him for sure, but not how to do his designs, his are too good."

One major detail that separates many independent animation productions from those that have been funded or commissioned is the nature of the production management itself. While in a larger sense, the *Ghost Stories* project was produced and managed by Scott Benson, who frequently maintained contact with all filmmakers in order to make sure each segment was on track, within the shorts themselves it was largely down to the director to take on the producer role as well.

"It didn't feel too unnatural to me, in this case, because there isn't a lot of money involved. The only people who got paid were the cleanup artists, because there was nothing to be gained creatively from that, so I wasn't going to ask them to do that for free. Basically I offered the rate that I got paid when I was doing my first animation job, which isn't very much but it's something, I guess, for students who weren't working at all. As far as producing, it came down to making a big spreadsheet and keeping track of shots and shot numbers, making sure I've got all the assets. In the end it was taking up half my day each day, working with artists and making sure they all had their stuff, which is a lot of energy, to sink into that."

The nature of small-scale auteur film production is often such that, when a larger team is formed, it is actually beneficial for the director and producer roles to not be mutually exclusive. While a competent producer is certainly capable of maintaining the artistic vision of the director, when they are one and the same person it's automatically easier to communicate precisely what is required of the visuals, style and tone. Being able to engage with each specialist team member firsthand with no buffer proved a boon to the production.

"The actual process was fine, I would actually feel weird if someone else was dealing with artists that were giving me help for free. I'd rather reach out to them myself and not have them at arm's length.

"We had some really strong design documents and animation guidelines for the process, the feedback, stuff like that. I really like systems, I use them a lot in my commercial directing, making sure everyone knows when feedback is and everyone knows what they're expected to show. I think that lets people relax and focus on what they need to focus on. Generally it was fine, sometimes Skyping, mostly email, a lot of draw-overs. I just let everyone have my Dropbox password and we shared a Dropbox, it was cool."

The end result of *Phantom Limb* is a film that feels like a singular vision, which far from being a slam on the contributing talents who brought it together is a testament to their ability to consistently maintain the directorial intent of the film. There is, however, no delusion that a film so successful in its execution can, without funding, simply come together without massive sacrifice to time and spirit. Though it was a worthwhile endeavor and an incredibly strong directorial debut, there will always be a personal toll.

"I kind of destroyed myself, sleep-wise, which is definitely one of the things that makes it hard to dive into it again. It's one of the reasons it would be nice to have funding, it's just that it takes a lot of pressure off that, having to be the bottleneck for everything."

Figure 10.13

An example of the notes animators (James Hatley in this instance) working on *Phantom Limb* would be supplied with. Image courtesy of Alex Grigg.

Work Ethic

The drive and self-determination that led to the successful completion of Robert Morgan's *Bobby Yeah* (Figures 10.14–10.16) sans funding or a rigid deadline goes back to his filmmaking roots when he was working on his student short *The Man in the Lower Left Hand Corner of the Photograph*.

"In my last year of college I just really put my head down. Something I just knew – and I think this is good advice to students generally – is to spend your student years trying to make a good film. It's the most important currency you can have when you leave, to show you can make a good film."

This attitude certainly paid dividends. The film performed well at festivals, earning top prizes, funding for subsequent shorts and ultimately carving the path of Robert's career. This domino effect is the most recurring aspect of almost every notable filmmaker's story; throwing themselves into a student project potential employers simply could not ignore. "By the time I got to *Bobby Yeah*, which was totally self-funded on my own, I already had a body of work, people already knew my work, and therefore there was an audience for it. It all comes down to that student film; if I hadn't made that, if I hadn't worked hard at college I really wouldn't have made any other films."

One of the by-products of *Bobby Yeah*'s improvised story development, as discussed previously, was Robert's ability to hand-build new characters on-the-fly whenever the action or a new scenario called for them. This too is a skill retained from his prior work, for which he has made a point of always sculpting his own puppets, "Because I don't think anyone would be able to do it in the way I like it. I think that people would probably be able to do it *better*, but it's not about 'better,' it's about being right. For the imperfections in the look, it has to be a certain way, so I will always sculpt the character myself."

A notable quasi-exception to the overall look of Robert's work would be *The Separation*, arguably his least independent short having been commissioned for a

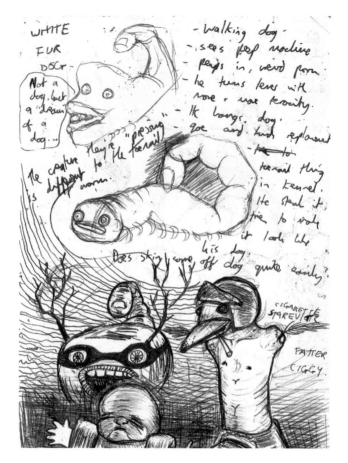

Figure 10.14

Bobby Yeah concept sketches. Image courtesy of Robert Morgan.

large budget by the Welsh cable channel S4C. Featuring additional design assistance from production designer Stéphane Collonge and slick cinematography by Philip Cowan, the film does stand apart as being more outwardly "produced," though at its heart it remains a Robert Morgan film through and through, with all the dedicated grotesquery that comes with it. Robert happily concedes that collaboration brings with it rewards of its own and that *The Separation* includes visual ideas he most likely would never have thought of himself, had the opportunity not arisen. The puppets themselves, however, remain purely his. "If I sculpt the puppets then I can feel like I've made them, I feel like they're my characters then. I don't think I could do those films if someone else had sculpted them."

Flashing forward to several years later, the production of *Bobby Yeah*, now acknowledged as one of his best works, more than anything went back to his early days as a student animator, working for the most part as a one-man crew.

"As far as the visuals of the film itself were concerned, it was basically me. I got a little bit of assistance here and there, such as my partner being a photographer who helped me shoot the exterior sequence; I wanted to have a moment where he suddenly goes outside. We're used to seeing dark, gloomy interiors in my films and being so bright and open on a sunny day really made for an interesting contrast, I think. We went to Dunderness because it's technically the only

Figure 10.15

Out for a jaunt – *Bobby Yeah* (Dir. Robert Morgan) exterior sequence thumbnail board/concept sketch to final film comparison ©2011 Swartz Can Talk/blueLight.

classifiable desert in the UK and I wanted something primal and basic, but very open. I also have a cinematographer friend Marcus who helped with the shots of the weird, psychedelic sky at the end of the film, which was created using ink in a water tank. The bit when the octopus bursts out of him, I got my friend Dominic Hailstone, a fellow director and a special effects genius to help me spruce that up a little bit. So there are bits and bobs along the way where friends where able to help out with particular bits, but essentially it was just me in a room."

To Robert, the progression of story in this way is largely instinctual, and consequently a process that cannot truly be planned out or intellectualized. "I think it's great when somebody says that my films have achieve a sort of nightmarish quality, because that's definitely something I aspire to. I suppose I would say that I'd really like my films to achieve that level of feverish delirium. But because nightmares are sort of irrational, you have to use an irrational part of your brain to do it, so in a way that's why I think I tried to do *Bobby Yeah* in a kind of stream of consciousness kind of way."

By going down this route the story serves to tap into the irrational part of the audience's brains, which makes the work divisive yet, to those on board with it, tremendously appealing. Had *Bobby Yeah* been traditionally scripted, it undoubtedly would not have carried nearly as much foreboding volatility, nor as much absurdist humor. "Very often when you try and write a script, there's a certain amount of sense that has to take place, so you're juggling plot with these horrific visuals. The nightmarish sequences, or the feeling you get, is very much to do with a certain escalation of images and, in particular, sound as well, to create an ambiance that is both dreamlike or nightmarish.

Also worth examining is the choice of medium itself. Save for the live-action *Monsters* (2004) and the mixed-media films *The Cat with Hands* and *Invocation* (2013), Robert's entire short filmography has indulged his first choice of stop-motion. With the advances of CG processes over the course of his active career, what are the elements of this medium that so lend themselves to, for lack of a more fitting term, the horror genre?

"To me the great, untapped dimension of stop-motion animation, which very few people have really truly harnessed, is the inherent uncanniness of it. Švankmajer's done it, as have the Quay Brothers and some others, but I'm surprised that not more people have tapped into it. I think a lot of people somewhat miss the point of it as well, they will try and be spooky and they end up doing a cartooney version of it which is not properly uncanny. I think the very nature of bringing inanimate objects to life and that kind of weird automaton way in which things move in stop-motion animation just lends itself to creepy or nightmarish filmmaking.

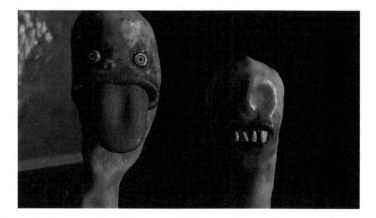

Figure 10.16

Still from *Bobby Yeah* (Dir. Robert Morgan) ©2011 Swartz Can Talk/blueLight.

10. *Keeping It Real*

Wisdom in Hindsight

Robert Grieves' perspective of what one might do differently if returning to a project is of particular note, having actually gone back and redone the film once before.

"A lot of the things that I would do again I did wrong in the first place because I didn't have the knowledge, so I would say storyboard it better. Don't rush in, take your time really getting it right. I put a lot of time into the storyboard, I just didn't know enough about film grammar.

"It depends on what's important to you, but I really wanted to make a film where all the storytelling was 100% visual. Obviously the music feeds into that, without a doubt, but maybe one of the reasons I didn't put the soundtrack on initially was that I wanted a film that, without the soundtrack, could 100% convey what was going on. I had got it to that point, where I could sit with people I respected who'd never seen it before and didn't know anything about it, who could watch it without the soundtrack and they fully followed it. At *that* point I knew that the soundtrack would only take it to the next place."

Something to consider throughout production is to what extent it's worth it to stay committed to our original vision if doing so impedes the production itself. In Robert's case, there is one area that he concedes would have made the whole process a lot less challenging. (Figure 10.17)

Figure 10.17

Sausage (Dir. Robert Grieves) backgrounds before and after coloring/texturing ©2013 Robert Grieves.

"The easiest thing would have been, by far, to use voiceover and dialogue. I think we worry about dialogue taking longer – or I do, anyway – because of having to lip sync, but lip sync is a whole lot easier to do than tell every bit of the emotional, narrative thrust through acting. I realized how hard that was and so I would say to anyone (or if I could go back in time and give myself advice when I was coming up with the idea for *Sausage*) would be to use voiceover and dialogue in it to at least *some* degree, because it just brings the audience along."

The use of narration in particular is something that independent filmmakers seem hesitant about. As writers like Adam Elliot have clearly demonstrated, narration can be far from lazy gimmickry if crafted well enough. Its success also hinges on the performer, as we will see in Chapter 12. The only real instance where narration should be completely avoided on principle is if it fails to add anything to the film itself. If the work speaks for itself visually, as the final version of *Sausage* proved to, then the addition of a voiceover or dialogue would be arbitrary and redundant.

"I saw so many films that were just labored with voiceover, where all the picture is doing is illustrating what is already in place, the narrative is there in the storytelling, in the voiceover, and you make some pictures to go along with it. I thought my film would be elevated above that for not using that 'cheap trick'; but audiences don't care about that! It's amazing, as much as I respect the sophisticated knowledge of the audience, that's one area people just don't care about."

The remaining constructive critique Robert has about the second, crowd-pleasing incarnation of *Sausage* would be its length. Cut down to six minutes from the original's runtime of eight, in Robert's view a purely visual story might better be served by something more succinct (between two and four minutes), if for no other reason than to make the production process itself less of a hardship.

Looking back at *Ernie Biscuit* (Figure 10.18) a mere handful of months after its completion, Adam Elliot has mixed feelings that lean more toward the positive.

"It was a bizarre five years. I think out of all my films it has been the rockiest and it's been a very inconsistent process, but I think in some ways it's a bit serendipitous. I went through a bad phase after *Mary and Max* where I really was disillusioned and I lost my enthusiasm."

Although it came at the cost of his original vision for the film as an elaborate feature with significantly higher production values, his unexpected detour into the world of independent animation seemed, ultimately, to be the shot in the arm required for him to rekindle his enthusiasm for animation on the whole.

"I'm only just starting to use the word 'experiment,' because with *Ernie Biscuit*, I really wanted to go back to basics, not just in terms of aesthetic but also just the process and the materials I used. I just wanted to try and go back to something a little bit more raw and organic. I really was quite happy if the film didn't get into any festivals or no one ever saw it, because it was more about experimenting and having total creative freedom and total creative control, without any broadcasters or government investors or distributors pressuring me. So probably I enjoyed the process more than I've been enjoying the finished result. *Ernie*'s certainly not my strongest film, it's very light, I think it's probably a little bit too long, some scenes are a little flat, but it's an experimental film. The audience probably don't see it as experimental but the way I made it was certainly very loose.

"I realized if I wasn't *enjoying* the process, particularly in animation which is such a slow shoot, and that if I didn't get that love back, it would certainly show in the end result."

Figure 10.18

Still from *Ernie Biscuit* (Dir. Adam Elliot) ©2015 Adam Elliot.

Inevitably, there will be moments during a production where maintaining any kind of enthusiasm for the process is more of a hard ask. Setbacks, delays and disasters need not even be the cause; sometimes there are stages of the production that are just outright boring. Such is the case with any task we embark upon that demands hard work, concentration and, if the deadline dictates as much, grueling hours. With tenacity, however, that impossible goal of making it to the other side with a finished film is reachable. In Chapter 18 of the book, we will hear from several filmmakers whose accounts of their own resolve should prove motivational enough for you to do likewise. Before that, though, let's look at some of the inventive and unconventional independent approaches to other areas of production.

Notes

1 This is evidenced by the fact that *Ernie Biscuit*, a film with comparable production values to 2003s *Harvie Krumpet*, was produced at a third of the budget over ten years later.
2 http://latenightworkclub.com.

11

Getting Comfortable

What is it that makes a film a comfortable watch? When considering the various disciplines of strong animated filmmaking, these should be simple enough to determine – an engaging script, appealing characters, a capable sound mix, seamless editing, expertly refined color palettes, a keen knowledge of dramaturgy and shot composition, and so on. Technically speaking, the more well-versed a filmmaker will be when it comes to the fundamentals, the easier a film will be to watch. In the world of independent animation, however, there are plenty of examples where films have taken an outsider approach, throwing off the shackles of traditional filmmaking and pushing the envelope to the delight of audiences worldwide. Sometimes, as we will see, films that are outright bizarre, challenging and seemingly horrific can, in a perverse way, elicit the same response.

Here, we will look at the ways in which films that are that extra step outside of convention have been successfully realized. To begin with, it's worth revisiting the world of abstract animation and one of its most successful offerings in recent years. Without telling a story or featuring characters in any literal sense, our first case study *Virtuos Virtuell* (2013, Figures 11.1–11.4) proved such a hit on the festival circuit as to pick up over forty awards during its astounding run.

Thomas Stellmach (Figure 11.5) is a filmmaker and animator whose prior filmography includes the Academy Award-winning animated short *Quest* (Dir. Tyron Montgomery, 1996) which he wrote and produced, as well as an extensive portfolio of commercial projects taken on during his time at the animation studio Lichthof, which he cofounded. Moving on from Lichthof in 2009 to focus on personal, more artistically driven projects, Thomas would meet artist Maja Oschmann (Figure 11.6) at an open day of Kassel's ateliers. Having both studied

DOI: 10.1201/9781003214717-11

Figure 11.1

Virtuos Virtuell concept sketch ©Thomas Stellmach.

at the Art University Kassel, though not at the same time, Thomas was intrigued by Maja's abstract artistic approaches, in particular her propensity toward music visualization, something the two shared a mutual enthusiasm for. It was not long before a creative affinity was realized, although there was some acclimation given their contrasting backgrounds – Maja's being solely fine art, with little by way of film production experience.

"It took time to understand our different interests and understanding of quality," says Thomas of the first handful of months of their collaboration. "That was an uneasy first step. Then suddenly, we understood one another. I wanted to make a project that achieved a special quality, so as to enter the international festivals. In my experience, I try to add more and more, to get something that nobody has seen before. Initially that was not easy to explain."

Once the pair came to an understanding of the scope of this potential collaboration, its focus needed to be determined. With the essential concept – to create an abstract piece that would interpret music through a hybrid of fine art, experimental film and animation – pinned down, Thomas found inspiration for its source via Kassel's Spohr Museum, the focus of which being the life's work and story of highly prolific German composer Louis Spohr.

"The purpose of the museum is to make him better known and push his name. He lived in our city for a long time and he did a lot of work, 170 different compositions, he composed ten operas (*Faust*, for example), a Requiem, a lot of violin concerti – really a wide range of different kinds of music.

"Because I listen to it during my work, music inspires me very much. I was listening to all of Spohr's different compositions, looking for a special kind of style that would be good for visualization, something which had a variety of dramatic aspects that change throughout."

The piece that ultimately proved most inspiring was Spohr's *Der Alchymist* (*The Alchemist*), a three-act opera originally composed in 1829–1830. Shortening the overture of *The Alchemist* to a seven-and-a-half-minute piece, Thomas wound up with a brief yet musically complex basis on which the moving visuals could be constructed. The dynamic range of the piece, with its wide variety of moods

Figure 11.2

Virtuos Virtuell concept sketch ©Thomas Stellmach.

and rhythms, allowed for a film far more abstract and visually arresting than originally planned.

"The first idea was to make an animated documentary about him, but when I read about his life, it didn't seem especially engaging, so I decided to visualize some music. So *Virtuos Virtuell* was my study about his life."

The finished film, composited for stereoscopic projection as per the museum's wishes, is a tremendously engaging piece of work that has clearly benefited from the meticulous attention to detail and time that has gone into every moment (more on this later). Presented as black ink on a white backdrop, the film increases in complexity and grandeur in perfect synchronicity with the music as it does likewise. Combining pure abstraction with the sensibilities of choreography and performance, it is also peppered with moments of pareidolia where more tangible forms can be glimpsed amongst the interplay between brushstrokes and random shapes.

"The idea began with a black ink stroke growing from an invisible brush. I did a lot of black and white drawings and abstract images to find something in that. During this step I met Maja and saw her very abstract paintings. To begin with, we didn't really know exactly what we would do together but we soon recognized that we could combine all of our different ideas and experiences. Together we developed a lot of the design for this film, especially the storyline."

Though an experimental piece largely open to interpretation, a storyline of sorts can indeed be picked up on. As the overture progresses, the ink stroke evolves from a mere visual throughline, eventually becoming a 'character' in and of itself, noticeably responding to the shifts in tone and mood within the music. To successfully achieve this, Thomas and Maja needed to determine the most appropriate style of movement for the ink, mainly through testing, trial and error and recording a great deal of footage of ink in motion.

"The whole composition is made up of a lot of separate material pieces that I put together with masks and blending. I tried to get the same density of ink and maintain the speed of the motion, sometimes adjusting it. In the end the audience should feel that there is only one graphic element, but in fact there isn't."

The next step was to develop a language where the two artists could effectively communicate their ideas to one another. Oftentimes their creative interplay would begin with Thomas's musical interpretations relayed through physical

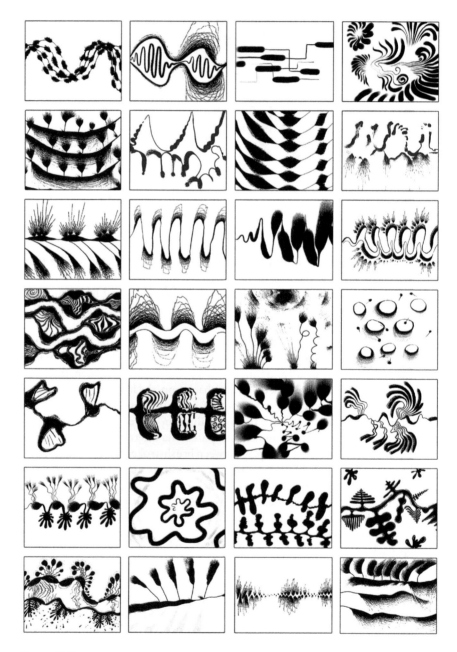

Figure 11.3

Virtuos Virtuell concept sketches ©Thomas Stellmach.

performance to Maja, who in turn would endeavor to replicate these actions through the ink itself.

"When I listen to the music of Louis Spohr, I feel that someone is sad. That was the idea, that this black ink stroke, the 'protagonist,' should be sad. The other 'character' would be its surroundings, so when I hear in the music the implication of something dangerous, something disruptive or disturbing, that sadness can become fear, for example. Sometimes we would split the instruments into two different 'characters.' What inspired me to choose this particular piece is that, when I listen to the first part, I can hear a dialogue between two different instruments. So the main 'character' would be woodwind and violin, while the other instruments that were deeper and darker – the contrabass, for example – might suddenly join the others and express 'danger.' I would explain to Maja that it could be something like that, where an outside force comes in and creates a sense dread, from which our 'character' will try to escape. She would visualise this with the black ink stroke, to move in such a way whenever there were interruptions or moments in the film that create panic."

One crucial moment in the film depicting such an "escape" also marks the transition from a flat plane to a three-dimensional environment, when the ink stroke seemingly breaks free of whatever threat has been introduced. Even when not viewed stereoscopically, the deftness of the film's 3D compositing (elaborated on in Chapter 16) clearly translates this extra level of dimensionality.

"We also needed to find words that we could use very abstract words to understand which sequence we would talk about. We separated every piece of the film into different sections and gave them each names – for example 'puddle skimming,' 'tulips growing,' 'dandelion sequence,' 'fire work' – this way we could collect all these pictures and recordings into special folders with those names, for easier reference. Over time we had developed a special language to understand each other and work together better."

The overall production was entirely taken on by Thomas (who went into *Virtuos Virtuell* with an already extensive career in film production under his belt) and Maja, developing and testing out the first ideas over the course of

Figure 11.4

Still from *Virtuos Virtuell* (Dir. Thomas Stellmach/Maja Oschmann) ©2013 Thomas Stellmach.

roughly six months. These tests essentially served as pre-production, with production (which consisted mainly of live-action filming of real ink behaviors in a variety of environments alongside digital brushstroke animation using a tablet) and post-production (the compositing of both elements) occurring simultaneously over the course of three subsequent years. This extended production time can be attributed to Thomas and Maja's discerning judgment as to when each shot or progression could be considered a success and, as such, usable in the final film.

"Every night I composited all of the layers of pictures and footage together and the next day we had to look them over. In most cases Maja would redesign every piece again and I would re-composite everything, usually three times!

"It looks very simple, but we would have to create a great deal of material for each shot to choose from. We weren't looking for the *best* footage necessarily but something which had some mistakes; we wanted the ink to have a sense of human behavior to it, so to get the ideal movement we were looking for there was a lot of preselection. Initially, it wasn't very easy for us to get the right movement. We would redesign it and change it, trying to keep the shape of the black ink stroke that Maja would have to draw again and again. Looking back, it seems hard to believe, but for us, it was so ordinary to go about it this way, having developed this feeling and language amongst ourselves."

To achieve the desired interplay between the music and the physical ink, it fell to Maja to breathe life into it, sometimes literally. Early experimentation involving breathing through a straw to control the motion of the ink proved promising but not reliable when dealing with longer musical notes that would last longer than breathing itself would accommodate. A variant of this approach, and one that proved more successful, was to "steer" the ink using an airbrush compressor, which also allowed for greater control over its behavior.

Experimenting with different materials, temperatures and surfaces also enabled a wider range of behaviors. "We started on paper, we also drew on glass, we mixed oil with black ink, we added some oil *on* glass – and the behavior of the

Figure 11.5

Thomas Stellmach retouches and edits thousands of ink film clips together with compositing software. Image courtesy of Thomas Stellmach.

11. Getting Comfortable

ink would change. We also turned the glass sheet vertically to get another result, for example. At one point, we used a syringe that was full of blank ink!"

The digital animation process was similarly labor-intensive, painting brushstrokes in time with each music segment using a software that could realistically simulate drawing inks, recorded "live" using a screen capture program. Frequently, the capturing of the perfect motion would prove just as elusive as when dealing with the unpredictability of the real-life, physical ink. One particularly troublesome two-second shot was so intangible as to warrant an astounding six-hundred takes before a successful outcome was achieved. Another major part of the compositing process was the removal (through masking in After Effects) of all the extraneous visuals that would accompany each piece of ink footage, such as hands, brushes and shadows.

The finished film premiered as part of the *1100 Years of Kassel* anniversary celebrations in February 2013, projected to a live accompaniment of the soundtrack performed by the State Orchestra of Kassel. As well as the film's highly enthusiastic response from festival audiences worldwide, its initial purpose – as a stereoscopic exhibit as part of the Louis Spohr museum – also proved popular, extending to an exhibit at the German Film Museum in Frankfurt and even being used as an educational tool to familiarize children with experimental film alongside works by such abstract pioneers as Len Lye, Norman McLaren and Oskar Fischinger.

Figure 11.6

Maja Oschmann blows the ink with an air brush tube. Image courtesy of Thomas Stellmach.

The Comfort of Discomfort

Although a tricky recipe to get right, the watchability of certain films can be enhanced by an element of unease. A psychological drama may be far better served by the power of what *isn't* seen onscreen, so that when some visual horror does present itself, it can be underplayed yet have maximum impact. By contrast, a film that is held together by shock value alone can indulge onscreen violence, gratuitous sexual content and strong language to far greater excess and wind up boring the audience. As demonstrated in the previously discussed work of Robert Morgan, independent animation can be a playground for the intense, the bizarre and the horrific just as much as it can be for the comedic or poignant, as long as it's in the right hands. Becky Sloan and Joseph Pelling's phenomenally successfully series *Don't Hug Me I'm Scared* is, on its surface, a simple sendup up children's programming, combining live action puppetry with animated vignettes, bold colors, boisterous performances, catchy melodies and simple topics such as the nature of love, creativity and time, amongst others. Its execution is so on-point, evocative of such iconic fodder as *Sesame Street, Rainbow* and *Yo Gabba Gabba*, that little would be required to parody or subvert the genre. The extra mile that *Don't Hug Me I'm Scared* goes is the integration not just of dry one-liners or vaguely adult concepts (as with the broadly appealing *Avenue Q*, for example) but elements of twisted, metaphysical storytelling, non-linear sequences of events, briefly glimpsed moments of loneliness and brutality as well as a somewhat purgatorial throughline that its online audience relish and latch onto in comments and discussion threads. Despite its beginnings as a quirky, independent short taking a (genuinely creative) swipe at "creative" types and seemingly predicated on an absence of continuity, Becky and Joseph have, in essence, cultivated an online fanbase that have created their own rationales and mythologies for what precisely the show is or means.

Shock value for its own sake, however, tends to fall flat. From my personal experience gauging audience responses to my own work, if any such device is used arbitrarily or for a cheap laugh, the audience won't be fooled and will probably respond negatively – or worse, with indifference. For no reason other than having the automatic writing style of a young man raised on shows like *South Park*, my thesis film (Figure 11.7) was riddled with crass language that I wrongly assumed would enhance its humor. Though the original seventeen-plus minute edit of the film did get some laughs at its various early screenings, the contrived edginess proved more boring than provocative. The reason was simple – it didn't need to be there. Having been assured that anything over fifteen minutes would severely limit the film's festival exposure, the easiest elements to trim out when excising three extraneous minutes were these self-indulgent moments, such as sweary dialogue and shots kept in simply because I liked how the animation looked, or had taken some pride in sneaking in a visual innuendo. The difference in response from the under-fifteen minute version compared to the original was palpable – festival acceptances and positive online feedback surged, and it was a stark lesson that, despite its remaining flaws, at its heart there was a solid little film there that was being held back by needless attempts to milk the gags and get a rise out of the audience.

I should hasten to add that the above does not constitute an outright condemnation of bad language or provocative ideas and concepts. If a certain visual tone matches up with a script boasting a foul-mouthed ensemble cast or distinctly

Figure 11.7

The rotting antagonist of *House Guest* ©2008 Ben Mitchell.

adult scenarios it can be a very entertaining watch indeed; one example that immediately springs to mind is Pierre Mousquet and Jérôme Cauwe's *Wind of Share*, an unrelentingly indulgent celebration of animated machismo, sex and ultraviolence that has proved to be a universal crowd-pleaser as far as international festival audiences are concerned.

Between making films and curating screenings, another psychological component I have also found muddies the waters of audience appreciation is best attributed to Poe's Law – a term coined in 2005 that refers to the line where parody and/or satire become undetectable from the genuine article, either through being expertly observed or from said genuine article's inherent ridiculousness. If somebody subscribes to a social or political ideology that is uneducated and facile, for example, it is much harder for a commentator or humorist to parody that person's outlook without coming off as subscribing to it themselves in earnest. Taking advantage of this lack of clarity purposefully has become one of the mainstays of "trolling"; simply inciting a reaction by espousing disingenuous opinions on a subject to watch the sparks fly. Where this comes into play as far as independent filmmaking is concerned can be down to numerous factors – a sharply satirical script needs to have its tone appropriately matched by the film's visual execution or the audience will be left scratching their heads.

An example that stands out in memory was a film that came onto my radar during a festival pre-selection in 2015. This film had some virtues, mostly in the modeling of the sets and props, but these fell prey to the weakness of the animator (who was also the director)'s ego. Any flow the film might have had was undermined by an insistence on lingering shots of the capable modeling work, from multiple camera angles, without any rhyme or reason. The animation itself was also hugely misjudged, being almost a masterclass in what *not* to do to the extent that, in conversation afterward, the audience struggled to determine whether this lack of skill was in fact deliberate. Where it primarily misfired was regarding the premise itself, dealing with a subject that is still considered a huge political hot potato in certain territories and hugely incongruous to the goofy, cartoonish character design. What was this filmmaker trying to achieve? If it was a dark, *South Park*-ian lampoon of social propaganda, it didn't work due to the misjudged style choice and incompetent animation. If, on the other hand, its social message was an earnest one (as turned out to be the case), it was equally a failure as there was no component to the story or visuals an audience could conceivably engage with or be moved by. Put simply, the film in and of itself was a pointless exercise, undermined by the laziness of its execution.

Such is the way different brains are wired, there will always be a certain subsection of the masses who won't grasp even an instance of obvious parody (there may be very well be, for example, a miniscule percentage of an online audience who might stumble across a *Don't Hug Me I'm Scared* short and be outraged, genuinely believing it was created for kids) but there is a limit to how accommodating we can be as filmmakers and storytellers. The purpose of distancing oneself from the trap of Poe's Law isn't to fetter our range of expression but rather consider alternative ways of communicating ideas, so that they might be clearer and perhaps even more impactful.

Odontophobia

Daniel Gray and Tom Brown (Figure 11.8) began working together while studying animation in Newport in 2003. "He was a young whippersnapper," recalls Daniel of Tom, "And I was a mature student there. We ended up working on a project in the second year in a group. We found that we worked really well together, so we did our final film together and have continued to work together from then on."

The final film was *t.o.m.* (2006), a staggeringly successful short that picked up twenty-five awards and over fifty official selections in the two years that followed. The film's performance made a name for the pair, who would operate as Holbrooks Films for over a decade; though both initially working from a shared space in Wales, they've each since moved on to entirely different continents – Tom in the US, Dan in Hungary. The film itself is a three-minute, firsthand account of a young boy's daily routine, beginning with predictably mundane rituals and observations that grow steadily more uncomfortable as the audience is informed that he methodically strips off various items of clothing at particular locations on his route to school. Throughout the film, the audience is led to become increasingly suspicious of the directorial neutrality and intent, until the final shot when all ambiguity is jettisoned; upon his arrival at school, the nude child is taunted with aggressive laughter from his congregated classmates. As university students, Dan and Tom's writing process when it came to *t.o.m.* would be largely the same process they would go on to adopt on subsequent projects.

Figure 11.8

Holbrooks portrait: Tom Brown and Daniel Gray ©Holbrooks.

"The way that we tend to write is we'll *over*-write, mostly, and then make the story better for just using the bits that we like," explains Dan, "For *t.o.m.*, we started off with this gross picture of this little naked beast in a classroom, on a desk. We had loads of sketchbook pictures that we'd make narratives around and made this overlong story about why he's naked in school. We'd write it all out, go through it and work out which parts seemed cheesy, or didn't work, focusing on what's interesting – chiefly, how does he actually *get* to school? The basic thing we were playing with was that we had a character delivering the narrative, which to the audience means he is the 'rule-setter'; what he tells you is what you believe.

"Animation is great because you can present your audience with anything and they come to it with a massive sense of innocence – they're ready to accept what you tell them. So he's giving you these rules, you're following it along and obviously it's 'normal,' even though it is in fact very weird, but everyone's going along with it. Then at the end we take away the narration, we pull the camera right back and we have this theatrical, almost pre-Raphaelite composition of the kids behind the fence and him on his own, on the other side. So 'normality' was actually on the other side of the fence and the innocence the audience has gone along with is taken from them."

That sense of being wrenched back down to earth almost serves as a wordless punchline moment, where it is not necessarily clear who the joke is on – the titular Tom of the film or the audience itself. Dan also notes the effectiveness of protracting the final shot on purpose, so as to compound the awkwardness of the moment. Reveling in manipulating an audience's emotions and expectations could be seen as malicious were it not such a strangely satisfying – refreshing, even – viewing experience.

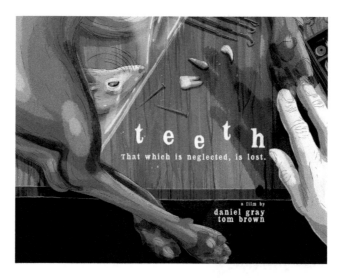

Figure 11.9

Teeth (Dir. Tom Brown/Daniel Gray) poster art ©2015 Holbrooks/Blacklist.

While *t.o.m.* could be seen as a test of to what extent an audience will go along with the farcically ridiculous, Dan and Tom's second film *Teeth* (Figures 11.9– 11.11), released in 2015, could be seen as an outright endurance exercise. The film shares certain similarities to their student short, such as a rich, painterly style to the backgrounds against harsh-yet-sophisticated foreground/character animation, as well as an introspective narration that guides the audience through an increasingly unsettling series of rituals and memories. In this later film's case, however, the unnamed and never fully visible narrator is an old man reflecting on a lifetime of dental masochism, in which he had set out to create the perfect set of dentures, methodically extracting his own teeth over the years and researching those of the animal kingdom for more optimal replacements. Perfectly delivered by veteran British performer Richard E. Grant, the compelling monologue that describes this inexplicable journey carries the viewer through an assortment of brutal visuals that tap into a primal urge to look away whilst simultaneously being compelled to keep watching.

"There's an interesting thing which I don't think I've seen elsewhere," observes Dan, "Where, during the moments of silence, you can feel the audience not breathing, almost. It feels almost heavy, on the back of your neck and I've heard some other people mention that as well. We wanted to really affect the audience obviously, and it was really nice seeing these unexpected ways that happened. The nervous laughing, as well – when people laugh at the 'punchline,' or the 'payoff,' half the laugh is from dark humor and the other half is from them thinking *Well, this has got to be the end*, which is interesting as well."

While uncompromising, there is a strange elegance and ethereal beauty to the film that somehow validates the nonsense logic of the main character and keeps the audience invested in the hope of some kind of resolution (will this elusive set of ideal teeth ever be completed and, if so, what then?). The directors are also careful to show a certain degree of restraint as to what is actually shown onscreen, never overstating the point by veering into outright gore but letting the audience's imaginations fill in the gaps, for maximum impact. This is best

11. Getting Comfortable

exemplified in one particular shot in which the obsessive lead scrapes a knife across his teeth. The image, when paired with horrendously accurate foley work, creates an all-too-palpable sensation in the viewer.

"It almost threatens the audience. Normally a film will escalate the gore and the disgustingness, so we put that visual there as a false promise, that we're going to *really* be this gross. So there's this tension, then, of people expecting us to keep ramping it up.

"As far as the development of the story goes, it's basically an allegory for short-sighted decisions. It was made around the same time as all the arts funding was being cut. Animation and art degrees were all being belittled as 'not necessary,' so *Teeth* was originally about the consequences of making the easy choices of closing these things down."

Without revealing the ending, consequences remain an important component of the film's resolution, though the denseness and heavy-handedness of the sociopolitical analogy ultimately turned out to not best serve the film. As with

Figure 11.10

Still from *Teeth* (Dir. Tom Brown/Daniel Gray) ©2015 Holbrooks/Blacklist.

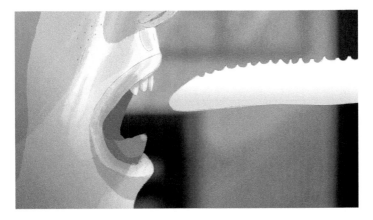

Figure 11.11

Still from *Teeth* (Dir. Tom Brown/Daniel Gray) ©2015 Holbrooks/Blacklist.

t.o.m., the refinement of *Teeth*'s final script comes from being pared down from a broader concept, so that only the strongest ideas at its core remain.

"We kept a lot of the symbolism but made it a little bit more vague, because the more specific you get with what you're trying to say, the less enjoyable a film can be. With both films we've used a pretty visual to hide this dark game we're playing, so with *Teeth*…well, everyone is squeamish with teeth. If someone were to hit their teeth with a knife or a spoon, you'd say 'Can you not do that?' So the film was a way of tapping into the audience's feelings of disgust. Plus, with the sort of message we were originally talking about, we *wanted* the audience to be disgusted and angry about it, almost. In a way it's subliminal, which is obviously not allowed in advertising and is frowned upon in general society – but it's what filmmakers do, isn't it? We have to play with the subliminal so as to be more aware of it."

12

Casting and Performance

Usually before an animation production can properly begin, not only will the casting need to have been sorted but the basic dialogue track should already be laid down. This isn't always the case – films with narration, for example, can get by with a placeholder track until the post-production phase – but either way the process of actually finding the right performers and getting the best performance out of them may very well fall on your shoulders when doing things the independent way. In this chapter, you will be presented with a variety of circumstances that have determined an independent project's casting success that should hopefully demystify the process somewhat.

Going It Alone

One obvious time-saver when it comes to casting and directing is to use ourselves in our work. And why not? Who else will know exactly what kind of performance we want our own characters to give better than us?

Well, slow down there. Of course, there's something of a chasm between knowing what's best and being able to execute it on our own. Just as we need to know our limitations throughout the visual side of an animated production, when it comes to the soundtrack we need to be equally vigilant – more so considering the increased likelihood that it will be territory outside of our usual field of expertise.

I write from firsthand experience in this regard as circumstances have regularly dictated I go this route for at least one character per each film of mine. At times, this has proved effective enough, though there are definitely instances

DOI: 10.1201/9781003214717-12

where I have regretted doing so in hindsight. A stilted, horribly affected attempt at a British accent plagues my MA thesis film *House Guest* and is completely at odds with the characterization of the character I voiced; a gruff, necessitous hunting enthusiast who lives on his own in the woods.

If you are playing more than one character, you may want to take the time to really consider whether or not your vocal range is up to the task. The first independent short I produced that wound up being successful enough on the festival circuit to sell for broadcast was *The Naughty List* (Figure 12.1), an animated sketch about dealing with higher ups not pulling their weight in the workplace, as depicted through an exchange with an anxious, beleaguered worker elf and Santa Claus. Turnaround time was tight and budget was nil (dueling circumstances that will be familiar to many I'm sure), so my workaround was to play both characters for the animatic, with an eventual plan to redub before lip-sync began proper.

The performances as recorded did not land as two separate characters, instead resulting in a voice clearly identifiable as mine affecting a clipped, fatherly voice for Santa and a cod-New Jersey drawl for the elf. When it became clear that recasting/re-recording simply wasn't an option, I experimented with various processing effects, eventually settling on simply pitching up the Elf (to accentuate his stature and frantic state of mind) and pitching down Santa (to accentuate his age and lethargic bulk) roughly 20% each way. By keeping the adjustment fairly moderate, the cheat is not immediately obvious; pitching up a voice by a semi-octave or higher, for example, will produce an identifiable *Alvin & The Chipmunks* effect, while you don't need to go too far when pitching any noise down before things start to sound outright demonic. By contrast, adjusting the audio by a smaller amount merely alters the tonality of the voice so that it becomes far less obvious as having originated from the same person. This option is what I've dubbed "the *South Park* cheat," in reference to the show's creators Matt Stone and Trey Parker's use of the same method in the pre-adolescent characterization of the main group of children they voice.

Certainly, the more authentic approach is to use a performer with enough vocal capabilities to not warrant any additional post-production trickery, or to use different actors per role altogether, but as a means to an end, this approach can be an effective compromise. Even performers as gifted as the great Mel Blanc

Figure 12.1

Still from *The Naughty List* (Dir. Ben Mitchell) ©2010 Ben Mitchell.

(the man who originated such iconic voice performances as Barney Rubble and Private Snafu, not to mention Bugs Bunny and the greater percentage of the entire *Looney Tunes* ensemble) made use of this technique – his characterization of Daffy Duck, for example, does not amount to a great deal more than a pitched-up version of his performance as Sylvester the Cat.

Taking the lead yourself can be achieved without the digital trickery of such a cheating little cheater as I, provided you have the chops for it. Hailing from Melbourne, Australia, animator Elliot Cowan[1] (Figure 12.2) is another independent artist, on top of those discussed in Chapter 8, to have created a feature-length independent animation project with minimal resources. Having spent eleven years in Tasmania working on TV commercials, the call to return to something more animation focused saw him move to the UK for eighteen months working for Uli Meyer before winding up in New York where he too caught the bug to make his own animated feature (there must be something in the water).

Earlier in his career, Elliot had developed *Boxhead and Roundhead*, a concept for a book package that failed to generate much by way of interest. As it turned out, there proved to be some life and audience appeal in the characters when they were repurposed for a series of independently animated shorts. Embracing a time- and cost-effective approach to the animation, *The Stressful Adventures of Boxhead and Roundhead* would eventually gain enough momentum to warrant their own longer-form outing (Figure 12.3).

This ultimately led to a slight reworking of the main characters, who had previously been mute entities. Though the visual style of the shorts worked well

Figure 12.2

Boxhead and Roundhead creator Elliot Cowan. Photo courtesy of the artist.

enough without dialogue, to carry anything longer than a few minutes, Boxhead and Roundhead would need voices and more thoroughly defined characteristics.

"They didn't speak originally, although in the later shorts, they do what I call 'indie speak,'" clarifies Elliot, referring to a nonsense language of murmurs and grunts. "They actually spoke to each other in the books that I had written, but at the time, I had no facility to record dialogue, so I abandoned it initially.

"Originally they were two very frightened characters that lived in this world where everybody hates them, but that also developed over time. One thing I was always trying very hard to avoid is, when you have the bossy character and the simple character it resembles *Ren and Stimpy*. I tried very hard to make sure it was not that relationship, that they were very close, that they needed each other and that it was a genuine friendship."

The initial plan when it came to the casting of the full-length film was to use placeholder voices in anticipation of redubbing the dialogue with bigger name actors down the line, something that ordinarily would not work given the specific timing traditional lip-sync requires. Though automated dialogue replacement is not unheard of in animation, it remains a laborious process ordinarily reserved for dubbing films and shows into foreign languages. The nature of *The Stressful Adventures of Boxhead and Roundhead*'s uniquely economic animation process did accommodate this, however, lip-sync largely being generated by single assets, manipulated in rough synchronicity to the dialogue of either main character. The point becomes moot, however, with the fact that no such big name actors would come to fill the roles. Instead Elliot took the reins himself while also taking the risk of bringing on friends and colleagues: "I've always done some voiceover

Figure 12.3

Still from *The Stressful Adventures of Boxhead and Roundhead* (Dir. Elliot Cowan) ©2014 Elliot Cowan.

12. Casting and Performance

work, so I knew it was going to be decent enough, but the plan was always that someone else was going to come and do the work. When that never happened I did all the voices except for a few, so my friend Jeremy Beck played Boxhead, while fellow animator Boris Hiestand and one of my students Carl Doonan also did voices. In the end, I liked that, and I had lots of experience directing actors, so that part was easy.

The fully voiced incarnations of Boxhead and Roundhead serve to match the key dynamic outlined previously. With Elliot's performance as Roundhead being a nasal, New York drawl ("It's basically Bugs Bunny if you listen to it, actually"), Boxhead needed to the straight character that could be played against effectively. With his own particular approach to voice directing, one that went hand in hand with his hopes for the overall tone of the film, directing the others proved relatively straightforward.

"I don't like 'reads,' I don't like feeling like the voiceover actors are in a booth, so it was nice and casual."

Making use of friends and acquaintances when it comes to your animated projects may not even be considered a last resort. Not to sell the vastly impressive abilities and performance ranges of professional voiceover actors short, but an independent production is significantly less likely to require such extreme versatility and it may very well be the case that somebody in your life has the chops to bring a particular character of yours to life. As long as you're not arbitrarily throwing the part to a boyfriend or girlfriend who can't act to save their life out of some sense of obligation, then there's no harm in canvassing the talent amongst your friends and colleagues. Don Hertzfeldt did as much in casting the leads for his *World of Tomorrow* series (Figure 12.4). Voicing multiple Emilys (an assortment of clones who travel back in time to escort the younger version of Emily 'Prime,' from whom they originated, around the future world they inhabit) was Don's friend and fellow acclaimed filmmaker Julia Pott – perhaps most known for her shorts *Belly*, *The Event* and the HBO series *Summer Camp Island*.

"Oddly enough," recalls Don, "I first met Julia on a stage at Sundance. We were each there with a film years ago and were called up to do a Q&A together after a program. So it was kind of cool to have *World of Tomorrow* play at Sundance after that festival had directly introduced us. Even though she has a great voice, she

Figure 12.4

Still from *World of Tomorrow* ©2014 Don Hertzfeldt/Bitter Films.

had never acted before. But she's funny…she can tell a joke, you can immediately tell she has really natural comic timing. So that was enough to know she could pull off the part."

Playing against Don's young (her contributions recorded between the ages of four and six) niece Winona Mae – another ingenious casting choice whose clearly unscripted dialogue perfectly encapsulates both childlike awe in the face of the mundane and childlike indifference in the face of wonder – Julia's detached, monotone delivery is a perfect match for the understated wit of his script and plays against her co-star's childlike exuberance perfectly.

Going Pro

In the previous chapter, we learned about *Teeth* (Figure 12.5) from Holbrooks Films and how its uncompromising and brutal visuals have proved strangely appealing to audiences worldwide. Finding the right voice for the film's challenging yet compelling story of a man obsessed by the functionality of his teeth was crucial, and success was found through English actor Richard E. Grant, known for such iconic roles in cinema as the titular Withnail of *Withnail and I* (Dir, Bruce Robinson, 1987). Securing such a high-profile name for a relatively independent outfit such as Holbrooks was mainly attributed to taking the direct approach, as co-director Daniel Gray recalls.

"We didn't have any money obviously, so we phoned his voiceover agent. Phones, by the way, are very good if you want people to respond – email is fine but with a phone call you can ask them what you want directly and they have to at least talk about it. A phone call is worth about ten emails, seriously, it's just so much easier. So we phoned up and we explained the project, that we had no funding, can we at least just get it in front of Richard E. Grant? That way, if he likes it, we can try to come to an agreement."

Given the nature of the film's dialogue being all narration, without cause for any lip-sync, Holbrooks were able to complete the bulk of the production before making this approach. As such, presenting a near-final version of *Teeth*, with finished picture, sound design and a scratch track for the eventual narration, clearly communicated the film's intent and value. As such, Grant was easily swayed

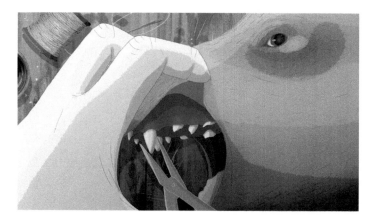

Figure 12.5

Still from *Teeth* (Dir. Tom Brown/Daniel Gray) ©2015 Holbrooks/Blacklist.

12. Casting and Performance

to be involved and lend his voice to the project. "We came to an agreement for a piecemeal amount of money and he came and recorded it. He was an absolute pro; we could have used the first take really but he did about four or five in the end."

Though a well-known actor on UK shores, Grant's performance in the film is not instantly identifiable. Far from a simple recitation of the script's narration as written, the unnamed protagonist (for lack of a more apropos term) is imbued with a husky melancholia, the abstract logic of his obsession tinged with ambivalent emotions. It is a fully charged performance, yet not remotely over the top. This is doubtless owed to Grant's long years of professional experience lending him an intuitive sense of character, despite the shortness of the film's length and the time available to record. Looking back, Daniel remembers it took minimal direction to bring this fullness of performance to the fore.

"The first time he read it through it was really nice, we could have used that easily. Then we asked if he could sound a bit tired and a bit old, and then he suddenly was!"

The end result undeniably makes an already strong film stronger and further strengthens the case for reaching out to a performer if you instinctively feel they are right for a film, no matter how unattainable they may seem. Generally speaking, for a lot of actors, animation can hold a certain degree of appeal and has an edge over other forms of independent film in a lot of respects. These include easier hours, no costume or make-up concerns and far less waiting around while technical issues are being ironed out, as would be experienced on a live-action set. As such, the seemingly impossible 'gets' of the acting world may be a lot more within reach than expected.

A similar case study is that of the late animator, filmmaker and storyteller Rosto, an artist whose output would span multiple narrative strands that were, by and large, all ultimately tied to the online graphic novel webseries *Mind My Gap*. The extent of this elaborate, mixed-media universe and its associated spinoff galaxies will be explored more fully in Chapter 15, though one of its less direct extensions is the 2011 half-hour independent short film project *The Monster of Nix* (Figure 12.6). The film, a story-within-a-story of the mysterious Langeman and troubled youngster Willy, originates from earlier projects such as the short films *Beheaded* (1999) and *Jona/Tomberry* (2005). It is also unique amongst Rosto's projects as being intended for a younger audience, primarily a dark fairytale rather than the intense and hallucinogenic work he is otherwise known for.

"I considered *The Monster of Nix* a children's film because I did it for my son, who was my biggest fan at the time. He wanted to know everything about the Langeman; who the forest creatures were who pop up in *Mind My Gap* and *Jona/Tomberry*. I had millions of stories to tell about them, because these universes are real – not externally, but inside me all these stories exist. I often don't use them in my films as narrative elements but more as snippets from those universes, but in this case I literally wanted to tell Max, my son, a Langeman story. So *The Monster of Nix* is related to *Mind My Gap*, but not part of the canon, so to speak."

Afforded some visibility and legitimacy by the festival success of earlier projects such as (*The Rise and Fall of the Legendary*) *Anglobilly Feverson* (2002) and *No Place Like Home* (2009) *The Monster of Nix* also boasts an impressive roster of voice talents such as Tom Waits, Terry Gilliam and Olivia Merilahti of European indie band The Dø. Securing such high-profile talent was more a matter of effective networking and mutual artistic appreciation than anything else, with Rosto having met Terry Gilliam in the States while touring with *Anglobilly Feverson* ("Which was very serendipitous, because I was actually looking for him"). Enamored of the film, the two maintained a friendly correspondence that made a voice role on *The Monster of Nix* a relatively easy sell when it came around, despite having not provided voices for animation since his own animated contributions to Monty Python. "I asked Gilliam because I thought his voice was made for this role." Rosto elaborates on the film's official website, "He felt rather uncomfortable about the singing. And that's exactly how I wanted this character to sound: scared and insecure. The poor bastard suffered but I got exactly what I wanted."

The notion of having Tom Waits supply the voice of Virgil S. Horn (*Mind My Gap*'s primary recurring antagonist) was an unexpected bonus, especially when considering the character's grand and darkly theatrical nature was largely inspired by the performance style of Waits himself.

"Virgil is both the God and the devil of this universe," Rosto expounds. "He created it, basically, which is why Virgil in the films has my face. I first create my characters, I then create settings for them, and then I have awful things happen to them, because otherwise, it wouldn't be interesting. So Virgil is my alter-ego, although in the films he's like an über version of me; he has a bigger nose, he's taller and lankier. However the character's voice in *Mind My Gap* isn't me, it's actually another actor doing the voice, but we always had Tom Waits as a reference, this sort of gravelly voice with a slight Romanian, Eastern European accent."

With the premise of *The Monster of Nix* partially removed from the canonical events of *Mind My Gap*, Virgil's depiction as voiced by Waits is notably different, portrayed not as a sinister, puppeteering deity but his spirit animal, "A giant swallow who hates being in a children's film, because he considers himself an *artiste*.

"I didn't originally want to write the music for *Nix*, so I was experimenting with several other composers to see if they could write parts – or maybe all – of the soundtrack. For Virgil I actually originally got in touch with Tom to see if he could write the leitmotif for that character, and maybe do the voice as well.

Figure 12.6

Willy meets Virgil (voiced by Tom Waits) in *The Monster of Nix* (Dir. Rosto) ©2011 Studio Rosto A.D/Cinete/Autour de Minuit.

For good reasons I ended up writing the music myself, but we stayed in touch regarding the voice, because I didn't know at the time when the production would begin."

Once the film was greenlit, Waits readily agreed to lend his voice to the character. Despite being facilitated by various streams of government funding, it remained a small-scale production with actors' fees generously waived so that the animators and artists brought on would not have to have their wages further compromised.

"It's amazing to see that so many people worked for free – or for not nearly enough. Nobody actually got what they deserved on this project, so artists like Terry, Tom and Olivia – or The Residents, for that matter – all worked for free on the project. I wouldn't feel comfortable giving the actors a lot of money with some of my animators working for practically nothing, that would be totally out of balance. Fortunately this was never actually a discussion, they actually proposed that I spend my money on people who really needed it, rather than on those who have a career and money in the bank already."

This generosity is not to suggest that the work and skillset of a voice performer is less artistically valuable than others who work on a film of this nature, but circumstantially speaking, it holds some water, especially when considering the actual time and labor involved. There is an obvious disparity between a handful of days working on VO for a project and the untold hours its crew of animators and artists will spend then bringing the performance to life. One certainly shouldn't approach a big name with the intention of getting free work out of them, but by pitching a project idea with all of its budgetary limitations worn on its sleeve, it may be that they are enthusiastic to work on it with some concession to their standard rate.

How you go about sourcing your voice cast is going to depend largely on exactly what type of production you are putting together – whether your film requires singing, narration, passion, high comedy, low comedy, understated nuance or pantomime theatrics are things to bear in mind when researching available options, as a performer who will shine in one arena won't necessarily be able to bring much to the other. One should not enter into this type of an arrangement with the expectation that a recognizable name on a poster will automatically increase the perception of the film's audience appeal by association. Indeed, Rosto was keen to not exploit their involvement when it came to casting and promoting *The Monster of Nix*.

"It felt very cheap to me that I would put on a poster 'Look! There's Tom Waits! There's Terry Gilliam!' So I underplayed it a lot as I had wanted to work with these guys because of who they were and what they would bring. But to see how little people actually *noticed* was slightly disappointing to me, at the time."

Fortunately, in the case of the examples we've explored in this segment, these casting choices were successful in so much as they manage to enhance the quality of the film from an artistic standpoint, rather than arbitrarily or cynically slapping a weak performance from a known celebrity onto a film's press kit. The major trap to avoid is the assumption that a film will automatically become more worthwhile through its voice cast (to hammer this point home, go ahead and look up the trailer for the 2012 film *Foodfight!*).

Adam Elliot's films have frequently boasted impressive casts, including *Harvie Krumpet* (Figure 12.7) narrator Geoffrey Rush, *Mary and Max* narrator Barry Humphries, not to mention Mary and Max themselves, voiced by Toni

Collette and the late Philip Seymour Hoffman, respectively. While these are tremendously accomplished names, the motivations for their use are miles away from the tendency in mainstream Hollywood features to cast whichever A-lister *du jour* is likely to have the most pulling power on a film's poster. In Adam's case, the performers chosen are sought after not because of their marketing potential, but because they are an ideal fit for the role. Once one has seen the performances Philip Seymour Hoffman and Toni Collette deliver in the finished film, it is impossible to imagine the characters played by anyone else. By comparison, many other films with broader subject matter and less developed characters tend to boast ensemble casts that are, for the most part, interchangeable.

"Usually by the second or third draft, I start to hear a voice in my head. It might be because that particular actor is popular at the time. For *Harvie Krumpet*, at that particular time Geoffrey Rush was everywhere, so his voice stuck in my head. With Philip Seymour Hoffman, he was not the narrator but his voice was probably the strongest in the film."

Adam's fondness for the Todd Solondz 1998 classic *Happiness*, coupled with Hoffman's recent Oscar-winning turn in Bennett Miller's *Capote* (2005), firmly positioned the actor as a frontrunner for Max. With a particular gift for playing the tortured, damaged and lovelorn, no other performer could hope to bring out the quiet, subdued tragedy of Max's perpetually lonesome existence, nor the glimmers of hope and depths of despair his epistolary relationship with his Australian pen-pal Mary bring about. Whether a major feature or student short, the principles behind Adam's casting choices have always remained the same.

"With my earlier films, what I've always gone for with the narrators in particular are people whose voices aren't necessarily obvious or immediately recognizable, but have a tone or a timbre to them that is immediately likable, not saccharine or overbearing. I really like the narrators to be anonymous – which is what a narrator is, an anonymous voice – but a comforting, authentic, believable voice, almost so that in the cinema the narrator is sitting just behind you, almost whispering into your ear as you're watching a film, so that you sort of forget that he or she is there, guiding you along."

Narration is a device a lot of filmmakers use, and one that receives some criticism as touched upon in earlier chapters. More to the point, it's a device that Adam as a writer enjoys and, as he sees it, if it works, then why not use it? The narration used in Adam's films is far from a crutch, nor is it overbearing, only ever contributing to the emotion of a scene rather than distracting from it.

"My narrators have all been different people, and certainly, some of them have started to 'act' in certain scenes – Geoffrey Rush became quite Shakespearian in one rehearsal – where I've had to try and pull them back. I always have to say to them 'Look, I don't want you to act, just pretend we're in a bar at 3 am and you're telling me about this uncle you have, or this pen pal you've got.' I really want them to be believable and authentic. Actors do understand that directors know what's best for their stories."

What essentially set the tone, on one level or another, for all of Adam's subsequent films was the casting choice for the narrator of his very first outing, the 1996 student short film *Uncle*.

"Originally, I was such a control freak and megalomaniac that I wanted to narrate my very first film, my student film *Uncle*, but the lecturers said 'No, no, Adam you can't act, you've got a squeaky voice and you'll ruin the film! You've got to get a real actor.'"

Figure 12.7

"Harvie" character sculpt for Adam Elliot's *Harvie Krumpet* ©2015 Adam Elliot.

Adam was pointed in the direction of Queensland-born actor William McInnes, a friend of the course lecturer then known primarily for portraying a Senior Constable on the Australian drama series *Blue Heelers*.

"I thought *No I don't want a cop, that's too macho, I want somebody who's got a poetic, tender tone to their voice*. She twisted my arm and he came in and, of course, was fantastic. Then he ended up in the next two parts of the trilogy.

"I still feel that I don't really direct the actors much, I give them a lot of freedom and room for spontaneity and improvisation because, again, I don't want them to 'act.' Often we'll just get the actor in with very little rehearsal time and we just let them talk. We record everything – we record the rehearsals, outtakes, anything that comes out – and then we piece it all together.

"I know most animators record the voices first but I record them last, I let the animation sort of tell the narrator the tone of each shot and scene, unless it's lip sync – but my films don't have much lip sync in them, so I have that luxury of showing the actors what they have done and letting them gauge the tone of their own performance. So they sort of self-direct, in many ways."

More than anything, the goal should always be to try and achieve a result that is believable and authentic, be it the unobtrusive, soft spoken narration of William McInnes evoking Adam himself or Philip Seymour Hoffman's gruff, at times distressed characterization of New Yorker Max evoking the real-life pen-pal on whom he was based. Suspension of disbelief is a difficult enough proposition when working in live-action, and an animated film will carry with it the added battle of getting your audience to engage with "this blob of plasticine," in Adam's words. When your blob is victorious, the intention is for the audience to rejoice along with it; when it dies, you want your audience to be moved. The skill of the animation itself can certainly cover some of the ground, but the competence of your voice actor can either make or break your characters' believability.

Note

1 http://www.elliotelliotelliot.com.

13

Thinking Outside the Lightbox

At the risk of sounding like the type of haggard old bore who sits rocking on his porch while nursing his inclement-weather-detecting joint pains: The times, they are a-changing. As touched upon in several prior chapters, independent animators are expected to perform to significantly increased expectations as far as presentation, originality and overall content of their work. If your film will truly resonate, it will be down to one of two things:

1   The stars aligning in the most gloriously unpredictable way imaginable, where by happenstance every stage of production comes off without a hitch and the final product communicates the genius of your work to a broad audience the moment it's put out into the world.
2   The comparatively less exciting prospect of heavily researching your proposed audience needs beforehand and reconciling yourself with the often excruciating and stressful juggling act of catering to the hypothetical masses while maintaining your core ideas and creative integrity.

So if you're confident the first will pan out for you (good luck with that), *mazel tov* in advance and you need read no further.

It's not completely out of the realm of possibility, sure, but it might not be the most realistic outcome to depend on. As for the seemingly dull second option – well, there's actually quite a lot to get enthusiastic about, so buck up and get happy. To keep up with the folks who are putting out work that jolt festival, online and television audiences awake, the main thing to try and stay aware of is how exactly audiences and consumers are relating to new media, and how does this directly inform the filmmaking process?

DOI: 10.1201/9781003214717-13

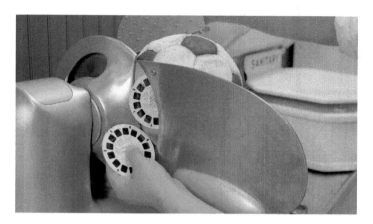

Figure 13.1

Still from *Submarine Sandwich* (Dir. PES) ©2014 PES.

The main spirit of this book, above all else, is to help animation filmmakers realize their full potential. Let's take pause before I continue: The phrase "realise your full potential" probably rings familiar, for good reason – it's bandied about as something of a catch-all in the vast world of "motivational" literature, the kind of phrase which, in its vagueness, comes across as all the more accessible. It has many brothers designed to similarly stir up the "get up and go" of its audience – "Be all you can be," "Take control of your destiny," "MANIFEST"! It makes my fingers ache to even type this kind of thing. Yet, fundamentally, the reason why these are so prevalent in literature is that they do yield visible, if largely superficial, results. Positive thinking, clear-headedness and determination do, generally speaking, assist tremendously in achieving certain life goals, and books on the subject fly off the shelves, so I'm in no position to besmirch them. Obviously, if I *did* have a book in me on the path to self-actualization, the road to spiritual fulfillment or the expressway to emotional empowerment, this wouldn't be it.

So sticking to independent animation, what exactly do I mean by "full potential" when it comes to your work?

Ultimately, it's what differentiates two main attitudes about filmmaking – the "nailed it!" attitude and the "that'll do" attitude.

The "That'll Do" Attitude

How many times have you seen a film – be it short, feature-length, independent, commercial or otherwise – that just sort of happens by? It may raise a smile, it may even engage you in the moment but, once it's over, there's nothing about it that lingers with you.

I'm not going to lie, as a freelancer I've not only witnessed directors succumb to this attitude in order to appease a client and meet a deadline; I've done it myself. As a director of my own films, I can appreciate moments in hindsight where significant improvements could have been made to a scene's timing, a line record, layout, musical choices and, of course, the animation itself (man alive, this last one can sting). Even the best animators who would leave the likes of me in the dust would – and should – regard their previous work with a critical eye. We learn best from our own shortcomings, and the biggest lamentation an animator will have about their own work is "Why didn't I redo that bit?"

Therein lies the difference – in the moment, we may have just been so sick of the frame, the shot – or the entire universe that the film itself takes place in – that we only had the energy to get through it and move onto the next scene. Once we hit the "that'll do" moment, it can be the most tempting thing in the world to just move on.

The "Nailed It!" Attitude

This, predictably, is the hallmark of a filmmaker who doesn't succumb to said temptation. The filmmaker who takes a step back and acknowledges more can be done to achieve perfection, even if that only amounts to erasing a flaw that might otherwise haunt them.

Give this matter some thought. Mull over the animators, directors, writers, etc. who have had a lasting effect on you. Why can't you get that scene, or line of dialogue, or musical cue out of your head? In the independent world, there are plenty of people who come to mind who so epitomize the "Nailed It!" approach, though naturally their work will seem flawed and riddled with inadequacies through their own eyes, such is the nature of this particular beast. Certain filmmakers produce work of such across-the-board satisfaction that pretty much everyone will take notice.

One such artist is Adam Pesapane, whose work put out under the moniker PES started strong, from the early days of his 2001 film *Roof Sex*, which depicted little more than animated furniture rutting on a rooftop. The overriding silliness of the concept was made authentic, innocuous and humorous in a way that endeared him instantly to audiences of all types. There's nothing perceivably dirty about the film, the attention to detail of the movement relating the cavorting furniture to animals in the wild (on the street, even) rather than any kind of threatening or debauched behavior. Yet so easily an idea of this kind could misfire if in the wrong hands, or executed with a more lackluster attitude. Comedic animation that relies on its subject matter alone oftentimes means the animation itself is rendered crudely or hurriedly; Not so with *Roof Sex*. PES's animation style and, perhaps most importantly,

Figure 13.2

Still from *Submarine Sandwich* (Dir. PES) ©2014 PES.

beautifully observed timing elevates the film as something noteworthy. The same applies to the greater part of his filmography, which includes *Game Over* (2006), a montage of familiar retro video game scenarios recreated using household objects; *Kaboom!* (2004), in which a military airstrike is similarly conveyed using trinkets and other found miscellany, and his "Food Trilogy" of *Western Spaghetti* (2008), *Fresh Guacamole* (2012) and *Submarine Sandwich* (2014, Figures 13.1 and 13.2), whose funding circumstances we touched upon in Chapter 9.

As is often the case, PES first acknowledged a sense of the greater impact his film work had on the world through their online viral success, especially when considering he was not the source.

"At the time of *Game Over* I was just releasing them as Quicktime files on my website, and this amazing thing happened where people just came to the site, ripped the files and threw them up on YouTube. At any given moment you could look on YouTube and see a hundred different versions of *Game Over.*"

The film had amassed millions upon millions of hits spread out over its multiple postings. Acknowledging that the online video craze was not about to die away any time soon, PES made the executive decision to release his own work via his own channel, ideally as a means to steer the public toward his other work while at the very least guaranteeing they would be of an ideal quality standard.

"Once I launched my channel, the very first film that got into that viral territory was *Western Spaghetti.* I was going on vacation over the fourth of July 2008 and was scrambling to get this thing online so I could go relax for a couple days, I must have posted it around 4 am. I was off onto my vacation the day after when all the emails started coming in, so I was totally out of the house for the whole weekend, at the beach. My email was completely shut down because of how many people and how many messages were coming through for that film, I had so many calls coming in on the phone, so much immediate response that it really became its own monster online."

While it would be impossible to quantify precisely how many hits earlier shorts such as *Roof Sex* (Figure 13.3) or *Kaboom!* may have had, the decision to

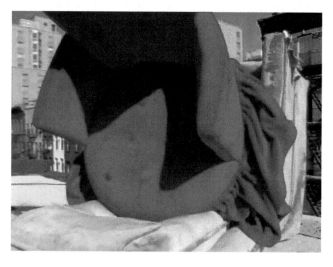

Figure 13.3

Still from *Roof Sex* (Dir. PES) ©2002 PES.

13. Thinking Outside the Lightbox

release work personal ensured a means of determining each subsequent film's level of popularity and audience engagement.

"I would say what's fascinating about *Western Spaghetti* (Figure 13.4) is that it actually got more hits per year six years on than it did the first year. Obviously, the explosion of social media since 2008 is responsible for some of that, but it is nice to see that people are still finding value to these films. I hope they continue to do that for a long time.

"The success of *Western Spaghetti* is more of a personal thing; I found that the substitution of objects as something I like to do fit really snugly with the cooking film genre, which is very ingredient-focused by nature. I was really pleased with the way that it was this nice little place for those ideas to live as I had been sitting on a lot of the ideas seen in *Western Spaghetti* – sticky notes as butter, rubber bands as spaghetti – for a while, not knowing what to do with them, so I gravitated towards the cooking show genre and went from there."

Though it was certainly helped by the encouraging response, the motivation to continue more crucially came from still more cooking-oriented film ideas. Taking inspiration from all around him, the basic concept of the second "Food Trilogy" short came from a pondering of the visual similarities between avocados and hand grenades while grocery shopping. Having recently moved to California and feeling compelled to stray from his Italian roots for a second culinary outing, PES traveled to Mexico to research recipes and develop his next idea.

"There's something in my brain where I fall in love with these ideas so much that I need to get them out into the world, so I set about making *Fresh Guacamole* coming from that seed of avocados and grenades. Okay, what do you make with avocados? Guacamole!"

As with *Western Spaghetti*, and indeed all of his popular work, *Fresh Guacamole* makes inspired use of household objects substituting ingredients, chosen for their visual resemblance and animated in such a way as to suspend disbelief entirely. The audience's brain knows on a literal level that they are seeing Christmas lights being chopped into an assortment of Monopoly houses, but they understand on a contextual level that they are in fact seeing peppers.

"I've almost thought of myself as a documentary filmmaker in some respects, it's just that I'm making these documentaries on the absurd. Even if it's two chairs

Figure 13.4

Still from *Western Spaghetti* (Dir. PES) ©2008 PES.

Figure 13.5

Still from *Kaboom!* (Dir. PES) ©2004 PES.

having sex, you'll notice all these films are shot very much as though I believe wholeheartedly that they're happening. I want my audience to take it as if I'm *really* cooking this (rubber band) pasta. *Kaboom!* (Figure 13.5) is basically like a history channel show, just with child's objects, and it's the sort of believability that I approach ideas with that heightens the absurdity and perhaps the response to it."

Real life consistently plays a role in the authenticity and believability of his visuals. Just as a character animator might study live performance or documentary footage for reference, so that their work can faithfully replicate a realistic style of movement, it's the examination of how real life objects look, sound and interact with each other that makes his work shine. Even when considering a film such as Game Over, which entirely references video game sprite animation, anyone of a certain age who experienced them firsthand will acknowledge a truly impressive fidelity to the timing, framing and even sense of mounting anxiety.

"Although there was really nothing to study in two chairs having sex, it really was just a sort of rhythm thing – how many frames forward or how many frames back in order to get that right. But with *Game Over* I used an emulator on my computer to record sequences of these famous arcade games and study them: How many frames does it take Pac-Man to die at the end, or what's the hold before the frog jumps each time? So I studied these things and broke them down to understand how many frames were used in the real game, so it was dead-on accurate when it comes to movement. It wasn't rotoscoped, I really just sort of studied the games so much that I understood what had to happen, then just recreated it.

"A film like *Game Over* is really built on my perception that what we remember most about these games is not all the wins we had but that thing that just drove you crazy, whether it was shooting centipedes down and then the spider just comes out of nowhere, or in *Space Invaders*, how even if you kill all the aliens so that you only have one left, he would come all the way down and get you. In stringing these famous death sequences together it was the notion that it was more memorable for how you died than how you lived, that was really the concept there."

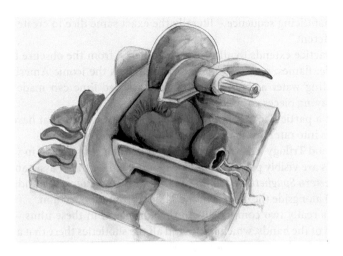

Figure 13.6

Submarine Sandwich concept artwork ©2014 PES.

To achieve the desired result is not just a matter of simply scooping up as many trinkets and pieces of household debris as possible and moving them around, as many PES imitators have demonstrated while effectively failing to grasp the central binding premise of his work. Ultimately, the choice of props and items boils down to what he equates with an elaborate casting session, one that can be held for months at a time, often branching off from one initial idea. As with the avocado/grenade epiphany that inspired *Fresh Guacamole*, the third film of the "Food Trilogy," eventually dubbed *Submarine Sandwich*, similarly took shape around an initial visual concept PES had envisioned, of putting a boxing glove inside a deli meat-slicer (Figure 13.6).

"I thought that was a really tantalizing image; boxing gloves always seem like cold cuts or fine Italian meats, so to speak, and putting them knuckle first toward the blade created a certain sort of palpable feeling." What followed was a series of musings on what could come out the other side, the 'meat slices' effectively. This automatically narrowed down variety of suitable objects to the very small and thin, such as patches, doilies and, in one particularly inspired instance, view-master reels (produced when the "meat" being sliced is a British soccer ball). The limitations of shape and size proved challenging, and inevitably some ideas come across stronger than others, "But at the end of the day I have to go with what I think is the best decision I can make at any given time. So there may have been multiple 'actors' considered for the role of onion rings, but in the end, a slinky gets the job.

"I guess a lot of people don't realize how much thought and how much work goes into trying to decide or uncover those associations – sometimes a great idea will strike you like a lightning bolt. If you recall, in *Western Spaghetti* I used dice as sugar cubes, but the connection there really stopped at a lookalike level. Somewhere in between there and *Fresh Guacamole*, I realized that a better idea would be to use dice for dicing – because that's what we say; we dice a tomato and we dice an onion. Then it became a question of whether or not, having used it as a sugar cube, could I use it again as something totally different? Of course the decision I made was 'Yes, I have to choose the best thing for every film,' so I chose that for that dicing sequence – literally the exact same dice to create something totally different."

This practice extends to all manner of objects, from the obscure to instantly identifiable; flames, oftentimes, are represented as the iconic American Candy Corn, boiling water as bubble wrap, while a sliced lime can made up Trivial Pursuit playing pieces encased in a golf ball.

"I have a particular fascination for these strange objects that have so woven themselves into our lives that we almost stop questioning them."

The "Food Trilogy" also incorporates a pixilation component, in which PES's own hands are visibly part of the process, animated (with the assistance of Javan Ivey in *Western Spaghetti* and Dillon Markey in *Fresh Guacamole* and *Submarine Sandwich*) alongside the objects in the same stop-motion fashion.

"There's really two components to the animation in these films – one is the animation of the hands, which is me, and all the subtleties there that are required to make it feel believable and not ugly. Then of course all the animation of objects that are based around my hands requires a partner, a teammate in the production. It's totally different to a film like *Game Over* where you just have your objects and don't need anybody else; this is more like two people who have to get on the same wavelength for months. Dillon and I had succeeded with *Fresh Guacamole*, he understands my tastes and things that I'm usually seeking to achieve in my animation, he's become a great partner in that respect."

When closing out his trilogy with *Submarine Sandwich* (Figures 13.7 and 13.8), PES himself is seen fully onscreen as the pixilated owner of a deli, a setting he had aspired to set the film in for some time beforehand, as made clear in Chapter 9.

"This film really started with a simple idea of how old athletic equipment always reminded me so much of cold cuts that I started envisioning a deli case full of these things, a sort of 'meat locker' so to speak; sort of cross between an athletic locker room and a deli, which was just an idea that occurred to me. I then started working on not just making a ham sandwich, but something bigger, a Submarine sandwich.

Having procured the deli case of his traditional Italian culture-steeped dreams, the vision for the film expanded to logically set it inside a realistic deli environment. With the notion of an on-location shoot rendered impossible by

Figure 13.7

Still from *Submarine Sandwich* (Dir. PES) ©2014 PES.

13. Thinking Outside the Lightbox

the production lengths and overall demands of the animation itself, PES set about building an authentic backdrop himself, choosing to favor authentic set-dressing over generic Hollywood prop house fare.

"It's just my nature to craft a space and make it personal, so I thought to myself *This is gonna be the only time I'm making a deli in my life, as far as I know, why not make it that place that feels like a home to me?* If I were to have a deli, this is what it would look like, it would have busts of the patron saints Dante and Beatrice and pictures of the Pantheon in Rome. That was the fun of it, for me, was making the space with all these old signs which are all real. I sourced those objects from around the world, from flea-markets to Craigslist to eBay. It made for a much bigger build – *Fresh Guacamole* and *Western Spaghetti* were purely table-top films and this one made use of a whole space. I don't think it makes the film any *better* for that reason, it was just what felt right for this particular idea."

There is certainly an element of the abstract in PES's films, in spite of being very simple to interpret and comprehend. As with other work we have discussed that could be labeled "experimental," without this structural foothold, the films could very easily fall apart. PES's filmography, and ultimately the reason why I feel he makes the most fitting case study for this chapter, serves to hammer home the duality of style and substance, all too often they are looked upon as being mutually exclusive.

"All the things that people say you always need for a successful film – characters, a story – I don't really buy that. If you can create a system where viewers want to know simply what happens next, if you can tap into that desire, *then* you have a short film, something equally viable in the world.

"I'm a big believer in traditional structures. I spend a lot of time working on trying to find a structure for my film that feels like it has that beginning, middle and end. I'm always looking for that inevitable conclusion to a film that feels like it *had* to go there, yet is not quite expected. With *Submarine Sandwich*, for instance, the big idea for me is in hiding the submarine itself until the very end.

"Transitionally I might say I would start the film by picking my bread out, cutting it and putting it down without revealing the submarine as I had this notion that if I held it to the end it would be more of a satisfying conclusion. Almost all my films have that priority on the ending, that sort of exclamation point at the end that makes watching the entire thing essential, or you miss out. There's all sorts of different examples of that, such as *Fresh Guacamole*, with the chip being dipped and cracked at the end. I think when I animate objects people are used to looking at certain structures that are familiar in one way and then all of a sudden I do something different with them, there's a sort of unexpected quality that makes people want to know what happens next."

While it is never fair to expect an artist to choose a favorite piece of work, when objectively assessing his back catalog to date, PES is able to impartially acknowledge one film in particular that fired on the most cylinders at once.

"I think *Fresh Guacamole* was one of those ideas that worked out particularly well, the puzzle of it fell together in a 'total' way that I have a particular fondness for. I'm too close to *Submarine Sandwich* to truly evaluate it fairly, but the nature of using a deli slicer was the challenge, because with a knife – which *Fresh Guacamole* is really about, a knife – there was a little bit more transformative magic. A deli slicer is more challenging in that it's almost like having two rooms separated by a wall, seeing what comes out on one side. It's magical but not maybe as magical as some of those instances in *Fresh Guacamole* where the

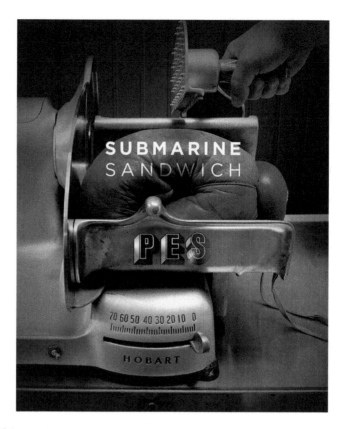

Figure 13.8

Submarine Sandwich poster ©2014 PES.

knife comes down and the objects become something different, but that's just me evaluating my own work. I think *Fresh Guacamole* just all worked out in the best possible way."

A seemingly indefatigable mainstay of the independent scene has, for decades, been film festivals, for fairly obvious reasons. The right festival can provide film-makers with invaluable exposure, networking opportunities and direct communication with a live audience to get a true sense of their artistic worth. There's no better context for a filmmaker to find out whether they have succeeded in impacting their audience than in a packed cinema, nor to determine precisely what form their audience will take. My own festival experience has shone a spotlight on the incongruities between the reaction I'd imagine a film might have and the realities of the matter; as someone who hopes his films will be funny, I can attest that it's a grounding experience to witness a moment you might assume had great comedic mileage play to silence, only for a throwaway gag you had never thought twice about beforehand bring down the house. Naturally, as with everything, there are many factors to be weighed against one another when it comes to festivals, something that will be explored further in Chapter 20, but a general home truth in this industry is that mass festival selection of a film is ordinarily a hallmark of its quality.

So how do you make a festival-worthy film? What do festival programmers look for in shorts that make them stand out? The best way to determine the answers to these is to seek insight from festival programmers themselves about what they look for and how they go about it.

Programmers' Perspectives

A misconception that has cropped up time and again is that festival programmers are the ultimate arbiters of what makes a film worthwhile. The truth of the matter is that these are individuals – or small groups of individuals – with their own tastes, artistic inclinations and unique ideas for what the voice and tone of their event should be. Compiling a fully rounded series of curated screenings that audiences will come away from feeling entertained or culturally enriched by is not as easy as one might think. It takes months of planning and logistics, and even then there may be some misfires among the selection.

Each festival will have its own specifics but, generally speaking, there will be three main phases programmers work through once the hundreds (or even thousands) of films have been submitted. Firstly an initial round of preselection, where key staff from a festival organization look over all the entries. For festivals that are more in-demand, sometimes this process begins between the opening and closing of their Call for Entries so as to not have to wade through an avalanche of submissions in one go, come the entry deadline. Sometimes the preselector(s) will be the main programmer or programmers of an event, sometimes they will be another team within the festival or recruited separately on a freelance basis. In any case, the preselection phase is to whittle down what has come through by eliminating films that don't fit the criteria outlined in the festival regulations or are objectively (sometimes subjectively, as is the programmer's prerogative) unwatchable. The second phase is usually when final decisions are made as to which films are eligible to screen and which, among them, are eligible to compete; oftentimes, festivals will have non-competitive fringe, supplemental or panorama screenings. Lastly – or sometimes concurrently – the selected films are divided up by what category of screening they belong to. Sometimes these categories are fairly broad groupings – for example, international competition, national competition, student films – and sometimes within each section will be thematic sub-categories: love stories, comedies, politically charged films and so on.

Unfortunately for filmmakers, uncontrollable issues such as timing and circumstance can be a major factor in whether a film is relevant or a fit for that year's edition of the festival it has been submitted to. For festival programmers and Artistic Directors, this can result in a lot of difficult decisions that need to be made as far as which films do and don't make the cut; as such, it's very important not to take rejection to heart (something we'll expand on later in the book). In this section, we'll hear from a range of festival programmers who have shared their insights on some key pitfalls to avoid when it comes to your films, so as to stand out enough to make it past that crucial preselection stage and be in serious contention for official selection.

The festival experts canvassed include Kieran Argo, whose roles in curation include having been the Animation Program Manager at Bristol's Encounters Film Festival as well as Producer of the British Animation Awards; Steve Henderson, Director and CEO of Manchester Animation Festival; Lauren Orme, Festival Director of Cardiff Animation Festival and its associated, year-round screenings series Cardiff Animation Nights; Chris Robinson, Artistic Director of the Ottawa International Animation Festival; Daniel Šuljić, Artistic Director of Animafest Zagreb; Marie Valade, Programmer at Festival Stop Motion Montréal; Nag Vladermersky, Director and Chief Programmer of the London International Animation Festival; and Tünde Vollenbroek, former Head of Program at Kaboom (previously KLIK!) Animation Festival.

From my own experience as a preselector for various events over the years, I've noticed that red flags tend to pop up in clusters around specific areas of either concept or production. The most prevalent by a country mile would be the issue of length and pace, an area in which filmmakers need to exert a lot of self-discipline.

Every once in a while, there will be a film that exceeds the twenty-minute mark, maybe even the half-hour mark, that legitimately engages the audience for its entire duration; but man alive, it is a once-in-a-blue-moon type deal when it comes to shorts curation. As Tünde Vollenbroek recalls, "Some films just go on and on for way too long. In some cases I've been tempted to call the filmmakers and ask 'Could you please just speed up the film by about 50%? Then we'd really like to select it!'"

Generally speaking, this is the attitude of most programmers, not just in regards to the film taking up so many minutes of programming space, but the other films that could potentially be doing likewise that are now at a disadvantage. "If you're going over twenty minutes," insists Chris Robinson, "it better be a goddamn masterpiece, because that's taking up spots for maybe two, three or four films."

"There is always limited space in any festival programme and so festivals like to celebrate the whole spectrum of what is available in animation," explains Steve Henderson. "For MAF at least, we would rather programme more smaller films than a handful of lengthy films. If you have a six minute film, it needs to be twice as good as a three minute long film, if you have a twelve minute film it needs to be four times as good because it is taking up the space that four films otherwise would."

When a film demanding more time comes along that is undoubtedly strong and will likely be a hit with the crowd, of course it makes sense to find a place for it. In the case of LIAF and some other festivals, this has actually led to special programs and competition categories solely intended for longer films. It stands to reason, then, that if a long film doesn't necessarily amount to a bad film, a short film won't automatically be good; if the best quality of a film is that it ends quickly, that's never a good sign. There's also no magic formula or sweet spot to shoot for when it comes to a film's ideal length, as it's crucially dependent on how you as the filmmaker are putting across your concept.

"Really whatever the length that best suits your story is fine," says Nag Vladermersky. "LIAF screen very few films that are under three minutes. There are some that we screen that are around the two-to-three minute mark, but generally I'd say the average length is somewhere between five and ten minutes. But if you've got a really, really great idea for a twenty-minute film and you know that it merits it, then go for it."

"If something is thirty minutes long and it's great then we'll select it, no question," agrees Daniel Šuljić. "Some films just need this time to develop to bring you into the story. The biggest dilemma is when we have, say, one longer twenty-minute film which is quite good, and then you have three shorter films, seven minutes each, that are equally good. If we would like to show all of them, but we only have twenty minutes left in the program, then we have to make a decision – do you show the one longer film or the three shorter films? We rewatch films over and over again when we're working on a final selection, it's always a discussion and we decide from case to case."

For Marie Valade, dealing in the more specific category of stop-motion animation and the unique demands of its process, the expectations on length are a touch more strict: "I think under ten minutes works well. If you have a four minute film it's easier to get it in, but at the same time, you cannot tell artists what to do! They do what they want and then either get picked up or not. Basically, if you're shooting for a twenty minute film then it needs to be really, really exceptional."

And as far as what qualities a longer film should have to push it into the category of "exceptional"?

"The same as a short one!" insists Daniel. "Innovation, strong images, clear story, emotional connection with the audience. If it's funny, it should be intelligently funny. So they're the same measurements as far as what we're looking for, from one minute to forty minutes (which is our limit for shorts, anything over is a feature, in our view)."

For Lauren Orme, a film more protracted in its telling "just needs a meatier story, really. Sometimes you'll get a longer, slow paced film, which will play really nicely in a cinema context."

"A good rule of thumb is to keep the audience hooked and not to outstay your welcome on screen," suggests Steve. "At the end of the day the perfect length to a film doesn't exist, it's the content of the film that matters most."

Strength of content, not coasting on basic, stretched-out concepts and taking your audience's expectation of being invested in the world of your film into consideration are areas that Tünde also insists are crucial, regardless of length; "Other examples are if there's one joke that goes on for way too long, or if the visual concept is really cool but there's nothing more to it, it could have been explored more, and thus it goes on for too long. Sometimes a concept/story just doesn't have enough meat on it for the length the film has – or for a film at all! A story/concept can be small, that's absolutely fine. But if you have a small story/concept, please don't make the film a second longer than it needs to be to convey that story/concept."

Kieran Argo's advice to young filmmakers is to turn to what has come before for guidance and analyzing the strengths of films that have proved successful in the past (in a large respect mirroring the main philosophy of this book on the whole): "Look at the quality of the production, look at how well they're put together, imagine what the storyboard would look like, imagine how the film was conceived, look at the design. Are the characters convincing? The technical aspect should always be scrutinized very closely, as well as the fundamental storytelling ability of it. Break it down into its component parts and scrutinize each aspect of the production as much as you can, from what you're given: You can read the credits, you can read the synopses and whatever other supporting info you're supplied with, you can use that to understand the film in its whole, as much as you can.

"I think films that are brave, films that stand out, that go out on a limb in a particular area – for example, design – they're the ones that jump the queue."

While looking back at what has come before as a jumping-off point for your own ideas is definitely a recommended approach, be sure to avoid simply imitating it on a superficial level. Sometimes when a film becomes a part of the zeitgeist in a major way, it can be a wonderful thing to see it inspire others in real time; the woolly aesthetic, for example, of Marc James Roels and Emma De Swaef's *Oh Willy...* (a beautifully bizarre tale of a man whose return to the naturist colony he grew up in marks the first step of an increasingly fantastic odyssey) had a significant impact on stop-motion production design and puppet fabrication, identifiable through the glut of needle-felted stop-motion films that followed in its wake. While many of these were original and inventive in their own right, with each year of preselection, there are inevitably a chunk of films that do little more than copy a visual approach or narrative concept of something popular that has preceded it without substance, originality of concept or unique spin of any kind. I cannot count how many *Black Mirror, Spider-Verse, Stranger Things, Love Death + Robots* or, most egregious of all, *Family Guy*[1] rip-off films I've seen over the years.

"It's great that we have so many wonderful shows, shorts and features that inspire us everyday," says Steve, "but the success that these inspirational projects have enjoyed is hard to replicate from scratch and filmmakers who put style first in order to recreate what they love as opposed to finding their own voice and style are doing themselves a disservice. Style isn't everything – the story is."

Similarly, Chris is "not interested in Pixar-copy films and stuff that you're making with a marketplace in mind, or as a calling card. It's really just about engagement."

Daniel Šuljić's priorities when it comes to programming are unique voices; directors who use innovation to put across ideas and concepts that festivals and festival audiences haven't seen before.

"When you have ambition, as all the festivals do, to show the newest films and try to trace the development of the art form, then you are not doing this if what you're showing is repeating somebody else. So yes, there are films that open the door for a whole new style but there is a difference between being influenced and copying. There is always a generation that makes something and inspires the next one, which in turn makes it on their own. If somebody just copies something, then it's maybe not so interesting. If they make something new out of it, then it becomes interesting again."

This is a sentiment that most share, including Tünde: "When a film tries too hard to be something else – style mostly, or sense of humor – and fails, it just feels like an empty shell. Make sure if you decide to attempt cliché or imitation that you do it extremely well."

"It's just a weaker proposition to me," adds Marie, "to have to reference something else. Something weird we see in stop-motion over and over again is that we receive a lot of films based on a character who is conscious of being a stop-motion puppet. It's a nice idea but it's been used a lot of times, so if you're going this way, you need to have a really good twist."

For Lauren, a film that wears its inspirations on its sleeve is not necessarily a bad thing, so long as the film comes across as authentic to the director's experience: "It can't just be 'I love *Steven Universe*, here's something that looks like it'; there's got to be something in there, something not necessarily unique – because I really hate that idea that every film has to be unique – but there's got to be something in there that speaks truth, or rings true."

We will be taking a more in-depth look at how you approach the sound and music for your film in a later chapter, but the importance of not rushing this area of production – or approaching it the wrong way – should also be addressed here.

"Many entries we see are let down by poor sound," laments Nag. "My advice would be to watch some of the films that have screened at festivals over the years, turn the image off and just listen to the sound – then watch the film again but turn the sound off. You can see how sound really enhances the film and is a vital part of it."

For Steve and the team at MAF, the value of well-crafted sound design actually takes precedence over the subjective competency or style of a film's visuals. "We have screened films in the past which are just lines dancing! We have an open mind when it comes to art style. However, we don't have much of an open mind when it comes to sound design, which is perhaps the most important thing to get right, regardless of the animated medium you use.

"When we watch our selections, we like to watch them all back to back and so it quickly becomes apparent which films have not put effort into their soundtrack and which filmmakers have opted to use the same free sound effects. You can't beat good foley, we'd encourage any filmmakers to design their own foley or find someone who can. A good soundtrack can elevate a film more than any visual can."

Programmers all have their own personal bugbears when it comes to this topic. For Chris Robinson, it's the well-worn dependence on a piano-based soundtrack, or songs arbitrarily set to visuals with no meaningful interplay, as is often the case with music videos. Marie Valade also notes how crucial a decent mix can be to the enjoyment of a film.

"You shouldn't need to turn the volume up or down during the viewing; I don't want to burst my ears and I don't want to not be able to hear anything." Another issue Marie cites are musical scores that try too hard to contrive an emotional response, instead overwhelming the film and negating its audience's potential to engage sincerely. "Just let me jump into your film. You don't need to force the emotion with a big orchestra; I like an orchestra, just not when it's over the top, trying to tell you what emotion you should have."

Another drawback in a film's soundtrack, agreed upon pretty much across the board, is when films substitute dialogue with 'um's, 'ah's and 'ooh's – it's one thing if a character organically reacts to their environment on occasion, it's another when every movement and moment is punctuated by an arbitrary grunt. This in many respects is emblematic of most major sound issues – that it has become noticeable to the point of distraction.

"Sound work is a supporting role," says Daniel, "and if it's great, you will not notice it. Fantastic. If it's great and you *do* notice it, and it works with the film, even better. But if you notice it and it's annoying, it can be the moment where we decide we don't want to select the film. So sound can really make or break a film."

Of course, having dialogue in your film is not without its own hurdles to overcome, most obviously the quality of the acting and the degree to which performers are a fit for the characters they play. From Daniel's perspective, heading up an international event that deals with a lot of English-language films, the mere audibility of dialogue can sometimes be an issue.

"Everybody speaks English (kind of) but if you send the film without subtitles and the narration or dialogue has been badly recorded and is spoken in a heavy accent, it can be a problem. There have been a couple of examples where we couldn't judge or select the film because we simply couldn't follow what was going on, so I would recommend that native English-speaking people include English subtitles. They don't have to be shown in the theater, that can be discussed, but add in the subtitles for the selection so that selectors – not only me from Croatia, but people from all over the world who watch it – will have a much easier task. This may make the difference between being selected or not."

An overabundance of dialogue can also be problematic, as Chris Robinson observes: "The reliance on talking has increasingly become an issue. I don't know if people just aren't trusting their visuals to convey what they want to get across but yeah, yappy films are my beef."

"When there's dialogue, there's often too much dialogue," agrees Tünde Vollenbroek. "Other times, a film has no dialogue at all but could really use it. I've come across many films that have annoyed me enormously with characters that either mumble too much or overact."

Overacting isn't necessarily the domain of amateur performers (their major issue being, if anything, not acting enough or at all); it can sometimes be a sought-after trait in professionals that, if matched to the wrong character or film environment, misfires completely. For Chris, "Sometimes having somebody who's too professional is maybe not the right way to go. I think what's so great about those old *Charlie Brown* specials is the natural acting, because it's untrained kids doing the voices. There's something really charming and engaging and real about that. That stuff I like."

The potential for an amateur performance to be an inspired choice for a film is something Lauren has also picked up on: "Sometimes you get your mate to record the dialogue and it can be really funny and good...but not a lot of the time." On the flip side, a performer who knows their onions and has been properly cast and directed can make a significant impact on whether or not the film sells itself.

"Some of the best films we get sent to us, you can tell that they've got actors who have got some experience and know where to put the different emphases on their voices," affirms Nag. "The right voices can really, really add to a film, as a bad narration can really do the opposite. A lot of films get sent to us that the animators have voiced themselves and it just lets it down."

When it comes to the final selection, Kieran Argo's bottom line when it comes to character-based, narrative shorts is how well the story is told.

"If they can tell the story in a compelling and engaging way, it doesn't *have* to be perfect or technically excellent. It can be forgiving in technique and many other aspects of production, but for me if it fails to live up to the title, if it doesn't convey a story, the narrative thread is lost. There are certain basic levels of competence that need to be set but the ones that really stand out are the ones that excel, principally, in storytelling. Sometimes the often overlooked importance of marrying sound and effects can tell a story better than the visual aspects, but combining good visuals with good sound is absolutely critical. The films that do that well, or have clearly put a lot of work and effort into that, are the ones that go up the priority list. The curator's role is not to be a gatekeeper in any way of refinement or quality, they really just have to make the painful decisions. The number of good films that have to be left out is always a bitter disappointment."

For many, the validation and personal satisfaction of making it into a festival's official selection is the ultimate goal. Others may be more incentivized by the prospect of winning awards, especially if they come in the form of financial assistance to support future creative projects, or are qualifiers for major accolades that would help ensure future career stability. Encounters is one of a number of festivals where winning films automatically become BAFTA eligible, a coup to any independent filmmaker. The ultimate decision, however, is rarely up to one individual, and on top of his programming duties, Kieran himself has also had firsthand experience of adjudication.

"What I think filmmakers sometimes need to remind themselves of is it's often the case that juries are not all signed up to the same decision. Conflict within juries has been known, as well as a few occasions where the best films sometimes didn't get awarded when they should have done. When juries are at loggerheads they may end up having to make a decision whereby the top prize goes to a compromise between the jury, rather than it being a collective, unanimous decision.

"A lot of filmmakers see the Audience Award to be much more valuable because that tells them that it's a hit with the crowd. It might be good to have the peer-reviewed thumbs-up from three or four well-respected professionals, but I think if I was a filmmaker I'd much prefer to have a thumbs-up from two or three hundred people in the audience. But it is the awards that still confirm kudos and status on a film, which is very useful in progressing the film's momentum around the festival circuit and how many awards it'll go on to achieve. If you pick up a top prize at Annecy – or other such benchmark festivals – and you're a filmmaker/animator you're going to have so many more festival doors open and undoubtedly pick up more awards.

The Online Crowd

The urge to share your film with the world the moment it is finished is no doubt especially tempting in an era where doing so is a very literal possibility. Long behind us are the days when the only evidence of your labors to share with the online community need be lo-res Quicktime files or horribly compressed 240p YouTube conversions sharing the same aesthetic appeal as early-onset cataracts. Nowadays, of course, our full-HD masterworks can be shared in all their glorious resolution, compressed by codecs sent from the heavens themselves, whose dainty touch yields barely a trace of visual artifact or blocky pixelation. I may be over-romanticizing a tad, but the key fact remains that, thanks to exponentially increasing internet speeds and the capabilities of video streaming services, there is already an established place for independent animation in this sphere, with the road ahead looking bright (Figure 13.9).

Filmmaker Jason Sondhi saw the writing on this particular wall back in 2007, along with *The Thomas Beale Cipher* director Andrew S. Allen. The two founded Short of the Week,[2] a website championing largely independent shorts of all genres and mediums.

"We thought it was a really strong opportunity for storytelling in the online space. What was really getting passed around a lot were TV rips and viral videos, we didn't understand why all these short films we'd loved seeing at film festivals weren't dominant. The conclusion we came to was that festival shorts are a very small, insular world, and there was no guide to point people in the right direction, to what was worth their time. With Andrew being an animator and myself being animation-inclined, a lot of our early curation really leaned in that direction, and we slowly became experts."

Another online platform taking the initiative to champion short film is Director's Notes,[3] founded the previous year by Managing Editor Rob Munday and Editor in Chief MarBelle. Rob would also join Short of the Week in 2009 as Managing Editor and, having accrued experience across online curation and within the festival sphere, his name is especially familiar to filmmakers and independent film fans who will likely have come across his passionate championing of the short film format in the years since. As an active participant in the online film community, he has helped to build, and as someone who has worked directly with innumerable filmmakers over the years to give their efforts a signal boost, he has a keen eye for work that is likely to stand out and gain traction if given the chance.

"I'm a strong believer that short films offer something very rare in a filmmaker's journey: an opportunity to make films without the restrictions they might encounter later in their career. With that in mind, I'm really searching for originality in a standout short. I want to be presented with new stories and introduced to new techniques and approaches, I want to experience things from a new perspective and gain insight into worlds and cultures I never knew existed. There are stories that would never have been told and production techniques that wouldn't exist if it wasn't for short film, and in my opinion, that's a really powerful thing.

"Online we do see genre trends and recurring themes that tend to be popular, so that does come into your headspace when considering the curation for your platform. However, it's really important to us that we never lower our standard just to accommodate these films."

As with festival selections, there are no guarantees when it comes to being selected for a profile or site pick, and for the same reasons, it shouldn't be taken to heart.

"We've passed on dozens of films that have gone on to be a huge success online, but even though we could recognise that potential, we ultimately declined those titles as they didn't align with our curatorial stance. It's a fine balance and other curators might have a different view here, but for the team at Short of the Week, we believe our curation is what sets us apart."

A particularly encouraging stance that both Director's Notes and Short of the Week share is the legitimacy and high artistic value of animation in the world of short films. It's rare these days, but there remain festivals and curation sites that minimize or exclude animation altogether. For Rob, animation

Figure 13.9

Sausage (Dir. Robert Grieves) would go on to receive a Vimeo Staff Pick as well as Cartoon Brew and Short of the Week Picks of the Day ©2013 Robert Grieves.

13. Thinking Outside the Lightbox

is "a personal favourite, so from my own perspective, I value it in the highest regard. I sometimes think if I could go back and do things differently I would have liked to be an animator…maybe it's never too late?

"I think all the festivals and online platforms I respect definitely see animation as a legitimate art form. After you've spoken to someone like Hisko Hulsing and he's explained his six-and-a-half year process of creating the short film *Junkyard*, how can you not? I also think we're seeing more and more animation being programmed alongside live-action, instead of sidelined into their own area and this is really refreshing to see. Animation is constantly exciting and full of innovation, isn't this what all programmers should be looking for?"

From his firsthand experience being involved in programming and award selection, Rob has witnessed instances of animation being a "token pick," or marginalized for the enduring myth that anything animated must be automatically "fun and childish."

"There are lots of great festivals and websites looking to disprove this notion. On Short of the Week we have channels dedicated to the specific animation formats (2D, 3D, stop-motion etc), but the animations also live within our themed collections (e.g. Love, Humanity, The Mind etc) next to our live-action films and we love the fact they do. There are some festivals trying to do this as well, but I do wish it was more commonplace.

"In general, I think animation is perfectly suited to the world of online. The average duration of an animated short tends to be considerably shorter than its live-action counterpart, and for an easily distracted audience (as we know is often the case online), that's a real bonus. I also think that a lot of those qualities that I look for in standout shorts (see above) can often be found in animation. There's a certain limitless freedom that seems to inspire animators into creating some truly groundbreaking and unforgettable films and that's the type of thing the internet tends to embrace wholeheartedly."

As with the festival route, naturally, with online curation, there are caveats that need to be met when it comes to sorting the wheat from the chaff. While it is an open forum for content creators to upload anything they wish, this creates a similarly oversaturated landscape as that faced by festival programmers. Jason's parameters for quality filmmaking come with their own ideologies:

"I think animators are let off easy a little bit, because people prioritize visual panache and technical excellence over storytelling. I do find this a little bit unfortunate and try to push back with my own curation where I can. As technology, tutorials and overall levels of expertise of young animators keep improving, I find myself looking to story more, looking to scripts that are funny or well-written and narrative structures that surprise, that are unfamiliar. On the other hand, the visuals are obviously super important as well. I've gotten to the point where, even though I'm not an animator, I have enough knowledge through practical experience of watching to be able to discern technique, to discern when someone is doing something new and what it is about what they are doing that is original. So I prioritize originality as well, pushing the medium forward in fresher ways, technique-wise. Also I have to prioritize my own aesthetic tastes, I love things that are beautiful, things that are bright, things that are fresh, things that take an idea such as abstraction or Eoin Duffy's minimalism and are able to execute it at such a sublime sort of level. Taking that initial germ of an idea and being able to decipher that in the work, what it is they're going for and then being able to judge aesthetically how they have been able to achieve or not achieve it."

Across the board, it's fairly easy to identify the main recurring qualities of contemporary filmmaking that curators and programmers are after. Possessing any or all of these can still not be enough if your film makes a certain vital misstep. The pitfalls of a film that might otherwise have had potential warrant special consideration, especially when it comes to originality.

"Avoid cliché in any form, whether it's visual clichés or writing clichés; there was a point several years ago where the concept of every short seemed to revolve around a chase of some sort, whether it would make sense or not. You don't want a short that purely serves as opportunities to flex your skill if you have the inability to think of the overall structure and come up with a satisfying ending. I also look for polish – something that has great design but has poor, blocky motion, those kinds of things I'll judge as bothersome.

"As much as you want to try to intellectualize and create a consistent schema for your own evaluation you do end up falling back repeatedly on intuition and feel. When something is fresh it hits you in an emotional place and you know it when you see it. When you don't see it sometimes you find yourself having to talk yourself into positive qualities that may or may not be there, or making excuses, but then you have to take a step back and realize *Oh, I'm trying to rationalize something that I am just not feeling.*"

Returning to the festival side, the major stumbling blocks can be a mix of practical limitations and overall work ethic, as Kieran Argo notes:

"Sometimes a film can tell a story well but the sound mix – the effects or the dubbing – is so bad that you just couldn't contemplate adding it into the mix. Just because you think you've cracked a certain technique or ability to do something, whether it's visual or audio, don't be too indulgent with it, be parsimonious, be disciplined. Discipline is absolutely critical. When a filmmaker cracks something, it's obvious when they work it to death, they'll just bash it until there's no life left in it. You've got to be very careful not to be over-indulgent in aspects of technique and ability. It's the less-is-more approach, often you can make a point by putting in more breathing space, more pauses, the whole nonverbal ability to tell the story and to convince people to make it resonate emotionally, you can use discipline to great effect in those aspects. So be disciplined. Self-flagellate!"

Notes

1 Seriously, folks – that show started in like 1999. Let's set our sights on something more recent, yeah?
2 http://www.shortoftheweek.com.
3 https://directorsnotes.com/.

14

Keeping Up

The number of platforms available to independent filmmakers of any medium and genre is bigger than ever before, and growing exponentially. Certainly, the days of physical home media could draw to a close soon,[1] with dwindling retail outlets in keeping with consumer demand. The many HD streaming or digital download resources available in their absence more than compensates, with the perks of supplemental features intact and even improved upon.

There is certainly evidence that festivals have been adapting to this philosophy. Bristol's Encounters Film Festival are among those who embraced the potential for web-based engagement with the incorporation of its supplemental online strand DepicT![2] since 1999. As its own competitive section within the larger festival, it challenges filmmakers to create exceptional work with a running time no longer than ninety seconds, a caveat to which Kieran Argo attributes its huge draw for international filmmakers.

"I think the length of ninety seconds for DepicT! is a good, do-able length, especially for live action. It's a bit more of a challenge for animation but again, it's down to discipline, to be able to do something that works in that maximum duration, to do that requires a lot of work. To do it *well* requires skill, requires a vision, requires discipline and it usually requires an element of collaboration as well."

Animators of note who have been shortlisted for the competition include Trevor Hardy (*Oops*), Felix Massie (*Can, Can, Can't*), Paul Hill (*Sun*), Joseph Pierce (*State of Nature, Big On Love*) and Nick Mackie (*Flimsies*) with prizewinning animators including Mole Hill (*The Fat Cat*), Matthew Walker (*Operator*) and Aidan McAteer (*The Gentleman's Guide to Villainy*), all of whom going on to further achieve notable industry success.

DOI: 10.1201/9781003214717-14

Figure 14.1

Still from *The Gentleman's Guide to Villainy* (Dir. Aidan McAteer) ©2010 Aidan McAteer.

"A lot of people are motivated to rise to the challenge so they can set themselves the feasible goal of an achievable kind of duration they can envisage completing in a decent space of time. I don't think you'd get that many people rising to a five-minute challenge because it's a different ball game. With anything longer than that you need to more seriously consider budget, how much you can realistically afford to do. Ingredients such as financial commitment, money and time have to be carefully considered before you embark on any project."

One filmmaker who certainly embraced the challenge and, in turn, reaped the rewards of DepicT! is 2010 winner Aidan McAteer, who used the competition as an excuse to make his first independent animated short since his college years.

It was also an opportunity to create something that would provide a refreshing change from his day job, which at the time was as an animation revisionist on the hugely popular *My Little Pony* reboot *My Little Pony: Friendship is Magic*.

"To be fair, it's a really good show, but it wasn't the most creatively fulfilling; I was taking other people's scenes and tweaking them, so if there was something the directors didn't like in a shot, I would make changes. It was paying the bills and I was happy to have it, but there were a lot of sparkles and pink fluffy clouds involved, which wasn't really my thing."

When that year's edition of DepicT! came across his radar, the feasibility of a ninety-second passion project without creative boundaries but a motivational deadline to work toward held great appeal to Aidan. On top of that, the idea of taking his own personal measures in broadening his filmmaking experience had long-term potential.

"People who are really good at stuff, who make strong first films, have inevitably been making 'short films' all their lives. I know that if you look at any good feature film director that you could name – Spielberg, del Toro, the Coen brothers, whoever – they've probably all been making films since they were ten or eleven with Super 8 cameras. So when the time comes to direct a feature, it's actually not the first film they'll have made, which I think is how they turn out so well. That was something else that I got in my head as well, so even if it didn't turn out to be the greatest thing in the world, I'd have made a film and built on my experience and when I would move on the next one would be even better."

Not only did this investment of Aidan's time and creative energies prove worthwhile when it came to winning the main DepicT! prize and subsequent exposure, it provided a track record that would serve to benefit his career years down the line; funding for his subsequent 2014 film *Deadly* was ultimately provided by the Irish Film Board's Frameworks scheme on the basis of his prior success.

Visually speaking, *The Gentleman's Guide to Villainy* (Figures 14.1 and 14.2) is poles apart from the sunny climes and bright colors of the *Friendship is Magic* universe, and not by chance.

"The film is sort of a visual catharsis; it's all angular, whereas there are no angles in *My Little Pony*. The animation boils and the backgrounds are really rough, charcoal-textured and messy. It's a black-and-white, 'silent' film, so I also put the old-timey iris around it. That kind of stuff was a kind of antidote, in a way, to the very cute, pink style of the show.

"There's something I really enjoy about super-short-filmmaking, where you can just take out all the unnecessary elements and leave just the kernel of the idea. If that's only one or two minutes, then that's fine, it's still going to be a good film. I have that sensibility, I guess, from having worked in commercials for quite a while."

Produced over the three months that led up to that year's DepicT! deadline, the element of haste when it came to the film's production certainly played its own part when it came to the overall design style. On top of the grainy, silent film aesthetic, the animation itself was simplified by having the characters appear entirely as cartoon modern-style silhouettes, with no extraneous details or elaborate facial animation beyond rudimentary mouth movements and dots for eyes. The sparseness of the film's backgrounds proved another labor-saving device, one which benefits the overall composition of each shot by not cluttering it or distracting from the main action. All told, each time or budgetary concession serves to support and enhance the "period piece" tone of the film. Concessions or no, in Aidan's mind, it is likely that the film would not have existed at all without the incentivizing nature of the contest and its parameters.

"There's lots of argument about this, but I'm one of those people who believes that limitations can create great art. I'm not saying *The Gentleman's Guide to Villainy* is 'great art,' but I do like having limitations, because I think it forces you to just direct your mind and focus. In animation, you can do anything, which is really daunting – 'I can do *anything*? Well…then what the hell am I supposed to *do*?' I find that almost too much, an overload. It's like entering something for an exhibition with no theme. In the case of my film, the limitations were good in two ways – firstly that they did inform the story I wanted to tell, knowing it had to be short; and secondly, that I felt like I could do it myself. So they definitely helped for me, I didn't find them a hindrance at all.

"I think if that film had been three minutes long, then it wouldn't have been as funny. It's a gag, basically, so I think I would have been laboring the point. I think it's a stronger film for being at ninety seconds."

Since its initiation, the internet has caught up to DepicT!, and with the notion of online film competitions no longer unique, the present festival model needs to adapt and embrace the new opportunities available to filmmakers and audiences

Figure 14.2

Still from *The Gentleman's Guide to Villainy* (Dir. Aidan McAteer) ©2010 Aidan McAteer.

rather than combat it. While some argue that festivals are a dying breed, Kieran's view is firmly the opposite.

"Festivals are an absolutely unique opportunity to see films in their proper environment, which is up on a big screen with optimum visual and audio reproduction, with an audience. A festival does give you quite a unique experience but there is such a wide variety of opportunity to see stuff. Those can be integrated with festivals, for example we open up for the Online Audience Award and the DepicT! competition is there to be seen online in advance of the actual festival. There are always opportunities to develop ways of expanding and developing those means of engagement, but as with all things there are only so many projects that a very small dedicated core team of people can take on. I think DepicT! is a fantastic example of how it really has developed and gone from strength to strength, where in the first few years of running it we had a small handful of entries, it literally runs into several hundred submissions now, a lot of those having been made specifically for the competition. You can never sit still, you've got to keep on looking at new ideas, new opportunities, new ways of doing things."

Group Effort

There is constant scope for change, adaptation and exploration in the world of animation. Films that might be considered conceptually avant-garde can remain fundamentally entertaining. In the following case studies, we'll examine prominent independent shorts from out of left-field that, in their inventiveness, have helped to revitalize short film as a medium, beginning with the contemporization of an old, established technique.

Jeff Chiba Stearns equates the process of an AniJam to the collaborative "Exquisite Corpse" games of the Surrealists, in which words or imagery are contributed by multiple artists without knowledge of the preceding contribution, to create an unusual final result. Applying this approach to animated film for the first time of note was pioneering Canadian animator Marv Newland, who brought twenty-two animators together to work on his 1984 short film concept *AniJam*, ultimately coining the term. The film features a single character trapped in a hallucinatory world, each animator in turn granted reign over his plight in their own style, with no knowledge of the events of the film outside of their own section save for the final frame of animation of the sequence preceding theirs, so the action carries on throughout with interruption. Jeff's interest in taking his own work to a new level following the success of *Yellow Sticky Notes* (see Chapter 7) took inspiration from this endeavor in a way that brought the most significant names of modern Canadian animation together, in some instances out of retirement.

"Marv is a legend in the animation field," affirms Jeff, "Especially independent animation – in Vancouver, he's really the reason why there's such a great animation community that exists, because a lot of people who worked at his company International Rocket Ship went off to start their own after it dissolved. I liked the idea of seeing how other people approached using sticky notes the way I had in 2007, basically just picking a day in their life and self-reflecting on it, through that documentary kind of process, documenting that one day in their life, so I thought it was time for an AniJam."

An extension of *Yellow Sticky Notes*, Jeff's proposal for *Yellow Sticky Notes: Canadian AniJam* (Figure 14.3) was to invite the most prominent Canadian animators he could think of to contribute an animated instance of self-reflection, executed in the same manner as his own in the original 2007 short.

"Marv was the first guy who I sat down with, because his film brought that process of collaborative animation into the fold. I think he respected that I came to him and said it was what I wanted to do, and when I asked if *he* wanted to do a section of the film he agreed! I had a list of Canadian animators who I wanted to work with and as soon as I knew I had Marv I knew I could get the majority of everyone else on board.

"At the beginning I was hoping to have someone from every major country in the world that are independent animation hotbeds, but what ended up happening was the majority of our funding came from Bravo in Canada, which stated it had to have 100% Canadian content. I figured it was a good starting point, to stay within Canada and go international if I wanted to expand the concept later. He gave me the contacts for Paul Driessen and I knew Alison Snowden and David Fine through my producer, so it was kind of easy to get them on board. Some people like Cordell Barker (Figure 14.4) - director of the 1998 NFB classic *The Cat Came Back* were really busy, but I didn't give anyone a time-limit, nobody had to do ten or twenty seconds of animation, they could do as much as they felt like, five seconds, thirty seconds, there wasn't no pressure to do a certain number of drawings. So I think a lot of people came on board because they thought it sounded like a fun, collaborative project (Figure 14.5).

"It wasn't a typical AniJam where one animator's last drawing becomes the first drawing for the next animator as with Marv's project; each section was bookended by a blank sticky note, that way everyone was working around the same time, so I gave everyone about three months at some point to finish up their animation. When they were all sent back I basically set it all down and organised

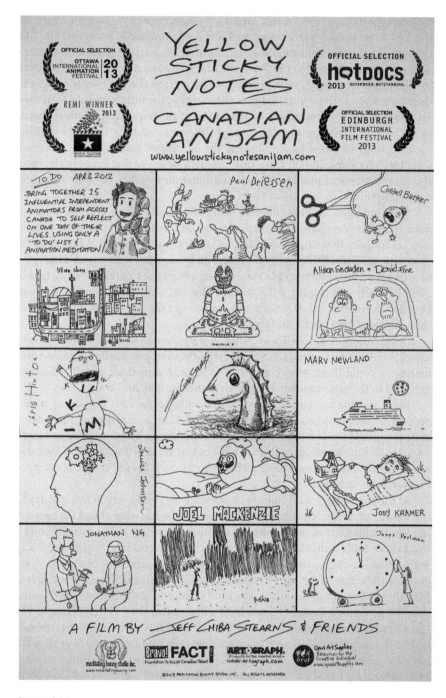

Figure 14.3

Yellow Sticky Notes: Canadian Anijam poster ©2013 Jeff Chiba Stearns.

it in chronological order. When you look at the upper-hand corner there's always a date, so it starts with Paul Driessen's earliest reflection when he was a kid and Janet Perlman's is in the future, so it makes sense that hers is the last sequence. Organizing it that way created a flow where just by chance or coincidence it could

Figure 14.4

Cordell Barker works on *Yellow Sticky Notes: Canadian Anijam*. Photo credit: April Barker.

Figure 14.5

David Fine and Alison Snowden work on *Yellow Sticky Notes: Canadian Anijam*. Photo credit: Lily Snowden-Fine.

be funny or serious. I just wanted to treat everybody equally, because even though some have won Oscars, it's more about each animator's own style."

The other animators brought on board were Jody Kramer, Chris Hinton, (Figure 14.6) Howie Shia, Malcolm Sutherland, Lillian Chan, Joel Mackenzie as well as Jeff's former *One Big Hapa Family* collaborators Louise Johnson and Jonathan Ng.

"Everyone had the same materials, I basically gave them a kit of around five-hundred sticky notes, a few black pens and a lightpad to use. The only rule was there couldn't be underlying pencil sketches, it had to be straight-up ink. Some people might've done roughs first and traced over the top, but for the most part when I animate it's rough, it's raw, it's sketchy and that's what I like, so I was trying to get them to open up and be free with that too.

"The funding was split up equally between the fifteen animators, the composer and the sound designer, so everyone got paid exactly the same amount. Then everyone just went to it. I think Paul was the first guy to send his in, it was amazing to hold and flip through his drawings! A lot of these animators were people who got me into animation and the fact we got Chris Hinton blows my mind because he's retired and lives on a farm in rural Quebec raising pigs now. Even though he had quit animation altogether, all I had to say was 'Marv Newland' and 'hand-drawn animation on paper' for him to come on board. It was really cool to get that calibre of animators together in one place, celebrating classical animation, drawing on paper."

As with the original *Yellow Sticky Notes*, the Canadian Anijam proved to be a hit at animation and documentary festivals alike. While it shares a more or less identical production approach, to Jeff, it plays more as a showcase film than a documentary, one which captures an era of Canadian animation heritage.

A variant on the AniJam concept makes use of the swiftness of online collaboration and how established artists can directly work with their audience. In 2010, Bill Plympton set about the visual reinvention of one of his most popular shorts, 2004s Academy Award-nominated *Guard Dog*, using an international pool of animators amongst his fanbase (Figure 14.7). Following a call on his website and social media channels, response to the proposed idea (in which every shot of the film would be broken down and assigned to an animator to reinterpret in the style of their choosing) was immediate and largely positive. Initial criticism on online forums suggested the project was exploitative crowdsourcing as the animators were giving their time for free. While it certainly isn't unreasonable to maintain a guarded attitude toward online solicitations of free labor from animators at an early stage in their career, the fundamental differences were clear to most. In place of remuneration was the legitimate kudos of association with a high-profile artist, a high-profile project and reasonable time demands, most assigned shots running for mere seconds. On top of which, each contributing

Figure 14.6

Chris Hinton (with assistant) works on *Yellow Sticky Notes: Canadian Anijam*. Photo credit: Katherine Reed.

14. Keeping Up

animator was rewarded with a hand-drawn frame from the original version of the shot they were assigned (Figure 14.8), an honorarium not to be sniffed at.

Following the success of the *Guard Dog Global Jam*, Bill has been keen to explore other such progressive enterprises, including a similarly collaborative reworking of his breakout hit *Your Face* and his own reinvention of a semi-lost classic.

"As I travel around the world, I'll run into someone who was part of the *Guard Dog Global Jam*, which is very exciting. I think it really does open up possibilities for new kinds of art forms and new kinds of filmmaking that I love. I reworked

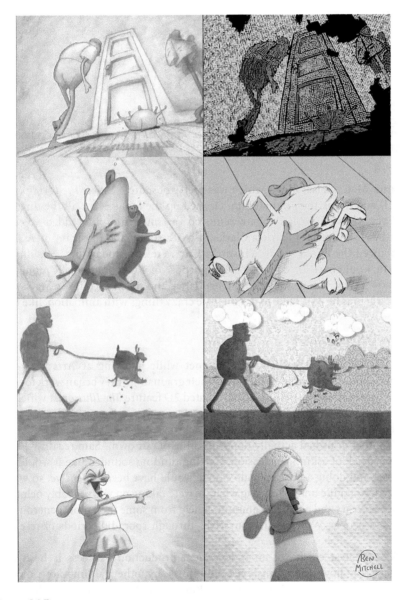

Figure 14.7

Shots from the original *Guard Dog* (Dir. Bill Plympton, left) and their re-imagined *Guard Dog Global Jam* counterparts (right) ©2004–2011 Plymptoons.

Figure 14.8

Original cel from Bill Plympton's *Guard Dog* (2004) – one of the unexpected perks of involvement in *Guard Dog Global Jam* was receiving a drawing from the original film ©Plymptoons. From the author's personal collection.

Winsor McCay's last film – which was pretty obscure – called *The Flying House* (1921) and I took the original film, cleaned up the footage, got all the dirt, dust and scratches off, added colour, removed the inter-titles and added voices by Matthew Modine and Patricia Clarkson. With sound and music on there it just revitalized the film, I feel if Winsor McCay were alive today this is the kind of film he would have liked to make. The purpose of it was not to make money, but to show a new, young audience the brilliance and talent of Winsor McCay and what a genius he was. I like to do fun little crazy things with animation, like that."

New Perspectives

Sam Taylor and Bjørn-Erik Aschim met while studying at Arts University Bournemouth. Immediately following their graduation, they began work together on Sylvain Chomet's traditionally animated 2D feature *The Illusionist* which was being produced in Edinburgh. After seven years of experience working alongside each other, the desire to make a film of their own began to take hold.

"Neither of us had actually done anything of our own." Sam recalls, "I think we were sick of asking permission. Getting funding sounded like it would take forever, and doing a postgraduate course would have been expensive, so we just started. Not quite understanding what we were taking on was probably helpful. It took two years and a massive amount of help from some incredibly generous and talented people. We funded it ourselves through sporadic periods of freelance work."

The greatest enemy of an independent production's success is hesitation. Considering how many films exist only in the hypothetical limbo of would-be creators' fantasies, very little is lost in taking the first steps to begin a film before the certainties of funding or production are set in stone. In the case of Sam and Bjørn's short *Everything I Can See from Here* (Figures 14.9–14.14), finished and released in 2013, taking such a plunge proved to be the right move.

Though the end result is visually sophisticated and indicative of an elaborate production pipeline, the duo's approach was relatively simple from the outset, sharing the load for the most part.

"Bjørn did all the painting and backgrounds in the film. Beyond that I think we both did a bit of everything, from character design through to animation, storyboarding, compositing, promotion and so on. We might not have achieved a perfect state of collective consciousness at all times – there were certainly disagreements – but I think the process of talking this stuff through was beneficial for a number of reasons.

"Firstly it forced us to justify our creative decisions quite specifically in each case. It also allowed us to get to know each other better and taught us about efficient methods of collaboration. I discovered, for example, that defining an illustrative style is something that is very difficult to collaborate on; it's so intuitive that it's difficult to talk about and always ends up coming back to questions of taste. In our recent work, we've generally assigned character design to one person in the team, which results in more of a distinctive and personal flair. It's our taste, but hopefully it also engages people."

As is often the case with the animation world, Sam's primary education came more from working on *The Illusionist* than the University studies which preceded it. The pacing of *Everything I Can See from Here*, which boasts a number of protracted, drawn-out shots to build atmosphere, is particularly informed by Chomet's film. For Bjørn, additional sources of inspiration came from his prior work for Aardman and Sony for the CG animated feature *Arthur Christmas*.

"The presentation of ideas, the packaging of your drawing is something that becomes very important when you work on larger scale productions. Directors and heads of departments just don't have time to react to something that isn't

Figure 14.9

Everything I Can See from Here (Dir. Bjørn-Erik Aschim/Sam Taylor) character concept sketch to final design comparison ©2013 The Line.

clear or doesn't read properly at first glance, they have dozens of meetings and tons of decisions need to be made every day. Ideas need to be visualized quickly and efficiently, being ambiguous or unclear kills your drawings instantly! It's heartbreaking when you've got a lovely rendered painting to show but nobody reacts to it because they don't understand the idea behind it. It's definitely something that I'm more conscious of now that I'm pitching ideas to my colleagues or to clients. Also, making a film means you'll have to talk about it for a long while after its release. If the idea is in any way unclear to yourself when you make the film you will be constantly reminded of this whenever someone asks you a question about it."

One unique quality of *Everything I Can See from Here* stands out to the audience immediately, that the film's aspect ratio has been purposefully subverted to 9:16 as opposed to the standard uniformity of 16:9. While wryly acknowledging the prevalence of many contemporary viral videos being filmed in this fashion (unknowingly, for the most part) using smartphones, what might initially come off as gimmickry proves to be an ingenious, contemporary spin on a viewing experience, which was been so adopted by mobile devices.

"The film is very specifically made for an audience of people who watch things online using their phones and tablets. This is reflected in the portrait aspect ratio and the fact we released the film online immediately," asserts Sam.

Figure 14.10

Still from *Everything I Can See From Here* (Dir. Bjørn-Erik Aschim/Sam Taylor) ©2013 The Line.

"We decided to make it portrait format half way through the boarding of the film." Bjørn adds, "We were both reluctant to re-do the boards but it was too good of an idea, so we went for it. It was a fairly straightforward process after that actually, no major problems. Max James van der Merwe, our 3D animator, flipped his monitor on the side and did the alien animation that way, which worked pretty well!

"I had just gotten an iPad and when we did our first test on the device it felt right. It was a different experience than watching it on a normal screen, almost like a moving comic, which was something that we got very excited about. It felt like not a lot of people had explored this form of storytelling yet."

The completion of the film was assured by corralling a team of eleven additional volunteer animators and a thirteen-person cleanup crew from a pool of creatives enthusiastic to see the project come together from the strength of its premise. A similar sense of enthusiasm for the end result pervaded the online community, earning the film a coveted Vimeo Staff Pick and exposure to an audience of hundreds of thousands thanks largely to word of mouth and social media. While hugely beneficial to the duo's visibility and reputation as artists, Bjørn's take on the future monetary potential of this form of exposure remains grounded.

Figure 14.11

Still from *Everything I Can See From Here* (Dir. Bjørn-Erik Aschim/Sam Taylor) ©2013 The Line.

"I think the sharing of videos online, in tweets, on people's timelines and Tumblrs has definitely opened up platforms for people who normally wouldn't have one, to get their vision across. I think that it's hardly a model that is sustainable for an artist though. The exposure is great and there's value in building an audience but there's practically no money to be made and very little incentive to keep making short form content beyond the pat on the back and a 'like' on your video. There's been attempts at getting people to pay and donate money for short form content online, like Vimeo's 'tip-jar' or Paypal's 'donate' button but apart from crowdfunding, there seems to be no sustainable model that could even get close to financing something like a short animated film."

To Sam, the exposure's primary benefit is also the spectrum of feedback and encouragement first-time filmmakers are given access to. "It's interesting how different forums have very different responses to the film. Vimeo is almost always extremely positive, which is partly a function of people wanting to self-promote.

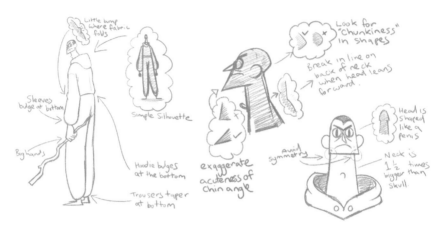

Figure 14.12

Everything I Can See from Here "Barry" character sketches ©2013 The Line.

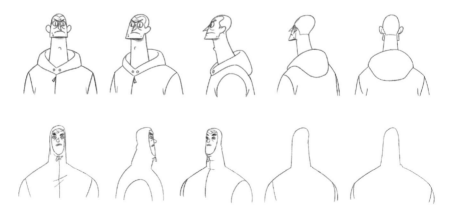

Figure 14.13

Everything I Can See from Here character turnarounds ©2013 The Line.

Some of the animation blogs had slightly more critical opinions, a lot of which was really insightful and instructive."

"Social media is a great tool to get people interested in what you are working on." Bjørn adds, "We're experimenting more and more with journaling our process online and being completely transparent about the filmmaking as we go along. Animation takes a long time and can be an isolating process. You just want to share something, get some kind of feedback, and the internet is great for that. But there's value in keeping a bit of secrecy about your work as well, the magic can quickly fade if you're sharing everything."

Another established, UK-based animation duo are the Brothers McLeod. Made up of siblings Myles, typically the writer of the pair, and Greg, who is responsible for their well-known and distinctive style of 2D animation and illustration, the pair have built up an impressive body of work spanning independent films, commissioned films, pilots, television series work, illustration projects, commercials and idents. Their division of labor is, by and large, rather cut and dry, as Greg explains.

"It varies from project to project how much we collaborate. Myles works on a lot of scripts for TV that I don't really have much input into unless he's gotten stuck for an idea. I do a lot of illustration and ident work which doesn't necessarily involve Myles, but for the big projects such as the short films, feature films and some of the bigger TV series ideas, we'll basically sit down in a room together and generate the ideas from spending time together. Then when the idea's kind of gelled he goes off and writes some stuff and I go off and draw some stuff, then we get back in a room again and so on, until eventually we end up with something. Even in production, he kind of co-directs and does a lot of the music while I do a lot of the sound, for post- production we work together, so there's a collaborative back and forth that works really well."

Although the notion of brothers working together has become something of a tradition in the world of film, the pair often field questions about the nature of their working relationship. Having invented stories with toys and playsets as most young siblings do, the pair naturally gravitated toward one another again

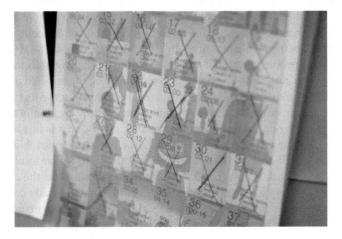

Figure 14.14

Everything I Can See from Here shot list ©2013 The Line.

Figure 14.15

Still from *365* (Dir. Brothers McLeod) ©2014 The Brothers McLeod.

in adulthood, shared influences and experiences building an intuitive sense of professional communication, not to mention ambition.

One such instance is the film *365* (Figures 14.15–14.17), an experimental piece that retains Greg's loose, cartoonish style with a pointedly out-of-left-field concept, having been animated in disjointed, one second increments each day over the course of the year 2013.

"I had started working on a film that wasn't really going anywhere," recalls Greg, "And wanted something that could be improvised. The idea of *365* just popped into my head one day and I just kind of started it without really thinking about it. The idea was that I would post an image every day on Facebook so people could follow it that way."

Once several of these images had been posted, Greg noted a visible interest that started to spread throughout social media. As with the primary motivation behind such work as Andy Martin's *The Planets*, the public awareness served as enough of a push to emotionally invest and commit to following through.

"Not doing it would mean I'd lose face, and the more I got into it, the more of my face I would have lost if I would've stopped. I think also, if I'm honest, there's an ego thing there, of 'Look what I'm doing, aren't I great for being able to do this?' Without being arrogant, hopefully! It was a reward system – if you make a film, you want people to watch it and enjoy it, and by sharing with them a bit of it every day, you get a little bit of a buzz. Now, watching the finished film with an audience is a whole different buzz. Aside from a couple of moments right toward the end in December where I just wanted it to end, in general, I really enjoyed not having to stick to one character or one scenario, every day was just a new thing which kind of suits my personality. It wasn't easy, but it was enjoyable."

The simple brilliance of the concept behind the film, which went on to win multiple awards and receive tremendous festival exposure, was the cornerstone of its feasibility. Very few animation projects could demand a daily commitment for an entire year, if for no other reason than the likelihood an artist can guarantee they'll be able to work from the same location. Greg's solution was simple and is one that has proved increasingly viable for independents – the setup of a portable studio that could be taken wherever he went. The demands of *365*s

　　　　　　　　　　　　　　　　　　　　　　　　　　14. Keeping Up

Figure 14.16

Still from *365* (Dir. Brothers McLeod) ©2014 The Brothers McLeod.

Figure 14.17

Still from *365* (Dir. Brothers McLeod) ©2014 The Brothers McLeod.

visuals, being little more than digital illustration, only required a laptop, animation software and a drawing tablet, and as such, accompanied Greg on his various travels whenever he was away from his office studio.

"It was really freeing. The technique I used for *365* was really basic, just hand-drawn straight into the computer, colored, then onto the next day. I really enjoy working like that and will probably work like that more in the future."

At the start of the book, we explored a range of storytelling approaches, from stream-of-consciousness experimentation to straight-ahead narrative. A project such as *365* certainly leans more toward the former, though as with such abstract fare as Robert Morgan's *Bobby Yeah* or Don Hertzfeldt's more avant-garde work, a structural backbone makes all the difference. Without even a small element of concession to audience habits, a film made up of three-hundred and sixty-five random, one-second sight gags could easily be unwatchable. Greg attributes his own sense of such concession to having worked alongside his brother for so long.

"Storytelling-wise, most of my short films have been non-narrative in a traditional sense, and *365* isn't at all. I think you naturally find rhythms, little tropes and little ideas. *Codswallop* had something of an emotional arc as Myles works a lot in television where you need to know story structure, so all the things he writes for have beats you have to hit. Myles really enjoys working with three or four or five-act structures, if you can get it right it's fantastic.

"We always do a talk about how you might have a subconscious idea that will just pop into your head, but to make it work in a film you have to consciously twist it. So there are bits like that in *365* where, at the ends of a month I would sometimes consciously slow it a bit, and at the very end there's definitely four seconds where I knew I had to give people that relief. So even though I do a lot of subconscious work, I still have to somehow organize it so it isn't just a load of stuff on screen. The issue when you're doing something that's very heavily scripted is that it's a different mindset where you have to heavily storyboard, create an animatic and know what it's going to be before you've finished. With a film like *Phone Home*, that is absolutely the right thing to do, because the comic timing had to be perfect. If I had done just any old thing it wouldn't have worked. I like working either way, it keeps it fresh depending on what the project is."

At this point in the book, it should be more than clear just how unfettered one's approach to an independent animated film can be. Not only that, the platforms and avenues available for your work are constantly evolving to accommodate these leaps forward in both technology and artists' progressive approach to their creative concepts. In the upcoming chapters, we will be further exploring just how conceptually broad an independent animation project can be, and how recent advances in technology are making the experience of viewing them more immersive than ever before.

Notes

1 Although I said the same thing in the first edition of this book and it's still kickin' around, so there may remain some life in it yet.
2 http://www.depict.org.

15

Combining Your Efforts

Next, we will explore the ways in which independent animation has embraced the mixed-media approach, something that has, over time, become a significantly more viable option for auteur production. Prior case studies have touched on this, such as Signe Baumane's tactile, hand-crafted sets and stop-motion environments for *Rocks in My Pockets* against which her signature 2D character animation is juxtaposed, not to mention the variety of stop-motion processes that define the work of PES. Here, however, we'll be looking at a handful of artists especially known for taking the combined approach throughout their respective bodies of work, showing just how adaptable and (at times) self-aware animation can be.

A key figure worth considering when it comes to mixed-media approaches would be Don Hertzfeldt, whose earlier work consisted almost entirely of drawn-on-paper 2D animation before organically evolving to incorporate live-action and analog film and camera processes to a charming, lo-fi effect. Though sometimes hilarious – one personal highlight being the protagonist of Don's 2010 short *Wisdom Teeth* (Figure 15.1) suffering hallucinations such as "prehistoric beasts" (toy dinosaurs being waggled around at the edges of the shot) – this approach also has the potential to be disorienting and unnerving, as in certain crucial sequences of his *It's Such a Beautiful Day* trilogy that denote the lead character Bill's rapidly deteriorating mental and physical health (Figure 15.2).

2014 would see Don take his place alongside Bill Plympton, Michał Socha and Sylvain Chomet (among others) when invited to contribute an animated "couch gag" segment for the twenty-sixth season premiere of *The Simpsons*. This opportunity, which saw identifiable characters from the show transmogrified into

DOI: 10.1201/9781003214717-15

Figure 15.1

Still from *Wisdom Teeth* ©2009 Don Hertzfeldt/Bitter Films.

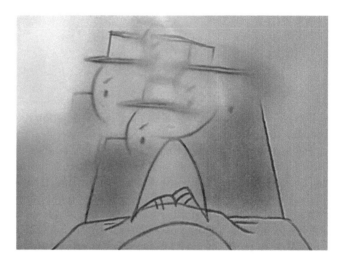

Figure 15.2

Still from *It's Such a Beautiful Day* ©2012 Don Hertzfeldt/Bitter Films.

alien-like creatures, simultaneously drew from minor elements of his preceding shorts while significantly foreshadowing his project to come, the ongoing *World of Tomorrow* series, especially with its depicting of a future landscape that has descended into comical – and occasionally poignant – surreality (Figure 15.3). These films would mark a shift away from analog processes, replacing his signature pencil-drawn lines for vector art and coupling the live-action backdrops with abstract CG moodscapes. This change in visual approach would bring with it some advantages as regards turnaround time, although Don's creative process would largely remain the same.

"My writing habits are the same of course, and I still work with sound the same way, which for me is always a huge part of the process. The main thing that

15. Combining Your Efforts

working with 35mm provided that digital does not is that unlimited range of happy accidents in the form of experimental images: running the camera back and forth over animation, lights, effects, and shaking it all up to see what you get. The way 35mm images blend is not the same as in the digital space, and you can really capture something beautiful that way without needing to visualize it all first. Most of the experimental effects and double-images in *It's Such a Beautiful Day*, the feature, wouldn't have been possible without 35mm. On the other hand, what I am really loving about digital is the speed. I can power through animating scenes now at record speed, and the very long process of carefully photographing every frame is also completely out of the picture. I made *World of Tomorrow* and the two minute piece for *The Simpsons* at the same time, and combined they still took exactly half the time as something like *Everything Will Be OK* did. Of course, the long waits and annoyances with the film labs are also gone. This probably all sounds incredibly obvious to anyone today in their twenties, but to me it feels like I'm on vacation."

Another director to look at is Daniel Greaves, whose 1991 short *Manipulation* would go on to win the Cartoon d'Or and an Academy Award the following year. Evocative (as many films have been, to varying degrees of success) of the 1953 Chuck Jones classic *Duck Amuck*, *Manipulation* is an early example of the "artist vs. creation" concept going one dimension further into more metaphysical territory, as the abuses inflicted on Daniel's hand-drawn, 2D animated figure grow considerably more complex, involving real materials animated using pixilation and stop-motion. Several sequences in the film (including its final moments in which the animated victim seemingly breaks free of the confines of the page) foreshadow the visual premise of the director's later short *Flatworld* (1997), produced for the BBC with a grander budget and scope. In this film, the protagonist Matt Phlatt, his pet cat and their fellow inhabitants of the strange titular universe are traditionally animated in 2D, albeit as cut-outs that stand upright in a stop-motion environment of hand-made sets. Beginning with a series of wryly executed nods to the process itself (e.g. shaving with a pencil eraser, turning sideways on to negotiate narrow openings, etc.), the film becomes progressively more elaborate, with an electrical storm opening portals through which television characters (also traditionally animated, but composited into the action to

Figure 15.3

Still from *World of Tomorrow* ©2014 Don Hertzfeldt/Bitter Films.

Figure 15.4

Still from *Mr. Plastimime* (Dir. Daniel Greaves) ©2014 Daniel Greaves.

suggest more dimensionality) appear and wreak havoc thanks to their own set of physical laws. To achieve the overall effect, all of the half-hour-long film's 2D animation was first animated on paper before being photocopied and glued onto meticulously cutout cardboard (with corresponding replacements required for each different frame of animation), to be then posed within the set and filmed as stop-motion.

"I suppose it's a kind of inherent restlessness in myself, that I keep wanting to try different things." Daniel reflects, "I quite like the challenge of doing something that's slightly out of my comfort zone and then learning from it. The bigger picture is to then accumulate all of these skills because they might spark something really special one day, when I've got all these techniques under my belt, as it were. That's why I jump from one thing to the other.

"I find that one film informs the next, so when it comes to an experience I've had making a film like *Flatworld*, which was incredibly labor-intensive work with cutouts involved, I know that I probably wouldn't do again! It looked good and it was exciting at the time, but once I've done something once I want to do something relatively different and learn something else."

The BAFTA-nominated film is part of a strong legacy of work produced by Tandem Films, the production company Daniel co-founded in 1986 that ran until 2014. The final project Daniel would produce as part of the company would be *Mr. Plastimime* (2014, Figures 15.4–15.8), a hybrid of stop-motion puppet animation and digital 2D in which a floundering mime artist unknowingly lives beneath his biggest – and only – fan. We previously learned in Chapter 9 that the film's successful completion was owed to crowdfunding, though the idea had existed for some time before the team at Tandem took the Kickstarter plunge.

"I had this image in my mind of a black and white, mime artist character, set in a particular era. I just wanted to do something that was quite moody. It was originally going to be a lot more slapstick in the beginning, but it changed into this romantic, atmospheric love story."

Though initially self-funded, the main impetus for crowdfunding a higher budget was Daniel's propensity toward using mixed media to strong effect. In the

15. Combining Your Efforts

Figure 15.5

Mr. Plastimime campaign page promo image ©2014 Daniel Greaves.

Figure 15.6

Still from *Mr. Plastimime* (Dir. Daniel Greaves) ©2014 Daniel Greaves.

case of *Mr. Plastimime*, the stop-motion puppets are imbued with an extra level of expression through the addition of hand-animated facial acting. Elsewhere in the film, the star-crossed neighbors find themselves indulging a mutual fantasy (while an accidental fire starts to spread in the woman's apartment) conveyed through an entirely 2D animated sequence where they dance the Tango, put together by Daniel himself with the use of live-action reference footage.

"As it was a fantasy sequence, there was a reason for it to be done in a different technique, for the two principle characters to be together. It also gave us enough time for the apartment to burst into flames, so when you come back to reality it's a shock, or a surprise at least."

While Daniel directed the entire film, not being a stop-motion animator by trade saw him among those taking on the additional 2D facial animation, using reference points built into the physical puppets as a guide, similar to the compositing approach of the NFB's 2007 stop-motion film *Madame Tutli-Putli* (directed by Chris Lavis and Maciek Szczerbowski), which would instead overlay live-action eyes to bring a more "human" performance out of the puppets. In the case of Mr. Plastimime, this hybrid approach was crucial to taking each character's range of expression to a place that would not have been achievable using stop-motion on its own.

"The animators said it would have been really difficult to sculpt the eye blinks and subtle expressions with these squashy shapes. I was quite concerned that they would have looked a bit blank, so I think it was worth taking a chance, even though it cost more. The thing is, the characters are in the film pretty much 80% of the time, so you've got to take perspective into account. We didn't use any technical, clever tracking devices, everybody just had to use their eyes and match it up, which was tricky because the eyes change depending on the angle of the camera."

Using Flash, the eye and mouth animation was applied straight-ahead to the stop-motion footage, with the opacity level brought down a touch so as to not be solid colors. Being able to discern plasticine textures through the 2D overlays keeps the end result from being jarring or incongruous – for the most part the facial animation comes across almost as having been physically painted on to the puppets themselves.

Harkening back to the days of *Manipulation* and *Flatworld*, Mr. Plastimime also indulges a certain degree of metaphysical humor in its references to the physicality of the animation itself, something of a Daniel Greaves trademark.

"I don't do it consciously but it has been pointed out – people say 'Your films really are about the process of animation.' In *Mr. Plastimime* you become aware of the technique when he walks into a lamp post and the plasticine squashes, for example. You can't pull the wool over the audience's eye – they're pretty clued up as to how these types of things are done – so I do like playing with the genre, but I don't want to be too heavy-handed with it. I don't want to make a big statement that this is a film about animation, it's just nice to occasionally remind the

Figure 15.7

Daniel Greaves using Flash to animate facial expressions in *Mr. Plastimime* ©2014 Daniel Greaves.

15. Combining Your Efforts

Figure 15.8

Still from *Mr. Plastimime* (Dir. Daniel Greaves) ©2014 Daniel Greaves.

audience that this is what the film physically consists of. So occasionally there's a little nod, almost like an in-joke, like the moments in *Flatworld* where the characters turn edge-on, but I try not to overdo it."

On reflection, Daniel cites his first short film outing *Manipulation* as perhaps the most harmonious coupling of animation approaches: "I had so much more control, because it was pretty much just me, so when it came to the point of combining the pixilated hands with the characters, I had an instinct of how far to move. As I was so familiar with the animation having done it myself, I had an instinctive idea of how much to move my hand, per frame. Because this was the early nineties, the days before computers, I didn't have video playback, I just had to sense how far to move my hands every frame. People have said it's remarkably smooth – it's actually quite jerky in places, but I think I got away with it, to a large degree."

Duality

Chris Shepherd, whose collaborative adaptation with David Shrigley *Who I Am and What I Want* (2005) we learned of earlier in the book, is another UK filmmaker who has frequently combined animation processes to remarkable effect. Two primary examples from his extensive filmography that come to mind are *Dad's Dead* (2003, Figures 15.9 and 15.10) and *The Ringer* (2013, Figures 15.11– 15.13), both of which are rooted in live action and visually emboldened via an assortment of captivating animation and visual effects. Although these films have a distinct visual edge, they succeed for both being strongly told stories.

"Story has always been my cornerstone," enthuses Chris, "I always think of story first and then think of what style it would be, based on how that might affect the audience. I'm not crazy about technique just for the sake of it, I always think *What's My Story?* and then *How Can I Tell It?* Then I'll think about what I want to do to the audience, do I want to scare them or make them laugh?"

Ticking both boxes, *Dad's Dead* is laced with dry wit while at the same time the events are catastrophized by the increasingly nightmarish overlaid animation. The film is a memoir about the turning point in which an unnamed, Liverpudlian narrator (Ian Hart) comes to realize his "best mate" Johnno (Chris

Figure 15.9

Still from *Dad's Dead* (Dir. Chris Shepherd) ©2003 Chris Shepherd.

Freeney) is not just an antisocial youth, but an outright sociopath. The film is presented as a sequence of POV memories with animated embellishments projected over them, begin innocuously and becoming progressively more disturbing; with each new unveiling of Johnno's real self, his depiction becomes ever more demonic and distorted.

"I wanted to tell a story about my environment. My previous film was very cartoony and I wanted to make something that felt real, more about memory." The backbone of the film is Ian Hart's narration, which had been recorded several years previously. Hearing Hart's performance of his own writing struck enough of a nerve that Chris initially had no desire to put it out in the world in any form. "I stuck it in the cupboard and shut the door on it! I was scared of it because it was so dark and I'm not a very dark person. But it was a good story and so when I got some funding to animate it I brought this recording back out and then made the film."

"It wasn't traditionally storyboarded. I did it very instinctively, five or six shoots over the year; I'd do some animation, then do another shoot, then edit, do some animation and do another shoot and so on, building it up like a painting."

Citing Francis Bacon as one of the film's visual references, the incrementally built-upon approach – some instances of footage having been shot three years beforehand in a tower block, with new footage subsequently composited in – makes for a film that manages to cultivate a natural flow to it. This can be attributed to two main consistencies – the narration that binds the action and the regular visual augmentation the animation brings to the film.

The latter is also a major component of *The Ringer*, an altogether different type of film yet still laced with a certain mix of comedy, darkness and pathos. Inspired by real life events, the film sees Christopher (Kieran Lynn), a young man working in web animation, re-encounter his estranged father Danny (John Henshaw). Unable to comprehend that his son's job does not bring with it any showbusiness pull, Danny's deluded hope and overbearing insistence that the two can work together on getting his mediocre screenplay *The Ringer* made into a film serves to dash any hopes of a clement reconciliation.

15. Combining Your Efforts

Figure 15.10

The increasingly demonic Johnno of **Dad's Dead** ©2003 Chris Shepherd.

"It's not a portrayal of reality; elements are real but it is fiction, and it's up to the audience to try and figure out what it's all about. I suppose in a way it's about reconciliation, but it's also in my mind a bit about dreams as well, the dream of wanting to go to Hollywood, the dream of wanting to make a big feature film."

The substory within the main narrative is that of *The Ringer* itself, a cliché-ridden stab at the gangster heist genre as filtered through someone with no real grasp of film or story structure. Indulging his father out of a sense of obligation that quickly wanes, the son can only envision the events described as a cartoon-ish pastiche modeled on the overstated grandiosity and color palettes of 1970s movie posters.

"It was something that I never would have done in a million years, the car chase, prostitutes getting shot, gunfire – normally, I'd run a mile from that sort of stuff. So I did it out of irony, but in the process of making the film, I realized how fun it was to make cars blow up and shoot people in the head – I can see why other filmmakers do it now! Even though the parallel story is quite weak and meant to be ironic, I like it, because whenever you make a film, you care about all the characters – Big Tony, the kid, Amber – even though they're not based in reality and are more like cartoon characters, I care for them just as much."

After their initial encounter, the interactions between Chris and his emotion-ally unstable father grow increasingly terse. The characters from *The Ringer* begin to bleed into Chris's thoughts as he starts to connect with them, eventually coerc-ing him to make at least some stab at inward reconciliation. The fantasy sequences

Figure 15.11

Still from *The Ringer* (Dir. Chris Shepherd) ©2013 Autour De Minuit/Polkadot Productions.

Figure 15.12

Still from *The Ringer* (Dir. Chris Shepherd) ©2013 Autour De Minuit/Polkadot Productions.

for the film, which was produced in association with Autour de Minuit, were predicated on live-action footage shot against green screen, later keyed, filtered and composited into 3D CG environments by a team of visual artists at ADV Studios in France. Lastly, a form of rotoscoping was applied, tracing line-art over every frame of the characters – a process that took over half a year – resulting in a striking, "moving poster" effect. While the film's strictly live-action sequences are strong enough in terms of the writing, direction and performances to be a compelling film, as with *Dad's Dead*, the visual garnish allows for a very effective insight into the main character's emotional conflicts and turmoil.

"Live-action and animation are very different." Chris reasons, "Something you show as being quite harsh in live-action you can put it into animation and it can become funny or quite mild, so there are all those considerations. If it's a dark comedy, you might not want it to become too heavy, so by showing it like a cartoon it just deflates it and almost brings a sense of sarcasm to it.

Figure 15.13

Still from *The Ringer* (Dir. Chris Shepherd) ©2013 Autour De Minuit/Polkadot Productions.

"All the films are different, but when I wrote *Dad's Dead*, it was as more of a straight play. Then when I did the animatic I would think about parallel narratives and ways to subvert the main narrative, building it up over time. When it came to *The Ringer*, I would see the film as I wrote it, the idea of this parallel world that would be animated.

Another shared trait with *Dad's Dead*, though buried perhaps a little deeper, is *The Ringer*'s tragicomic sensibility. The humor, underplayed, though it is, keeps the film from being maudlin melodrama. Danny's attempts to bond or find common ground with Chris, for instance, are strangely endearing for being utterly devoid of logic. Toward the end, when the film's main narrative (now intertwined with that of the fictional universe within) goes from threatening to poignant, the shift in tone is felt all the more.

"I feel that with comedy you can convey something quite dark while keeping the audience on board. Even when I try to be serious the films always end up being funny, it's become one of my things. I suppose the other thing I've always tacked on are themes around nostalgia and imagination, because you can use the animation and live-action combo to go to a higher sensory plane, by showing your fantasies in a way that you can't do with live-action on its own.

"I do love live-action because with that it's all about subtlety. I always say that in animation you can kill somebody by dropping an anvil on their head, that's totally acceptable, but in live-action you can kill somebody with something small, a *look* even, and in the next scene, they're dead or gone. I've done purely live-action films as well, such as *Bad Night for the Blues* (2010), but the magic of live-action and animation combined is that anything can happen. That's quite an exciting thing, to have that extra arsenal of tools to make something come to life."

Splintering Off

One particular series of independent, mixed-media projects from the Netherlands serves as a prime example of how storytelling and a multitude of art forms can come together to form entire creative universes. The work of Dutch artist Rosto is legendarily grand in spectacle and often the talk of many a major festival, combining rich soundscapes, arresting musical compositions (from avant-garde to straight-ahead rock), a plethora of epic, sometimes metaphysical interwoven story strands and unforgettable visuals. While Rosto's later projects boast bolstered production values through significant financial support from a variety of funding bodies, all of his work retains a crucial independent and artistic spirit at its core.

Animation was always an important part of Rosto's process, going back to his childhood and a home studio setup involving his father's 8 mm camera and friends who would financially contribute to materials costs so as to be involved. The technological limitations of the time put his animation inclinations temporarily on hold. "It took forever to do all the animation, shooting all these cels and then sending it off to a lab and having to wait three weeks for it to come back – only to discover that it was all out of focus and underlit! After a while I gave up and started to shoot horror movies in my teenage years." With the advent of video briefly reigniting a pre-digital enthusiasm for filmmaking, it wasn't until the arrival of the Amiga ("A miracle machine!") that animation was permanently brought back into his life.

"I first started doing the drawn animation thing again, then very slowly the hybrid approach came in. By now I was a more stubborn young man who decided

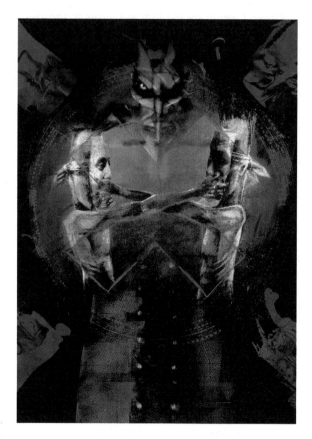

Figure 15.14

Artwork for Rosto's *Mind My Gap* ©Studio Rosto A.D.

that I don't *have* to choose to become a 2D animator – or graphic designer, or musician – I can actually combine *all* these things!"

The mixed-media roots of Rosto's highly complex artistic universe can be traced, at least visually, to his online web series *Mind My Gap* (Figure 15.14), which takes the form of a multimedia "graphic novel" detailing the troubled journeys of Diddybob and Buddybob, best friends and presenters of the fictional television show *Living Interior*. The story begins in a 1998, Flash-animated webisode *Map1: Highway* which sees Diddybob on a mysterious road journey, having left his life and Buddybob behind, for reasons unknown. Set to mostly still illustrations and rudimentary animated sequences, the narration and dialogue is unforgiving, at times coyly self-aware of its impenetrability, yet the story is absorbing enough to entice the viewer into attempting to fathom its mysteries. The saga concludes fifteen years later in 2013 with the two-part, full-blown live-action/CG metaphysical epic *Map13: XIII* and *Episode13: XIII* (episodes 25 and 26 of *Mind My Gap*, respectively). These two concluding chapters are best known on the animation festival circuit as the single piece *Lonely Bones* (Figure 15.15), itself the second part of a parallel series of short films.

Before exploring those, however, it's worth examining the long path to Rosto's status as one of Amsterdam's most successful and intriguing independent artists. Though *Mind My Gap* is where the story ultimately begins, the creative seeds were sewn some time before through music, not animation.

"The graphic novel was actually inspired by songs I had written in the mid-nineties," says Rosto, "Although I didn't realize at the time that my entire career would spring from it! When I wrote the first songs around 1995 with the band The Wreckers – as we were called back then – it was all very intuitive. The only thing that I knew was that it was about landscapes, crossroads – there was no concept behind it other than those elements."

Several years later, as both the nineties and The Wreckers as a real-life band were coming to an end, these compositions became the springboard for something altogether more complex. From the very first episode, it is clear that *Mind My Gap* does not follow any established patterns or frameworks that Flash-based web animations were known for at the time. Certainly, it makes use of the advantages of the medium – the addition of sound effects, music and recorded

Figure 15.15

Still from *Lonely Bones* (Dir. Rosto) ©2013 Studio Rosto A.D/Autour de Minuit.

performances help tremendously in the adaptation from its original print incarnation, as does a certain level of interactivity allowing the viewer to switch from one narrative strand to another. Though the official website self-effacingly refers to these early episodes as "obsolete," the concept of this type of digital storytelling "a dinosaur" in an era where the internet has "evolved into a dominating household commodity," they are a valuable study when it comes to several areas of artistic development and approaches to storytelling. As Rosto recalls, "This was basically right after the birth of the internet. I was pioneering, while not really understanding what I was doing. You have to understand, this was the nineties – the internet seemed like it *might* be here to stay, but we didn't know at the time whether or not it was just hype."

Though not "tech-savvy" by his own admission, Rosto's motives for embracing the internet's potential in a manner far removed from the glut of web animators rising to popularity at the same time came from seeing a documentary on the subject. "I realized a couple of things. Firstly, that this was probably going to be big, and the 'big boys' would probably try to hijack it and make it theirs. So we, the 'little people,' had to be there first – it was like the Wild West, basically; whoever gets there first claims their territory.

"The other thing I realized was that even as an independent artist or filmmaker, you're never *truly* independent, because you need the money people on your side. Even if you don't do it with big budgets, if you make your own small, guerilla projects, you still need the blessing of curators, festival directors or whoever else might own a platform where you could put your work on display. They still have to be your friends, your fans or supporters, so you depend on their tastes."

Rosto's sense of territorial obligation paired with the open-door potential of distributing his work on the internet (nowadays a common practice) led to the breakthrough revelation that there were truly no limits – subversive, individual or personal – on whatever form it might take. "That I could publish it online and have the world be my audience was amazing! Now we're so used to it, but back then literally all possible platforms and stages were owned by people whose help you'd need to get work published."

That very evening the efforts to adapt *Mind My Gap* – which had already started in print form as a running series in two sibling Dutch magazines – began, converting the artwork and dialogue to an online Flash slideshow with music and sound, teaching himself the fundamentals of HTTP to be able to create and upload the first episode all in one night. Bound by the same technical limitations of the era, early episodes are barebones affairs less than a megabyte in size to allow the online audience of the time to be able to watch them uninterrupted. Though visually minimal, the uninhibited, auteur nature of the stories more than compensate for this. "The early days were fantastic in the sense that it literally felt like, on a more political or philosophical level, what I was doing as a *truly* independent artist mattered. It was great to discover that, as soon as *Mind My Gap* became more of a body of work, there actually was an audience out there, in the world. What I do is what you could call 'boutique,' it's a niche that is certainly not for everyone, but as soon as you have all these quirky individuals who are potentially interested in what *you* are interested in, suddenly you have a substantial audience."

Learning, largely via emails, that this ongoing mixed-media project had some resonance and a growing fanbase boosted Rosto's confidence to progress the stories of *Mind My Gap* without compromise, regardless of their intricacies or inaccessibilities. The stories became as adventurous and unpredictable to Rosto himself as they were to their eventual audience, yet certain components ensured the narratives did not go so far off the rails as to become tedious or off-putting. Chief among these was the musical foundation of the series.

"There was no master plan except for the songs. On a narrative level, I had no clue as to what would happen in the next episode. I wanted it to be as adventurous and as creatively challenging as possible, so I basically just took my time and, just like a musician would, followed the material and played with it and surprised myself. I deliberately did it like this because having everything sketched out and knowing what I'll be doing for the next fifteen years of my life sounds like a nightmare to me."

As the freeform approach to telling Diddybob and Buddybob's story continued to gain momentum, additional narrative strands branched out of *Mind My Gap* in the form of the short films *Beheaded* (1999, Figure 15.16), *(The Rise and Fall of the Legendary) Anglobilly Feverson* (2002) and *Jona/Tomberry* (2005). Rosto acknowledges this trilogy as representing more or less the start of his career as an independent filmmaker.

"The first little short *Beheaded* is a three-minute musical piece about Langeman, one of my characters, losing his head – I consider that my first successful film. I had been trying to make films all my life, basically messing around, trying to find my voice, trying to imitate others, all the stuff that you should do as a young person. *Beheaded* was my first film where I felt "This is me; I did this for me; it's as honest as possible; I'm not trying to please my mother or my girlfriend or any of these demons looking over my shoulder whenever I'm creating something.' It was a three-minute little sweet nothing, but for me it was a breakthrough."

The film certainly succeeds as a natural progression of the graphic novel webisodes, combining the simple-yet-affecting visual of the Langeman's disembodied computer-generated head singing his lamentation against a backdrop of densely composited typographical elements, following an introductory scenario

Figure 15.16

Still from *Beheaded* (Dir. Rosto) ©2005 Studio Rosto A.D.

combining both asset-based and hand-drawn digital 2D animation. While the film would not achieve the same success as those that came after, it laid an important foundation for the subsequent works to build on.

"After *Beheaded* was *(The Rise and Fall of the Legendary) Anglobilly Feverson*. In *Mind My Gap* there is an episode where the 'director' character refers to a storyboard for his film. People thought I was just messing around, but it actually was a real storyboard for a real film that was, I suppose, my breakthrough. *Anglobilly* finally gave me a spot in the independent short filmmakers' landscape." Further cementing this spot was the concluding film, 2005s *Jona/Tomberry*, which went on to win a major prize at the Cannes International Film Festival. This trilogy of films embraced the established characters and sense of structural lawlessness from the graphic novel universe while adding additional elements, such as an hallucinogenic reincarnation of Rosto's nineties musical outfit, later to be rechristened Thee Wreckers. Paying tribute to the band from whose music these stories had sprung, the animated counterparts of band members Wrecker Walley, Wrecker Folley, Wrecker Rooney and Wrecker Rosto are shackled and chained demonic specters who quickly become a key visual of *Mind My Gap*'s expanded universe. "I had now immortalized them by taking their 'souls,' making them into characters and doing a studio project of all the songs that we wrote in the nineties, this time recording them properly."

The strength of this visual concept, paired with the crucial role the songs played as a catalyst for these adventurous film ideas, ultimately led to another supplemental story strand, a tetralogy of shorts in which Thee Wreckers ultimately take center stage. The first two of these films, *No Place Like Home* (2009, Figure 15.17) and the aforementioned *Lonely Bones*, are firmly a part of the *Mind My Gap* storyline, functioning both as works of avant-garde film to be appreciated in their own right and/or as an elaborate coda to Diddybob and Buddybob's journey. The third short *Splintertime* (2015, Figure 15.18) focuses on the journey of Thee Wreckers themselves, chauffeured in an ambulance following the events of *Lonely Bones* through a vast, seemingly unending tundra by a dancing nurse, again a meta-nod to the band's real-world origins.

"Often there will already be a backstory or a legacy of some sort. The nurse was our 'mascot' when we were *The* Wreckers in the nineties, because for the

Figure 15.17

Still from *No Place Like Home* (Dir. Rosto) ©2009 Studio Rosto A.D.

15. Combining Your Efforts

Figure 15.18

Splintertime (Dir. Rosto) ©2015 Studio Rosto A.D/Autour de Minuit/S.O.I.L.

first demos that we recorded I designed the covers for our cassette tapes. I found this 'kinky' nurse in a sixties magazine who was doing nothing special except for just sitting there and pulling on her clothes a little bit, which I found fantastic, in a way – what is kinky about that? I liked that visual a lot, so every time we put out a release on a cassette, there was a nurse. It always seemed to make sense, these guys in black – The Wreckers – wrecking stuff, and then a nurse in white comes in. That visual disappeared for a long time and with Thee Wreckers she doesn't play a part until that ending of *Lonely Bones*, when suddenly there she is again."

Portrayed in live-action by dancer/choreographer Nina Nestelaar, the CG-accentuated features and frenetic movements of the nurse serve as one of the most striking visuals of *Splintertime*, and as such, the character's organic origins are notable when considering idea generation. Indeed, many of Rosto's most affecting visual concepts have sprung from the real world, adapted in such a way as to occupy a limbo between documentary filmmaking and outright fiction (though it is certainly closer to the latter). The final sequence of *Lonely Bones*, for example, is laced with acknowledgments of the production process itself (in which the elaborate CG backdrop alternates and occasionally disappears completely to reveal the green screen studio and crew - Figure 15.19), while the fourth and final entry *Reruns* recreates the interior of Rosto's grandmother's house in a digital space using old Super 8 home movies shot by his father for reference and tracking. Other recurring visuals in the preceding films, such as the motif of various forms of a cross, inform the visuals of *Splintertime*, though whether these are conscious or subconscious decisions elude even Rosto himself. "Did I create these things or did they just fall into place? I never know how that works, but that's why I call my work intuitive, it often feels like I just found these ideas somewhere. My own intuition is basically a repository of everything that has happened to me in my life. Did I find these things there? Did I borrow them? I don't know, but at a

Figure 15.19

Still from *Lonely Bones* (Dir. Rosto) ©2013 Studio Rosto A.D/Autour de Minuit.

certain point these things click, they are all aligned and then it's as though the universe is telling me that they are ready to be used in my next project."

These ideas generally manifest themselves as combinations of elements from preceding projects, oftentimes perfectly suited to the variety of combined approaches that has become something of a signature style. Though the tetralogy has at the least some elements of consistency, be they the musical foundations, the characters or each film being able to identifiably lead into the one that follows, the lack of any hard and fast "rules" to the mythology of Rosto's universe has been its most creatively freeing aspect.

"It's interesting to me, because the graphic novel is now finished and it sort of has its own internal logic, but everything grew organically and there is still a lot of stuff in there which is contradictory and doesn't add up or lead to anything. I see some things where I go 'Wow, I never realized at the time that this actually makes a lot of sense' because I had just done whatever pleased me, whatever I found interesting. There are also other leads that I see that are basically red herrings, things I found interesting at the same, got bored with and dropped."

The actual visual execution of the films chronologically increases in sophistication, with the funding circumstances as overviewed in Chapter 8 playing an obvious part. However from the rudimentary assortment of animation processes visible in *Beheaded* to the lavish HD spectacles of *Lonely Bones* (Figure 15.20) and beyond, Rosto had always embraced the limitless potential of cross-media filmmaking, even eschewing such labor-saving approaches as motion capture for comparatively complex pipelines of 3D tracking and rotoscoping overlaid on top of live-action performances, so as to preserve the unique look and nightmarish quality of hybrid animation he has established.

"It may be that how I do it is time-consuming, which could be a case for motion-capture, but I don't find that especially interesting. If I want the characters to look like real people I don't see why I can't just shoot a real person. Sometimes I want them animated, because there's always a difference in what an animator brings to a character, it's never the same as live-action unless you

15. Combining Your Efforts

Figure 15.20

Still from *Lonely Bones* (Dir. Rosto) ©2013 Studio Rosto A.D/Autour de Minuit.

rotoscope it. An animator can bring an otherworldliness to a character, which you cannot do in live-action. So I never really understood, except for time efficiency, why I would use motion capture."

16

Audience Interaction

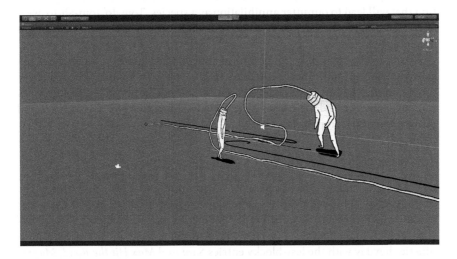

Figure 16.1

Constructing the interactive *PLUG & PLAY* app in Unity. Image courtesy of Michael Frei.

It's often been pointed out that Orwell's vision in his 1949 novel *Nineteen Eighty-Four* of an interconnected society without privacy has indeed panned out, but the role of calculating governmental forces drumming a hive-mind mentality into us has been enabled by our own adorable narcissism. Mankind, as it turns out, is far less collectively at ease when not being seen than when we're screaming "Look at us!" Orwell evidently didn't predict the deep-seated emotional comfort

DOI: 10.1201/9781003214717-16

that high numbers of vlog subscribers and social media followers would induce, the near-sighted fool.

This state of affairs has bled into how we engage with the world around us, to the point where entertainment sometimes just isn't entertaining enough. A night in watching television rarely goes unaccompanied by a session of pithy, hashtag-accompanied editorializing over social media. As a smoker might fidget in a conversational scenario where they're unable to light up, the rest of the world does likewise when its socially indecorous to reach for their phone as it temptingly vibrates with news of how many "likes" their pithy editorial remark has received. Our brains – or simply our fingers – have been reconditioned, it seems, to be constantly occupied, and alongside the exponential rise of video games, from hyperreal, decade-spanning franchises to cutesy, faddish ephemera is an interesting and relatively new trend within animation itself – interactive storytelling.

Interactive media may have hit a stride within most of our lifetimes – some of you readers may even have muddy, half-buried memories of the long-long-ago, a troubling era before every household had even a dial-up connection to the internet.

Nowadays, however, digital interactivity has gone to the other extreme, becoming a component of pretty much every child's cognitive development; there's something vaguely eerie about seeing a drooling infant intuitively know exactly how to swipe at a tablet browser to get to the next *Morph* episode, but that appears to be where we're at. We may be witnessing the dawn of a new evolutionary stage, in which being attuned to technology in such a way advances our entire species; or it may be that our utter dependence on constant stimuli via our smartphones will in fact become a worldwide pandemic of crippling addiction that will lead to our utter annihilation as a species. Tomato, tom-ah-to, we'll cross that bridge when we get to it. In the meantime, how do we take advantage of it as animators?

Perhaps unsurprisingly, the world of independent games development has proved one of the most ideal bedfellows (Figure 16.1). In many respects, there is a sense of mutual intent, to creatively appeal to a niche (while potentially voluminous) audience and to serve as a platform to showcase ability, work ethic and talent to potential employers.

Adventurous Spirit

One happy resurgence has been that of the point-and-click adventure game. Having been established by video game pioneers Ken and Roberta Williams, this medium was powered forward by development companies such as LucasArts with games like *Maniac Mansion* (1987) to something of an early-to-mid-nineties heyday with the less-blocky entries *Sam and Max Hit the Road, Maniac Mansion: Day of the Tentacle* (1993) and the long-running *Monkey Island* series (1990–2010). These games at the time were incredibly sophisticated and the closest approximation gamers could get to a fully interactive cartoon. That they had teams of highly skilled animators taking care to craft wonderful instances of classical, physical comedy instead of the standard, generic sprite animation one expected from games at the time helped sell the experience enormously, not to mention the first major inclusions of wittily scripted voice acting. Though 2D animation soon fell by the wayside in favor of 3D polygonal graphics, for a time, there was quite a significant ripple effect in game animation – Doug TenNapel's

Figure 16.2

The Adventures of Bertram Fiddle cover art ©2014 Rumpus Animation.

Earthworm Jim (1995) and Michel Ansel's *Rayman* (1995) applying similar degrees of visual brilliance to platformers. Indeed, even more recent entries in the video games world such as *Night in the Woods* (2017), *Hollow Knight* (2017), *Cuphead* (2017) and *Knights and Bikes* (2019) still prove how effective 2D animation can be in a modern gaming era.

Rumpus Animation, the Bristol-based animation studio whose independent music video work we looked at in Chapter 5, took a similar initiative by drawing upon a property they had incrementally developed over the course of a decade. Bertram Fiddle began life as the titular explorer of Rumpus Creative Director Seb Burnett's MA film *The Films of Bertram Fiddle*, produced at the University of the West of England's Bristol School of Animation years before Rumpus was firmly established. The original film, predominantly serving as a character design and illustration showcase, did not take flight in and of itself, though the hopes of finding a fitting avenue for the character remained.

"I had an idea about making some kind of film based on a Victorian explorer, and over the course of that year, I developed Bertram as the main character. I made a short film where he gets lost on his way to Great Yarmouth and finds himself up in an obscure part of England that no-one remembers."

After what Seb dubs the "amazing non-success" of the film, the character was further developed over the course of several, equally non-successful ventures. With humor deemed "too old" for children, and "not smutty enough" for most remaining online avenues catering to the sixteen- to twenty-four-year-old male audience, it became clear that Bertram Fiddle would be a harder sell than anticipated.

"We then considered doing a Kickstarter to fund our own series. We estimated that we'd only need £800 to do a whole series – our budgeting has never been a strong point – so luckily we didn't do that. Afterwards it kicked around for ages, we continued doing other work, I continued writing more Bertram stuff, my pile of different ideas and different characters continued to get bigger."

The universe of Bertram Fiddle was further developed during Seb's participation in Animation Sans Frontieres, a course that allowed him to develop the project for production, a step that coincided with studio discussions of the possible merits of branching out into interactive work. The culture of self-published apps, books and games as a way of selling one's ideas without requiring the assistance or permission of a major broadcaster held significant appeal, especially to a studio with designs on getting a television or web series together. Upon returning from Animation Sans Frontieres, the studio took the initiative to pitch their idea to Starter For Ten, a regional funding scheme that had been recently set up to support new creative businesses in the South West. After succeeding in receiving starter funds, Rumpus went on to pitch for additional financial support via Gameslab, a game-development fund initiated by the UK-based investment scheme Creative England. After eight years of the character's incremental development, *The Adventures of Bertram Fiddle* was created (Figures 16.2–16.5).

For a character to have survived eight years of, in blunt terms, rejection, only to persevere and finally break through in an interactive medium says something about the character's staying power. While the timing or circumstances were never right for Bertram Fiddle to have his day as a funded short, series or comic book, certain qualities of the character and his world translated effectively to the independent games world.

"One was I didn't have a clue what I was doing! There were a lot of technical issues, and also it was that when you're doing an animation you have complete control over the scene, you know exactly what will happen and when, and that's

Figure 16.3

The Adventures of Bertram Fiddle gameplay footage ©2014 Rumpus Animation.

16. Audience Interaction

it, it won't change. Whereas when you're making a game it's much more open-ended, you can set certain things up but you can't completely control it. You're not making something for an audience, you're making something for someone to play, so that took a while to get my head around. Then games have things like bugs – when we ported it to PC some of the audio files just vanished, for example; a little animation clip disappeared so we had to re-set that up. When you've done an animated film, it's finished, you can't go wrong, you're done. But with a game it never ends!"

As with all independent ventures, much by way of the promotion itself falls to the creators, who were able to ensure a launch on the games distribution platform Steam via an online campaign, as well as a spotlight focus on various online publications such as Adventure Gamers. With the increased coverage comes increased demand, though that in itself presents its own issue when considering how many platforms need to be accommodated.

"There's so many different variables – when it comes out on iOS people ask if it's coming out on Android. Once it's out on Android people ask when it will be out on PC. Then they'll still complain, because they have a Mac or use Linux. With animation it tends to come out and then you can just watch it, you don't put it up on YouTube only for somebody to demand you put it up on Vimeo, or Dailymotion, because they only visit those sites."

Looking back on the ambition of taking a short film premise and applying it to the unknown territory of interactive media, Rumpus by and large have a good sense of which lessons they've learned are the most essential.

Figure 16.4

The Adventures of Bertram Fiddle storyboard excerpts ©2014 Rumpus Animation.

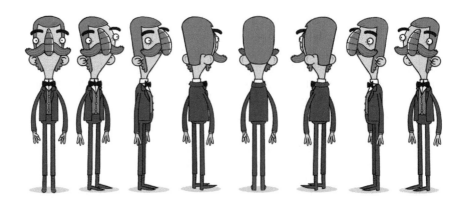

Figure 16.5

Bertram' character turnaround assets for *The Adventures of Bertram Fiddle* ©2014 Rumpus Animation.

"I must admit, the planning is something I left to the last minute," confesses Seb. "It happens in animation, where you have your last couple of weeks when you get everything finished, address what needs changing, and you do it. With a game you can't really leave it that long, you need to constantly keep testing and playing, deadlines need to be a lot closer than you might imagine.

"Everything you do, you'll have to learn to spend two weeks testing it and making sure it hasn't broken; testing what you've already done, whether it actually works, if it's fun to play or if it makes sense. This is especially important in an adventure game that's all about puzzles, you have to make sure people can actually figure out how to solve them. A lot of adventure games have an internal logic that only makes sense if you're a developer – that if you combine a rope with a bit of bramble it will make a pigeon – whereas you would never have thought that unless you already knew it. That's something that took a lot of time, making sure things are in a place where people can find them and you're not just going back and forth too much. But also you want it to be difficult enough to be a challenge."

To Defy the Laws of Tradition

A native of Switzerland, Michael Frei's journey into the world of animation is an atypical one. Though not necessarily the most traditional route, it did begin with the skill of visualization when he started an apprenticeship as an architectural draftsman at the age of fifteen. After four years of appreciating the drawn side of that industry, the strict rigidity of straight lines and mathematical precision that construction plans entail, coupled with the complete lack of creative freedom, was ultimately not what he was looking for in a long-term career.

The world of animation existed as a relatively vague concept – outside of Disney movies, Michael was exposed to little else at a young age. As his enthusiasm for draftsmanship waned and he began to take on a variety of more experimental projects that involved recording himself as he drew, eventually a self-started desire to learn more about animation began to manifest itself. Following his apprenticeship, he took the advice of a friend and looked into what options there were to study animation, eventually starting a course at Switzerland's University of Lucerne. The traditional processes and fundamentals of animation, as it turned out, were something of a brick wall themselves.

16. Audience Interaction

Figure 16.6

Early *PLUG & PLAY* concept sketch Image courtesy of Michael Frei.

"I was quite disappointed after the first year, because they have this classical approach to animation – start with an idea, do a storyboard, then a character sheet, then do your layout, then key frames, then in-betweens and maybe some color – so it's a very linear process. It appeared to me that it was training to work in the industry, a little bit, so I took a year off after that because I wanted to do my own stuff. Eventually I had to do something serious so I studied one year in Tallinn, Estonia, which was very different than Switzerland. In Switzerland we don't really have an animation history; we have French-speaking artists inspired by French animation, we have German-speaking artists who are not influenced by anything in particular, so it's a bit scattered. In Estonia they have some animation tradition, it's a very small country but they have an animation scene that's quite big considering the size of the country, with some studios that are still producing quite original work. The people there really do their own thing, they don't care too much. That's where I started to make my very own films."

Michael's fundamental issues with the traditional approach to animation production should be familiar enough to some with an independent bent – being one link in a production chain. The idea of having to refine one's area of interest into specialist expertise rang too familiar to the architectural work he had left behind.

"It was clear what I had to do – and it was kind of boring. Although I really like it at some times and find it rewarding to watch when it's working, I'm not a born animator. When I animate something, I try to animate until it's finished, I scan it and I watch it and I just do that once. I really hate pencil tests because they ruin that."

The enthusiasm Michael did have toward animation was pretty much entirely limited to independent production and the possibility of creating his own film while being in control of every aspect of it. Investigating the wider independent scene led by proactive individuals and small teams, the idea of figuring out a process that worked best for him and on his own terms held far more appeal than figuring out what to do in the classical animation process.

"Because the process is very predefined in the industry – there's a department for story, a department for animation and so on – there's too little interest in experimentation, I think. That was also how I got into this interactive approach to animation, it was just for me a logical addition to having a vocabulary to tell something through animation. I was not interested in gaming necessarily, it was just one more tool to work with."

Michael's first film *Not About Us* was produced as part of a year-long exchange program at the Estonian Academy of Art, under the mentorship of lauded directorial duo Priit ("his feedback was mostly no feedback") and Olga Pärn. One area of guidance that benefited Michael during this time was the broadening of his scope of influence to include the work of numerous independent Japanese animations, something that helped develop his own style.

"I had problems drawing after my apprenticeship because I was so used to constructing everything I was drawing, so when I started animation, where there are character sheets, where every proportion has to be right and where everything has to be on-model, I started to construct everything; boxes with a circle inside to make a head, it was ridiculous. In Estonia, with drawn animation, quite often the drawings are loose and 'ugly.' I tried to just get away from constructing my drawings and just draw a character fifty times a day until I just had a feeling for it."

Even with the new exposure and experience, the imprint four years of architectural apprenticing had made on Michael frequently saw him gravitating toward geometry based design work. While this had no adverse effect on *Not About Us* (the film's bold look and unique energy earned it a modest festival run, winning several awards and was capped off by a Vimeo Staff Pick upon its release, something of a holy trinity for independent films), for Michael's own sense of artistic direction, he was keen to try something new. When it came to his Lucerne graduation film *PLUG & PLAY* (Figures 16.6–16.12), he actively eschewed the formality and parallel lines of his earlier training by creating the entire film on a trackpad, which made any attempt to draw a completely straight line impossible. While *Not About Us* had performed well, *PLUG & PLAY*'s response was phenomenal, winning over fifteen major awards and screening at over sixty international festivals in its first year of release (the eventual festival count would far exceed one-hundred). A prime example of how abstract, experimental filmmaking can be not just entertaining but witty and subversive, *PLUG & PLAY* takes place in a universe of

Figure 16.7

Still from *PLUG & PLAY* (Dir. Michael Frei) ©2013 Michael Frei.

detached, arguing voices and a society of not-quite-androgynous (some have plug sockets for heads, others have plug pins) characters. What the film doesn't possess in terms of conventional narrative it makes up for in spades with curiously poignant dialogue, well-considered timing and – a particular rarity in abstract filmmaking – slapstick physical comedy. The interactive potential for *PLUG & PLAY* was on Michael's mind since the early stages of the project, although initially just as a hypothetical option.

"I remembered afterwards that before I got into animation I was also interested in interactive design and had applied for that as well, so I had to actually decide whether to go into interactive design or animation. To me animation was just kind of my hobby and I thought *Okay, it's probably impossible to earn a living like that, but if I do it in the beginning of my life that's okay*. If you study interactive design then you most probably will have a job in the industry, you'll make some money and so on, but once you're earning money, you're stuck. That's what I found out through many of my friends, that once they start to work commercially and have a regular income it's very difficult to go your own way, to say 'no' to money."

Amongst the various case studies we have already looked at in this book, we've seen a hefty variety of ways in which the storytelling process of a film can be approached – scripted, visual, non-fictional, meta-fictional, interpretational, abstract and, most recently, with interactive considerations. When it comes to Michael Frei's overall artistic process, along with his methods of idea generation, "storytelling" is not a word he is fond of. As he sees it, the term narrows down what a film in and of itself *is*, an issue that proves a particular concern when extended to transmedia projects.

"At that point *nobody* gets what it means anymore. But I think I have a more open approach, by which I mean I call it 'narrative' more than 'story.' I try to develop a system that works, a world that works to certain rules like our own world, and if everything somehow works together then I have a film. With *PLUG & PLAY* I tried to have very few visual elements as well, to make it simpler to develop it further into this interactive experience. In general, that's what I think I'll try to do in the future, to make a narrative out of minimal visual elements. It's not that I start with an overall concept of what I want to tell and then I try to

Figure 16.8

Still from *PLUG & PLAY* (Dir. Michael Frei) ©2013 Michael Frei.

To Defy the Laws of Tradition

do that, it's more playing around with visual elements until I've found something that is meaningful to me.

"The filmmaker Royd Anderson has a not-so-very different approach to film-making but how he tells stories is just different enough to feel as though it is totally from another world. It's more like a theatre play. I really like his approach, I think he also avoids the term 'story' and I think that's very interesting. His films were definitely an influence, in how they transport emotion. That's why I go to the cinema, not for the story but to relate to something."

The absence of "story," as many would define the term, does not hamper the effectiveness of the final film – as abstract as it is, the visuals are not so obtuse or ineffable that an audience cannot make their own interpretations as to their meaning. The interactive version of *PLUG & PLAY* took roughly two years to put together following the completion of the movie, made possible in large part due to the positive festival reception and prize money it had picked up. These festival-enabled funds were also supplemented in part by Swiss Television.

"In Switzerland there is some government funding for animated short films and for animation in general, because in Switzerland the industry is so small that it wouldn't work without a funding system. So it turns out with *PLUG & PLAY* that there is a chance to get some revenue from doing such work. I was quite surprised, I didn't anticipate something like that but I think it's possible to still make something for a niche audience that people are willing to pay for, even though it's hard."

The terms of accepting the funding were that the developers themselves had to be Swiss. Reaching out to Zurich University of the Arts, known for having a prominent games design course, it soon became apparent that the option of working with students would not be practicable on top of their course workloads. Eventually Michael's search led him to recent graduate and independent games designer Mario von Rickenbach.

"I sent him the film when it was finished over email, we met at the beginning of 2013 and just talked about what we like between these interactive, game-related worlds. I'm really not a gamer but there were two games we both considered

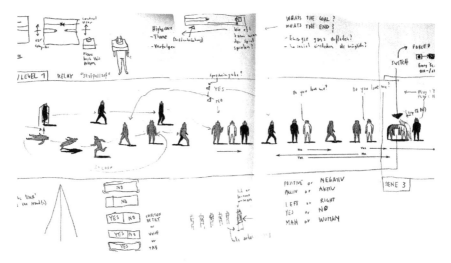

Figure 16.9

PLUG & PLAY app concept sketches. Image courtesy of Michael Frei.

favourites, *Windowsill* by Vector Park and *BlaBla* from the NFB, so these were what we wanted to go for. We definitely didn't want to turn it into any particular game genre that was already out there, we just wanted to make an interactive experience that could really stay true to the film. We didn't really know how to do that, there was a lot of experimentation and prototyping, and it took an incredible amount of work in the end. It was only possible because of how much Mario committed to the project."

It was clear from the outset that the project would need to be done for the love of the medium rather than any financial gain. Following a series of working and prototype sessions, Michael ultimately found himself moving to Geneva to work on the final project with Mario full-time from May 2014 to February 2015, when it was released to accompany the online premiere of the original film. The production of the game itself required a great deal of experimentation, Michael not having gone into the project with a clear and rigid concept of how it should turn out. This freeform approach was pointedly different to how he had put together the original film.

"I try to figure out everything in my head before I start to animate because I'm a lazy animator and I just want to animate what I have to. With the game it's completely different, with almost every scene that is in the movie we made a prototype, we started just taking the animation that was the easiest to take out of the movie and tried to make something out of it. In the beginning, we only had this figure running left and right, trying to figure out how to interact with it. That turned out to be one of the most difficult scenes, in the end."

The interactive experience was gradually pieced together by each scene from the film, deconstructing them from how they were originally presented and reconstructing all the pieces together in Unity. Out of necessity certain workarounds needed to be developed, such as modifying the frame rate from the original film's twelve-per-second (considered way too slow by today's standards for interactive media) to a more accommodating sixty. As well as the film's frame-by-frame animation, Mario and Michael also made use of Unity's digital puppet system, as well as certain elements such as the game's interactive cables rendered in 3D CG using a 2D shader.

"We also combined some of these techniques, so there are scenes where the legs are frame by frame and the upper body is a physical puppet. Where all these techniques are combined, we made this process of going from one step to another.

"You might have seen the finger simulator, it was an earlier test on how to interact like that, and the cables were coded by Mario, he worked on them for one month until they felt right, so it was a very slow process of making a scene, making a prototype, advancing to another one, going back to an earlier scene with new ideas or a new technique, until everything fit together. The difficulty was that we wanted to have clean cuts, like a film would have; this is something you see very rarely in games. We didn't want to have cutscenes, instead when we developed a whole new system, where you have to plug in cables to advance from one scene to another. So that was the only thing we actually added in the game that was not a component of the original film. That was to solve a lot of the problems that we had, because every path has to be motivated by something, in a game or interactive experience, otherwise it feels awkward.

"With the game the problem is it never really feels finished, you can always think of ways to make it better. After a certain number of updates you have to say

Figure 16.10

Constructing the interactive *PLUG & PLAY* app in Unity. Image courtesy of Michael Frei.

16. Audience Interaction

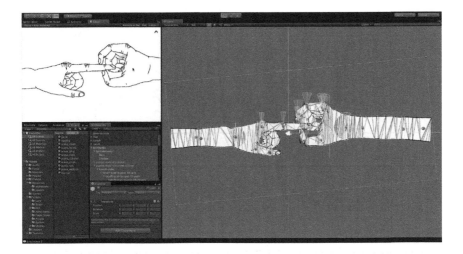

Figure 16.11

Constructing the interactive *PLUG & PLAY* app in Unity. Image courtesy of Michael Frei.

'That's it,' otherwise you could work on it forever, but we were very happy with the response we got."

Having the original film version of *PLUG & PLAY* to compare it with, Michael has had a direct insight into just how different either project's audience response has been. While the various online communities that support and showcase independent film tend to be positive and constructive, customers who have paid for a game will make no bones about airing any and all grievances they might have with the experience.

"When I show the film at festivals and I get comments about a film they are always filtered. Because you're in a room with the audience there's a certain social dynamic that changes depending on which country you're in. I find it very interesting to watch gameplay videos, there are lot of videos of people playing through the whole *PLUG & PLAY* experience and will just tell you what they think, unfiltered. It's very funny to be in someone's head as they play, it's interesting how different it is to the reactions I had gotten before.

"I think there are some flaws maybe that we already know of but it's quite funny that people don't really see them. Another critique we got which was surprising to me was there were people thinking I had just made a game to make money, that it is either too expensive or too short. These are the main complaints you get online."

In spite of the naysayers, Michael would continue to explore the opportunities available for filmmakers to expand their film work into an interactive realm, his subsequent project *KIDS*[1] similarly being released in several formats; a short film officially selected for over 150 international festivals including Annecy, Berlinale and Clermont-Ferrand; a three-part touring installation/exhibition; and an interactive game, again in collaboration with Mario von Rickenbach, co-produced by Playables, SRG SSR and Arte.

Similarly, symbiotic relationships between independent shorts and accompanying games are on the rise, one defining example being London studio Animade's *Ready Steady Bang*.[2] Starting life as a basic one or two-player reflex test app, the sprite design of the dueling cowboys each player commandeers is

Figure 16.12

Prototyping the interactive *PLUG & PLAY* app. Image courtesy of Michael Frei.

minimal yet fluidly animated, with thirty comically animated death sequences in rotation. The originality and perfect timing of these basic animations prove so appealing that merely compiling them in sequence makes for a satisfying micro-short – *Thirty Ways to Kill a Cowboy* – on its own. As more games – with more sprite elements -- were introduced in the wider ranging follow-up app *Ready Steady Play*, more short films in a similar vein, such as *More Than Just a Hobby* and *Queue the Cowboy*, were produced as in-studio offshoots, facilitated by the stark minimalism of their design while again animated with beat-perfect comic timing and smoothness. While serving as additional advertising for the games, their value as entertaining shorts is owed to their structural discipline and ability to get their point across clearly and quickly, a similar trait – though very different in terms of design approach – to fellow webisodic animation producer Ant Blades, as seen in Chapter 6.

Further exploring what precisely makes an animated project interactive, Ant's own *Singing Christmas Hedgehogs* from 2011 (Figure 16.13) is also worth considering. Without having any traits that could see it considered a "game," strictly speaking, it serves more as a cleverly updated spin on the now antiquated Flash webtoons that would offer viewers prompts to determine the events or outcome of an animation (spoiler alert – whichever way you went, there was no happy ending for the frog in that blender). By 2011, YouTube had become more of an automatic go-to as far as the general public were concerned, though only offering a platform to host videos without any in-built interactive buttons. Instead, Ant makes ingenious use of the website's captioning and annotations options that allow viewers to either skip to a certain time in the video being watched, or a new video altogether.

"When you're working, you're always trying to think of new approaches." Ant explains, "Every advertiser comes to you and says they need something new that hasn't been done before, and there are a limited amount of things in your toolbox to try and make use of. In this case it was something that not many people had done, that whole kind of annotation journey, taking you through different stories. I was mostly thinking about that from playing with these annotations when I worked at YouTube."

The interactive experience of *Singing Christmas Hedgehogs* is facilitated by eleven separate video uploads, seven of which being the alternate final outcomes.

Figure 16.13

Diagram indicating one possible outcome for *Singing Christmas Hedgehogs* ©2011 Ant Blades/Birdbox Studio.

The first is a "character selection" menu where the audience is presented with three hedgehogs in a snowy field. Depending on your choice, one of three subsequent videos will play, presenting three options (that occur as the timeline progresses or can be skipped to using YouTube's annotations – labeled within the body of the video itself – in lieu of buttons) as to either how you want your hedgehog dressed, or what you want it to sing. Each of these choices lead to a final punchline video promising a song from your hedgehog, after which any viewer would be hard-pressed to not wish to return to the start and explore the alternatives.

"The actual initial idea was that there would be three hedgehogs – I think they were called *Adventure Hedgehogs* – that you could dress how you wanted, as superheroes. You'd see there would be, for example, a princess or someone who needed rescuing and how you needed to get there, it would look like there was going to be this massive journey ahead of you. You then chose what superpowers you were going to have, whether you'd be a knight, or perhaps a ninja, but then when you started your quest, you'd take one step and get run over by a car, however you dressed your hedgehog or whichever one you chose. That was going to be the gag behind it.

"When it came to doing a Christmas idea, I think I was all out of any good ideas, that was when I thought I could maybe just repurpose that one. It did well in terms of clicks, people clicking around again and again, to try all of the outcomes, so that was a good kick off for the first year of the studio."

Notes

1 https://playkids.ch/.
2 https://animade.tv/.

Reinventing the Wheel

Here, we will look at some contemporary examples of independent films that stand out for having a particular visual edge, whether through dynamic use of color, contemporary design sensibilities or inventive approaches to shot composition, cinematography and dramaturgy. Granted, virtually every film that has been discussed is visually striking, to some degree, and in truth, I could dedicate some words toward each on the matter in the instances where I haven't done so already. In the interests of simplification, I will limit my indulgence in this regard, beginning with one of our earliest case studies, Adam Elliot.

The instantly identifiable nature of Adam's sculpture work also goes hand in hand with a particular sensibility when it comes to his use of color. When used at all, in fact, color is sparse and often heavily desaturated. This resistance against a "chirpier" visual approach began with what Adam refers to as a "purist ideal" during film school that he would only make black and white films ("I was a minimalist at 25 – I was *full* of ideals!"). This determination was followed through with his first trilogy of shorts *Uncle*, *Cousin* and *Brother*, though when the opportunity to tell a broader story came about, he found that matter not entirely in his hands.

"By the time I got to *Harvie Krumpet* I was convinced by the government funding bodies that I couldn't keep going with black and white, that if the film was going to have any commercial potential, it had to be color. So I gave in."

It's hard to say whether or not sticking to his guns would have made a better or worse film. Despite its tragic side, when compared to the quiet, bleak universe of his first three darkly comic offerings, there is a far sunnier disposition to *Harvie Krumpet*, with more outright comedic beats and a notably feelgood ending. That

DOI: 10.1201/9781003214717-17

Figure 17.1

Original "Max" puppet demonstrating use of spot coloring in *Mary & Max* (Dir. Adam Elliot) on display in Annecy, 2014. Photo by the author.

the world of the film is one of color – albeit desaturated to the point of being near-monochrome – does not feel like a negative thing, or one that goes against the film's artistic intent. Certainly, the presumed commercial potential paid off, the film winning an Oscar for Best Animated Short Film in 2004.

The domino effect of this success ultimately led to 2009's *Mary and Max* (Figure 17.1), a film that boasted its own unique color palette. Set alternately in New York and Australia, the look of the film shifts from black and white (with occasional instances of spot-coloring for effect) to a sea of beiges and browns, respectively.

"With *Mary and Max* I put up a battle again, I wanted it to be completely black and white and they said no. So I suggested that maybe Max's world could be black and white using color as a device, that we could create these two different color palettes, and one can be grayscale – as New York in the 70s was a very concrete environment – and the other can be brown – as Australia at that time was very brown; everyone had brown carpet, 'Mission Brown' was the most popular color at the time.

"With *Ernie Biscuit* (Figure 17.2), I wanted the film to have a nostalgic, photographic (as in an old photo album) feel. I wanted it to have a heavy vignette round the edge, I was even going to add scratches and more dust to the final grade but in the end I resisted that. Then also, because I wanted to clear my head of color, I wanted to go back to black and white. The film is set in 1966 which was pre-color-television in Australia anyway."

Though *Ernie Biscuit* wound up a companion film to *Harvie Krumpet* rather than *Mary and Max*, the black and white world Ernie occupies is at odds with the

17. Reinventing the Wheel

Figure 17.2

"Ernie" character sculpt for Adam Elliot's *Ernie Biscuit* ©2015 Adam Elliot.

muted color world of Harvie's. Yet more than anything, the story itself is what binds the two, as similar tales of migrants adapting to life in Australia. More importantly, to have produced *Ernie Biscuit* in color simply to be consistent with its cinematic sibling would go against Adam's fondness for his chosen aesthetic.

"I love high-contrast looking films, I love black, I've always tried to…again I see watching a film as a multisensory experience, there's the aesthetic but there's also the poetic nature of the dialogue, but also I want people to almost 'smell' and 'taste' certain scenes. Of course, they're not actually doing those things, but I want it to be a full sensory experience. I love films where one of the elements is taken away, so you have to rely on your other senses. Another thing about black and white that's very honest in a way is that you can't hide as much. Every film I make I would prefer it to be black and white, but just because I love black and white films and I love narrated films, though for purely selfish, indulgent reasons."

Rising High

Switching focus to an artist with an altogether different slant on design, not to mention story and visual execution, Adam Wells has taken on a series of self-started, auteur projects with his own visual edge owed largely to his background in CG motion graphics. A champion of Cinema 4D, a software package with its feet firmly planted in both the animation and mograph world, Adam gravitated toward it for its array of advantageous character animation solutions.

"I actually didn't want to do any character animation really at all, because it was really hard to do, so my solution was to mainly do little loops with simple characters and see if I could tell a story using looping images. I enjoyed working in motion and Cinema 4D, back in 2010, definitely seemed to have its own aesthetic. I think that the fact that I was still learning the software comes across in my early work. It's not something that many people do and I've moved away from it a little bit as I've gotten more comfortable with actual animation, which is a shame because I think it's interesting to blend the two."

Adam's first film which established his style to the independent community was 2012's *Brave New Old* (Figure 17.3), in which an assortment of simply

Figure 17.3

Stills from *Brave New Old* (Dir. Adam Wells) ©2012 Adam Wells.

Figure 17.4

Still from *The Circle Line* (Dir. Adam Wells) ©2013 Adam Wells.

designed, cuboid characters inhabit their own insulated, compartmentalized worlds the audience is alternately given glimpses of through the side panels of a cube which perpetually rotates. Each tableau we witness explores a variety of topics, on one end impenetrable (yet aesthetically satisfying) abstraction, on the other more accessible themes of travel, technology and relationships. The prevailing themes of compartmentalization and our ambivalence toward the rise of technology (along with its potential for societal alienation) are recurring themes in Adam's subsequent work, which includes 2013's *Risehigh* and *The Circle Line* (Figure 17.4) followed by 2014's *Fake Expectations* (Figure 17.5). Though it is a subject ripe for criticism and satire, Adam's attitude to said technologies, contributing as they do to the films' creation, distribution and reception, is largely fond.

"I personally quite like technology. It's kind of fun, isn't it? There's not much you can do to change it, the genie's already out of the bottle so everything's much more fragmented and will continue to be so. I'm constantly excited by my iPhone, so I'm probably not going to martyr myself. I can try as much as I can to be conscious of it, but I've been very fortunate because I have a skillset that can work for me commercially and can also make my own animations so I'm quite satisfied as well. Being this fortunate means I'm not really in the best position to judge the wider picture."

This grounded sense of balance in Adam's attitude benefits his work in several ways, chief amongst them the absence of sanctimony; there is no hypocritical condemnation of the technologies that have reshaped human habits, merely a series of well-observed and good-natured visual gags around the habits themselves. In 2014's *Fake Expectations*, one of the main subjects of exploration is the validity of art, something Adam has seen to be conflictive when it comes to how his medium is regarded in the independent animation world.

"On social media I've seen some independent 2D animators being very sniffy and sneery about CG animation, asserting that 2D is not dead. From my point of view, it's been a little bit left behind because it's the mainstream, so people who are kind of drawn to creating fringe work always want to work on the fringes and are slightly dismissive of CG animation. It's hard to say if they're dismissive of it as an aesthetic, because it's so established or because it can be quite technical and they feel cut out of it.

Figure 17.5

Still from *Fake Expectations* (Dir. Adam Wells) ©2014 Adam Wells.

"There are a few different factors: Technically, it's different from drawing frame-by-frame, sure, but a lot of animators use After Effects in a similarly technical way to create rigs, for example. I've looked at festival selections and it seems a very small percentage of selected films are CG. Considering it's supposedly the dominant production method, it's clearly seen as 'for cinema,' while other methods are for the independent artists.

"Because it's a newer medium as well there's so much potential to experiment and try new things. The stuff I'm working on at the moment is poly cel stuff, trying to retain that CG aesthetic while animating in a much more close-to-the-bone fashion. But ultimately I feel as though the independent sector's very derisive of CG animation and dismisses it as children's stuff. People who are into independent film and animation tend to be, I always feel, drawn to more traditional aesthetics because it meshes more with the personality of independent animation."

The complexity of Adam's work is owed in many respects to multiple sources of inspiration beyond just animation and design. The physical impossibilities of *Brave New Old*'s (Figures 17.6 and 17.7) key visual motif, made possible through a combination of CG modeling and extensive masking and compositing in After Effects, took inspiration from the high-concept physical manipulation of the video game *Portal*. Adam's 2013 film *Risehigh* (Figure 17.8), a twenty-minute mini-epic where the audience travels up a tall building, glimpsing the goings-on inside each apartment along the way, was informed in part by Terry Gilliam's *Brazil*. Predominantly, Adam's key visual concepts and approaches to production are born out of a passion for theater and set design. The progressive work of troupes such as Punchdrunk[1] and You Me Bum Bum Train,[2] who make pains to further the art of immersive theater by combining interactive environments and installations with traditional performance, is of particular resonance. Oftentimes, it is the visual concept for a film's environment that serves as the first germ of Adam's creative process.

"Whenever I have an idea for a set piece, I'll generally end up designing films, stories and ideas around that set piece, which is probably a naughty way of doing it. It may be why some things hang together differently to how they would in other people's films, but I like it. There's a good core to build off of and set pieces always help me with that (Figure 17.9).

Figure 17.6

Brave New Old (Dir. Adam Wells) shot render ©2012 Adam Wells.

Figure 17.7

Brave New Old (Dir. Adam Wells) press shot ©2012 Adam Wells.

"I've tried different things on different films, just because I'm trying to figure out what works really well. In *Brave New Old* I went through it in a very linear way, I just kept storyboarding the plot with rough, setup ideas of things I had been brooding about for a long time. There were also visual remnants from commercial pitches that never went anywhere that I thought were great mysterious ideas, people pulling levers and stuff like that. The cube-headed characters were designed for simplicity's sake, trying to determine what I could technically achieve at that stage, to make them as simple as possible so I could animate and manipulate them in many ways. I kind of got stuck at the end and decided to make it a quandary everyone in the audience could stroke their beards to."

Were it not for the themes introduced throughout the film and the visual sophistication of the closing shot, the perceived absence of an ending would most likely not be successful; even when dealing with conceptual abstraction, a film needs structure, something Adam gave extra consideration toward with his follow-up film.

"*Risehigh* (Figures 17.10 and 17.11) was a bit different. I kind of arced that out a little bit more, came up with a beginning, middle and end and drew what were almost flow-diagrams for the characters. I knew where I wanted them to go, where I wanted them to start and how I wanted it to look. I then filled in all the blanks in a spreadsheet, which went from bottom to top as with the building in the film, so every floor of the building was represented by a rung on the spreadsheet that had a description of what would happen on that floor. The other stuff is made up as I go along, slightly. Generally, I'll see little visual ideas that I'm keen on and try to think about how I can integrate them into a plot."

The structural nature of CG animation brings with it several creative benefits. The freedom to tinker with the film's environment before, during and after the animation itself brings with it significantly more options than composited 2D animation and especially stop-motion, where there's very little opportunity to

Figure 17.8

Risehigh (Dir. Adam Wells) shot render ©2013 Adam Wells.

return to the film, so to speak. Adam's process has proven conducive to embellishments and experimentation, creating densely populated and detailed environments that invite repeat viewing. "Generally before I start building there's not much room for improvisation but most of the films I've made up until now I've built as physical spaces. *The Circle Line* I had built as a giant shopping mall, and when I built that there was a lot of 'real estate' that I hadn't quite worked out yet that wasn't super important for the plot. It's almost like leaving a page out of a book, I go back and fill those bits in, which can be really hard, although I think that may be one of the things you can do in CG animation you can't do as well elsewhere. It's like writing, you don't know fully until you've actually written something how it might feel; ideas lead to ideas.

"For practicality reasons it can't be one project file because it slows the computer down, but it will be designed as one file. So if you pasted all the elements together, it would all be in place, but I can't actually render that because it's impractical. *Brave New Old* required so much compositing to make the rotating

Figure 17.9

Character animation using flat planes in Cinema 4D for *The Circle Line* (Dir. Adam Wells) ©2013 Adam Wells.

cube that there's a different file for almost every shot. I *could* do the compositing in the Cinema 4D project file but again it would slow things down unnecessarily, so *Brave New Old* was wholly composited, whereas *Risehigh* I managed to make use of lots of in-software compositing by using Boole expressions. Doing compositing can be a real head-scratcher, it just requires lots of planning to make it work."

There are two prevailing approaches to character animation evident in Adam's work, the first being shape-based geometric constructs with rotatable pivot points as opposed to traditional, inverse kinematic rigging. This approach is seen in *Brave New Old* and the quasi-robotic occupants of the world of *Fake Expectations*. Adam's alternate approach applied to *Risehigh* and its shorter follow-up *The Circle Line* sees the characters rendered as flat, two-dimensional entities devoid of any detail save for their polygonal, Cartoon Modern-esque outlines. This approach gives the films more of a mixed-media feel, although the process is achieved within the same software.

"It's animated on flat planes, which is a weird cheat as I like the idea of being able to do it frame-by-frame in the software but I really like the idea of 'drawing' in the 3D environment. Using geometry is so much quicker, so *Brave New Old* and *Fake Expectations* had much easier character animation than *Risehigh* or *Circle Line*. For those I wanted to try and keep the polygonal aesthetics while taking advantage of stuff like those weird smears and blurs you get with old animation but don't really see as much of in CG, you tend to see motion blur instead.

"In my new work I'm now designing characters to be much more naturalistic looking, because what I find with those characters is I like them and they're fun to do but they're not very empathetic. They leave people a bit cold, I think, because they're quite abstract. I do like that but if you're trying to inspire people into feeling an emotion you need something that people can grip onto a bit more."

The major risk Adam has taken with his work is just how much it amounts to. With *Brave New Old* and *Fake Expectations* averaging out around the ten-minute mark, and *Risehigh* nearing twenty, these projects are clearly enormous undertakings for one person (outside of music and sound, the films are by and large put together entirely on his own). Ordinarily, longer animated shorts can backfire by losing their audience's attention along the way, a pitfall Adam has effectively sidestepped by keeping the action so consistent and varied. The remaining concern is the drain on one's personal time such an undertaking demands, an aspect that Adam is fairly level-headed about.

"I've managed to trick my brain: When I do commercial work, which is how I make my living, there are often really strict deadlines. I was looking at these crazy deadlines and thinking *I just made a minute's worth of animation…in a week! And it's pretty good stuff. Why can't I do that for myself?* So I just forcibly did it, working really fast and not getting too bogged down sometimes, because it's really easy to get really bogged down in ideas. If I get stuck on something for too long I'll try to move on, otherwise staying focused for so long can be pretty difficult. I really enjoy modelling with music on, which is controversial because lots of animators don't, but I get more done because I can just relax and do the work, then go back and fix things without music on if I need to. But if I didn't have the music or the podcasts, I wouldn't get it done because I wouldn't be entertained while I was doing it."

We all may find ourselves in a better position when freelancing as we can allocate, as Adam does, a certain amount of time to our film work. If a work lull

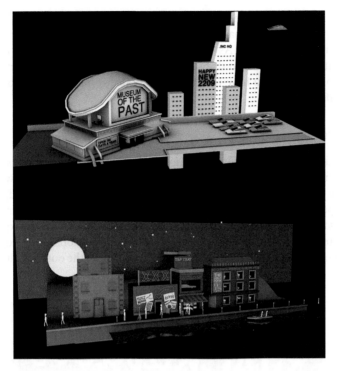

Figure 17.10

CG sets constructed in Cinema 4D for *Risehigh*. Image courtesy of Adam Wells.

Figure 17.11

Still from *Risehigh* (Dir. Adam Wells) ©2013 Adam Wells.

appears every once in a while, it's a good use of one's time and keeps the creative muscles relatively flexed.

"It's tough work on days when you just want to sit around and play video games, but once you've done it enough you develop this mentality where you feel like you're failing if you're *not* doing it."

The need to work does not necessarily have to be constant either. It's far more advisable to let your personal work benefit you when the time is right, rather than force it and risk burn out. As long as our creative impulse remains, it's a good idea to take the odd break and absorb what's around us every once in a while. As Adam points out: "You have to fill up your brain with stuff before you can spit more stuff out."

Retro Vertigo

While Adam's work features the odd nod to the past, his filmography is rooted in its contemporary sensibilities. Yet great things can also be achieved when marrying the tropes and conventions of animation's golden age with the edgier, more frenetic pacing of our current film landscape. Montreal-based Benjamin Arcand's *Wackatdooo* (Figures 17.12–17.17) grew from a series of animation experiments made during his work breaks, centered around a traditionally styled, 2D animated dancing cat created for the fun of it. Pleased with the outcome, it occurred

Figure 17.12

Wackatdooo poster ©2014 Benjamin Arcand.

to Benjamin that an entire animated, musically driven short "about a cat going crazy and dancing around" could be a very real possibility.

"I had tried to make a short film before and had to stop at a certain point, because it was pretty hard. So *Wackatdooo* was a challenge I set for myself, whether or not I could do a film on my own, with no production company or money whatsoever."

Having not followed through on the earlier attempt at a completed short, Benjamin credits his intervening industry experience as the guaranteeing factor of *Wackatdooo*'s success, as well as a clearer knowledge of how one's ambition for a project can be more realistically achieved. Although the finished film holds together perfectly, the pre-production process was something of a staggered affair.

"I started to storyboard it, but mostly just as rough story panels on pieces of paper. I was just getting the heavy ideas out, still working on it when I had breaks, until the point where I decided *Okay, let's do this* – I think around February 2012. I started to do the boards, going with my thumbnails I had done and building the story straight-ahead in the animation software, not using storyboard software, just the animation timeline."

The freeform, unrestrained mania of the film is influenced by such early animation pioneers as Ub Iwerks and the Fleischer brothers, with the sight gags and overall visual quality serving as an ode to Warner Bros. animation stalwarts Tex Avery, Bob Clampett and Chuck Jones, not to mention the contemporary spin on their approach seen in shows like *The Ren and Stimpy Show* in the early nineties. This is perhaps most notable toward the end of the main musical segment, where the frantic nature of the fantasy world becomes an increasingly overwhelming nightmare.

While the production of *Wackatdooo* would be assisted in many respects by the music at its core (see Chapter 19), another major contributor to its visual appeal is the bold and inventive approach to its use of color. As the piece increasingly gives way to fantasy elements, color palettes alternate between highly saturated analogous schemes to more understated complementary schemes, with occasional monochrome backgrounds jumping from one point of the color wheel to the next with each shot – sometimes even within the same shot as the fantasy gives way to manic hysteria. What gives these freer, more playful instances of color use more impact are the comparatively restrained and disciplined palettes of the bookending "real world" scenes, an area assisted by fellow artist Edith Lebel.[3]

"Sometimes I like to do everything because every aspect is fun, but also I think it gives a film a nice touch to bring a different vision to it. I went and looked for the strongest people, and Edith is very strong with colour and she wanted to do it, so I was happy. Another reason would be that it helps with the workload – I mean, just painting the city background would have taken me forever – but I do think the film is better with an outsider vision."

Maintaining the spirit of the original test sequences from which the film developed, *Wackatdooo* was animated straight-ahead in Toon Boom (with textural and film grain overlays to enhance the richness and "retro" vibe of the film), flying in the face of the conventions of animation where pre-vis and meticulous planning are considered crucial. This manner of tackling the visuals pairs well with the overall vibe of the production and the events being depicted – beginning as a cathartic, post-workday dance session, the lines between reality, fantasy and dreams are blurred to the point of non-existence, until the main character's

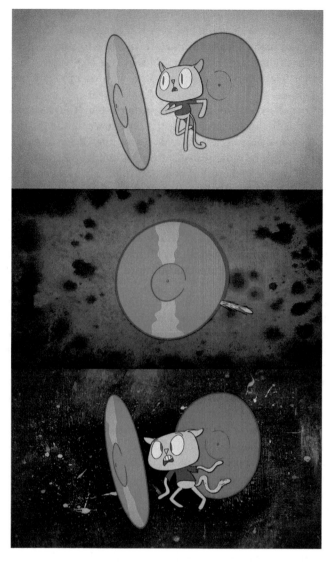

Figure 17.13

Demonstrating the impactful use of color during a sequence in Benjamin Arcand's *Wackatdooo* ©2014 Benjamin Arcand.

morning alarm brings him back to the real world. As such, the absence of a need for continuity allowed for Benjamin's approach to each shot to be more or less unfettered, save for a certain degree of visual continuity to keep the film anchored on a subliminal level.

"Animating straight-ahead doesn't suit every kind of film story for, but mine was pretty simple. I think the main advantage to the animation was that I sometimes scenes were created purely out of ideas for transitions, 'let's see what we're going to do next', from shot to shot. So I like the straight-ahead approach, although it can create some continuity problems in a way, and of course you need to wrap it up at the end. I had some trouble working out how the film was going

Figure 17.14

Wackatdooo background layout by Benjamin Arcand, background painted by Edith Lebel ©2014 Benjamin Arcand.

Figure 17.15

Wackatdooo animatic sketch ©2014 Benjamin Arcand.

to finish – all I knew was that I wanted him to wake up, so at the animatic stage I left the ending a bit open, when the alarm clock is ringing."

The coda of the film manages to tie everything together with a cleverly paced, three-punch ending that frees the musical enthusiast cat from the hell of his job by sending him instead to the hell of his fantasies, to his eternal delight. Bookending the main musical number of the film with two "real-world" scenarios that are

Figure 17.16

Still from *Wackatdooo* (Dir. Benjamin Arcand) ©2014 Benjamin Arcand.

Figure 17.17

Wackatdooo jump sequence ©2014 Benjamin Arcand.

playfully subverted by the time the credits roll proves an effective means of lending the project more substance from a story perspective; though the bulk of *Wackatdooo* is a wordless dance number, the overall piece works structurally as a film.

"I think that sometimes when there aren't enough limitations you find yourself going in all directions without enough structure, but in this film at least I had a small setup. It wasn't a crazy story with thousands of characters, so since it was pretty simple it worked."

As with many of these case studies, the time and effort spent on the film has been advantageous to Benjamin's career and future prospects, as well as his own personal artistic development.

"I've been contacted for a couple of projects and job opportunities, and there are possibilities to maybe pitch for short programmes at major networks. The main benefit was that I came away from the project with more skills; by making the film, I've improved much faster than if I had been just working on some TV show. I decided to not take on any work for a period of time while working on the film and at first I was a bit scared about losing opportunities, that maybe it was going to be hard after the film was done, but now things are even better than before."

Figure 17.18

Alex Grigg. Photo courtesy of the artist.

Late Nights

Few collaborative efforts so encapsulate the spirit of independent animation while confirming the creative possibilities this book celebrates than the Late Night Work Club, a rotating collective of animation talents who released their first multi-artist anthology *Ghost Stories* in September 2013. The film's genesis was the coming together of fifteen likeminded animators based around the globe, corralled by illustrator/animator Scott Benson, as contributor Charles Huettner recalls.

"Late Night Work Club was started by me, Scott, Eamonn O'Neill and Eimin McNamara. We were just talking on Google Hangouts about freelancing and frustrations with that. Scott just sort of pitched to us this idea of doing Late Night Work Club and we were really into it and it just kind of blew up from there."

These first conversations ultimately led to a callout among the indie animation community, with Ghost Stories' contributors eventually comprising thirteen animators – Jake Armstrong and Erin Kilkenny (*Mountain Ash*), Louise Bagnall (*Loose Ends*), Scott Benson (*Last Lives*), Sean Buckelew (*The American Dream*), Ciaran Duffy (*Ombilda*), Conor Finnegan (*Asshole*), Alex Grigg (*Phantom Limb*, Figure 17.18), Charles Huettner (*The Jump*), Eamonn O'Neill (*Post Personal*), Dave Prosser (*I Will Miss You*) and Caleb Wood (*Rat Trap*).

Having been working in animation for roughly four years, Alex Grigg's experience had largely been limited to commercials, feature work and assisting on other people's shorts. Having reached a point where he was able to take time off from paid work, the opportunity to direct a film entirely of his own was met with tremendous enthusiasm.

"I had just moved to London, which was a huge influence on me, getting out and doing my own stuff, finishing my own work for the first time. Having been in Australia previously, the only people who made and finished personal work were people who got funded by funding bodies. That seemed to be the only way to do things, and then I got to London and everyone I met was in the same position as me, they'd all be freelance animating by day but they'd all have finished films or interesting projects to their name, without having to wait for permission from anyone. So it was kind of a perfect storm."

Alex's first job out of school had been as an animator on the short film *The Cat Piano* (Dir. Eddie White and Ari Gibson) in Adelaide. It was on this job that he cut his teeth on animating in Photoshop, a software he continued to gravitate toward throughout his subsequent work and involvement with the Late Night Work Club. Bouncing around the Australian industry saw Alex take on work as varied as commercial CG animation and motion capture for video games before eventually landing a job at Nexus in London. This last move proved something of a culture shock in terms of his perception of what constitutes an independent animation director.

"That is something that doesn't happen in Australia at all, there aren't really freelance directors here – you own a company and then you're a director, that's what director generally means now, in Australia. So I worked everywhere just generally as an animator, and about the time I moved to London I was sort of losing interest in just animating, I felt a little bit like I was watching someone else work all day. So I broke out, got my own studio space, turned down work, started making my own and then spent maybe four or five months on my film."

Said film was *Phantom Limb* (Figure 17.19–17.21), Alex's contribution to the Late Night Work Club's *Ghost Stories* anthology, in which a man finds himself plagued by guilt manifested as the haunting apparition of his girlfriend's arm, which has been detached in a road accident. From the outset, Alex knew that the opportunity and motivation to direct his first short was not to be taken lightly, and made the potentially risky decision of taking an extended period of time off from freelance work. For some independent filmmakers, this level of dedication can be the only guarantee that a project will receive the proper attention it deserves to come together successfully.

"It's weird to talk about money but it's obviously a reality of making personal projects. I think that at a certain point I stopped being afraid of not getting freelance work. Eventually you know that when you finish a job you get another one

PHANTOM LIMB

Figure 17.19

Phantom Limb character sketch ©2013 Alex Grigg.

17. Reinventing the Wheel

relatively quickly, within a week or two, and after that happens a bunch of times you just lose the fear. There is always a hustle but it is really liberating, not having to worry. Also I'm pretty frugal generally, so that I can take time out to do this sort of stuff. I'll save a lot of money when I work, then live on those savings while I do other stuff, which is cool."

Alex is the first to concede that this way of life is not for everyone. Whether one's circumstances require constant work and constant frugality, or the notion of losing the stability and quality of life we're accustomed to is frightening (or perhaps just impractical) is something we can only determine individually. Aside from the occasional monetary award at festivals, *Phantom Limb* did not wind up generating much by way of revenue; as is so often the case with independent shorts, any perceivable monetary value is far more likely to be measured by the increased visibility and career prospects a successful short can put in motion. With a career already established, for Alex the venture was more worthwhile for artistic growth and development of new skills it brought about.

"If it had turned out that everyone hated it, I might not feel the same way, but people were into it, so it's a relief! Even if they didn't like it, I wouldn't have regrets about it. That's one of the things people don't talk about, because they have this idea that there's this gift, 'natural talent' or something, and I think it's a really dangerous point of view. It's as though there's this narrative that they give people and if you struggle at all, if you fail or you're not seen as gifted from a young age, then people think you're not as good. I find that really damaging. I have this view that the things that differentiate me from somebody on the street are not my ideas so much as my discipline in learning a craft to make them happen and having an interest in actually making something out of those ideas. I think that everyone has interesting, cool thoughts about stuff, so I sort of hate that myth of the artist. It comes down to the concept of failure – people will tell you failure is important, but they don't like seeing it. They think less of you."

All fifteen contributing Late Night Work Club artists were given the same theme of "Ghost Stories," but unlike other group collaborations (such as the varieties of AniJam discussed previously), there were no parameters when it came to style, materials or execution, nor was any film required to transition from or

Figure 17.20

Still from *Phantom Limb* ©2013 Alex Grigg.

to either which bookended it. The end result is an anthology of completely individual stories, despite a binding premise of sorts.

"I'm lucky that they gave us a theme. 'Ghost Stories' sounded sort of spooky and cheesy, as in 'campfire tales' or whatever, so I actively tried to do something that wasn't that, but *Phantom Limb* did turn out to be a pretty literal ghost story I guess. I think we all had a similar reaction to be honest, we were all on a similar wavelength except for one or two of the films.

"I think that something that saved me a lot in the process was having a really understandable premise. I tried to set up the premise really quickly and early on and then you just kind of play with it at that point. I don't know if I wanted it to be more *complex* originally, I think I just wanted less of a straight narrative. I wanted it to be a little more dreamlike, but I think that my mind just works in ordering things into an understandable package, so inevitably it became a pretty straight narrative. That was important to this film."

The dialogue in the film is scarce, though effective in its scarcity. As a storyteller, dialogue did not fall within Alex's comfort zone, which saw the visuals taking the lead.

"I really respect people who can do dialogue well but they tend to be people that write words. Maybe it's a cheat to just use visuals because I spend all day practicing that specific craft, so it becomes more natural. Films that I have made since *Phantom Limb* have been completely visual. I start by going into it with designs and fully finished storyboards so as to present a story I am interested in exploring. I want to be more playful visually rather than lock myself in with storyboards and a really tight animatic. I don't have any preference when I watch films, I tend to think either way can be a crutch, whether using a lot of dialogue or not. I don't particularly like narration unless it's really well done; if the film itself isn't balanced then it feels like a bit of a wasted opportunity."

Figure 17.21

Excerpts from the *Phantom Limb* storyboard ©2013 Alex Grigg.

17. Reinventing the Wheel

While consistent with the overriding theme of its fellow *Ghost Stories* segments, *Phantom Limb* would go on to much success and visibility as a standalone film, both online and at festivals. In spite of it not being narratively or stylistically beholden to the other shorts involved, Alex was initially hesitant to split it off from *Ghost Stories*, maintaining that the ideal way to experience it is as a chapter within the overall anthology.

"I think *Ghost Stories* is more than the sum of its parts, plus the reason any of us got any attention at all is because it felt really aspirational and new. I think that we were all keen to keep it as part of the anthology for as long as possible, especially on the internet, so we kept it like that for about a year. That way we weren't competing against each other, we were always supporting each other.

"If we had all individually released our shorts it would have been more of a flash in the pan and whizzed by, like all internet shorts seem to do. Just being part of a big group felt like it gave it a lot more weight. I was really grateful to be a part of that. Then, on top of that, it was my first film. I was a really big fan of all of the other people's previous films and knowing that I would be up next to them made me push myself a lot harder, because I didn't want to show myself up. I can't speak for the others but it was very important to me personally and I'm really glad I was part of it."

Notes

1 http://punchdrunk.com/
2 http://bumbumtrain.com/
3 http://edithlebel.blogspot.com/

18

Perseverance

Figure 18.1

Filming stop-motion animation for *Planet Six* Photo ©2013 Andy Martin.

The tenacity of self-producing an animated film – especially when one is also taking on the roles of director, lead animator, both or more – should be more than evident at this point. A declaration of commitment is pretty much meaningless if you don't stick around to actually commit and, as we've seen and will continue to see, follow through is more vital to a film's success than any funding scenario or distribution plan.

One project truly demonstrable of how independent work can be truly comparable in quality to that of studios is Andy Martin's *The Planets* (Figures 18.1–18.6).

DOI: 10.1201/9781003214717-18

An exception to the earlier-touched-upon philosophy that an animation career can hinge entirely on a smash-hit student film right out of the gate, Andy came into his own a fair while after his graduation, working within the freelance sector until his skills and ability eventually led him to be taken on by Strange Beast, a division of London-based Passion Pictures.

Andy incrementally segued into animation from studying motion graphics, itself branched off from graphic design. Growing up with an enthusiasm for the character-driven children's fare of Peter Firmin and Oliver Postgate such as *Bagpuss* and *The Clangers*, it's no surprise that his twelve-part anthology film *The Planets* is notably character-driven with supremely palatable visuals and a light, general audience-accessible sense of the absurd. Beginning life in January 2013 as an illustration project in which he made a point of drawing something new in his sketchbook every day, cleaning it up in Photoshop and posting the results on Tumblr, several weeks in it was suggested by one intrigued follower that the visuals he was coming up with would look impressive in motion.

"I had a week where I wasn't doing anything so I animated the first planet and thought it would just be its own little special thing. Then I changed the whole style for February because I knew that to stay interested I would need to mix it up. After I animated the second one I figured I had something here, that it could be a series, something that would provide a deadline at the end of each month. By putting up something new every month, people might start getting interested and by changing the look every month, then *I'd* stay interested in what I was doing and have a big catalogue of styles that I'd done and different directions of animation I'd explored."

This method also pushed Andy to hone his skills as a storyteller, working on the fly to write achievable stories in the limited time (working alongside a day job as well as real-life obligations) he had allowed himself. "It was a challenge that, at the end of it all, seemed to come together quite nicely and had a feel of one whole thing."

Figure 18.2

Character sketches for *Planet Two* Photo ©2013 Andy Martin.

Each monthly film focuses on the lifeforms and general activity of a previously undiscovered planet, each one unique in tone and animation style, though bound by a strong comedic thread. Planet Eleven, for example, is inhabited by frantic alien cyclopses, animated using cardboard cut-outs; Planet Nine is occupied by destructive, childlike superheroes rendered in pixel-art; Planet Six is under threat from its own warring, claymation society; and so on. The final film, edited together from the twelve micro-shorts that preceded it, not only serves as a design portfolio and artistic showcase in its own right but, most importantly, succeeds enormously as a film. To preserve the journey's sense of development, the anthologized edit shows all the planets chronologically.

"It seemed logical to do it like that, although given there's no running narrative between them I could have mixed them up, except for the last planet which needs to go at the end. Planet Nine with the digital, 8-bit superhero characters, that was the one that really hit people and turned a corner, it was towards the end of the project that it got Staff Picked, and then people really started noticing what I was doing. I could have started off with that one but I didn't want to put that at the front, just because it felt nice the way that they ran together, in the order they were. This way you start and end with the musical ones, Planet One and Planet Twelve.

"So from the start of not knowing where it went, the project eventually came to a point where I knew what I wanted to do with it and then once I'd finished the twelve individual ones, I just needed to package them all and I did the space in-between bits where I got all the planets together and we moved from one to another which seemed like quite a nice device."

Another benefit of having an anthology film is just how much wider its exposure has the potential to be. While, of the twelve micro-shorts that it consists of, some certainly work better than others as standalone films (Andy cites Planets Six, Nine and also Four, in which a society of robots who have taken over "find harmony and discuss philosophical matters of enlightenment, beauty and magnificence," as being particularly resonant with audiences), all of them possess a uniquely identifying strength. Planet Seven, in which sheeplike creatures ponder the banality of their existence is, while minimally animated, notable for its dialogue; the entirely musical Planet Two is a character-based mograph extravaganza reminiscent of the best that onedotzero and Pictoplasma have been known to showcase.

"I think if you come into some of them on their own, they come across more as sketches than narratives. The ones that are narrative, that have dialogue and voices in them stand alone better than the ones that don't. Some festivals have just chosen individual ones to show. They were all made to be individual parts of a series, so I'd assume that if you saw one of them on their own, or found it in the middle of the project you would see that a film titled Planet Seven indicates there are at least six more of these. That's what I hoped would happen."

Despite the high professional standard of the film's overall look and feel, *The Planets* serves as another example of a film created without adopting a methodical, studio approach. Pre-production consisted of little more than sketches and doodles, dialogue more often than not scribbled in notebooks or recorded into a phone while out walking the dog rather than scripted. Andy equates his creative process more to that of writing standup material.

"Sometimes I'll just speak into the microphone, acting out stuff to see what works. I listen to a comedy podcast where comedians interview other comedians

Figure 18.3

Character concepts for *Planet Nine* ©2013 Andy Martin.

about their writing process, how they came to do what they do and how they technically write the material. Very rarely is it that people just sit down at a desk on a computer, typing stuff out. Some of them do that, I think people who specialize in one-liners will have a topic and write a load of things that work with it – that's a sit-down thing. I think a lot of them go onstage and try stuff out, they start with a nub of an idea as a bullet point and then start talking round it and seeing what works and what doesn't. I don't have the kind of audience that I stand in front of, but I do try to take a bit of that on, where I'll act it out so that I can see that it works. When you write stuff down it can turn out more like literature, rather than the way people talk or the way a character would interact. You write more words than you need, whereas I think if you just try it out and say stuff then you will get the natural rhythms of speech."

Figure 18.4

Character sketches and still from *Planet One* ©2013 Andy Martin.

A quality of Andy Martin's work that is clearly evident in *The Planets*, and works significantly to its advantage, is its broad appeal, something generally synonymous with simply "playing it safe." In Andy's case, the fact that his film plays just as well as part of a late-night screening as it does at an early morning children's program (I can personally attest to this, having witnessed both circumstances during its 2014 festival run) is a testament to his authenticity as a filmmaker. The film doesn't contrive to be child-friendly, nor fashionably design-oriented or edgy; it simply is what it is, from sketchbook to the screen.

"I usually just make stuff that isn't that offensive!" Andy muses, "In my own work, stuff with lots of swearing or sex and violence doesn't naturally come out of me. I like it in other people's work but I think if I tried to do something like that it would feel forced and would be awful, because it wouldn't represent who I am and the kind of thing that I would want to make. I really love films like David OReilly's *The External World*, but I could never make a film like that, I could never push it as far as he could, so mine tend to become quite family-friendly. *The Planets* seems to appeal to adults as well as kids which I think is good because I don't really aim them for kids, but kids seem to like my sense of humor."

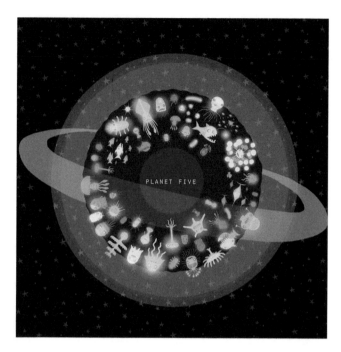

Figure 18.5

Planet Five cover image ©2013 Andy Martin.

The accessibility of a film like *The Planets* to younger audiences highlights what generally separates the wheat from the chaff when it comes to effective children's programming. It is easy (perhaps even difficult not) to pander and condescend to children if they are your intended audience. Yet the films, shorts and television shows that stand out are the ones that invariably make a point of not doing so. Oftentimes, it is merely the absence of explicitly adult themes that deems content to be engaging to children. From the uncompromising verbosity of Oliver Postgate's writing in the sixties and seventies to the unabashedly vanguard premises of more modern shows such as Joe Brumm's *Bluey*, children evidently respect not being talked down to.

"If I tried to do *The Planets* as a film for kids, trying to think of stories that would appeal to boys aged seven and eight, I would probably start patronizing and it wouldn't appeal to them, it would be all wrong. I'll more likely do something that I think is a funny idea, stories reflective of aspects of life such as war, reluctance, regret, belief, all these starting points, they then become really simple ideas and jokes that appeal when I show other people. If I thought *Okay, this is going to be targeted at this specific age group* I would just fail miserably! Whereas if I do something that does appeal to them, then that's a happy accident."

The aforementioned David OReilly is nowadays known for some truly game-changing contributions to the contemporary art, animation and design landscape, notable work including the conceptually adventurous video game experiences *Mountain* (2014, Figure 18.7) and *Everything* (2017) as well as animated sequences for Spike Jonze's 2013 feature film *Her* and directing the *Adventure Time* season five episode *A Glitch Is a Glitch*. All of his personal projects have maintained a pointedly unconventional independent sensibility, oftentimes subverting convention (*Mountain*, for example, asks not for engagement but meditative passivity

Figure 18.6

RUNNING! Character cutouts and still from *Planet Eleven* ©2013 Andy Martin.

from its players; beyond minor input at the start, the experience largely plays out on its own), the roots of which can be seen in his very first animated offerings.

Beginning his career at Kilkenny studio Cartoon Saloon, the animation powerhouse that would give the world such films as *The Secret of Kells*, *Song of the Sea*, *The Breadwinner*, *Wolfwalkers* and *My Father's Dragon*, David would find himself alternating between on-the-job training and Flash animation before finding himself more involved with their 3D department. Following this stint, David would study in Dublin for a year before moving to London. As with most young animators' careers, the road ahead was initially a bumpy one.

"There were parts of it that were really high and parts of it that were really low. That kind of goes with the territory with any city I think, but I started out with a really nice situation. I was working with people I wanted to work with for a long time. Then there were periods when I was working on my own stuff and that was really great too. Then there were periods where I was just going fully broke and needed work and couldn't get it. So it was definitely a roller coaster, because when you start out, your priorities are a bit different. I didn't expect necessarily that I was going to go and make a bunch of short films or anything like that. At that time I just wanted to get really good. I wanted to improve my craft. So that was what I was working on."

Early, relatively high-profile opportunities that came along included *Szamár Madár*, a music video for the band Venetian Snares, created in part to push himself more toward CG animation, something he'd developed an interest in. While enthusiastic to develop and produce concepts of his own in his spare, David

Figure 18.7

Mountain ©2018 David OReilly.

credits his formative commercial experiences as being a contributing factor in the development of his technical proficiency.

"I definitely learned things about design, character design, technical things about Photoshop and 3D. It's hard to disentangle what was filtered in and what was just from my own stuff I was doing in the evenings. And also what you do, that's kind of to rebel against the thing that you're 'forced' to do. So you have these different combinations of stuff. The style that people are most familiar with was something that came on quite a bit later, three or four years after various experiments in different directions. For a while I was a concept artist, I was doing appealing concept art, like big Photoshop paintings. So that stuff would be very unfamiliar to people who are only exposed to my 3D work. But when you do that kind of thing you learn a lot about layout, and how to arrange things, and how to balance stuff out. Just lots of things that filter into the work that's more experimental, and more formally playful."

Among his earlier projects was *RGB XYZ*, an episodic, lo-res, CG glitch-art nightmare fugue of bewildering camera movements, speech-synthesized dialogue and dizzying color palettes, created from 2005 to 2007. Coming together before platforms such as YouTube were commonplace on the internet, each segment would be released on the now-defunct website Technicolon as embedded Quicktimes.

"It was kind of difficult to watch." David recalls, "It was a strange website that had films, comics and blog entries, all from this character who's in the film. So the initial response was a Cartoon Brew article that came out about it, and that was the first press I had ever gotten in the animation world. The comments are a mixture of people loving it and hating it – and not quite sure what to make of it."

With the initial press attention occurring before the five-part series had concluded, the reception that eventual full edit of *RBG XYZ* met with would prove to be a promising start, premiering at the Berlin International Film Festival (Berlinale) and earning itself a Special Mention.

"I was really amazed that other people would enjoy this. It was the first time I really had any kind of feedback, I'd been working for so much in the shadows up until that point, for about five or six years, so I didn't know what to expect. But people were really surprisingly interested in what I was trying to do with it,

18. Perseverance

Figure 18.8

Still from *Please Say Something* ©2009 David OReilly.

in ways I didn't expect. So it was positive, it was a surprising thing and it was encouraging."

The following year David's next project *Please Say Something* (Figures 18.8 and 18.9) would similarly embrace a propensity toward stark, uncompromising CG design while ultimately proving more audience friendly. Despite being easier on the eye, the film remains an uncomfortable yet compelling experience. Ultimately, it is a portrait of a toxic relationship between a cat and a mouse who exist in an isometrically designed hellscape, and was also told in episodic increments during 2008 on blip.tv, a video platform that has since ceased to exist. The combined episodes would eventually be put out as a ten-minute short, premiering (and winning) at Berlinale in 2009 and later released on a wider variety of streaming platforms to huge success; alongside subsequent work including 2010s *The External World*, the film would go on to prove enormously influential on the CG and design landscape for years to come. Producing these earlier works in chronological increments proved an important motivator for David when it came to following through and bringing them to an eventual finish line.

"I did a lot of things like that, that were built up in these modular chunks that connected to become short films. You're always trying to measure the tasks you give yourself. It's a balancing act – if it's too small, you just get weaker and you're not challenging yourself. And if it's too great, then you just won't bother doing it. If you say to yourself 'I'm going to make a 10–20 minute short by myself,' that's usually a really intimidating thing for an animator, depending on the type of animation you make. But if you say 'I'm going to do one minute and it's going to be 20 seconds here and 20 seconds there and 20 seconds somewhere else,' it's much easier for you to break that down. That was the sort of method I figured out."

Approaching the film's production in this way, eschewing the more traditional method of planning out a fully realized story prior to the start of production, brought with it a degree of uncertainty. Although risky, this quasi-improvisational approach ultimately paid off.

"I didn't know how it was going to end when I started it. It's strange because, as with any story, things are kind of inevitable, if you've constructed it correctly. The fact that it works is kind of a mystery to me, but then it's because you're working that slower process of doing one thing, committing to that and moving on. It's quite unusual in the animation world to work in that way. But it does allow

Figure 18.9

Still from *Please Say Something* ©2009 David OReilly.

you – well, it forces you – to commit to certain constraints. It also allows you to really absorb what already has happened and to really analyze it, which you can do in the process of writing in abstract form. The fact that I had done it in this slower way made it easier to construct a narrative out of it, because I was aware of all of the mechanics in play in a very real, visual way. For me it was a very helpful method. Also, I was animating and building and rigging, the whole process, this whole period of time was just myself. So I created a process that I could manage and not get too bogged down by."

Staying Power

While there is laudable perseverance when it comes to filmmakers in Andy Martin, to set themselves an unshakable goal that ensures their commitment for an entire year (such as Greg McLeod's *365* project discussed earlier in the book), a short film idea can be just as well served with a slower-burn approach; Emma Birch and Peter Williamson's short film script *Being Bradford Dillman* (Figures 18.10–18.12) also took nearly a decade to successfully adapt into an animated short.

Emma, whose creative partnership with Peter began when she joined the Soho-based, independent stop-motion studio Loose Moose, used writing as an exercise to keep her creative juices flowing, having found herself largely settled in the admin side of animation production. Peter, largely working on character design commissions and commercial briefs, had a similar itch to scratch, and so the two paired up for what was originally planned out as a three-minute short. A series of ultimately unsuccessful funding applications proved invaluable in terms of addressing areas of the film that could be strengthened.

"It was after being shortlisted for a couple of funding schemes that the team at Loose Moose thought maybe there was something a bit more to our idea," Emma recalls. "They encouraged us to continue to develop it during times when the studio was quiet."

Though the film slowly marinated, progressing to the point of fully developed characters and story, circumstances led to the project being shelved for three years. As her time at Loose Moose drew to a close, the planets eventually aligned nearly ten years after the project's initial conception. The catalyst came from the arrival of recent graduate Daniella Orsini (later of Catfish Collective)'s showreel, which showcased her unique approach to stop-motion, cutout animation.

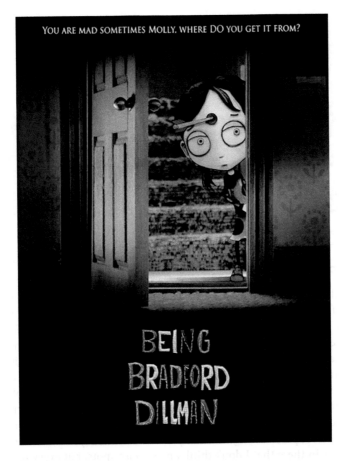

Figure 18.10

Being Bradford Dillman (Dir. Emma Burch) poster ©2011 Emma Burch/Loose Moose Ltd.

"We really liked Daniella's animation style and thought it would fit the story perfectly, so it was one of those happy coincidences. We called Daniella in and she agreed to help, so we wound up completing the film before I left Loose Moose."

What made Daniella's contribution so essential was the laborious style journey the film had gone on throughout its development. The story is of Molly, a young girl who becomes obsessed over her Mother's drunken admission that, at birth, she had been a boy. Her alternate self is manifested as Bradford Dillman, an imaginary friend with whom she forms an uneasy sibling bond. Over the years no visual approach to telling the story had seemed like a fit, or least not one that could be constrained within the limited available resources as an independent project.

"We had looked at lots of different styles of animation. We'd even gone through the process of having people build Molly as a 3D CG puppet. Obviously, I would have loved to have done stop-motion, but from years of experience watching Loose Moose, I knew that was way out of our budget. I think I had even tried to turn my hand to Flash at one point to try and get it made, using Pete's designs, but everything that we tried lost the charm of Pete's original ink illustrations. He used to do them with ink and cartridge paper, so they'd also have a nice texture to them, and something was just lost."

Staying Power

Figure 18.11

Still from *Being Bradford Dillman* (Dir. Emma Burch) ©2011 Emma Burch/Loose Moose Ltd.

Daniella's approach served to succeed where Flash had failed, retaining the textural feel of the designs and animated from multiple print-outs. Given the narrative thrust of the short, mainstream television shows such as *Family Guy* proved helpful research when evaluating the economics of the character animation and approach to set construction. The film sets were built with sitcom production in mind, the cinematography combining theater views with characters typically set at ¾ angles, creating a tactile environment with the depth of a 3D stop-motion production in which the 2D printed characters could perform.

"It's a quite naïve, simplistic style, but it works graphically for the piece. There are always a couple of shots you think you'd do differently and there are a couple of mistakes in there that I don't think anyone else spots, but every time I watch it I always only see those details. But generally I'm very proud of it, as a first film, and because it took so long to get into production I'm just glad that we completed it! It ended up being a little bit rushed towards the end as time and money ran out, but I figured that it's better to have a finished film people will enjoy than an unfinished masterpiece that nobody's going to see. Something I've always carried with me that Pete once said is not to dwell and just make sure any lessons learned you apply to your next project. You just have to keep moving on and keep learning from your experiences."

As aggravating as spotting mistakes can be – especially if it isn't until after the film is done and out there – a strong story will make great strides in masking them as far as the general public is concerned. We are all, as Emma reasons, only human at the end of the day. On reflection, the protracted production of *Being Bradford Dillman* was the best thing for it, and as a back-burner project, it had the opportunity to mature creatively as Emma and Peter themselves did, as well as resulting in a more considered, fleshed-out story. The experience of the studio environment itself also played an important part in the film's maturity, Emma cutting her teeth by osmosis through observation of directorial talents such as Ken Lidster and Ange Palethorpe.

"I don't think you jump on your first idea and then be impatient to make it." Emma reasons in summation, "Development is essential, I think, to make strong and compelling work."

18. Perseverance

Figure 18.12

Still from *Being Bradford Dillman* (Dir. Emma Burch) ©2011 Emma Burch/Loose Moose Ltd.

A similarly protracted development process also served to benefit Daniel Gray and Tom Brown's 2015 film *Teeth* (Figure 18.13), the first pass at the story being written nearly eight years previously during a train journey returning from the Annecy festival. In the interim Dan and Tom, collectively Holbrooks, would largely work on commercials, though as the years went by they would see the expectations of advertisers transition from short, simple messages to elaborate, sometimes quite lengthy endeavors with parallels to short film production. Projects such as *Parcel* for Red Cross New Zealand and *Safe in Your Hands* for Allstate's LGBT campaign *Out Holding Hands* kept the pair practiced and helped refine their own working dynamic as filmmakers.

"Our working process sort of naturally comes from working on the commercials together," explains Dan, "So if there's a commercial which suits Tom's way of working more he tends to do more of the art direction and I'll stay back and do more storyboards; if it's something that suits my art direction then I'll do that.

"I guess we have a certain conflict about the way we work, not in an argumentative way, but in the sense that my natural aesthetic is completely different from Tom's. Where they meet is always quite interesting, because they *shouldn't* really meet. We basically try not to overanalyze it!"

Though there were some initial funding prospects to help get *Teeth* off the ground, these would ultimately not take flight, leaving the pair to rely on their own resourcefulness. The eventual coming together of the film was the result of simply dedicating time, enthusiasm and effort to a project they believed had legs. Knowing they had the skills to cover the visuals themselves meant that the only real consideration in lieu of a budget was cracking on with it. When bringing on other talent was concerned, such as background artist Leland Goodman and sound designers Antfood, the directors were able to offer incentives such as festival attendance and a more artistically varied showreel in lieu of remuneration (the old line of free work being "great for exposure" can actually be quite appealing in the rare instances such as this where it happens to be true).

This approach largely epitomizes the spirit of many other case studies we've explored in the book – as so many people have shown, devoting a regular portion of your free time to such projects will incrementally bring it to fruition.

Figure 18.13

Still from *Teeth* (Dir. Tom Brown/Daniel Gray) ©2015 Holbrooks/Blacklist.

In terms of being psychologically committed to following through on a passion project, working toward a self-set deadline will always help. Major festival entry deadlines are often a strong motivator, especially if you have a particular hope for your film to get its premiere at a specific event. When it came to ensuring that *Teeth* would reach its finish line, Tom and Dan made the decision to seal their fate by sending a rough, work-in-progress cut of the film to the Sundance Film Festival, so as to set an unshakeable deadline for the finished product should it be accepted – which, as it turned out, it was.

Even if you need to work a day job, there is always time in the evenings and weekends for our hobbies and passions. As Dan breaks it down, "Do as much in your own skill set as possible towards the completion of the film until you reach a point where there's something you can't do. For example, with us we can storyboard everything, we can do the animatic, so we did everything slowly until we got to the point where the next step was just to *make* the film – which, again, we could do. So we started making the film and then it was finished by accident really. Once you've started it all tumbles into place and you enjoy it! If you're a writer you write every day, if you're not a writer you don't – it's the same with filmmakers.

"The classic Kickstarter scenario you see these days is, some guy will have some character designs and a story and he's asking for money to make a film. He's a filmmaker, he can do everything – the storyboards, animatic, everything – yet goes to Kickstarter. It almost looks like they want it as a job, and making short films shouldn't be a job. They're not going to get you a house or anything like that. It's something you put yourself through, because you enjoy it. Then, once you release it into the world it's great to just sit back a bit and see whether other people like it or hate it; if they've interpreted it completely wrong or gotten it spot on. It's a fun little world!"

Hurdles to Overcome

Another serious risk when it comes to putting yourself in the position of taking on a major creative project can be burnout and, with it, feelings that you're not achieving what you should. This can strike at any point during the production of a single project or be the result of an accumulation of frustrations over several.

Figure 18.14

Still from *The Meaning of Life* ©2005 Don Hertzfeldt/Bitter Films.

As has been addressed earlier, it's important in terms of overall reputation to not vent your frustrations in a hostile or damaging way if pitches, submissions or hopes for how your film is received don't turn out how you'd liked, but that doesn't mean your mental health or self-worth should suffer either.

As other artists, such as Joost Lieuwma, have previously attested, sometimes the dissatisfactions accrued over one project can ultimately prove to be a positive influence on how we approach our next. While Don Hertzfeldt's 2005 short *The Meaning of Life* (Figure 18.14) represented a tonal shift from his more outlandish comedies to a more cerebral and introspective approach, one that clearly informed the look and feel of his hugely acclaimed *It's Such a Beautiful Day* trilogy-turned-feature film, its production was not an especially joyful one for the director himself.

"I think *The Meaning of Life* was more of a game-changer in learning how I am least comfortable making a film. I'm happy with the final product but I was deeply unhappy making it. It took far, far too long to finish, it was the most technically difficult thing I'll have ever attempted, and the story (or lack of a traditional one) did not allow me to improvise or really change anything as I went along. So it was often incredibly grueling for me to work on, and then the amount of time I thought it would take to complete doubled. It was mainly a big lesson for me in how *not* to make a film – knowing what sort of project I am happiest making, what sort of project best reflects my strengths – and because of that experience, I'm probably a much better (and happier) filmmaker now. So it was sort of like my own personal animation boot camp. I like it, but it can be difficult for me to watch because knowing what I had to go through still sort of hurts my heart."

From his experience across commissions and independent work, David OReilly (Figure 18.15) has been through his own ringer and has some reflections on not allowing our self-doubts to overwhelm us.

"Life can be tough. I don't think anyone's response to the world is ever 'wrong,' from their point of view, but I do think it's important. I think the most important thing, maybe even more important than actually making work, is preserving your engine, making sure that you're maintaining your person, your organism

Figure 18.15

Still from *The External World* ©2011 David OReilly.

and your relationship to your medium. That very simple, basic thing of just wanting to get up every day and make something, that simple thing that gets you excited about making things – when that's poisoned, it's very hard to fix it.

"I've been in situations like that, I've seen it and I've felt it, where a certain individual – it's not always a client, some people have teachers, for example, who can be so self absorbed and self righteous and mean and bitter that they turn their students off what they're good at, their own talents. You do remember the bad times, not only in your career but your whole life, you remember those things. To a certain extent, you need to experience bad things in order to know what a good thing is.

"These are things that everyone will go through, but I think just by seeing these things before they're coming, knowing that outcomes – particularly in the commercial realm or when you're when you're doing jobs – can have certain consequences and they can poison this relationship that you have to your work, you can better avoid them. Every situation is different, but I do think in terms of priorities it's not only just making the best work, it's making sure that, if you really want to do it, you look after yourself. That includes not only managing your stress, it's things like your diet and exercise, it's managing the distraction of TV and internet and social media and email, it's making sure that you're productive and that you have this positive relationship with your work. It's not often talked about, everyone sort of has to figure this out for themselves. But I do think longevity is a thing that's worth caring about."

"I think it's probably even a particular thing for people in animation, or in independent games for that matter, because you're going to have a pretty unique lifestyle, you're going to have to disappear for huge periods of time and have this incredible discipline for committing to one thing. Because of that simple fact, there's extra potential for that to put you in a situation where you're going to have to worry about maintenance things. It's going to affect your personal relationships; it's going to affect your health. So yeah, these are things that are worth talking about."

To summarize on a motivational note, I'll hand it over to Andy Martin, director of *The Planets* (Figure 18.16), for a nugget of crucial advice on how to keep the experience of personal projects fun and rewarding:

Figure 18.16

Still from *Planet Eight* ©2013 Andy Martin.

"If you've got an inescapable deadline you have to finish by a certain date, it can't be bent because you have a client – so the way that I did it with *The Planets* was assume that millions of people were waiting for the films to go online, even though they weren't, but that gave me pressure to make sure I got something done. Again what helped was changing the style every month so I had a whole new cast of characters to play with. That made it a lot more fun for me and helped me stay interested in it."

19

Your Two Most Important Characters

It's said that an animated film's music and sound make up the greater percentage of its effectiveness. This proclamation may irk some of you who have bled, sweated and cried through countless hours of animation production, only for some noise-making outsider to swoop in and be granted more than half of the credit in what may take a fraction of the time you've put in. In spite of this, the statement remains painfully accurate, and possibly even understated. As many an auteur, independent, student and even studio film has proven over the years, whether your animation consists of virtually inanimate stickmen or rivals the production quality of a Disney feature, a botched sound mix or music score can make it unwatchable.

Outsourcing

When it comes to finding a composer for your film, be discerning, if possible. When turning to friends, students, young professionals or those who've even carved a career in sound or music for themselves, there remains the same potential for lack of talent or ability you'll have doubtless witnessed in your own industry. You want to find yourself engaged in a creative partnership that will benefit the production, not just pad out one another's CVs.

Referring to an earlier case study, a strong example of this principle is the constructive relationship between Melissa Johnson, writer and co-director of the autobiographical film *Love in the Time of March Madness* (Figure 19.1), and the film's composer and sound recordist Albert Behar.

"Albert converted his bedroom into a hip sound studio with a really beautiful, old-fashioned microphone, and I got into this makeshift booth (his mattress and

DOI: 10.1201/9781003214717-19

Figure 19.1

Still from *Love in the Time of March Madness* (Dir. Melissa Johnson/Robertino Zambrano) ©2014 High Hip Productions/KAPWA Studioworks.

boxspring propped up on their sides – with red velour curtains draped over them to 'make it sound better') on the hottest day of the summer. It was just brutally hot, so swampy that we would have to take breaks where we would put on the air-conditioning unit in his wall and crowd around it to cool down so we wouldn't pass out. I'd practice my lines and then turn it off and do five or six minutes of recording. Then we'd turn the air conditioning back on and cool down again."

Having frequently collaborated on projects that preceded *Love in the Time of March Madness*, Melissa cites their rapport and mutual respect for one another's craft as being conducive to their creative process.

"I love working with Albert – we have a long history of collaborating together. I know his music very well, when I heard what he came up with for *March Madness*, it got me fired up: 'Yep, that's exactly right!' Sometimes when we were stuck in production I'd go off and play the music by myself to get back into the right headspace.

"Those moments, those are the true moments where you connect with your artist friends, where it's not about the money, it's not about awards or anything external. If I'm going to entrust the story of my love life and a range of funny and painful and awkward moments growing up, who do I really trust to represent me in a way I'm really comfortable with? Without question, I put myself in exactly the right hands, with Robertino and Albert."

As with animation or, frankly, any of the creative arts, somebody who has taught themselves in their bedrooms – or even simply hobbyists – can prove to be just as gifted and able as accredited professionals. A degree or list of credits is no guarantee of competence or work ethic. Nor should either of these be disregarded, as there are many dueling factors to consider. To begin with, more than anything you need to make sure that whomever you work with has a reciprocal respect and understanding of what you wish to achieve with the project and how you both can benefit from the experience, financially and/or artistically.

- Get to know them personally, build up an understanding of their background and a clear sense of their working methods to help determine where any creative affinities might lie.

- Research their body of work thoroughly. When self-promoting, what projects of theirs are front and center? Are these projects similar to yours, as far as story, style or even production conditions do? What projects of theirs seem weakest, and why? Being keenly aware of one another's limitations as well as your skills will help keep expectations reasonable on both ends.
- Respect the artistry and skill of their craft and keep your expectations reasonable. It's aggravating to us when, as animators, a client makes farcical, unreasonable demands on what is possible or acceptable within an established budget. A client you'll want to work for time and again will be clear, communicative and understanding, so extend that same courtesy to other artists (this applies to all of your crew, to be perfectly honest).

Composers' Roundtable

For this section, we'll hear from several composers who often find themselves veering toward animation – frequently of the independent variety – to get some vital perspectives on the process from their end.

Berlin-based composer and sound designer David Kamp is the founder and primary creative force behind Studiokamp, a highly reputed one-stop shop for sound and music services whose clients have spanned "visual artists, companies, galleries, NGOs and cultural institutions worldwide." David has worked with such outstanding animators as David OReilly (*Please Say Something*), Joseph Wallace (*Salvation Has No Name*), Réka Bucsi (*Love*), Nicolas Ménard (*Wednesday with Goddard*), Robert Löbel (*Wind, Link, Island*) and Nikita Diakur (*Ugly, Fest, Backflip*) among many others, developed a fascination with music from a young age.

"I ran around recording things with a tiny cassette recorder as a kid, and (poorly) played various instruments (drums, cello, guitar, piano). After school, I wanted to study something to explore this medium further, so I ended up studying Electronic Composition at ICEM at Folkwang University of the Arts. There I learned a lot about sound and music: technically (acoustics, studio technology, coding, and DSP) and stylistically (music theory, instrumentation, composition techniques). Being exposed to a wide range of genres there, especially avant-garde 'art music' and experimental 'new music' composers of the past and present, truly opened my mind to sound art and what could be considered music."

Another composer frequently drawn to collaborating with animators alongside (and sometimes hand-in-hand with) his commissioned work is Philip Brookes (Figure 19.2). Based in Wales, Philip has frequently collaborated with stop-motion director Anna Mantzaris (beginning with her student short *But Milk Is Important*, co-directed by Eirik Grønmo Bjørnsen, as well as subsequent shorts including *Enough* and *Good Intentions*) as well as providing sound and music for the films *Creepy Pasta Salad* (dir. Lauren Orme), *Marmalade Is Missing* (dir. James Nutting) and *Peregrine* (dir. Daniela Shearer). Philip's first musical dabblings began in his adolescence when his older brother moved out, leaving his guitar behind.

"I used it to teach myself enough to start playing with friends. One of those friends gave me some recording software. I would sit on the landing of my house, multi-tracking instrumental, ambient music. Little did I know, this would form the style I would later use in films. I would play in bands which taught me so much about discipline, expression, patience and musical/human dynamics. I was kicked out of school, but worked my way through college to university, where I met an animator called Eirik Grønmo Bjørnsen. I worked with him and then he moved back to Norway and he made *But Milk Is Important* with Anna Mantzaris. I taught myself piano for that film, a film that opened the door for what I do today."

Skillbard Studio, a two man music and sound design collective comprised of Tom Carrell (Figure 19.3) and Vincent Oliver, boast an impressive portfolio of work for top-tier corporate clients and institutions that sit comfortably alongside their scores for independent animated shorts. Among these, notable projects include Sophie Koko Gat's *Slug Life*, Alex Grigg's *Phantom Limb* and *Born in a Void*, Frederic Siegel's *Honour* and Sean Buckelew's *Lovestreams*.

"We haven't studied classically," Tom affirms, "but I feel that once you do it for 10–15 years, you do a lot of self learning. We both really enjoy learning and self teaching, we've picked up so much. We've also had a few composition lessons to fill in gaps we had. I would say a lack of classical training definitely hasn't held us back in our industry."

"I used to co-run a record label and Tom was in a fantastic band that I wanted to release," recalls Vincent, "So that's how I'm aware of Tom. Then when I started doing music for things, I was talking to a guy about a cartoon and describing how I thought it should sound and it was basically Tom's band. So instead of ripping him off, I invited him to come and join me on the project and it just worked. So every job since that I invited him on as well. Then we became one thing quite quickly, actually. It clicked so naturally that after one project we were a company."

"I think we definitely complete each other in what we do," adds Tom, "We don't really divide our responsibilities, with every project we're just passing stuff back and forth all the time, and tweaking what each other has done. It's been working really well so far."

You often produce work for animated productions, can you explain the appeal of animation as something you've gravitated toward?

Phil Brookes: "Thinking back to how I got into animation, amazingly (and luckily), I think animation found me. It sucked me into this incredible, crazy, creative world that I love (Figure 19.4). I've learnt so much about animation and have grown to love the many forms it takes. I'm forever grateful to the people who make it. Their imagination, hard work and dedication to their craft has inspired and bought the best out of me. I love the expressiveness of animation and it's limitless potential. This has urged me to create things I would have never dreamt of. Creating a Middle Eastern inspired soundtrack for a Ted-ED lesson is something I would have never imagined doing as a little kid in Wales."

David Kamp: "I grew up with comics, always liked animation but during my time at Folkwang randomly stumbled across this whole independent animation world that I overlooked before. I was not interested in the blockbuster type of animation coming from Disney and Pixar but fascinated by the more personal, artistic projects. I realized how unique many of the films are and how close to the director's vision the finished film tends to be. I was also fascinated by the effort, craft, and commitment to realize an animated film independently. One of the George Schwizgebel shorts, Jeu, blew my mind back then and still does.

"Regarding my involvement, I like how each film is unique in its aesthetics (and animation technique, look, etc.) and, consequently, the kind of sound world it needs. This keeps it exciting for me even after many years and 100+ projects in

Figure 19.2

Phil Brookes composing for *But Milk Is Important*. Photo credit: Leanne Brookes.

this area. I also really like how animation requires me to build everything from scratch. There is no production sound; the film's acoustic reality (whether realistic or abstract) has to be invented each time."

Do you consider yourself an independent artist?

DK: "I feel like I am a strange mixture of artist and designer. I do my own sound artworks that are exhibited at Galleries, but I also do commissions and commercial work with clients, like the audio logo I designed for The New Yorker or soundscapes for Museums. Then there is the work with animation filmmakers, which sits somewhere in between: I get to bring my creative ideas for the sound, but in the end, it is about the film and the director's vision for it. On the other hand, often, the filmmakers come to me because they liked how I approached the sound for previous animated films and are actually interested in my ideas for their film. That often leads to a very collaborative creative process.

"But back to your question: I am independent in the sense I own and run my studio without any outside capital or 'boss,' which means I get to pick the kind of projects I work on, the balance between 'art' and 'commercial' and how much I want to work overall – this aspect of independence is something I really like, and I can't imagine doing it any other way at this point."

PB: "As a musician and sound designer I've always considered myself independent. Out of financial necessity and then later on through the DIY ethos I was proud of in the music scene I was a part of as a teenager. During a project however, my role is to compliment the director/client's vision to the best of my abilities as part of a team."

Vincent Oliver: "I think, creatively, we certainly approach it with an independent spirit. We try to do as much in-house as possible, find our own ways of doing things and keep creative control over bits and bobs that some studios might not. We even cast voiceovers sometimes, but yeah, we try to be professional as well." (Figure 19.5)

If so, is having independent sensibilities a good fit when working with independent/auteur animators (as far as communication, mutual understanding, etc.)?

DK: "Yes, I think so. One difference between bigger studios and me is that filmmakers have a very direct line of communication to me – there are rarely any agents, producers, assistants in between. This also means fewer misunderstandings or superfluous communication. As a project progresses, especially when I repeatedly work with directors, we develop a mutual understanding when talking about sound. This can be very helpful when discussing sound details."

PB: "Yes, having the drive to create all the music and sound myself from the ground up, recording all the instruments, effects, voices, mix it and master it etc. This draws so many parallels to many of the animators I've been so lucky to have worked with and how they work, from the animatic to the final piece. Especially with the stop-motion animators I've worked with."

VO: "We get invited onto a lot of people's portfolio projects, their short films, their passion projects, I guess because we're interested in doing things a bit weird and… arty? I don't want to use that term, but I can't think of anything else. You know, we're not like a sausage factory, doing advert music and whatnot, over and over."

Tom Carrell: "It's very homespun what we do, and on a lot of these independent shorts that we've been lucky to work on, we've put so much more work into it than a

Figure 19.3

Tom Carrell. Image courtesy of Skillbard.

19. Your Two Most Important Characters

more mainstream industry post house in Soho, for instance, might have time to do. It's been much more hands-on craft, where we've been recording all the assets and designing all the sounds rather than reaching for presets and that kind of thing."

Are you usually involved during production of a film/project or only once the final animation has been completed – or does this pipeline change across different directors/projects?

DK: "That depends on different aspects, including schedule, the type of film and its (visual) production process. Some things clearly profit when I am involved early, such as films based on music or rhythm, for example. For other, more atmospheric and less musically driven films, I prefer seeing something closer to final to be directly inspired by the picture's mood when designing sounds and ambiances. But I can be very flexible and usually go with what makes sense for the project."

PB: "This, like a lot of elements to my job, has the potential to be different across the board. However if I get the privilege of being asked when I would like to join the project, I always ask for the animatic or story board. The earlier the better, even if nothing is created until a more fleshed out version of the animation, I'll be thinking about how to approach the sound/music and communicating this with the film maker."

TC: "I'd say it really depends. For music, we enjoy getting involved really early, but for sound design, especially foley, we really like to wait until stuff is pretty much finalised because otherwise we end up having to do things twice. Essentially, if we're doing sound design to a rough animatic and then the animations get finished, then we have to redo everything or tighten everything up. But music is more fluid."

VO: "With music it's nice to get involved super early with animatics, put something out rough and then animators work from that and get inspired by it. Then later they pass it back to us. So if we get involved early, there's often a period where we do some sketches, and then nothing for a little while the animator does everything else, then another intense period of finishing it and progressing."

To what extent are you generally involved with sound design, and if a project you've composed for has a separate sound designer, do you have a working relationship with them during production (and vice versa, if you've worked on sound design for a project with a separate composer)?

DK: "For most of my projects, I handle all audio. Meaning: Music (if any), Sound Design, Foley up to the final mix in the required format – mainly stereo and 5.1 for cinema these days even though I can mix and deliver anything up to Dolby Atmos from my studio. I have had projects where I got a foley artist or other sound designer, musicians, etc., involved, but the more traditional split between music and sound design is pretty rare for me.

"Being in control of both also has advantages since I can compose something differently, knowing which sound design I plan to add later and the other way around. Having said that, I recently worked on *Terra Incognita* by Adrian Dexter & Pernille Kjaer made by IKKI Films and Sun Creature studio in France, where I did not compose the music. And years ago, I made a commercial with Studio AKA where composer Jóhann Gunnar Jóhannsson composed the score. I am open to these collaborations, but it did not happen very often in the past, and I really enjoy doing 'the whole package,' so I did not actively pursue such collaborations. But since the short films I work on tend to get longer recently, this might happen more often."

PB: "A few years ago I started taking on projects as both a composer and sound designer and now I'd say 9/10 projects I work on, I'm doing both and creating all sound. I've really embraced the sound design element, Foley, vocal work, the lot. For me it's all coming from the same place creatively and each in turn inspires the other. Which is very interesting, because previously my communication with anyone else on the sound side was little to nothing as I usually just communicated with the director/producers."

TC: "I think people just tend to come to us as a one-stop shop in a lot of the projects we've had, but we're doing more and more music nowadays where other people are doing the sound design. So that is happening more, often on very commercial adverts, or they might be using a sync track or library music or something and we're just doing the sound design and not handling music. Sometimes that happens."

VO: "But we'd often edit the music in that case. So there will be some interplay between sound and music, where we will make space somewhere for something to shine through. However, ideally we would do both. Then we know if something's important in sound design, we'll move the music out of the way or time the music around it and make sure everything works together. We like to do sound design-ey music and music-ey sound design, so sometimes the line between the two is a bit blurred. We're quite cartoony in that respect."

What advice would you offer animators as to what to consider for a strong working relationship with their composer/sound designer?

DK: "Get familiar with each other's work and talk about what you want the audience to feel. Sometimes, concrete sound examples (be it from the sound designer/composer's work or other sources) make it easier to get on the same page. Sound can be very abstract, and the shared vocabulary of sound designers and filmmakers can sometimes contain the same words, but both mean different things by it. I found that sometimes filmmakers use audio technology or music composition terms but actually mean something else. Sometimes it is better to discuss sound or music in broader terms, more general emotional descriptions, or visual metaphors. A good composer or sound designer will know how to translate those into music and sound.

"Schedule time for exploration, don't get your sound designer or composer involved only at the very end. Give them a chance for input early on just in case some things can be explored while the visuals are still being created. Sometimes these early discussions helped with edit decisions avoiding issues down the line."

PB: "I love the challenge of working for all different types of animators. Some I have the pleasure of working with regularly, some only once. I think a clear creative vision serves any project well and helps the sound to support that vision. Most of the time I personally feel the onus is on the sound to deliver as we are providing for the animator.

"I've been blessed with a very small amount of behavioral complications. The ones that were complicated were due to inconsistencies in creative vision. There's nothing wrong with changing your mind, that's of course part of the artistic process, but with limited time and resources, it can become problematic. Especially when communicated poorly."

VO: "Maybe one thing to bear in mind is what the composer is getting out of it. You need to balance what they're receiving financially against how they're gonna feel about it creatively, how much control they get put into it and how proud they will be of it afterwards versus how much credit they'll get in the end. I remember early days, when I was doing things that were largely favours, I would feel bad about not being able to do exactly what I wanted, because I wasn't getting paid, I wasn't getting any awards for it because I'm not the director, or accolades generally. So I really wanted to feel like the score is mine, which is something I learned is not the right way to feel, it is always best to follow what the director wants every single time. But it's something the director could keep in mind, when dealing with a composer."

TC: "There's classic communication stuff that composers talk about when giving advice to directors. Often composers want to talk about the story in emotional terms, and have directions about how something should feel, rather than the director actually try and talk in musical language. Because music is so subjective, often things can get really confused if the director starts talking about certain chords they want to hear, or instrumentation even. Myself and many other composers feel that if they're just told what the story's trying to achieve and what emotion is required it's a much better footing to achieve what is actually needed, in a more open way. You can come up with more interesting, creative solutions and not be stuck trying to talk about very literal music theory, which can be quite limiting."

VO: "Yeah, it's surprising how many directors feel kind of shy talking about the music and sound. They feel like they need to use musical terms and they will often apologise because they don't know how to talk about music very well. And they should resist the urge to feel like they need to sound clever in a musical sphere

Figure 19.4

Phil Brookes composing for *But Milk Is Important.* Photo credit: Leanne Brookes.

and, as Tom says, talk about the story and what it needs to achieve rather than how it should sound. We've had an example, when we were doing sound on something where we kept hearing 'it needs to sound more lo-fi and muffled.' We didn't really understand what was going on, so we kept rolling off the top end and giving them something that sounded less good. And it turned out what they wanted was a 70s vinyl/tape feel, which is not necessarily lo-fi or sounds bad, but they kept giving us terminology about how they think it should sound – 'muffled,' 'old' and 'worn.' We could have given them a really lovely tape-saturated, crisp, 70s-feeling thing if they had talked about how it should feel in those terms. One very practical thing is, once you've given the composer – or sound designer, whoever – the film, if you edit after that, make frame-by-frame notes of what you've chopped or added, because that could save an awful lot of time. We've worked on films where I might estimate 50% of our time has just been retiming things. Sometimes it isn't always obvious where the edit is, so nudging everything back and forward to figure that out can be very time consuming. If you just write 'I chopped a bit at 11 seconds,' then we'll at least know where to hone in on."

When you watch independent films (or any films, for that matter), what are some common mistakes or pitfalls filmmakers fall in when it comes to how they've used music and sound?

VO: "I don't suppose I would ever think of it that way. I think sometimes something will strike me and I'll go 'Well, that's an interesting choice.' But I don't mean that as a euphemism for 'They've done that wrong.' I personally always like it when something stands out. A lot of people will say the composer's done their job when you don't notice it – I've never agreed with that. So when something seems like a mistake, I often like it that way."

DK: "One small thing that continually annoys me in animated films is when every character movement triggers a verbal reaction: 'hu? ugh! arrgh! oh!,' etc. I've been guilty of that too, once or twice.

"Very often, less is more. The first question should always be which visual element or action actually needs a sound and which doesn't. This adds impact and relevance, and focus to the elements with sound. I also think music should be used for a reason and not wall to wall. Silence can be powerful. Loudness too, but only relative to something else. If everything is loud for long periods, it just becomes painful – an experience we probably all had with some blockbuster movies in the cinema.

"Of course, there are no hard rules for anything, and there is no absolute right or wrong, except for some very dull technical aspects. If you feel like your film requires something obscure, precisely the things considered common mistakes and pitfalls could make it unique."

PB: "From conversations I've had with people who aren't in the film industry, I know how obsessive and absurd I can be about sound. I hear the same police radio communications in so many films and computer games. I hear door squeaks, knocks, punches, screams. I understand completely though, it's budget and time, sometimes you don't have much of either and you have to deliver. Perhaps though, a pitfall can be treating sound as an after thought. When I think of life changing films, the film maker has thought a lot about the sound. Then again, who am I to say? One person's pitfall is another's masterpiece and that's what I love about art. There shouldn't necessarily be any rules."

Figure 19.5

Vincent Oliver. Image courtesy of Skillbard.

TC: "I notice cliches a lot and that's one thing I get annoyed about, when watching TV especially. Also, just on a really technical level, the mix – people are often very shy with the levels of the music. For very good reasons, but at the same time it's a shame because all this stuff gets pushed down and then has way less impact. One of the things that can be really noticeable is when a composer has gotten very close to a temp track. There are some really good video essays about that kind of thing. A lot of big, mainstream movies have been really at risk of overdoing that, and sometimes you can really tell because a lot of the time they've temped it with a really idiosyncratic score, and then just asked the composer to go really, really close to it. Or the composer hasn't had much time to do the score and they'll just copy the temp. But yeah, temp stuff is a big thing with composers. I would prefer never to use temp but it can be a useful tool to communicate what the director needs, because music is so difficult to talk about. It's really useful for someone to actually be able to throw something against the film and see if it's working or not, and convey how they want something to feel. But then you risk getting stuck in this really uncreative avenue if you have to deal with it."

To get a clearer understanding of this crucial stage of production, we can look back at some of the films we've previously explored.

Being Selective

As pivotal a role as music can play in a film, in some instances it achieves more in its absence. Adam Elliot's student short *Uncle*, along with the companion films *Cousin* and *Brother* that followed in swift succession, are notable for being almost entirely without any music whatsoever. Rather than a pre-planned artistic choice, the reasoning behind this was largely the same as that which determined the minimal look of the films.

"As a student filmmaker you have to be very economical, so with *Uncle* my aesthetic was purely based on lack of money. None of the characters walked and they talked very little, and similarly, I just knew that I wouldn't have money to purchase music rights. I could have gotten some friends to compose something but I've never been a fan of composed music, because I like to know what I'm going to have well in advance."

The absence of music in Adam's original trilogy does not come across as a budgetary choice, however. Allowing William McInnes's understated performance as the films' narrator to sit in the sound mix on its own, accompanied infrequently by minimal foley work, on top of the ever-present audible film hiss (another artifact of the time period in which the films were made, again perhaps an unintended result of the small budget but responsible for an atmosphere that would be near-impossible to recreate authentically with a digital sound mix) adds tremendously to solemn tone of the film. Although certain limitations remain, the added resource makes for a sudden contrast when it comes to Adam's lengthier 2003 short *Harvie Krumpet*. In a similar way that the increased budget affected the visual production values and color palette, the soundtrack also comes across as more ambitious in its scope.

"I think it wasn't until *Harvie Krumpet* that I was brave enough to start using music, and in that film the music came first. I knew that I wanted Pachelbel's *Canon in D Major* in it somewhere because it's such a cliché, and Respighi's *Ancient Airs and Dancers* as credit music, but I also knew I wanted the song *God is Better than Football, God Is Better than Beer* because that was such a ridiculous song I used to sing at Sunday school when I was forced to go to church. So all of that music ended up in there. Then with *Mary and Max*, I've always been a big fan of Penguin Café Orchestra. It's such nourishing music, universal and timeless and all those things that I love. I know it had been used a lot in advertising and documentaries, but to my knowledge, nobody had ever used it in animation."

In a rare instance of true filmmaker indulgence, a significant chunk – $300,000 – of the film's budget went toward the music rights for *Mary and Max*. It was undoubtedly a worthwhile investment, as the aforementioned nourishment of iconic Penguin Café Orchestra tunes *Perpetuum Mobile* and *Prelude and Yodel* became a huge part of the film's identity during its marketing as well as within the movie itself. Also rounding the music picks are Bert Kaempfert's *Swinging Safari* and Pink Martini's haunting rendition of *Que Sera, Sera*, all used to maximum effect at crucial points in the story, alongside a number of original cues composed by Dale Cornelius. Adam's shift from mainstream production to independent filmmaking when it came to *Ernie Biscuit* ultimately meant that the luxury of music licensing was not nearly as available as it had been before.

"The only piece of music I really paid a significant amount of money for is the music at the beginning and end of *Ernie Biscuit*, which is a very cheesy number one hit from the 70s, from a Dutch detective series called *Eye Level*, by an English orchestra. The rest of the music in *Ernie Biscuit* was purely off the internet where I think it cost me $100, but not of any high sound quality. I think that's one of the things that lets *Ernie Biscuit* down is because I was experimenting with new materials with a really limited post-production budget, so I think not just the music but the sound overall is pretty average."

A film whose storytelling approach is some distance remove from Adam's is *Sausage* by Robert Grieves (Figures 19.6 and 19.7). Without dialogue or narration, the story's timing is hugely dependent on the character animation and visuals. One work around when taking this approach is to start with a piece of music that will facilitate the timing along the way. As Robert had such a clear concept of how the story would pace itself (having made the entire film twice), the entire film's

Figure 19.6

Still from *Sausage* (Dir. Robert Grieves) ©2013 Robert Grieves.

animation was produced without any sound whatsoever, and attempts to score it with a temp track of found music during production only served to complicate the process. As all the sourced music that fit thematically came with its own structure, it proved impossible to find a way to match up cues to the visuals being created. The final film, however, is presented a glorious, rich score by Dan Radclyffe that matches the film in tone and playfulness and syncs up perfectly to each action beat.

"What you're enjoying is the genius of the composer." Robert assures, "It wasn't an easy journey, I went through a few different people but I found the right guy who was someone who could just riff off of things in a really spontaneous way. I had a wonderful experience as well with the music where I had sat with the composer for about three days in his studio and we just worked through everything together, so I just shadowed him. I *hope* I gave him enough space that he felt he was making his thing, I'm pretty sure he did as it is definitely his soundtrack. I was just there making sure things stayed narratively on-track."

There is an element of risk in having a composer go off on their own with notes – especially ones that are purposefully vague; it's unreasonable to assume your composer will telepathically know exactly what will work, and an unfair expectation to place on him or her. As talented as any composer is, it's an outright impossibility to get into your head as a director. Robert Grieves's own attitude on the matter is more or less the same.

"With *Sausage* I really needed to be there, he'd put some mood in there and I'd say 'It sounds cool but it really doesn't reflect the motivation of the character at that moment' and it's stuff that you don't necessarily know until you hear it."

The latter point is worth considering – a director without a musical background is, in fact, quite likely to not have a pre-existing idea for the film's score that will tangibly exist. This makes the burden of a composer even greater if they are flying blind with no frame of reference for what you're hoping to achieve or evoke. The solution – or, at the very least, the springboard that will bring a solution closer – is to consider what is already out there.

Other options available to filmmakers in need of a musical accompaniment to their film, if not a meticulously composed score, can be relatively affordable, if not outright free, though this can be perilous too. Grabbing a piece of music you like from a website that lists it as "free to use" is not exactly a binding legal contract, so it's always best to do that extra bit of homework to make sure that slotting a piece of production music into your film is in fact legal to do. If you have

Figure 19.7

Still from *Sausage* (Dir. Robert Grieves) ©2013 Robert Grieves.

some spending money, purchasing tracks to use from online production libraries won't break the bank necessarily, though there a fair few formalities that can eat up a lot of time if you are working without a dedicated production manager to handle that side of thing. For the sake of argument, the most advisable low-to-no-budget approach is to canvas online royalty-free music libraries that will often-times charge a single fee for either a single piece of music or library collection. Another alternative is to eliminate the middleman and go straight to the source, as Aidan McAteer found himself doing when on the hunt for the perfect piano accompaniment to his silent movie-era tribute *A Gentleman's Guide to Villainy*.

"I've never met Kevin!" Aidan says of the film's music scribe Kevin MacLeod, "But he's a fantastic man." Via his online outlet Incompetech[1] the composer licenses his own music, a practice among composers that is becoming more and more common. In instances such as short films with credits sections and online video descriptions that allow for him to be actively credited, the use of a free Creative Commons license to use the music is a possibility. "It's an incredibly generous thing to do.

"I was looking for music, knowing I didn't want dialogue – which also helped inform the silent movie aesthetic – because if I recorded dialogue I most likely wouldn't do it very well. As far as music goes, I kind of noodle a bit on the guitar, but I can't *play* anything. So I was looking for royalty-free music when I came across Kevin's site, which had a silent movie section. I found this track which was the appropriate length (another thing where DepicT!'s ninety-second limit helps), it was a great exercise in so far as what I could use and what I could make out of it, with the resources available."

As per the conditions of the license, MacLeod is given due credit as the film's composer, Aidan later getting in touch to show him the final result. "He may not have even known that I was even doing it until he'd seen the final thing, but he was very happy with it."

Self Sufficiency

The above serves as another example of the ever rising benefits of intercontinental collaboration and how independent creatives the world over can support one another. Of course, it's entirely possible that you happen to have your own clear understanding of sound design, score composition or both. In my auteur film work,

19. Your Two Most Important Characters

Figure 19.8

Still from *Planet Twelve* ©2013 Andy Martin.

I've often found that having a sideline career in music and sound production has facilitated the easiest path to a finished film. Taking on these roles on top of directing the film is a time-saver in the sense of eliminating lengthy discussions on what you aim to evoke. Now I'm not suggesting that everyone go out and train themselves to be composers or sound artists, and truth be told, it may be the best thing for your film to step aside and let someone else take on the role rather than spread yourself thin. If a film of mine, for example, called for country music, folk songs or an elaborate, classical score, I would not think twice about bringing in a composer more suited to these genres as I know they are not my strengths. Sometimes going it alone is the most suitable route for your film's identity.

Andy Martin, himself a musician as well as an animation director, was able to apply his own ability when closing out his anthology film *The Planets* (Figure 19.8), by rounding off his year-long endeavor in traditional film fashion, with a musical number.

"None of *The Planets* was particularly well planned except for the last month, Planet Twelve in December, where I knew exactly what I wanted to do: I knew I wanted it to be a song, I needed it to tie everything up, to include what we'd seen and it have some finality to it so you knew this was the end, a full-stop."

After a first pass at a song in July, deemed unlistenable when played to his family, his second attempt proved a lot more fitting and thematically in-line with the rest of the film.

"It has a bit of pathos and melancholia as well as being quite funny, which is what I wanted it to be. I gave myself a little bit longer to animate that planet as well, because I didn't have another one starting afterwards."

Supporting the notion that relinquishing control even with a musical background of one's own can be the most advisable option, Benjamin Arcand's *Wackatdooo* (Figures 19.9–19.11) benefited from handing over the reins to a composer he instinctively knew would do a better job. With music ever-present throughout the film, Benjamin originally timed the animation-in-progress to a placeholder soundtrack in the form of jazz standards from the early twentieth century, knowing the final accompaniment would be in the same stylistic vein and tempo. Using this as a springboard to help inspire how the beats were timed out, this straight-ahead storyboard organically morphed into an animatic.

Figure 19.9

Wackatdooo character animation ©2014 Benjamin Arcand.

"I did a couple of the scenes using the placeholder music. There's a double-bounce walk at one point where I knew I wanted that tempo, so I stuck to it. Let's say it was an eight frame beat, I would write it down and when it came time to record the real song I asked the composer to keep the music to the tempo, using a metronome."

Taking on music and sound duties was composer and drummer François-Xavier Paquin, a longtime friend and bandmate of Benjamin's over the years. With a musical background of his own, Benjamin's reasons for reaching out to an outside composer are simple – "He's better than me at music! He has a master's degree in composition and jazz performance. He also likes cartoons a lot, and cartoon music, so with me going into cartoons it worked well.

"I could not have done what he did, I don't know about jazz, as a musician I play rock-and-roll guitars. So he went ahead and composed all the parts for it, then we hired some jazz musician friends of his. We had a very low budget, I mean it was like fifty bucks and a few beers! They were kind enough to make it because it was short and sweet, and since they're all pros they came in and only needed one day for each session. In the first session we had the rhythm section – just banjo, upright bass and drums. After that, we went with the trombone, saxophone, trumpet and that was it! It only took a couple of takes for us to have everything we needed."

Once the final music was composed and recorded, Benjamin used the new musical backdrop to tighten up the timing of the animatic, remedy any story or continuity issues and, once the proper flow of the film was firmly established, begin work proper on the animation. As anyone who has seen the film will attest, François-Xavier's considered work on the music absolutely brings out the best in the film's equally dynamic visuals, something that may not have been achieved otherwise.

Back to *The Planets*, the primary advantage of having an awareness of music composition and performance as far as director Andy Martin is concerned is just how much it can assist with timing, something crucial to all animation production. Being your own film's composer can feed into the creative process from both ends. Animation on a scene, for example, can begin with a set tempo and tone, which can then be compositionally embellished to complement the visuals once they have come together.

"Generally I do the music first and then animate to it but I can switch between the two. The animation might kick off an idea that I think would be nice to add punch to in the music, then I can go back to the music and do them in tandem with each other. I try and do funny stuff and I think having a sense of musical timing helps with comedy timing, I think they usually work hand in hand:

19. Your Two Most Important Characters

Figure 19.10

Still from *Wackatdooo* (Dir. Benjamin Arcand) ©2014 Benjamin Arcand.

Figure 19.11

Still from *Wackatdooo* (Dir. Benjamin Arcand) ©2014 Benjamin Arcand.

You've got a build-up and then a release with music, it's the same with a joke. Also with storytelling when you want something that feels plaintive and emotional, there's a way of doing that with music (switch it to a minor key and it feels sad, a major key, you're upbeat). Similarly with design and storytelling, you can take these basic elements and fundamentals and apply them to both things.

"I think having different disciplines helps give your work an individual tone to it. The music side for me gives my films just a little touch that's very much my thing. If I used an outside sound designer I'd probably have a beautiful soundtrack, probably better than what I can do, but I think it would lose that feel of what I have when I do it myself. How you want something to look and sound is not necessarily how it will come out, but in striving to do that you can achieve your own unique style."

This philosophy is especially relevant to the film work of PES (Figure 19.12), in keeping with the careful approach taken with his animation we explored several chapters ago. While the choice of bric-a-brac and household objects used to represent, amongst other things, food preparation, certainly goes a long way in terms of selling the film as believably surreal, the true suspender of disbelief is the diligence when it comes to his sound design. It is a process that appeals both to him and his audience.

"I think there's a particular degree of fascination with the sound design that I do that brings it together. It takes one thing and makes it believable. Very realistic sound design is something of an unsung hero that makes the images come to life, and it *really* makes the jokes come alive. It makes something happen in the viewer's brain that I think is interesting, which is that you're seeing one thing – a grenade, for example, with someone cutting into it – but *hearing* an avocado."

The combination heightens the authenticity of the scene tremendously – if heard on its own, the sound would strike a listener as nothing more exceptional than standard kitchen ambiance; similarly, if viewed while the audio is muted, the transformative quality of the animation remains but doesn't carry with it nearly as much impact. It speaks volumes about compensatory power of sound and just how much of a role it plays in how our brains process our environment. We clearly see a grenade being sliced, but the sound of an avocado instantly transfigures the reality of the film and makes it seem like the most natural thing in the world.

"That's an interesting thing. There's a sort of mystery about it that is one of the beauties of stop-motion; that everything is visually one-hundred percent realistic because it's a photographic medium, and the sound can be very realistic, yet the concept is completely fanciful, so there's a collision of the hyperreal and the surreal."

One of the common audience reactions to work such as PES's is an inherent degree of satisfaction that comes with them. For reasons similar to the inexplicable neurochemical responses that induce satisfaction when we pop bubble wrap, certain visual and auditory combinations can prompt a certain sense of gratification. More often than not, this works against us when we experience the opposite reaction triggered by bad sound design (something we'll explore later in this chapter), but in the films of PES, the execution makes for a very fulfilling watch.

"I don't think about this while I'm shooting or creating sound, I only try to create the most satisfying sounds to match the picture that please me. I was curious to see that there was this whole community of people who study and look at my work, focusing on that one element of the 'satisfying' sounds, such as the snapback of a slinky, the crinkling of this, the crunching of that...I don't really

Figure 19.12

Still from *Western Spaghetti* (Dir. PES) ©2008 PES.

19. Your Two Most Important Characters

profess to do any more than match the picture with the sound, but it's funny to see the responses."

Another example of a bold, visually driven film whose success ultimately hinges on the sound would be Greg McLeod's *365* project (Figure 19.13). As with Andy Martin and PES, sound is an area of production Greg chooses to take on himself.

"I did the sound in general, every day, because I've always loved it. I've always been in recording studios and have always enjoyed sound."

Given the freeform nature of the project, and that literally each second of sound design was isolated from whichever preceded or followed, a certain degree of international collaboration came into play. Sound designers Tom Angell, David Kamp and a host of others donated an assortment of one-off noises that found their way into the mix, including vocal contributions.

"We had people like David Tenant and Adam Buxton who we were doing other work with, we would just ask them to give us a word to use. I recorded things out and about, so there were also some found sounds. I think the really important thing was that each mini-one-second movie had its own one-second soundtrack that was very specific, because if there'd just been music over it all I don't think it would have had the same impact. If you try to watch it without the sound on it, it's almost impossible, your brain almost needs the sound there to anchor the timing. With sound you can actually make a second feel longer than it is, which is quite interesting, so I had a lot of fun with that."

Another director who will actively seek to get their hands dirty when it comes to the sound mix is *Bottle*, *Move Mountain* (Figure 19.14) and *Hi Stranger* director Kirsten Lepore, whose films all boast arresting soundscapes. In a similar manner to the work of PES, *Bottle*'s expertly crafted foley work absolutely infuses the impossible sand and snow beings with life, not through auditory anthropomorphization (such as adding humanistic sounds or voices) but by retaining their material qualities. Despite the slight time-lapse judder of filming the animation outside, the sound is authentic enough as to sell the characters as "alive" instantly. Similarly, *Move*

Figure 19.13

Still from *365* (Dir. Brothers McLeod) ©2014 The Brothers McLeod.

Figure 19.14

Still from *Move Mountain* (Dir. Kirsten Lepore) ©2013 Kirsten Lepore.

Mountain embraces a highly considered approach to the exterior ambiance, though with the addition of musical elements such as its acapella score and party sequence.

"I don't know the exact quote,[2] but someone once said that sound is 70% of an animation – which I think is true. It's so disappointing when a good animation has a lackluster soundtrack, or sound that was thrown in as an afterthought. You can describe a space and situation with sound the way visuals cannot. Because of this, I always take great care with my soundtracks, and have always done all the sound design myself. I usually have a professional check my final mixes and create my 5.1, but I do all the design and the rough mix alone, for the most part.

"I did, however, collaborate with my friend and former CalArts classmate Paul Fraser on my first sound pass of *Move Mountain* and on several client projects. He always does an amazing job and brings some really interesting sound work to the table.

"In terms of music, I also like to collaborate with my sisters (my sister Chelsea is a really talented composer) mainly because they totally get and share my musical tastes. Our mother is a music teacher, and we each grew up playing several instruments, so it seemed to make sense to collaborate. I also have a hard time trusting other musicians since I usually have a super specific idea of what I'm looking for musically. If you haven't already noticed, I'm a bit of a control-freak."

Approaches to Sound Construction

I shall not pretend for a moment that a comprehensive breakdown of how to tackle your sound mix can be put across in a few paragraphs. As with other areas of this book that refer to the hard graft of production itself, with sound, there is a great deal of territory to cover for which further reading and research is highly advisable. That being said, as sound design is something of a personal passion – and bad sound design something of a personal bugbear – there are certain key areas worth discussing as a springboard for further education on the subject.

Think about the use of sound in wildlife documentaries, where you are witnessing animal activity such as lions engaged in a territorial scuffle that would necessitate filming from much further away than normal. Beyond a certain distance, it becomes impossible to record audio with even the most high-end equipment, yet in the documentary, the sound of the fight can clearly be heard. So what happened there?

19. Your Two Most Important Characters

This will usually be the result of a clever combination of sound design and foley artistry. The foley artist's role is to invent or replicate the landscape of sound, sometimes in real time and with the aid of props (the name of the practice originates from its inventor Jack Foley, whose approach to sound production for film set a precedent as far back as the 1920s). For example, literally dragging objects or even oneself through a sandbox brought into a recording studio would be timed to match the video of a lion being pulled across the ground by its opponent. All sorts of different approaches can be used to create sound that works on film, even if its source is wildly different from what is being seen onscreen. Also worth mentioning, alongside the multitude of short documentary vignettes, one can easily search for online to observe the process, is Peter Strickland's 2012 feature *Berberian Sound Studio*, a wonderfully dark work of live-action fiction in which Toby Jones plays a beleaguered foley artist who reluctantly spends his days smashing up produce to create sounds for a barbaric Italian slasher film. One moment of my own foley work I'll afford some personal pride toward is, after much trial and error, happening upon the sound of torn, cooked chicken flesh timed to a character getting out of a leather couch his bare skin is stuck to (Figure 19.15). Just for the record, it doesn't always have to be gross, but if it works, it works.

In animation, there is always this potential to combine conventional approaches with cartoonish embellishment, as there's a little extra artistic license granted than when dealing with live-action. To illustrate this spectrum, take two obvious examples from popular culture: On one end, *The Simpsons* uses, for the most part, genuinely authentic sound design to ground it in a certain reality; when a character such as Homer is hurt, the thud of his fall or the crunch of his bones is realistic enough to give you a very real idea of his pain. On the other end, when a character from a classic *Looney Tunes* short is squashed, blown-up or propelled in whatever manner deemed fit, the sounds chosen more often than not have no grounding in reality, coming from props, instruments or vocal performances, sometimes with additional modifications such as being sped up, slowed down or reversed. If dealing with narrative, the approach you'll wish to take with your film will most likely be somewhere between these two camps, contemporary animation for older audiences generally tending to lean more toward the former, more realistic end of the spectrum, with children's and pre-school animation more the latter.

Figure 19.15

Still from *House Guest* (Dir. Ben Mitchell) ©2008 Ben Mitchell.

Out in the Field

Gathering your sounds online may not be the best route for your film, especially if you are after specific audio that cannot be categorized by metadata alone. You can sift through hundreds of footsteps, splashes, crunches or creaks and all the while the exact sound you're after may prove elusive. The other complicating factor of gathering sound from multiple sources is the likelihood that they will have been captured under fluctuating conditions with equipment of varying quality. If your character sounds like they're in an open field one moment and a coffee can the next, audiences will notice instantly. It's a very identifiable instance of lazy inconsistency, yet remains a pitfall of indie animation to this day.

When dealing with a typical narrative short, good sound – as with good editing and most of the post-production process – carries with it the burden of being pretty much thankless. The best response an authentic sound mix can get is none at all. Our brains are wired to always take in the elaborate array of incidental sounds constantly around us, so if the sound mix has been successful to the point of suspension of disbelief, your audience shouldn't even notice it. Yet the slightest mistake when it comes to quality or timing will stick out like a sore thumb. The dices are not loaded in the sound designer's favor, but that's the way it's gotta be, I'm afraid.

While there is a great deal of nuance and artistry that separates competent sound design from expert sound design, the mainstays of *in*competent sound design are far more blatant. With that in mind, I'll wrap up this chapter with three major hazards that should be easy enough to sidestep from the get-go:

The Hiss Factor

All recording equipment will pick up a certain degree of hiss, which is usually a combination of ambient noise or even the internal mechanism of the microphone itself. In a professional studio environment, this will be negligible, but if combining professionally recorded dialogue with an assortment of field-recorded or

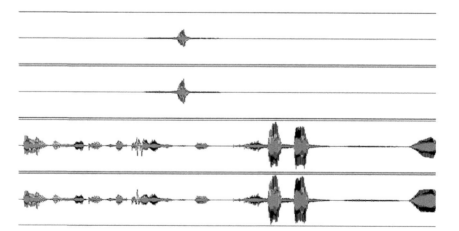

Figure 19.16

The top audio track features an externally-sourced sound effect being added to the mix. Note the visible auditory hiss that surrounds it - removing this will make the sound effect far less jarring.

19. Your Two Most Important Characters

externally sourced sound effects, the varying degrees of hiss accompanying each effect can be jarring. Ideally, you should just toss a low-quality sound for one recorded under better conditions, but if that's absolutely not an option, there are some workarounds.

Noise reduction is an advisable first port of call and a function of most audio editing software. The process essentially examines the waveform of the ambient hiss of selected audio on its own when no sounds or dialogue are present, then once identified, eliminates it, leaving only the dialogue or sound effects remaining. The drawback of this process is that the remaining sound can be distorted as a consequence; if the hiss is quiet, the difference won't be too noticeable, but if filtering out loud ambiance, your end result will wind up sounding horribly muffled or underwater. A combination of software capability and the recording itself will both be at play here, so it's worth evaluating whether or not this is the best solution on a case-by-case basis.

For very short sound effects, you may not need to filter out the hiss for its minimal duration, but it's crucial to take out any before or after hiss so your sound effect isn't essentially screaming out to the audience "Oh hi guys! I'm not from around here! What's shaking?" The hiss will be easily identifiable as part of the waveform itself (Figure 19.16) and, as such, easy enough to isolate and silence. To eliminate the risk of a pop effect (more on this next), you may need to bookend the effect with a very brief fade-in and fade-out.

The Pop Factor

Another sound issue that will furrow your audience's brows comes from splicing in audio haphazardly. This, along with the aforementioned hiss factor, is a common issue for those who create their soundtrack within the animation software itself, by just dropping effects and dialogue onto a timeline. I implore you, *don't do that*.

This makes sense as far as getting your timing right, but if you don't want to undermine the hard work that's gone into the visuals of your film, you'll really want to export the timed audio and give it proper mixing attention. One area being: Get rid of clicks and pops. So what are these, and what causes them?

They're essentially the result of a waveform that has been hastily cut or edited, so the sound will begin at a point when the waveform is not on the central amplitude line. The point at which the waveform jumps in the illustration will create a click (Figure 19.17), the further apart the jump, the more aggravatingly noticeable.

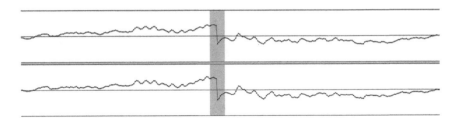

Figure 19.17

The highlighted dip between points of a waveform denotes a hasty edit. If left as-is, this will create a "pop" in the soundtrack.

This largely explains why the audio on a vinyl record will start to crackle and pop over time – the frequent running of the needle over the groove of the record, whose shape has been etched in based on the waveform of the recorded audio, will eventually cause physical wear and produce tiny gouges which have the same auditory effect as these jumps illustrated above. Okay, we get it – I'm old.

What's most infuriating about this issue when left in is just how much of an easy fix it is. Even if the sound required is sudden and abrupt, applying the smallest fade or even manually editing the points of your waveform will take no time at all and have no auditory effect save for eliminating the pop itself. Some software even has an automatic means of detecting these pops and clicks and will do it all for you in one pass, so there's really nil excuse. Smooth out your pops, people!

The "Oh God, My Ears" Factor

Dynamic range: It's a very gentle art, my friends. This is basically the difference between your film's quietest and loudest moments, and when done right, it can massively improve the authenticity of your film's soundscape (Figure 19.18). When done wrong, your film will have the comfort level of an internet screamer video. The two main offenders in this arena are non-ambient sound effects, especially when gathered from multiple sources, whose volume levels have no bearing

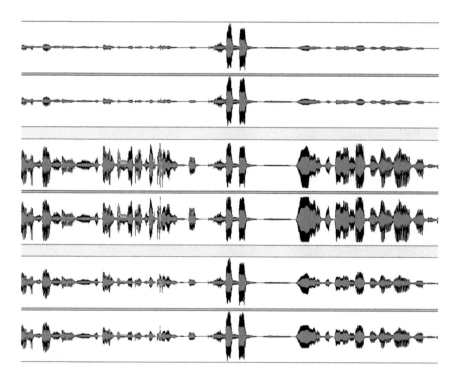

Figure 19.18

The top audio track shows recorded dialogue with a high dynamic range where the two instances of louder noise will stand out too much. The middle track shows the same audio after being highly compressed, giving the entire dialogue track consistent volume. The bottom track shows a medium level of compression, where a change in volume remains if the impact of it is desirable, while not being so vastly different in volume as to give the audience a heart attack.

19. Your Two Most Important Characters

on reality. When taking on your own mix, really take the time to consider how prominent or obscured each instance of sound should be, and whether it carries across when viewed with the animation.

The second major slip-up frequently comes with dialogue. The volume difference between a quiet, thoughtful rumination and an emphatically projected speech of passion will be substantial, and you will most likely want to curb it depending on the quality of mic or recording conditions. Applying compression to dialogue is perhaps the best way to keep these discrepancies curtailed so as to not be jarring (important point – compression and normalization are not the same thing). In both instances, be sure to test that your dynamic range translates to different listening scenarios, from the tinny speaker of your smartphone or laptop to the loudest studio/stereo equipment you can get your hands on. Most crucially, don't purely mix your sound with or without headphones – be sure to test it thoroughly under both conditions throughout.

Notes

1 https://incompetech.com/
2 "A truth whispered among animators is that 70% of a show's impact comes from the soundtrack" – Michael Dough.

Putting Yourself Out There

After weeks, months, perhaps even years of blood, sweat, tears and whatever other bodily fluids you may have sacrificed along the way, it finally happens. After every shot has slotted into the project timeline, after every hair-pulling liaison with various members of your post-production crew has borne fruit, after the absolute, final, this-is-it, no-more-tweaking, definitive render announces its conclusion with its life-affirming "ding" – you've done it. You have yourself a film, my friend.

Bask in it. Give it a watch and revel in its completion. Show it to your folks, your friends, that barista you fancy, prove that all this time you haven't just been making up that you're a filmmaker to appear bohemian. Or do none of the above and just catch up on what's sure to be a long stretch of much-needed and well-deserved sleep. Contented, blissful sleep.

Now wake up and get going, because it's not over yet, not by a long shot. Thought you'd make a film and the rest would all slot into place, did you? Ah, sweet delusion. Allow me to bring you back to crushing reality.

Much as a curmudgeon like myself enjoys delivering bad news, in truth, this reality isn't especially crushing, nor does having a finished animation shackle you with obligation. It is, after all, your film and you can do with it what you wish. You may want to just gift it to the world as a video upload literally minutes after its completion, which is certainly a route many have taken and gone on to receive acclaim. For many contemporary filmmakers, their work may solely belong in browser windows or tablet and smartphone screens, but to many others – yourself possibly included – the mileage a film can have, not to mention the life it can lead once out of your hands and in the world, is something you may

DOI: 10.1201/9781003214717-20

Figure 20.1

A bygone era; various screeners for my films produced between 2008 and 2010, before festivals mercifully switched to digital projection. Photo by the author.

wish to be present for. Seeing firsthand how the public receives your art is one of the most beneficial experiences one can have when it comes to artistic growth, so get your film in front of people and be there to see how they react.

Why Submit Your Film to Festivals?

In this day and age the only response to the above question is a predictable "Why not?" In the digital age the festival landscape is ever-changing and, with each iteration, the process of film submission gets increasingly simpler and more streamlined. From a personal frame of reference that goes back to the long, long-ago days of the late-noughties, submitting to festivals still proved something of a hassle. More often than not it was a requirement to deliver films on physical media (Figure 20.1), which involved a case-by-case grappling with shipping costs and international customs parameters, not to mention hand-writing/signing entry forms, statements, labeling DVDs and CDs and multiple trips to the Post Office. Then, with a film having been accepted, screening formats were usually again limited to the physical – a progressive festival would maybe play DVDs, while others were still piecing together programs from miniDV tapes or the wonderful world of DigiBeta. Going back less than a decade further and some festivals were still dealing with VHS. Bearing all this in mind, the ease of filling in online forms, transferring HD content and the variety of organizations set up specifically to simplify the process make festival submission something of a no-brainer today.

One such organization is animation-festivals.com,[1] a website set up by Slurpy Studios Producer and Managing Director Aaron Wood in 2009. The site serves as

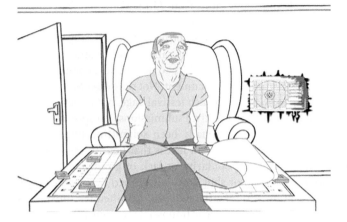

Figure 20.2

Still from *Death by Scrabble* (Dir. Katie Steed), the film whose festival run put animation-festivals.com in motion ©2007 Katie Steed/Slurpy Studios.

a festival directory for filmmakers to browse events in order of name, event dates, submission deadlines, territories and entry fees. While similar directories exist, animation-festivals.com prioritizes those that are exclusively animation or have animation as a major category.

"Although you can submit your animated film to most festivals, we preferred the idea of meeting likeminded people." Aaron reasons, "Animators will most likely want to meet other animators more than live-action filmmakers. So we put this list together, not just for people to submit their film, but so they could actually look up festivals, even if they just wanted to visit them."

The directory began life as a database made up of information collated by Slurpy's Creative Director Katie Steed during the festival run of her multi award-winning student film *Death by Scrabble* (2007, Figure 20.2). Keeping tabs on the performance and progress of the film, Katie took the advisable approach of keeping an Excel spreadsheet documenting every festival the film was sent to, with each event's respective URLs, contact information and decision as to whether or not the film had been accepted. As films are generally considered eligible for most festivals during the first two years of the completion, this approach is recommended so as to avoid resubmitting to the same event two years in a row.

"At the end of the film's festival run Katie had an Excel spreadsheet of around two-hundred festivals. At the time we considered just putting it on the company blog, as a useful list of festivals for animators. We later realized that we could turn this into a more substantial website and keep it updated, specifying that it was just for animation festivals."

While daily maintenance of a three-hundred-plus festival database would have proved unfeasible, Aaron's prior background in website design enabled him to build an open-to-all interface so that anyone with a festival to add might register and submit it. With notifications in place to let Aaron know if any contributors were abusing the system, the directory was able to grow and stay up-to-date relatively simply. This system also ensured that festival directors could edit and re-edit details of their events should circumstances change from year to year.

"That's probably why it's still going today, because of that feature. Otherwise there's no way that it would not have become outdated very quickly. We always welcome feedback and suggestions from filmmakers and festival directors, and we like to implement anything that will improve the user experience. Overall, the feedback on the site remains very positive; that it is easy to use and navigate, which has resulted in us sticking to the same interface and layout. However, one feature that we have added is the ability to download a complete list of the festivals and their details, as a CSV document. Not only does this save the filmmaker time from having to go through each festival page, but it serves as a nice starting point for them to record their festival submissions in a spreadsheet."

As somebody who has personally been submitting films to festivals semi-regularly for over a decade, one sad fact is that not all festivals are everlasting. Sometimes due to lack of popularity or lack of governmental backing, events need to become bi-annual or shut down altogether. Even some of the major festivals have been known to take the odd year off when circumstances have been particularly tough. Though it's near impossible to implement an automated system that would track which festivals go extinct or get put on hiatus, Aaron has a three-pronged approach to making sure animation-festivals.com stays on top of things and keeps its listings as relevant as possible.

"First of all it can come from having a good rapport with festival directors who will get in touch personally and explain that a festival is no longer running and the reasons why. The second way is similar in that festival directors can also go in and simply press a 'delete' button that will send an email to me with their reason for removing it. Then there are those types of festivals that do just disappear and nobody knows what's happened to them, and that's a manual consideration. Once a year I will go through and check the links for each website to see if the festival is still running, and then it's a matter of me just taking it down manually if not. It's a shame that some of them come to an end – it's especially a shame when it's a purely animation festival that has closed its doors."

As well as festival listings websites such as animation-festivals.com (Figure 20.3), online submission options have steadily increased, with virtually all major festivals presently accepting digital submissions, either through their website or, more frequently, through submission portals they have partnered with. Sites such as Shortfilmdepot, FilmFreeway, FilmFestivalLife and Festhome among others are specifically set up to streamline the submission process, in most (but not all) cases charging small fees per submission that roughly approximate the postage costs of physically sending materials. Not all of these platforms will be the right fit for you, your project or your budget, so use your best judgment when it comes to taking this route, should you decide to. Either way, it is definitely worth investigating all available options as the more festivals you initially approach will increase the likelihood of an official selection early in your film's two-year "'lifespan."

Many filmmakers incorporate a marketing element into their festival submission strategy. Some materials such as stills, posters, director biographies and headshots are solicited by festivals as standard, although usually for potential future use should the film be selected. While it is definitely advisable to put together an electronic presskit (an easily updatable document or accessible online space collecting the materials mentioned as well as additional relevant information, such as awards won, festivals selected for, director's statement, press quotes and behind-the-scenes/development materials) for your project, bear in mind that it will likely not have much bearing on whether or not it will make it through preselection as, by and large, programmers will be so deluged by entries that they won't have time to look at much more than the film itself; for many,

Sign In | Register

animation-festivals.com
HOME TO 262 INTERNATIONAL ANIMATION FESTIVALS

Search   GO!
                    Advanced Search

HOME   FESTIVALS   SEARCH   ADD FESTIVAL   CONTACT   MORE...

About animation-festivals.com

WHO WE ARE

animation-festivals.com is a hybrid of Wikipedia and the Yellow Pages, but for animation festivals!

We are a small, but dedicated team, who aim to provide the International animation community with a constantly updated directory of festival listings. The website is completely free to use; our only request is that if you see a listing that is either out of date or incorrect, you edit it. That way the community constantly benefits.

NO ONE ELSE LIKE US

animation-festivals.com was born out of the need for a comprehensive directory of animation festivals around the world. Unless you have been in the animation industry for a number of years and built up your own database of festivals, there are very few places, if any, where you can find up to date festival listings all year round.

Whereas there are many film festivals out there, and it is not difficult to obtain a listing of *these*, it is a time consuming task finding out which ones accept animation. Students, producers, directors and others do not have the time or resources to search for the relevant festivals amongst all the others.

animation-festivals is a very specific online resource which aims to take this headache away. But we can't do it without your help...

WHY WE CHOSE TO OPEN IT UP

Animation and film festivals the world over come and go in relatively short spaces of time. Some festivals are fortunate enough to run annually year after year, while some only have a life span of a year or two. animation-festivals.com wants each and every festival (that showcases animation) to be listed, regardless of its regularity. Festivals that run only once or twice can chose to be removed after the festival ends at the click of a button.

As this kind of resource could not be managed by a few individuals, we created a site which works very much like Wikipedia, and allows listings to be update by festival directors and employees, students, animators, producers, studios, local event coordinators, production house, and YOU!

INTERESTED IN ADVERTISING WITH US?

DOWNLOAD OUR SPONSOR PACK FOR MORE INFORMATION

NEXT 5 DEADLINES

1   Big Muddy Film Festival
    28 Nov 2015

2   4th Mumbai Shorts International Film Festival-2015
    30 Nov 2015

3   Chicago Underground Film Festival
    1 Dec 2015

4   Holland Animation Film Festival (HAFF)
    1 Dec 2015

5   Cine-court anime
    5 Dec 2015

MORE FESTIVALS ▶

Figure 20.3

animation-festivals.com site interface. Image courtesy of animation-festivals.com.

they prefer to go in blind anyway as this avoids the issue of being influenced by a project's prior performance.

"I think it's dangerous when you start to select based on outside performances," suggests Chris Robinson of the Ottawa International Animation Festival, "If you want to be taken seriously or have something unique about your event, then replicating what another festival is doing isn't the healthiest way to approach programming. There's many times a grand prize winner at, let's say Annecy, didn't even make the cut in Ottawa – and vice versa.

"I never look at promotional materials. Sometimes I read the synopsis if I'm just utterly confused. I really just try to go right into the film. I mean, of course, people put their laurels on at the beginning but that really has no sway on it."

Nag Vladermersky of London International Animation Festival's attitude is much the same: "When the entries come in, I try as much as possible to watch the films as-is, without any prior knowledge of where they've screened. I just want to see it for myself without preconceptions, so it doesn't hinder my idea of whether it should go in or not. I mean, if you know in advance that a film screened at every other festival you may think, 'well obviously it's really popular, I have to put this in as well.' So I try to exclude those thoughts."

As Animafest Zagreb Artistic Director Daniel Šuljić notes, the fact the festival programmers frequently attend other international events the year round will inevitably mean that some films will already be on their radar, to an extent.

"When you've seen a film previously you may have built an opinion of it already, but what it comes down to is we are watching these films *now* and we are deciding *now* which of them we think are the most interesting for competition programs. If they were selected for other festivals previously, who cares? We're selecting for ours."

Something that gets brought up less often is the possibility that submitting to a festival with a highly successful festival run already behind you might actually work against getting selected at festivals. This isn't out of snobbery but rather acknowledgment that, with the limited programming space their event has, the selection will likely be more valuable to a film that is equally strong but not necessarily had as many opportunities to be seen.

This is not to say that you shouldn't bother adding this information at all. For one, a positive response to art that you have worked hard to create is something to be proud of. It can also help your film further into the selection process, if not at the start; for Nag, there is some value in having the information to hand, even if it likely won't be his first port of call, as it can give a more rounded view of a film's engagement and accessibility at the later stages of curation where harder decisions need to be made. "With our competition films there's around 150 films that get in, so when I get to the stage where there are really difficult decisions about having to get rid of some films because there's too much, then I will look a bit more into where they've screened, and that might then make me take that into consideration. I watch everything once without looking at all the promotional stuff that people sent in, then when I get down to a shorter list, then we'll look at that stuff. It's always great to see nicely put together press packs or stills, information about what other work that filmmakers have done, their websites, et cetera. So I think it's very useful, but not at the very first stage."

At the very least, it is advisable to upload some basic information with your film entry, especially if you are submitting through a platform such as FilmFreeway that makes the process of attaching supplemental materials easy. On occasion I've come away from adjudicating a film submission completely baffled by what the director was trying to achieve, only to find the information page completely bare and thus no help at all in giving the work any helpful context that might support its case.

Discussions with festival programmers themselves can also prove enlightening. An early indicator of just how disparate one festival's identity can be from another's occurred during the festival run of my second film *Ground Running* (Figure 20.4), a micro-short that began life as a series of animation exercises so as to cover ground I'd not managed to in my preceding thesis film. Though it never took flight on the festival circuit in the same way as my other films had done, it did get screened across the world and would receive, for the most part, a positive audience response (think polite chuckles rather than carrying me out on their shoulders chanting my name). While chatting with programmers of two UK-based animation festivals that took place a month apart from one another, both independently commented on its retro, cartoony feel, one as a compliment, the other as a criticism. In terms of one festival's identity, the idea of a retro and

Figure 20.4

Still from *Ground Running* (Dir. Ben Mitchell) – the troublesome second film ©2009 Ben Mitchell.

cartoony animated short was a refreshing harkening back to an era they wished to celebrate as an effective juxtaposition to the avant-garde contingent of their official selection; to the other, "retro" was synonymous with archaic and somehow less artistically relevant. Granted, the selection committee saw enough in it to include it, but the impression I got was that my film stood out as far more of an oddity in the latter festival's program than the former. Of all the criticisms I would level at the film myself – and, trust me, they are multitudinous – my personal artistic sensibilities will always see me defend the cartoony side of animated film as something that has no reason to not sit alongside work deemed more socio-politically or culturally valuable.

If every festival shared this personal ideology, then the landscape would be a fairly dull one; a sense of identity is important. Festivals that focus on films with a certain tone, or have a clear idea of what they want to evoke when compiling a program of multi-genre films, are ultimately stronger and more memorable for their conviction.

It is sometimes the case that a festival's definition of what your film is to an audience might not necessarily line up with your own. When it came to the festival exposure of *Love in the Time of March Madness* (first explored in Chapter 4), co-director Robertino Zambrano would come to learn of a wider categorization than anticipated:

"I'd always just thought that we'd enter this into the animation category, and then people were telling us to enter it into documentary categories. That made me think a little bit about *Okay, why, and why animation?*"

The power of animation as a storytelling tool, especially when dealing with non-fiction as its source material, is exemplified by the visual approaches taken in *Love in the Time of March Madness* (Figure 20.5). Not least down to Robertino's flair for conveying non-literal and intangible concepts that writer and co-director Melissa Johnson's narration intimates.

"I feel like animation is almost more honest than a live-action storytelling approach," explains Robertino, "You're not choosing the perfect depiction of this story, rather you're providing some sort of medium for the viewer to bounce off what the narrator is trying to tell. It leaves it open, like reading a book, but not as far as watching a movie of a book, it's somewhere in-between. When a live-action movie of a book is made, it almost goes too far in its manifestation of a story, by trying to convince the viewer that this is how it looked and happened. In opposition to that, an animation is honest about itself being a pure depiction of an idea or event."

The film itself definitely works on multiple levels that broaden its appeal – the drily witty observations and musings present in the script delivered by Melissa's narration give it a great deal of comedic value, yet at the same time its honesty about her very personal struggles infuses it with subtle pathos. Given the fluidity of the animation and its lack of boundaries, in some programmer's eyes it could even be considered experimental. Certainly that it has toured the States, played at major international festivals and won major international awards is indicative of a wider appeal, regardless of how the film itself is categorized.

"A lot of people initially wondered how to program us and we didn't really care." Melissa says, "We were happy to be included however the programmers saw fit for their showcases. It's definitely not just animation, we know that – but is it narrative, is it documentary? For me, it's like the filmic equivalent of creative non-fiction; it's a true story told in a narrative style, and the animation just amps that up. I love the grey areas between scripted and documentary – I could talk about this stuff all day long.

"It's kind of emblematic of the metaphor of the film itself; I may be pushing it here a little bit, but what you see in our film is what you see in yourself, whatever you want to bring to it. We're quite open to however you want to categorize us, I'm not hung up on that at all. But the perspective the audience brings to the film says, I think, a lot more about them."

Of course it's fine to propose a whirlwind festival tour in which you charm peers, contemporaries and industry bigwigs alike with your talent and assortment of personable *bon mots* as your ticket to visibility, but as with so many areas of discussion presented in this book, some pragmatism is required. Realistically speaking it probably won't be the case that every festival will cover your travel

Figure 20.5

Still from *Love in the Time of March Madness* (Dir. Melissa Johnson/Robertino Zambrano) ©2014 High Hip Productions/KAPWA Studioworks.

and accommodation, and even if they do, there are likely to be expenses accrued alongside the probability that, while you're away from your home turf, you won't be working.

How you fine-tune your outgoings to best suit your circumstances depends on your own judgment. If, after all, animation is the industry you're enthusiastic to commit to for the remainder of your professional career then animation festivals, conferences and markets should definitely be given consideration from a professional standpoint. There's even cause to justify money spent on or at said events as business expenses, though it's best if you go ahead and run that sort of thing by your accountant first. If you get in trouble for trying to pass off a weekend of cheeky pedalo racing in Annecy as a business trip, then waving this book in an auditor's face and saying "Ben told me it was okay!" probably won't help you out much as an excuse.

Rejection: How to Deal

Everybody who takes a shot on something that runs the risk of rejection will agree that it is never fun. You're being told, in essence, that your film is bad and that you as a filmmaker should pack it in, right? Wrong.

I remain aghast at the number of sincerely talented filmmakers I've seen over the years who have not only given up on getting their project seen but on filmmaking altogether, simply from having been rejected by the first handful of festivals they submitted to. I cannot stress enough how important it is to *not be discouraged* by an initially slow response. As with the travails and turmoil of applying for funds discussed earlier in the book, when it comes to festival visibility, you have to embrace the fact that you're playing a numbers game. Even if a festival is frosty in their response, and the ones you should take seriously won't be, that only speaks to the individual tastes of its programmers; it's not a full assessment of the quality of your work. Context is all, so bear in mind that while sifting through submissions, programmers will have a very limited context for the circumstances and directorial intent behind your film. Trash to some is treasure to others, as the saying goes, though in the world of subjective film appreciation we could say that amateurishness to some is playfulness to others, maudlin sentiment to some is heartfelt poignancy to others, caustic juvenilia to some is refreshing edginess to others, and so on and so forth.

As outlined in the introduction, the primary intention of this book is for filmmakers to be able to take the lessons learned from the case studies and apply them to their ongoing/future projects, so as to stand out in the crowd. As such you, the reader, may be wondering why the notion of rejection is even being brought up. The fact of the matter is, as strong as your film is, it's statistically impossible to achieve 100% success,[2] even for established veterans of the animation world. Films that have been rejected from the most prestigious of competitive film festivals have gone on to win major awards and cement the future careers of their directors – but that can only happen with persistence and not being dissuaded by the first bumps in the road. Even for those who seem to have the world handed to them on the proverbial platter have, in all likelihood, been put through the ringer a fair few times. The fact is that we are all of us far more inclined to share our successes than our failures and setbacks, so for every festival inclusion you see attached to a film, it is entirely possible that there have been the same number of rejections – likely far more (Figure 20.6).

Figure 20.6

Sunscapades poster – though oft-rejected, with perseverance it eventually accrued enough official selections to fancy up the layout a tad ©2020 Ben Mitchell.

To offer up some perspective, let's again heed the advice of our veterans of animation festival programming we met earlier, many of whom are no stranger to rejection themselves.

"I've written books, and I've had a lot of rejections before somebody picked one of them up. It's just part of life. Festivals are highly subjective – there might be something that I didn't like, or we didn't like, about a film that maybe another festival will like. So you can't let it bother you too much. When I started, I felt there was this mystery to the jury, or the selection committees, that they were these godlike figures who were like a Supreme Court. No, they're just human beings like the rest of us."

-Chris Robinson (Artistic Director, Ottawa International Animation Festival)

"I'm sure those rejection emails or letters can be very disheartening but if you really want to have a career, or get into the world of film festivals, you just have to persevere. From a festival point of view, we get to see 2500 films a year and choose around 150–200 to screen in competition screening. So around one in ten get into the festival, which is tough, but just keep at it and talk to other filmmakers, other animators, go to festivals, make yourself known. We get films from filmmakers who have put stuff in every year for the last ten years, and eventually, there'll be something that just catches our eye. So keep at it."

-Nag Vladermersky (Director/Chief Programmer,
London International Animation Festival)

"As a filmmaker, it's so much work to make animation and it's easy to get discouraged. Two or three of my own films have not been successful, but then I do a new film. A new film is a new deck of cards, and from film to film there can be a really big difference in the number of selections and the quality of the festivals. So keep doing it, that's the only thing I can say. Persistence is the most important virtue in art. Just work and you will find your audience."

-Daniel Šuljić (Artistic Director, Animafest Zagreb)

"It really isn't meant as a personal slight, even though it can sometimes feel like that. The most important thing to remember is that this decline doesn't mean you've made a bad film, you've just made something that isn't right for that particular festival or platform. Really, that last sentence is essential in maintaining your sanity as a filmmaker."

-Rob Munday (Managing Editor, Director's Notes/Short of the Week)

"It's always a good idea to target the right festivals as opposed to sending the film to everyone and wasting money on submission fees. If you've got a film that's abstract and you send it into a festival that shows mainly narrative-based work then chances are that you won't get in. There might be other reasons that your film doesn't get selected. We have to reject hundreds of amazing films every year for MAF because we simply don't have the space in our programme, so don't assume that your film is bad and nobody else will want it because no two festivals are the same."

-Steve Henderson (Director/CEO, Manchester Animation Festival)

"Sometimes films get missed out just because they didn't fit with how we were approaching the program. Maybe some festivals will have a theme for the year; it's not strictly the 'best' 100 films that get into the festival, it's about what plays well together and the flow of the program. And on top of that, it's ridiculously subjective. So our team might love something that the Encounters team would hate, or we might hate something that the MAF team would love. We've all got different tastes."

-Lauren Orme (Festival Director, Cardiff Animation Festival)

"You need to get the film out there and don't be disheartened, don't just try it in five festivals, then forget it if it doesn't work. There are always subjective decisions for what goes into a festival, so a festival that might be good for one film might be bad for another. A film can be hugely successful and win a top prize at one festival and not be selected for two dozen others, so any advice to filmmakers or whoever's in charge of submissions to festivals is don't give up, keep at it."

-Kieran Argo (Animation Programmer)

Film as Discourse

The festival environment can prompt not just new filmmaking but also active discussion on the topic. Many festivalgoers will walk away from a film screening or presentation feeling inspired in the moment, and the hope remains that there will always at least be a small percentage of those who will act on it and follow through with new work of their own. Steven Woloshen, whose output would already be considered prolific, was moved to create an abstract film in the vein of his established style as a reaction to *Spiral*, a parody of the abstract film genre directed by Bill Plympton in 2005. *Spiral* was allegedly inspired by a screening at ITFS Stuttgart of *Film-Wipe-Film* (1984) a near-half-hour abstract short by Paul Glabicki, in which the audience grew visibly impatient. In Bill's film, the artistic expression of the animated shapes is met with hostility by an unseen cinema audience who eventually resort to violence despite the pleas of the shapes themselves, who insist they only wish to entertain.

Though the film serves as light satire on a subsection of festival culture rather than any kind of malicious condemnation of the abstract film genre, Bill initially used the moniker W.P. Murton so as to not upset experimental filmmakers he knew and respected. Steven elected to counter *Spiral* with a piece of his own, using similarly good-natured chicanery.

"Us experimental filmmakers are kind of at the bottom of the heap, we don't have a lot of people standing up for us. So what I did was I created a fictitious film archive and contacted Bill Plympton for a copy of his film *Your Face* to be part of it. So I paid for the film, he mailed it to me and I took a pair of scissors, cut it into little bits, glued it onto film and made an abstract film out of it."

The end result, titled *Rebuttal* (Figure 20.7), was later screened at the Ottawa Animation Festival, under the pseudonym Luther Cartier ("Luther being the name of our cat and Cartier the street we lived on").

"I open up the floor to anybody who wants to talk about the subject. I think there are a lot of people like myself who work in an experimental way, who don't want to be ridiculed for trying something new. He takes it in good stride, because he knows the debate's more important than what side you take. So sometimes his film *Spiral* plays *with Rebuttal*, so the audience can get a sense of what both sides of the story are. It's a way to open up a debate so we can talk about these things.

Figure 20.7

Still from *Rebuttal* (Dir. Steven Woloshen), featuring manipulated footage from Bill Plympton's 1987 classic *Your Face* ©2005 Steven Woloshen.

20. Putting Yourself Out There

"Does experimental film *belong* in a competition setting? So many festivals recognize that you can't judge an experimental film in the same way you can a narrative film, there are all these issues that have cropped up, we should look at things a little bit differently, we should let people explore in workshops, let people talk about these things, let debate happen. So maybe it's going on, slowly. Annecy now has an award for non-narrative, experimental work, so that means it's opening up. Already there are so many festivals around the world that already recognize that there are so many different types of filmmaking. Thank goodness!"

While several major festivals still require submitted films to not yet be publicly available online, this is becoming less and less of an essential caveat as the years go by. Some festivals have recognized that online hosting is indeed the best means of generating buzz for a film in this present climate of audience engagement and word-of-mouth via social media. Even if an audience is familiar with a film already online in full, that has achieved a measure of viral success or significant media attention, that does not automatically mean that the opportunity to see it in a theatrical setting won't be a draw (every screening I have seen of the long-online *Don't Hug Me I'm Scared* films, for example, has never failed to get a strong reaction from a festival audience). Bringing it around again to a positive note, *Story from North America* co-director Garrett Michael Davis has a reassuring take on the long-term ramifications of a solid festival run and its associated exposure.

"When I was in school, an artist I was acquainted with gave me some really great advice: Spend your last year of school making something you can 'take around' for a while. In terms of animation, that's pretty clear – just make a good animation. There are so many animation festivals that are not as competitive as full-blown film festivals where people are showing projects that cost thousands or millions of dollars. People should know that it's not hard to get your films screened, even if it's only five seconds long. Festivals and events are always looking for things to screen, and if you make something good, it will continue to work for you for a long time."

Notes

1 https://www.animation-festivals.com – you probably could have worked that one out for yourself, to be fair.
2 In truth, "success" is such a subjective term that it would be disingenuous to present it as a realistic goal by everybody's definition. I define the success of my own work as films that have made people laugh, been sold for broadcast and been a tremendous boon to my freelance career; to some, however, the fact that they've not won major awards from certain institutions or achieved online viral success would, by their definition of success, make them failures. But why you gotta hate?

21

Distribution

A Brave New World

As we near the end of our examination of the independent animation scene and the multitude of lessons that can be learned from its artists, our last stop will be the matter of distribution itself. Throughout the book, a number of options have already come up, such as online platforms to showcase and potentially monetize your films. For some that is a realistic option, as indie legend Don Hertzfeldt has found through the online release of recent projects such as *It's Such a Beautiful Day* (the 2012 indie masterpiece that accompanied the launch of Vimeo On Demand) and his *World of Tomorrow* series. Don weighs up the primary digital distribution options available to independent filmmakers thusly:

"I think Vimeo genuinely cares about quality of presentation, and their 90% revenue share to the filmmakers was unprecedented. Independent filmmaking is in a constant state of 'evolve or die.' Which is good, it probably keeps us from getting too comfortable. A question that everyone in the industry will constantly be asking from now on is, 'how do people want to watch movies these days?' There are so many different methods to see something now and they will always be changing with new technology. *It's Such a Beautiful Day* (Figure 21.1) had a long and healthy life in theatres, we did the DVD, Netflix, vimeo, itunes and, in some countries, television. As long as the quality stays high I want to give people every possible option."

Don Hertzfeldt's vantage point is from perhaps the most conceivably popular end of the independent animation spectrum, so while it is healthy to aspire to be as accomplished a filmmaker as he, in terms of an early project paying immediate dividends, one should keep expectations grounded when approaching such a distribution platform. Observationally speaking, the pattern a majority of

DOI: 10.1201/9781003214717-21

Figure 21.1

Still from *It's Such a Beautiful Day* ©2012 Don Hertzfeldt/Bitter Films.

independent animators and filmmakers alike have fallen into goes roughly along the lines of:

1. Finishing a film (kind of crucial)
2. Aiming to premiere it at a major festival
3. Submitting it to festivals en masse (a process made easier should stage 2 have proved successful and your film been received well) to increase its award prospects and international visibility
4. Release the film online, for free, following its two-year festival-eligible period and pending any contractual obligations to distributors and others who may have purchased rights in the interim
5. Next project!

It won't necessarily be red carpets and champagne, but it can be immeasurably valuable to your reputation, career prospects and likelihood of producing more work down the line with a wider array of resources, so as to drive your art and passion even further forward.

You may of course wish to be the master of your own film's destiny and take the reins when it comes to how, when and through which avenues it will be released. The easiest approach to take for this of course being to upload it to a streaming platform and hope for the best. Sure, it's entirely possible that somebody of influence might stumble upon the film by happenstance and give it a signal boost, or that the algorithm of the platform it's on will happen to be in your favor and recommend it to a ton of people. Unfortunately, the more likely outcome is that, without a strategy in place, your film will be a droplet lost in an ever-expanding ocean of content and may go years without finding much by way of viewership. For some guidance on how best to approach this vital stage of your project, let's turn to Rob Munday, indie film champion and online shorts specialist who we heard from earlier in the book.

Tips for an Effective Online Release: A Q&A with Director's Notes and Short of the Week Managing Editor Rob Munday

- **Should filmmakers allow for a certain amount of time in advance of their online release to start reaching out to blogs and playlists?**

  "There was a time when an online release felt very much like an after-thought. Something you didn't give a lot of attention and usually came at the end of a festival run when filmmakers were either tired or focusing on new projects. At Short of the Week, we've been promoting the approach that filmmakers should be considering their online release as early as possible and thankfully that message appears to be getting through.

  "An online release should be planned as part of a film's festival and distribution strategy, and you should look to find a release partner as early as possible in the journey. The earlier you have that locked in, the more prepared you'll be when the time comes to release your work online. We've seen films submitted months before they want to go online and we've had others that submit and want to go live as soon as possible, we definitely prefer the first option here. It allows more time for planning and discussion and both parties have the necessary headspace to work out the best options for that release.

  "I guess the short answer here is apply to festivals and online at the same time...if your budget allows it."

- **In this day and age, can you think of any disadvantages there might be of releasing a film before (or in lieu of) a complete festival run?**

  "The only disadvantage I can think of relates to premiere status, I know there are some top tier festivals that still ask for films in their programme to be 'exclusives' and that they haven't been screened else-where. My advice here would be to give this consideration in your festival and distribution planning, look at the festivals you're submitting to and check what their policy is with online films, will it affect your chances of being selected? A lot of festivals are fine with your film being online and I've spoken to a lot of filmmakers who, in hindsight, wish they would have released their film at the same time as a festival screening, to build on that buzz. The timeline used to be festivals then online, but again, it feels like this is changing."

- **As an online curator, is it important to cultivate ongoing relationships with directors whose work you've showcased in the past?**

  "I can only speak from my personal experience here, but I think it's essential. As co-founder of Directors Notes and Managing Editor of Short of the Week our network of previously featured filmmakers helps drive everything we do. From short film recommendations to project updates, those filmmakers help us find new content, provide industry insight and strengthen our brand. Short film is often seen as a stepping stone in a filmmaker's career and although we see it as much more than that, we love hearing news of how this work has helped them progress in their professional journey and we're always proud to share in their success."

- **Would you recommend any prepared promotional materials (such as the kind festivals often request, presskits/stills/bio, etc.) be supplied with films being sent for consideration?**

  "At the submission stage, it's not something we ask for on Short of the Week, but I know platforms like FilmFreeway (which is a really important tool for festivals and online platforms) have the option to upload a lot of this information, so it's good to have it prepared. In general, I think it's good to be ahead of the game and have an EPK (electronic press kit) ready before you submit, as it will make your life easier down the line. When you find a release partner and start planning to put the film online they are going to ask for all of these elements anyway, so why not have them prepared, organised and online, so all you have to do is send a link when they are needed."

- **From a strategic point of view, would you say it's better for a director to simultaneously release their film across all available platforms (including social media that permits longer videos) or to stagger the release? And what would the notable advantages/disadvantages to either be?**

  "We have a whole article about this on Short of the Week, it's called the 'Be Everywhere All At Once' strategy[1] and, as you can probably gather from the title, it's based around the idea that a simultaneous release across multiple platforms is the best approach when bringing your film online. If you would have asked us this question five years ago, we would have almost certainly recommended focusing all your attention on one platform – usually Vimeo – but through our own experiences, we've found this somewhat limiting.

  "The advantages of a multi-platform release are pretty simple: each platform has a different audience, so take your film to them, instead of expecting them to come to you. Vimeo is very much based around your network and that coveted Staff Pick, whereas YouTube is all about Keywords, Search and that notorious Algorithm, having success on one won't hamper the other. The same with social media, putting it on Facebook isn't going to affect your view count elsewhere.

  "We've helped countless filmmakers with a multi-platform release and while you can't expect everyone to become a viral hit, we've certainly seen some excellent results. Films like *Lost & Found* by Andrew Goldsmith & Bradley Slabe, *Garden Party* by lllogic Studios and *Negative Space* by Ru Kuwahata & Max Porter have found huge audiences on Vimeo and on YouTube. In terms of disadvantages, it's more work, there's no avoiding that. You have to know what works on each platform and how to best find an audience there. It's not easy becoming an expert in these areas, it takes time and research. Again, this is where a release partner can help you, we already have the audience and we already have the knowledge, so we can work with you to get the best from your release."

- **Should filmmakers make a point of researching/targeting specific sites that may be more inclined to include their work or go ahead and do a full blast?**

  "We're all aware that there isn't a lot of money in short film and if you take into consideration that to submit to most online platforms there's a fee involved, I would certainly advise doing your research when it comes to planning which outlets you'll send your film to. Just like on the festival circuit, each online platform will have its own curatorial guidelines, which will guide its selection process. On Short of the Week, for example, we have a narrative-first approach to our curation, where story is key, so we don't really accept music videos, comedy sketches or commercials. We love seeing short film used to push new techniques and experiment, but if a film is devoid of a strong narrative hook, it just won't be for us.

"With that in mind, research is going to be really important to ensure you aren't submitting to sites where your work isn't a good fit. Have a browse of existing content on the platform you're thinking of submitting to and see if your film shares the qualities of those being championed already. The majority of platforms will spell out their minimum requirements for a film to be accepted, so make sure you adhere to these before submitting. It's also worth noting that there are certain platforms dedicated to specific genres, so if your film falls into one of these that could influence your decision to submit."

- **Are there any other etiquette tips (dos and, more importantly, don'ts) when it comes to how filmmakers should approach blogs and curators when they're ready for an online release?**

"Always try to go through the official routes when sending your film for consideration, I know everyone loves a waiver or a freebie, but the fees involved with submissions are often what helps keep these platforms afloat. We do understand that a lot of short filmmakers don't have the budget to submit to every festival or outlet they'd like, but it's always worth considering the time, commitment and admin costs it takes for a platform to accept and watch screeners.

"It feels like we're entering general everyday advice here, but always try to be considerate and respectful. When corresponding with outlets and their curators, just keep in mind that this isn't personal, no one is looking to belittle your work or demean your craft. Most of us who work in curation, whether online or at festivals, chose this profession because of a love of filmmaking and the very last thing we want to do is damage your confidence or stifle your creativity. Just because a film is rejected by a certain platform, it doesn't mean it's a bad film, it just wasn't right for that particular line of curation. Try to keep that in mind, before sending an abrasive response if your film is declined."

- **Does festival performance (or positive prior media coverage) have any bearing on whether or not a film is considered or do you prefer to go in blind where possible?**

"Personally, I prefer to go in blind. I even try to avoid a synopsis before viewing a film, as I think sometimes they can spell out a film's aims and either make you see it in a different light or spoil the impact of the narrative.

"Festivals do play a vital role in our curation though, as we try to attend as many as possible to check out programmes and meet filmmakers, so I'd be lying if I said festival performance didn't have an impact on our content. Through attending events and being immersed in that festival circuit you see certain titles again and again and it's impossible to avoid all the hype around certain films, but it's fair to say that can have a positive or negative effect.

"It's also worth highlighting that just because a film does well at a festival, it doesn't mean it will experience the same success online. We've seen a lot of festival favourites bomb online, as the audiences are very different. As online curators, our favourite films to programme are the ones that come out of left field, with no festival background and no prior knowledge, and blow you away with their innovation, craft and storytelling. These are quite rare though, and in some instances premiering online can result in these films being picked up by festival/distributors afterwards."

- **Online programming has very much been embraced at this point. From how you've seen films be received over the years would you say the currency of a high performing online release is comparable to film festival exposure/awards at this point?**

"I agree with this to an extent, but it very much relies on what your goals were in making a short film. Selection and awards on the festival circuit means recognition from industry peers, where online success comes from a more general audience, but also offers the opportunity to reach a broader viewership. What I would say, is that when it comes to developing your career, both can have an impact. We know talent scouts and agents are involved in the festival scene, but we also know, from our own experiences and contacts, that they monitor what's happening online. I think festival success provides recognition for a filmmaker, whereas online success can be a good indicator of the interest in a certain premise or storyline – as you've already proved, it works by drawing in a big audience. It also depends on the project, more commercial, mainstream works might not fit suitably into a festival's ethos, but they can thrive online and in general, these might be the projects that see more development opportunities.

"I'd like to finish this point on a little bit of a tangent, but I think it's important that we start to set new metrics when it comes to evaluating the success of a short film. Festival accolades and millions of views are gratifying to receive, but are they the be-all and end-all in your filmmaking career? Again, it's about identifying your goals and acknowledging what you hoped to achieve with your project. Only you really know if it's been a success (or maybe I've been reading too many Buddhism books lately?)."

Book Smarts

Tünde Vollenbroek, whose curational insight we benefited from in Chapter 13, is also known for her work as a writer, board member of the European Animation Awards,[2] a continuing relationship with the Kaboom Animation Festival (of which she was previously Head of Program) and Producer at the Amsterdam-based Studio Pupil[3] among other creative hats she wears. With their portfolio of commissioned work spanning animated sequences for documentary series and cultural events, collaborations, adaptations, children's series and feature films, the studio is also driven to internally produce their own passion projects.

One such endeavor would be *Tabook* (Figure 21.2), directed by Studio Pupil co-owner Dario van Vree in 2016 and released online the following year after an encouraging festival run. Channeling the studio's ethos of combining entertainment with

Figure 21.2

Still from *Tabook* (Dir. Dario van Vree) ©2016 Studio Pupil.

social awareness and education, the short depicts a young lady whose interest in erotic literature is at odds with the judgmental behavior of her fellow bookshop patrons. Racking up (at the time of writing) nearly a million views on YouTube alone, the online release was a several-pronged approach that, in spite of its overall success, came with its unavoidable share of hiccups along the way.

The first step was to put it on the radar of certain platforms ahead of schedule so as to give them a heads-up; as Rob Munday mentioned above, expecting a prospective release partner to immediately put themselves in a position to promote your work on the day of its upload without any prior heads-up is less likely to pan out. Another strategic element that tied in neatly with the studio's values was to time the release so it went up on the second Tuesday of October – International Face-Your-Fears Day.

"I thought International Face Your Fears Day was a good day because it's not too well known," reflects Tünde. "If you released it on Valentine's Day, no one would notice, because there are too many things on Valentine's Day. I think, looking back, International Face Your Fears Day was maybe a little bit too small to really make an impact, but some press picked it up because of that."

As Rob Munday observes, "In general, timing an online release around particular holidays or national days won't have a huge impact when it comes to finding an audience, but there are, of course, exceptions. In the build-up to Halloween for example, people do tend to seek out something spooky or sinister to watch and then on the flip-side, there's really no point in launching a film on Thanksgiving or Christmas Day, as in certain parts of the world you'll be missing out on a huge audience.

"Some of the larger awareness days do help bring in viewers, but you really have to make sure that your film has a strong connection to the message of the campaigns, otherwise, it could come across as underhanded self-promotion. What I would say is that these awareness days do offer online curators a great opportunity to shine a spotlight on underrepresented areas deserving of a little more attention – something they should be doing anyway, but a reminder can never hurt. Diversity and representation is key in programming and short film is an area of filmmaking that should be at the very forefront in this regard, so if you're telling an important story, which needs to be heard, you probably won't even need to time your release with a particular event or day."

In anticipation of *Tabook*'s scheduled upload, Studio Pupil would send out a press release linking to a prepared film teaser, the intended result being that press outlets would schedule a post for the day of release. This approach would ultimately misfire, with press websites merely posting up the link to the teaser; by the time the film itself was online, most outlets had moved on. For Tünde this highlighted the importance of a timely press blast, and the inclusion of a link to the full film. Other strategies that proved fiddly involved creating bespoke, International Face Your Fears Day memes using clips from *Tabook* with the intention of distributing them over social media as sponsored posts (paying the platform a certain amount of money to guarantee a targeted signal boost). Incorporating this more formal advertising element into the plan proved to be something of a drain on time around the launch, although the team found Facebook specifically yielded some worthwhile engagement.

"Thematically it really connected with people on Facebook. We advertised for €200, targeting certain countries where people were not too conservative, but also not yet too open minded, around age twenty to forty-five, female, and then we also targeted people who liked the *50 Shades of Grey* page on Facebook."

In a short time the Facebook version of the film would accumulate views in the hundreds of thousands on its own, with roughly a fifth a direct result of the sponsored boosts; from there, word of mouth – in the form of thousands of shares and viewers tagging friends in the comments section – would do the rest. The team were also delighted to see positive discourse and enthusiasm for the subject voiced by those with whom the main theme of the film resonated.

"This is exactly what we wanted to do with the film. We wanted to open up conversation and people shared it as a kind of 'coming out' – 'I like bondage, and that's okay.' That, I think, has been my favorite part of the whole promotion plan. On Vimeo you can like and you can share the link with people, but it's not as easy – or not as common – to tag friends or share it on your timeline. It all depends on the film. For *Tabook*, it really has this theme that connects on a personal level with people, so that really, really works, but maybe for another film it would not."

Director Dario van Vree would also take the film to the online forum Reddit, initially finding that it would quickly be lost when posted to larger subreddits. Ultimately, it was from sharing the link with smaller communities that the film would eventually be discovered and reposted by an influential user, leading to a significant spike in its Vimeo stats. As with its Facebook success, the most gratifying upshot of this development was the conversations and reactions it yielded, as Tünde recalls.

"The amount of views on Reddit was cool, but what's even cooler was reading the discussions. There were so many users there, getting in arguments – but also friendly conversations – there were over a hundred comments, and we were reading them all, things like 'I really liked the style, but I also really liked the message,' 'I really liked style too, but what is the message?' Then the other person replied with this whole story about what they thought the message was. So that was really cool for our filmmaker hearts.

"We also had a little strategy for YouTube, but that was more of a long term strategy because we initially wanted to focus on Vimeo, Facebook and Reddit. For YouTube, I visited my friends at Frame Order (Figure 21.3), who kindly shared their knowledge about tags – because that's the most important thing on YouTube; people go on there and they type in some search tags to search for the film that

Figure 21.3

Still from *Cartoon Box #21: Frank the Fat Horse* (Dir. Joost Lieuwma) ©2016 Joost Lieuwma.

they want. The most useful advice that I got from Frame Order about YouTube was that you have to find your niche in this kind of endless universe that YouTube is.

"For *Tabook* the niche was hard to find, because it is about bondage and sexual preferences, but the world for this on YouTube was really dark. That also showed us that it was really important to make and to spread *Tabook* because apparently this relaxed way of talking about bondage was really not available online yet."

Another detail Tünde credits the team at Frame Order for making her aware of was formatting the actual content of the film in a way that best suited online audiences, as well as further considerations regarding its thumbnail presentation that YouTube users would be more likely drawn to.

"We made an internet edit of the film, shortening the beginning and the end, as much as possible. We originally had our logo animation and credits at the beginning of the film for the festival version, but for the internet edit we cut it off so it just starts with the title of the film. When people click something online, they want to see exactly what they expect – 'Okay, this is the film that I clicked on.' That was really important for the amount of views, because if people click away then it really brings that down. If you don't give the viewers what they want, then they will go away, and your film won't be promoted on the platform as much as it otherwise would.

"We also made different stills for different platforms, because what we found is that the YouTube and Facebook audience is really more the wide audience that don't really care about whether it looks really pretty or artistic; they would actually rather have it look less artistic, but more approachable. So the poster image for YouTube and Facebook has the main character, this girl with really big eyes, looking at you (Figure 21.4). Then for Vimeo we had a still from the film that showed more of the paper art backgrounds and had more of an artistic vibe. That was also interesting, to check what works for which platform on which audience."

Closer to the film's launch, its YouTube reception was relatively modest, though in the respectable thousands. In the long-term, *Tabook* would indeed find itself a huge viewership on the platform, the algorithm eventually working in its favor (as indicated by the comments) in a major way several years later with June

Figure 21.4

Tabook social media thumbnail poster ©2016 Studio Pupil.

2020 seeing a massive surge in its view count, nearly half a million of which over two days alone.

An inconvenient truth when it comes to online content is the ease with which unscrupulous viewers can rip content and repost it for their own gain. During its waves of popularity, Tabook would wind up one of the many animated shorts to endure this fate, something that, to Tünde, underscores the importance of a multi-platform release from the get go, as it can be tricky to demonstrably assert your ownership of the content if some sneaky bugger has illegally uploaded it first. For Joost Lieuwma of Frame Order, manually dealing with the regular occurrences of content-theft resulting from the popularity of his web series *Cartoon Box* would not even be an option:

"This is one of the things that I learned to let go. If I would report every illegal upload, I wouldn't have any free time at all. For YouTube I work together with an MCN (Multi Channel Network). They have access to a content ID tool, which means that if someone is illegally making money with one of my videos, the money will be transferred to this MCN automatically."

Reflecting on the push for online distribution that Studio Pupil put into *Tabook*, Tünde has some suggestions for those who may wish to do likewise, but whose time and resources may be more limited:

"Online promotion is a lot of work, but if you're thinking about it I would say to analyze the potential that your film has on different platforms, because every platform that you publish it on requires a lot of work. If you have a really artistic, ten-minute film then I would just put all my energy into Vimeo and getting that strategy right and maybe approach some press websites who are into this kind of film. But if you have a really approachable film, where the art is not really prominent or important but the story is really fun, then focus your attention on YouTube or Facebook. Just look at where the potential is and then put the time in there, because there's no one promotional strategy that works for every film."

Partnering Up

Mind My Gap creator Rosto (Figure 21.5) would be a perfect example of how one's self-funded roots in independent animation can, with perseverance and genuine

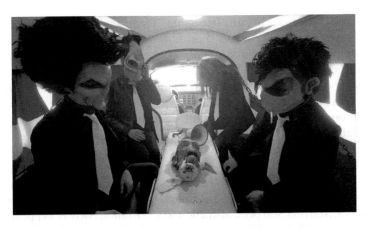

Figure 21.5

Still from *Splintertime* (Dir. Rosto) ©2015 Studio Rosto A.D/Autour de Minuit/S.O.I.L.

creativity, translate over time to becoming a valuable commodity in the eyes of funders and distributors alike. Benefiting from a decade-plus of personal work and auteur projects that made a name for himself with online audiences, a string of bizarrely compelling and successful animated films brought him to the attention of the festival circuit and France-based film production company Autour de Minuit, an organization founded by Nicolas Schmerkin with a keen eye for visual innovation and mixed-media projects. As well as taking on distribution of his films, from 2011s *The Monster of Nix* on Autour de Minuit maintained an active involvement in Rosto's output, ambitious films that tick all the boxes of the company's mission statement and plenty more. After his untimely passing, the company continued on his legacy by crowdfunding one of Rosto's unrealized passion projects, a physical release of his *Mind My Gap* hardback graphic novel adaptation with an accompanying soundtrack album *Songs From My Gap.*

When approaching – or being approached by – a company that can help facilitate funding and distribution, it's important to consider whether or not you are an artistic or ideological fit. In many respects, this should be easy enough to determine – a production company known for specializing in content for younger audiences will most likely have no interest in a project for adults, and vice versa – though it is always worth researching a company's overall remit. Even if, on a surface level, producers and distributors boast a broad canvas of projects, as Autour de Minuit could be seen to at first glance – a thorough examination of their project portfolio will reveal enough recurring elements and give you a sense of their overall standard of quality. A little bit of research can ultimately save you a lot of time in the long run if you are in the market for a serious partnership.

Another company whose brand has become synonymous with independent animation of a high caliber is Miyu Productions,[4] a Paris-based production company founded by Emmanuel-Alain Raynal working alongside fellow Associate Producer Pierre Baussaron. In 2017, Miyu would partner with Luce Grosjean of Sève Films to form Miyu Distribution,[5] an avenue through which some of the best contemporary shorts and emerging talent have had their visibility amplified through international sales and festival distribution. This distribution slate extends to any and all shorts made by Miyu Productions itself, with Luce taking the lead on new acquisitions.

"It's one of the bases of our partnership," Pierre explains, "that Luce will distribute every Miyu Productions short film, and also take others on her own. Obviously, when she decides to take a film, she sends us a link and we discuss it, but she's pretty independent."

"It's her editorial line but we are in communication every time she discovers a great film or film director," says Emmanuel-Alain. "At the same time, when we have the opportunity to see a great film, we send her a link to recommend it, if it doesn't already have a distributor and we think it would be cool to take it."

While Miyu's production base is focused on development of its own projects, Miyu Distribution maintains the original spirit of Sève Films in focusing on student films and independent shorts, and has built up an enormously impressive roster of work from the likes of Špela Čadež, Will Anderson, Sarina Nihei, Daria Kascheeva, Martina Scarpelli, Michelle and Uri Kranot, Nicolas Keppens, Shoko Hara, Imge and Sine Özbilge, Britt Raes, Chintis Lundgren, Paul Driessen and Nadja Andrasev, among many others.[6]

From her work as an advocate of animation shorts, Luce has developed a keen eye for what makes a film a valuable commodity, what its distribution options may be and how filmmakers can benefit from whichever avenue they pursue.

"I would say that it's really important that directors figure out what they need. What are they aiming to do after this film? From there, they can think about how they will approach the distribution. If they need a job, they should find the most efficient way to have producers and agencies see their work. Releasing work online can maybe be a good strategy, but if you want to do other shorts, increase your directing knowledge and make yourself more well-known in that sense, it's important to consider the festival circuit. Of course, directors can combine both approaches and they should think about not releasing their film too early in the process. If their dream is to be a Vimeo Staff Pick, then sometimes it's better to have a festival run behind it as that can validate your film.

"I think it's important, especially if you made the film during your studies, to take feedback as a way to understand what will be best for your film. If your film isn't perfect, that doesn't mean that you're not going to be a great director, it just means you have to make another film! You just need more time, and that's okay. It's not about the number of festival selections that you will receive or the number of views. If you have no Vimeo Staff Pick but you have been shared in other websites and niche blogs where people will be able to see and discover your style, maybe that will be better. If you only have ten selections in festivals but from them you meet a new producer who will produce your next work, that's more important."

Earlier in the book, we explored some of the rookie mistakes and pitfalls animation filmmakers are advised to avoid so as to increase their festival exposure. When it comes to acquisition and distribution (both of which are heavily entwined with the festival landscape itself), many of these familiar concerns will still apply.

"One of the things that frustrates me about short films that we cannot distribute will be the length. Sometimes directors push their films over fifteen minutes where they could have easily cut out four or five – or just rethought the project. Shorter films will be easier to distribute. Long duration is not sexy for sales or festival selection, because it's harder to find room for a film if it's longer.

"The voices can be really bad, especially if it's people trying to make something not in their own language. Also from my perspective, when I see films that are trying to be like Hollywood shorts, they'll have English dialogue (because English is considered better for international film distribution). You can tell when an American accent is faked; trying to be something that you're not isn't good.

"Another frustration is when people try to build – or jump on – a trend; when a subject comes along that's 'cool,' people will make films that are too similar. A film can have great design or a great director but if it's too similar to what other people have been doing it won't be as easy to distribute the film."

Assuming your film has avoided enough of these stumbling blocks to be a prospective darling of the festival circuit, it may very well be that the time and resources available to you mean that devoting yourself to submission blasts or seeking out potential buyers simply isn't tenable. It may also be that a distributor, by virtue of being far more ingrained in the industry through the very nature of the work they do, will automatically open more doors for your film. If building this type of relationship is among your hopes for your film, getting the ball rolling early on is crucial.

"We prefer it when people approach us during post-production," suggests Luce. "We don't like it when the film is already out, because if it's been sent to 50–100 festivals then it's a much harder process for us. If the film already started its life in festivals then we're more likely to say 'no'; if it's at the beginning then we're more likely to take it.

"I think doing your own distribution can be really rewarding, but what you learn from working with a distributor is avoiding the traps, avoiding the bad festivals, so you win back time for the distribution process. It's important to have distributors who can explain the way the film can be best distributed. Some films that are self-distributed do great in festivals by themselves and that's great to see, it really depends on the quality of the film and the director who is behind it."

Reinforcing some of the points we addressed in the preceding chapter, Luce subscribes to the belief that a physical festival or market environment can be more conducive to striking a rapport and building relationships with potential partners, be they on the production or distribution side, as well as the benefits of engaging your audience in person.

"You don't meet the same people when you put films online that you're meeting when you're in festivals. I wouldn't value one audience less than the other, but I do think that meeting people in real life will increase not just your network, but your creative process. And I love seeing animation film directors at festivals, because they're really precise in their process and when they all speak together about the way they work it's super exciting. You can see how they are getting stronger.

"I think people should always go to festivals to be sure that they meet people and stay in touch. People will be more likely to give you time and will take time to answer your questions in person, so in that sense it's a good strategy. Two festivals you should attend if you want to meet distributors are Clermont Ferrand and Annecy, but they are also super crowded. I recommend smaller, cosier festivals where you can meet people who, at a larger festival, wouldn't otherwise be available. For example, Fantoche is amazing, it's really easy to meet everyone in the same place. Anibar is great, Anifilm in Liberec, Turku Animated Film Festival as well. Whenever you're stuck in a small town I think it's great, because then you will get to see everyone. There are also bigger festivals that have this kind of energy, like Animafest Zagreb. These are where you'll find the best opportunities to meet professionals who will be there to hang out with filmmakers, which is precious."

Emmanuel-Alain concurs that Annecy – along with Cannes – "are obligations every year. It's important to go to festivals because it's a good opportunity to see films and to discover some directors, but also to meet some co-producers. When you are in front of someone and you talk about anything and drink some beers, maybe you can bring up 'Oh, by the way, I have a project, maybe it would be good to co-produce with you.' It's like a concentration of opportunities–, which is important.

"And as far as animation is concerned," adds Pierre, "Annecy is the place where everybody goes. Usually it's the craziest week of the year, because we can meet with a lot of co-producers we're working with – and meet with new ones there might be new projects with, et cetera. So Annecy's definitely where the activity is at its peak."

Unexpected Developments

You'll recall that Aidan McAteer's first attempt at making a short film since college, *A Gentleman's Guide to Villainy*, was a success as far as its immediate purpose of winning DepicT! was concerned. This began a snowball effect that saw the film being selected for a number of high-profile festivals including Annecy, which in turn resulted in a Swiss television broadcast deal. This seemingly surreal turn of events is, if not readily available to everyone who has ever made a film, not as uncommon as you might think. Festivals partnered up with film markets would not exist were there not accredited buyers in attendance, and even if independent films don't seem to be a valuable commodity where you live, chances are they might be to some other parts of the world. Depending on your territory, there may also be short film distributors and sales agents that actively solicit precisely the type of independent short you have made. Though bear in mind such businesses won't appreciate having their time wasted, i.e., if they state in their remit that they are on the hunt for documentary shorts, nobody will benefit if you slide an animated music video under their noses. Also, you should keep your wits about you as regards anything involving a contract – it may seem like an old cliché, but relinquishing ownership of your intellectual property is not something to be entered into hastily. Even "non-exclusive" agreements that have caveats that, while reasonable and most likely beneficial to your project's overall exposure, may be easy to overlook and accidentally breach. Remember that no matter how laid back (obviously when it comes to animation there's really no such thing, but you know what I mean) an independent animation project's production might have been, things will become exponentially more formal the moment that distribution deals are in place.

In Aidan McAteer's case, once *The Gentleman's Guide to Villainy*'s TV contract and festival exposure had run its course, it joined its animated short film brethren online, its most valuable upshot being clear to the director: "It just gave me confidence to say 'Now I'm a filmmaker!'"

Bill Plympton, whose words of seemingly out-of-reach advice proved true to Aidan, has his own thoughts on the matter of distribution in the wake of his 2013 feature Cheatin':

"I'm a little old-school on this but I've come to the realization that digital distribution is a much more democratic and profitable way to make money. In the past you always had a theatrical release, then a DVD release, then – way down the line – video-on-demand or a digital release. Now people are just going straight to

Figure 21.6

Still from *Cheatin'* (Dir. Bill Plympton) ©2014 Plymptoons.

the digital release stage and they make their money that way, through YouTube, Vimeo or Netflix. It's really changed for the better for younger people, or people who are independently minded. They don't have to deal with Hollywood, which is a Godsend because Hollywood is such a rapacious place that they will take your film, distribute it and make lots of money you will never get to see. It's really a very scary position to be in, to spend four years of your life and all your money on a film that becomes a success but then you don't get any of the funds from the movie theatres or TV sales.

"With *Cheatin'* (Figure 21.6), if we would have gotten a million dollar – or even half a million dollar – advance then we probably would have made a deal, taken the money and ran – forget about royalties! Since we never did get a really big advance we decided to do what's called a 'Service Deal,' in other words paying a distributor to get it out to theatres, to get publicity, the chance for some good reviews and some good word of mouth. Then we take the film back and do the DVD and the internet sales ourselves – that's where we hopefully cash in and make a profit. It's all theoretical and it depends on if it's a good film, if you get good distribution on the internet, find the right home for it. That's the important part to make money, is to get a good home for it."

Similarly, Bill's protégé-turned-independent feature director in her own right Signe Baumane learned some hard truths when it came to getting *Rocks In My Pockets* (Figure 21.7) out into the world:

"Looking back I could say that making the film was the easy part! When you're making a film, you're doing something that you are good at, you know what you're doing, you have experience, you have ideas, it's a creative process. It's challenging and there are hard days and easy days and all that, but when you come to the stage of distribution and marketing, that is something I'm not good at – and I found myself having to do it, day in and day out, for a year and a half, when I should have been making another film.

"We have different distributors for different territories, so strictly speaking we don't have to do anything, because there is a publicist for when we had a theatrical run and the distributor takes care of the business side."

What was most important to Signe and the *Rocks in My Pockets* team was the opportunity to use the project to connect with people, person-to-person. As

Figure 21.7

Still from *Rocks in my Pockets* (Dir. Signe Baumane) ©2014 Signe Baumane.

Figure 21.8

The Naughty List poster ©2010 Ben Mitchell.

indicated by the film's social media following, there was a sizable interest from people who were willing to come out and see the film theatrically.

"These are people who wouldn't know that the film exists if it wasn't for social media. So we felt compelled to try to reach out to those who might be interested and it turned out to be a very effective marketing strategy. Even if the New York

Times gives a film the kind of big approval that a lot of people see, they won't necessarily go to a movie after they read it because the next day it's about another movie. When you go home, open Facebook and see a friend saying 'I'm going to see *Rocks in My Pockets*' it becomes more personal, so that was our strategy; No distributor can do this type of person-to-person marketing."

Bill Plympton frequently insists that the most advisable way of profiting from a short film is to keep production costs at a minimum. From firsthand experience, I can confirm that you needn't be as established and internationally revered as the Bill Plymptons of the world for this to be true. My 2010 short *The Naughty List*, (Figure 21.8) produced over a quiet, two-month period when commissioned projects were sparse, received some negligible financial support to assist with the post-production and coloring, but could largely be considered an unpaid, entirely auteur affair. Though the process of getting it out in the world was a slow-burn one, eventually it sold to enough territories for broadcast to make back more than what my income would have been during the time it was made, as well as the various postage, submission and transfer fees incurred. If I had devoted, say, six months or more to the production and subcontracted a crew to make it a slicker, more polished affair, it's certainly *possible* that the more professional production values would have increased its salability, but the risk would have been far greater. Taking this to a further extreme would be my 2015 short *Klementhro* (Figure 21.9), produced over two weeks between gigs and probably my most barebones endeavor to date; granted, it's also one of my most annoying films to date and confused the hell out of people, but when it did get some positive attention, then turning a profit was a breeze. Looking at your film as an investment in this way and from the get-go can be a very helpful determining factor when it comes to the budgeting phase, not to mention your approach to the production itself. Assuming you as the director or main contributor to an independent film or passion project will not be paid, the time and skill you put into it still has value and it's completely reasonable to want to recoup this investment.

Pixar have more than proved that a short animated skit can be a success when made with a big budget, while many an independent animator has equally proved that it can function just as well when scribbled on a napkin if the premise, timing and execution is properly thought through. Admittedly, the low budget approach

Figure 21.9

Still from *Klementhro* (Dir. Ben Mitchell) ©2015 Ben Mitchell.

virtuos
virtuell

EIN EXPERIMENTALFILM ZU EINER KOMPOSITION
VON LOUIS SPOHR
AN EXPERIMENTAL FILM ON A COMPOSITION
BY LOUIS SPOHR

VON THOMAS STELLMACH UND MAJA OSCHMANN

ORIGINAL VERSION
LIVE VERSION
MAKING OF /
TV-SPECIAL

Figure 21.10

Cover art for the *Virtuos Virtuell* (Dir. Thomas Stellmach/Maja Oschmann) DVD/ BluRay, sold via the film's website virtuosvirtuell.com ©2013 Thomas Stellmach.

to filmmaking is not for every artist, and definitely not for every film. In the case of Thomas Stellmach and Maja Oschmann's filmic tribute to Louis Spohr *Virtuos Virtuell* (Figure 21.10), a level of visual sophistication was required, not to give it a superficial glossiness, but to treat its subject with respect and fully immerse the audience into its illusory world. As a consequence, the project required significant financial backing (as discussed in Chapter 9) which in turn was a significant motivating factor when it came to approaching distribution. With over twenty-five streams of financial support in total, Thomas could determine in hindsight that approximately half of the film's budget had been covered.

"When producing this film I counted every hour, and at the end I knew exactly how many hours I worked on the project. I counted from this the cost, which was 114,000-€. We had managed to get half of that from funders, the other half came from the time I spent working on the film."

Given the film's experimental qualities, higher budget and the ever-changing landscape of short film sales, a more targeted and traditional approach was warranted to achieve significant financial success. On the heels of the first leg of *Virtuos Virtuell*'s festival run, Thomas released the film on DVD and BluRay, purchasable online via the project's official website.[7]

"I sold 1400 DVDs which was a successful outcome. I also took the time to send it to 350 festivals, out of which 180 chose the film for competition. Doing that was also a huge job, and a major reason for the film's success was because of the time – over two years – that I put into the process. It seems to me that usually filmmakers won't invest quite so much time for that side of things. Of course there are companies that can take on the work of sending the film to festivals as a service, but I didn't use that option, I chose to do it by myself. It might seem to be a bit crazy, to take so much time to do this, but I'm an enthusiast! I love my products, I love my films and I try to send them out so that people can see them."

Thomas Stellmach's sentiment is one that I certainly hope all of you reading can relate to. Whether or not your film proves to be profitable or propels you to international stardom, that you followed through on creating a piece of art is a success story in itself. Hopefully through the array of case studies, personal stories, masterclasses and tips this book has gathered together, you will have come away with a film that is something even more – a standout animation project that makes a significant mark on the ever-inspirational independent scene and leads to the exciting first step of your next creative journey.

Notes

1 https://www.shortoftheweek.com/news/be-everywhere-all-at-once/
2 https://animationawards.eu/
3 https://studiopupil.com/
4 https://www.miyu.fr/production
5 https://www.miyu.fr/distribution
6 Honestly, I could happily sit here and list all of their directors, but my word count on this book is limited and I don't want to come off like a total kiss-ass
7 http://www.virtuosvirtuell.com

Recommended Further Reading

Every animator can benefit from having a personal library of reference material, whether to brush up on the fundamentals, further familiarize ourselves with specific software processes or as a means of exploring entirely new avenues. Assuming most will have started off with such obligatory tomes as *The Illusion of Life* (Frank Thomas/ Ollie Johnson) and *The Animator's Survival Kit* (Richard Williams), here are a few personal recommendations that deal with the practice of animation itself. Obviously when it comes to building up your own resources, you'll wish to consider which animation role (writer? Director? Producer?) you're best suited to, which medium (stop-motion? 2D? CG?) you dabble in most, what type of project (short? Feature? Interactive?) you wish to pursue and which software (I'll stop asking one-word questions now) you gravitate toward. While I could put together a book's worth of book recommendations – from cultural histories and critical analyses to specific software walkthroughs – when it comes to the territories this book has covered, the following should further assist you on your journey, whichever direction you wish to go:

Animation: The Mechanics of Motion
Author: Chris Webster
Focal Press
ISBN: 978-0240516660

Timing for Animation
Authors: John Halas and Harold Whitaker
Focal Press
ISBN: 978-0240521602

Action Analysis for Animators
Author: Chris Webster
Focal Press
ISBN: 978-0240812182

Action and Performance for Animation
Authors: Derek Hayes and Chris Webster
Focal Press
ISBN: 978-0240812397

Acting for Animators
Author: Ed Hooks
Routledge
ISBN: 978-0415580243

Stop-Motion: Craft Skills for Model Animation
Author: Susannah Shaw
Focal Press
ISBN: 978-0240520551

Prepare to Board! Creating Story and Characters for Animated Features and Shorts
Author: Nancy Beiman
Focal Press
ISBN: 978-0240818788

Dream Worlds: Production Design for Animation
Author: Hans Bacher
Focal Press
ISBN: 978-0240520933

Ideas for the Animated Short
Authors: Karen Sullivan, Kate Alexander, Aubry Mintz and Ellen Besen
Focal Press
ISBN: 978-0240818726

Make Toons That Sell (Without Selling Out)
Author: Bill Plympton
Focal Press
ISBN: 978-0240817798

Directing for Animation
Author: Tony Bancroft
Focal Press
ISBN: 978-0240818023

The Game Narrative Toolbox
Authors: Tobias Heussner, Toiya Kristen Finley, Jennifer Brandes Hepler and Ann Lemay
Focal Press
ISBN: 978-1138787087

Digital Storytelling
Authors: Carolyn Handler Miller
Focal Press
ISBN: 978-0415836944

Hybrid Animation
Author: Tina O'Hailey
Focal Press
ISBN: 978-0415718707

The Foley Grail
Author: Vanessa Theme Ament
Focal Press
ISBN: 978-0415840859

Designing Sound for Animation
Author: Robin Beauchamp
Focal Press
ISBN: 978-0240824987

Voice-Over for Animation
Authors: Jean Ann Wright and M.J. Lallo
Focal Press
ISBN: 978-024081218

Index

Note: *Italic* page numbers refer to figures and page numbers followed by "n" denote endnotes.

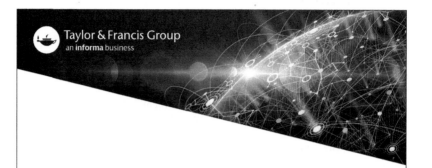

Taylor & Francis eBooks

www.taylorfrancis.com

A single destination for eBooks from Taylor & Francis
with increased functionality and an improved user
experience to meet the needs of our customers.

90,000+ eBooks of award-winning academic content in
Humanities, Social Science, Science, Technology, Engineering,
and Medical written by a global network of editors and authors.

TAYLOR & FRANCIS EBOOKS OFFERS:

A streamlined
experience for
our library
customers

A single point
of discovery
for all of our
eBook content

Improved
search and
discovery of
content at both
book and
chapter level

REQUEST A FREE TRIAL
support@taylorfrancis.com

 Routledge
Taylor & Francis Group

 CRC Press
Taylor & Francis Group

||||||||||||||||||||||||

9781032103112